Businessmen have always had a strong inclination to avoid competition and regulate the market. Helen Mercer traces the evolution of British competition legislation designed to discourage such practices, from 1900 to 1964. Textbooks frequently attribute the dynamic behind the development of this legislation to an undefined 'public opinion'. Helen Mercer disagrees. She contends that competition policies have been shaped by the strategies of powerful business interests – at home and in the United States. Trade unions and organisations of labour have provided a consistent pressure on governments to legislate on private monopoly, in the face of sweeping criticisms of free enterprise. This book makes extensive use of archival sources to give a detailed analysis of government–industry relations. In the course of this it sheds new light on Britain's changing industrial structure, and offers pointers to the likely outcome of business regulation in Britain in the future.

Constructing a competitive order

Constructing a competitive order

The hidden history of British antitrust policies

Helen Mercer

University of Glasgow

Published by the Press Syndicate of the University of Cambridge
The Pitt Building, Trumpington Street, Cambridge CB2 1RP
40 West 20th Street, New York, NY 10011-4211, USA
10 Stamford Road, Oakleigh, Victoria 3166, Australia

© Cambridge University Press 1995

First published 1995

Printed in Great Britain at the University Press, Cambridge

A catalogue record for this book is available from the British Library

Library of Congress cataloguing in publication data

Mercer, H. (Helen)
Constructing a competitive order: the hidden history of British
antitrust policies / Helen Mercer.
   p.   cm.
Includes bibliographical references and index.
ISBN 0 521 412927 (hc.)
1. Trade regulation – Great Britain – History – 20th century.
2. Competition – Great Britain – History – 20th century.
3. Monopolies – Great Britain – History – 20th century. 4. Pressure
groups – Great Britain – History – 20th century. 5. Pressure groups –
United States – History – 20th century. I. Title.
HD3616.G72M47 1995
338.8′0941 – dc20 94-9622 CIP

ISBN 0 521 41292 7 hardback

SE

Contents

Tables

Acknowledgements

First of all I must acknowledge two major intellectual debts: to my father, Eric Mercer, and to my partner, George Hallam, who have shaped my understanding of economic history. In addition, my father has made innumerable suggestions on drafts of the book, and my partner has been an unfailing source of enthusiasm and encouragement, ideas and insights. On the subject matter of this book I have been much influenced by the pioneering work of W.A. Williams and Gabriel Kolko.

Much of the original research for this book was undertaken in completion of my doctoral thesis, supervised by Geoffrey Jones then at the Business History Unit, London School of Economics, now at Reading University. It was made financially possible by an ESRC linked studentship for two years and by the academic support provided by the Business History Unit under Leslie Hannah. I would like to thank them for their support at that early stage. Since then I have received much help and advice on draft chapters for the book. At Leeds University Malcolm Sawyer made invaluable suggestions on a draft of the book, and Mike Collins read the whole thesis before I started revisions, also being very encouraging. I would also like to thank the many people who have commented on my work over the years and given their support, and especially Jim Tomlinson, Neil Rollings, Larry Butler, Katrina Honeyman, Peter Nolan and Kathy O'Donnell. Needless to say, I alone am responsible for all mistakes, hyperbole and polemic.

Many people involved in the events described here agreed to be interviewed, although not all are cited. In this regard I would like to thank Dame Alix Meynell, Mr William Hughes, Lord Thorneycroft, Dame Elizabeth Ackroyd, Sir Alan Neale and Mr Raymond Colegate. Denys Gribbin, who has worked on this area for the war-time period gave me valuable help at the start of my thesis.

I owe a special debt to the staff of the Public Record Office, Kew, for their willingness to answer my requests and for the general service that they provide. I would also like to thank the archivists and librarians at the Modern Records Centre, Warwick University, the British Library of

Political and Economic Science, the Labour Party archive, the Bodleian Library and Nuffield College, Oxford, Churchill College, Cambridge, the Pilkington Archive, St Helens, and the W.H. Smith archive at Abingdon.

I would finally like to thank my family for their patient support, and special thanks to my daughter for reasons too numerous to mention.

Notes on conventions used and abbreviations

Unless otherwise stated all primary sources cited are Public Record Office references, e.g. CAB87/3, BT64/318, see bibliography for more details.

All secondary sources are cited with place and date of publication, unless the place of publication was London in which case only the year of publication is given.

The reports of the MRPC are cited in full in the bibliography, but given abbreviated titles throughout the text.

Abbreviations

FBI	Federation of British Industries
MRPC	Monopolies and Restrictive Practices Commission
PEP	Political and Economic Planning
RPM	Resale Price Maintenance
TUC	Trades Union Congress
RPM	Resale Price Maintenance
BPP	British Parliamentary Papers
BHR	*Business History Review*
Bus Hist	*Business History*
CBI	CBI Predecessor Archive
EHR	*Economic History Review*
EngHR	*English Historical Review*
EJ	*Economic Journal*
JCH	*Journal of Contemporary History*
JEEH	*Journal of European Economic History*
JEH	*Journal of Economic History*
LPA	Labour Party Archive
Parl. Deb.	Parliamentary Debates (Hansard) House of Commons Official Report 5th Series
Parl. Deb.(Lords)	Parliamentary Debates (Hansard) House of Lords Official Report 5th Series

1 Introduction

as a general principle of organisation I prefer the diffused initiative and quasi-automatism which go, or can be made to go, with private property and the market ... This does not imply ... any blind belief in the existence of economic harmonies. I have argued already that, within the present framework of law and institutions, I see no guarantee of good results from the free play of private interest. It does imply, however, the belief that, rather than to proceed by destroying the market and enterprise system, it is better to proceed by trying to improve it. It implies that, rather than stake all on the dubious prospects of overall collectivism, it is better to retain existing mechanisms, but to erect around them, so to speak, a system of laws and institutions within which they may be made to work the right way. It implies, that is to say, a belief, not in a spontaneously harmonious free enterprise, but rather in a deliberately constructed competitive order.

This idea of a competitive order is by no means a simple notion. It is not just trust-busting – although there are many 'trusts' which I would like to see bust. It involves the systematic revision of the whole apparatus of law and order – the law relating to patents, the law relating to restraint of trade, the law relating to limited liability and corporations, and many other branches of the law – with a view to creating conditions which tend to maintain effective competition, where it is technically possible, and to control monopoly in the public interest where technical conditions make monopoly inevitable. It involves the search for new methods of fiscal control, not only for the purpose of stabilising aggregate demand, but also for the purpose of correcting and supplementing the operation of the incentive of relative prices, where analysis discloses that this incentive works badly

L. Robbins *The Economic Problem in Peace and War* (1947) pp. 81–4.

From the end of the nineteenth century in advanced capitalist economies large firms, cartels, 'trusts' and all manner of collusive organisations were supplanting the 'invisible hand' of the market by regulation of markets. The 'rise of the corporate economy' had an impact on economic thought and policy which cannot be understated. Joan Robinson has summarised its significance:

Generally, in the orthodox scheme, monopoly is a Bad Thing. For most economists

1

competition is absolutely essential to the justification of laisser faire; it is competition which equates the margins, distributes resources so as to maximise utility, and generally makes the whole scheme work.[1]

If the market could no longer be relied upon to harmonise private and public interests, the state, many economists argued, had a responsibility to do so. Hermann Levy, an early pioneer of research into the 'trust movement', stated: 'a revolution has broken out in the most important areas of industrial organisation and ... this revolution calls for new departures in economic and political thought and policy.'[2]

But what direction was policy to take? Since the 'trust movement' emerged in Britain, governments have been sympathetic to 'bigness' in economic organisation, to the economies of scale, amalgamations, rationalisation and the concentration of production.[3] In the interests of competing on a world market dominated by the industrial giants which arose in Germany and the United States British governments have encouraged the opportunities which the integrated corporation was seen to open to the reduction of costs, increased efficiency, export competitiveness and extended research and development: a highly sanguine view.[4]

British policy has had marked preference for self-regulation by business, while state supervision or regulation of monopoly has proceeded along two principal lines: nationalisation or competition policies. Nationalisation was arguably the British form of antitrust: the manifesto of the Labour Party in 1945 argued that this was the solution to inefficient private monopoly in the industries concerned. One American regulation theorist points out that all regulation of private industry by government involves some interference with and limitation of the full exercise of the rights of private property.[5] Nationalisation simply carries the intervention in private property to an extreme. Also, since the 1940s, Britain has developed a corpus of competition legislation designed to regulate the behaviour of private firms and to promise safeguards to the public from monopoly abuse through encouraging competition. It is this which is the subject of this book.

The ideological justification for competition policies owes much to neoclassical and liberal economic thought. By the 1940s many such economists viewed the world with alarm: economic man was born free, but everywhere he was in chains. Soviet collectivism was knocking on the gates of Western Europe, socialists in Europe proposed wide-scale nationalisation, the nazi economic system had enthroned monopoly and cartels with state support. To oppose the Scylla and Charybdis of socialism and fascism liberal economists like Lionel Robbins, Friedrich Hayek, John Jewkes and George Stigler began to develop and disseminate the notion of 'a deliberately constructed competitive order'. The state was to provide the legal and institutional framework within which the competitive forces could best proceed. Robbins, for instance outlined a Keynesian but laissez-faire state which would not usurp the field of private enterprise, but would define the rules and limits of the game.

But there is something very odd in the notion of a 'competitive order', indeed in the idea that the state should create competitive conditions which are supposed to occur naturally. The whole idea raises two key questions. First, what is the likely outcome of trying to create competition? Why greater monopoly? As Joan Robinson again asserts:

> But competition, surely, is the main cause of monopoly? How can it be that to lower prices, expand markets, undersell rivals, is a Good Thing, but that the firm that succeeds in overcoming these difficulties and remains in possession of the field is a wicked monopolist? The objection to restrictive practices, and the main justification for the present campaign against them, is that they restrain competition and keep inefficient producers going. If the campaign succeeds, competition, driving out the inefficient, will create more monopolies. Is that what we want? And if not, what do we want? What are the rules of the game?[6]

Nor does monopoly suppress competition: it may stimulate still more intensive oligopolistic competition.[7] The conscious attempt to encourage competition in one area has prompted monopolistic tendencies elsewhere. In both Britain and America the effective outlawing of cartels in 1956 and 1890 respectively became one element in the subsequent merger waves in those countries.[8] Indeed, antitrust policies in Britain and elsewhere have generally been aimed primarily at certain forms of collusion.

It has not infrequently been remarked that the word 'antitrust' is a misnomer. In the USA the Sherman Act of 1890, although responsible for spectacularly busting a few trusts, was actually anti-cartel.[9] In Britain, similarly 'antitrust' policies have never been motivated by hostility to large-scale industry or monopoly itself, only to such practices which may be judged against the 'public interest'.

The second problem in the notion that the state should construct a competitive order lies in the fact that, for those liberal economists espousing the idea, the involvement of the state to regulate business, even in the interests of competition, must be like calling on Beelzebub to drive out Lucifer. Summarising the classical liberal view of the state Galbraith writes: 'Any union between public and private organisation . . . means that public power has been captured for private advantage and profit.'[10] Indeed the trend towards monopolistic forms of economic organisation has prompted calls for state regulation, while at the same time endowing those very organisations with the power to control and direct the nature of that intervention. In a 'market-oriented system', as Charles Lindblom says, business stands in a privileged position in government and politics by reason of the dependence which government has on successful business activities.[11] Accretions of business and economic power carry with them greater political power.[12] Thus the government intervenes when the very forces it seeks to control are in a position to influence the nature of that intervention.

These two considerations are at the core of this book. It therefore takes issue with existing accounts of the evolution of competition policies in Britain. These, operating with a belief that competition policies have been introduced in the 'public interest', have presented a 'whig' image of the gradual and progressive development of improved and enlightened perceptions of the problem of monopoly since the 1930s.[13] To them progress is manifest, not in the extent of competition or efficiency now present in the British economy, nor in the ability of past and present legislation to develop competition, but in the change of outlook which they identify between the 1930s and 1950s. Thus they tend to see the dynamic of the history of competition policy as one of outlook, of changing and improving perceptions of the problem. Although not all are Keynesians, they possess Keynes' faith in the power of economists to influence governments, at least in the fullness of time. As Keynes said, 'I am sure that the power of vested interests is vastly exaggerated compared with the gradual encroachment of ideas'.[14] They therefore approach the subject with the standpoint of the reformer: until recently most accounts of the evolution of policy were preludes to recommendations on future policy.

The key element in their understanding of events is an emphasis on the role of 'public opinion' or 'the climate of opinion' in forcing policy developments. For instance the Monopolies and Restrictive Practices Act of 1948, following a period of government support for cartels and rationalisation in the inter-war period, was introduced because, 'the climate of opinion had changed.'[15] John Jewkes found the change baffling: 'The postwar disposition in Britain to place greater reliance upon competition must rank among those mysterious and unpredictable switches in broad economic thinking, so numerous in history, in which irrationality has played at least as great a part as rationality.'[16] For others it was the Civil Service and the 'liberal-minded bureaucracy' which carried the 'banner of free competition', or the role of economists in government.[17] A similar approach is adopted towards the subsequent Restrictive Trade Practices Act, passed in 1956, although here accounts recognise that legislation accommodated the demands which organised industry made.[18]

British analyses of the evolution of antitrust policies continue, therefore, to be at a similar stage to that of American writers of the Progressive Era who believed that 'public interest was the raison d'etre of economic regulation'. Since then, however, American economists and historians have established that businessmen agitated for and benefited from regulation.[19]

This book challenges orthodox interpretations of events in Britain. It argues that the potential strength of 'public opinion' is actually greater than competition theorists admit. Popular views of the trusts may be illustrated by the rash of fiction on the theme at the turn of the century. Writers like H.G. Wells foresaw a social and political nightmare, often leading to revolution.[20] For most of this century the most coherent critique of private monopoly by a wider 'public' has been articulated by the labour movement – the Labour Party, the trade unions and the Co-ops. Accounts of German and American antitrust have already developed this point. Britain, in common with Germany, has a strong labour movement which, as in Germany tended to criticise not monopoly per se, but private ownership of monopoly. Such movements channelled much popular anti-monopoly feeling away from the solution of antitrust and towards that of nationalisation.[21] Contrariwise in the United States, antitrust enforcement was used to deflect calls for socialist reform.[22]

Thus to the extent that antitrust embodied a 'public interest' it was to preserve the legitimacy and dynamism of the capitalist system. Leslie Hannah describes competition policy as 'a means of strengthening the case for private enterprise by increasing the competitive pressures within the capitalist system'.[23] Hans Thorelli's study of American antitrust argues that it 'was intended to safeguard the freedom of enterprise in general; to achieve this purpose it was found necessary to limit in some degree the freedom of action of the individual businessman or firm'.[24] Competition policy promises that, should there be evidence that the 'public interest' has been harmed by monopolistic organisations the matter will be investigated and appropriate action taken. The issue is removed from the hands of popular campaigning bodies and transferred to 'independent' tribunals operating with the consent of at least a section of the business world. Competition policy is, in part, an alternative to more drastic solutions to the 'monopoly problem', which would interfere with and challenge private ownership of production.

This book also applies to Britain the conclusions of American writers who see regulatory bodies as a forum for settling disputes among businessmen. A study of the vigorous enforcement of antitrust legislation under the 'pro-business' Eisenhower administration argues: 'The Antitrust laws protected the American businessman: he could carry on his endeavours without being subjected to organised group pressures or monopoly power, but if he was injured by violation of one of the laws, the Antitrust corpus afforded him a chance for redress.'[25]

A vast American literature details the power of business interests to influence the nature of their own regulation. At a general level Lindblom again argues: 'even the unspoken possibility of adversity for business operates as an all-pervasive constraint on government authority.'[26] More specifically a left-liberal school of historians and a right-liberal school of economists conclude that vested interests have 'captured' the bodies set up to regulate them, either while the machinery of regulation is in the process of enactment or after a period of operation by the regulatory body.[27]

This book sees business pressure as fundamental in determining the nature and timing of British competition legislation. The study of government–industry relations in Britain has been influenced by the concept of a 'corporate bias': a continuous contract between government, industry and the unions, with no one group possessing a preponderance of power.[28] This book, however, balancing the influence of industrialists and the various groups composing the labour movement in Britain, demonstrates the predominance of the former. The very form of monopoly, and ensuing business strategies, in Britain was the key influence on the type of competition policy enacted.

In addition it places the evolution of policy in an international context. It was not only domestic businessmen who sought safeguards against monopoly powers – so did overseas businessmen especially, in the key period of the 1940s and the 1950s, those in the United States. We know that in Germany and Japan, occupied and administered by the United States, the 'American-style free enterprise system' found legislative expression in the 1947 anti-cartel ordinance in Germany and the Deconcentration and Anti-Monopoly Laws in Japan of the same year. (In fact in neither country did these laws survive the opposition of indigenous business leaders, nor the impact of the Cold War on American plans for these countries.)[29]

The evolution of British antitrust policy was part of the process of welding Britain into the new world order which the Americans were trying to establish from the 1940s onwards. This was neither a smooth, nor a necessarily successful process, nor was America the only international player with which Britain had to deal. In fact the debates about competition policy, especially after the Second World War reflect also deep ponderings about Britain's future world role, caught between America, Europe, the Empire, and the Dominions.

It is not only ideas but forms of economic organisation and economic interests which are the focus of study and through which I hope to lay bare the real dynamic of British competition policy and in so doing to controvert some present free market myths.

Outline of the book

The main weight of the material concentrates on the period between 1940 and 1964. This was a formative period for Britain's current competition legislation, and is also a time when there is a wealth of government, business and personal records available to paint a detailed picture. Chapter 4 is devoted to war-time Reconstruction discussions, and chapter 5 to their culmination in the 1948 Monopolies and Restrictive Practices Act passed under a Labour government. Chapter 6 looks at the interpretation of policy under the first Monopolies Commission and chapter 7 analyses the passage of the 1956 Restrictive Trade Practices Act in the context of changing business strategies in Britain. Finally chapter 8 examines legislative moves against resale price maintenance from the inter-war period to 1964 when it was abolished.

Two chapters set the scene. Chapter 2 indicates the actual extent and nature of the British cartel system between 1880 and 1956. The thrust of British competition policy up to 1965 was directed against cartels rather than large firms, and hence some idea of the problems which policy-makers felt they were tackling is needed, and cannot be gained elsewhere as the historical evolution of British cartels has been a neglected area of study. Chapter 3 indicates the main outlines of British policy on 'monopoly' up to 1939 when the main story begins.

2   The British cartel system, 1880–1964

People of the same trade seldom meet together, even for merriment or diversion, but the conversation ends in a conspiracy against the Publick or in some contrivance to raise prices.

Adam Smith *An enquiry into the Nature and Causes of the Wealth of Nations, 1776* edited by R.H. Campbell and A.S. Skinner (Oxford, 1976) I.x.c.27 p. 145.

Some definitions of cartels:
'Planned Trading: the unwilling tribute paid by Capitalism to Socialism.'
'Social Security for Shareholders'.

Dalton Papers 7/6 unsigned memorandum by an official at the Board of Trade, 30/9/1944 giving Dalton definitions of a cartel in preparation for parliamentary questions.

Recent accounts of the historical evolution of the 'corporate economy' in Britain have focussed primarily on the development of the large firm. The history of cartels has received only cursory attention, although recently the significance of price-fixing in the 1930s has been re-assessed.[1] Yet cartels, international and domestic, were arguably the dominant form of market control from the 1930s to the early 1950s, and together with a critical level of concentration of ownership and technical development created a culture of collusion. It was against this widespread cartelisation that the Acts of 1948 and 1956 were directed.

This chapter traces the interwoven development of cartels and concentration in British manufacturing from the 1880s to the 1950s. It looks at the development of the British trade association system before commenting briefly on some views of the causes and consequences of restrictionism in British manufacturing especially in the middle years of the twentieth century.[2]

A cartel[3] is a collusive strategy which, because the associated firms remain nominally independent, does not end the competition among them, 'rather is the arena changed'.[4] It differs therefore from the amalgamation (formed by merger or takeover) which, while part of a competitive strategy, does end, more or less permanently, the competition among the firms who amalgamate. This combination of collusion and competition among the firms in the cartel is its unique feature. A secondary feature is its extreme flexibility. Each cartel agreement can choose from a wide range of restrictive activities – restrictions on sales attached to patent licences, price-fixing, division of markets, regulation of capacity and output to name but a few. This 'pick 'n' mix' element in the cartel and its specific choice of restrictive practices makes it a vertitable weather-vane, not only of the economic climate generally, but of market conditions in specific trades.

As the terms of the cartel are relatively impermanent and unstable, cartels require a specific set of conditions to secure the loyalty of as wide a section of the trade as possible in order to reap what may be short-term benefits. They are more successful where the organisation *of the trade or product as a whole* is possible, and hence in conditions where the number of firms is manageable.[5] Whereas in the 1950s it was unusual for a large firm to control 70% of the production of a commodity in Britain (though some did) it is rare to know of a cartel that did not. Cartels may thus appear more monopolistic, but their success and longevity will frequently depend on the existence of large firms, willing and able to regulate the trade. The definition adopted here is intended to emphasise the development of large firms and cartels as a unity of collusive behaviour, or as Hannah has expressed it, cartels as the complements to mergers.[6]

Much evidence on cartels gathered for this survey concerns the development of trade associations. The terms 'cartel' and 'trade association' came to be used almost interchangeably in British economic literature of the 1930s.[7] Domestic cartels were generally organised through trade associations which combined two roles: as private market-regulating bodies and as representatives of their trade with the government. If the Association wished for government recognition it had to claim to be as representative of the firms in a trade as possible. Most estimates of the extent to which a trade association 'controlled' a particular market are therefore based on the trade association's own, possibly bloated, account. However, measurement of these trade associations is useful. They proved to be long-lived, and between the 1930s and 1950s moved to an integration horizontally and vertically of all stages of production and retailing in a given trade. There thus emerged a recognisable system, which combined economic control with political influence. Hence description of the growth of this system means that an idea of the *potential* extent of market regulation by private industry can be obtained. Most importantly, the politico–economic character of the trade association system is crucial in understanding the evolution of British competition policy in the 1940s and 1950s.

Table 2.1. *Calculations of the share of the largest 100 firms in manufacturing net output, 1907–78*

Dates	Share according to Hannah (%)	Share according to Prais (%)
1907	15	
1909		16
1919	17	
1924	21	22
1930	26	
1935	23	24
1939	23	
1948	22	
1949		22
1953	26	27
1958	33	32
1963	38	37
1968		41
1970	40	40/41
1978	41	

Source: L. Hannah *The Rise of the Corporate Economy* (1983) pp. 180–81; J.S. Prais *The Evolution of Giant Firms in Britain* (Cambridge, 1980) p. 4.

Cartels and concentration in Britain in the twentieth century

Compared with Germany and the United States, Britain was a late developer in the moves towards concentration and collusion at the end of the nineteenth century. In the United States, the largest 100 enterprises already accounted for 22% of net manufacturing output in 1909, a position not reached in Britain until the 1920s (see table 2.1). In Germany the 'trust' movement became noteworthy from the 1870s, and the great Rhenish–Westphalian coal cartel began around 1876–7. The German Kartell-Commission estimated in 1905, in the first official investigation into cartels, that there were 353 associations.[8]

It is, of course, possible to cite early developments in Britain. The United Kingdom Soapmakers' Association was founded in 1867, the National Association of British and Irish Millers was formed in 1878, and there were several attempts at price-fixing in the iron industry in the 1880s and early 1890s. However, these were generally short-lived, and local to overcome a recession in the market, especially that of 1885. The Royal Commission on the Depression in Trade and Industry of that year gave only a small hint of any tendency to combination and agreement: rings in steel and the international agreement on rails were mentioned, and criticisms of railway rates aired.[9]

The increasing number of agreements in the 1890s were local, limited to textile finishing and the iron trades and frequently needing to invoke trade union or workforce support, such as the short-time agreement in the Yorkshire dyeing industry between 1894 and 1896 or the Birmingham Alliances in metal goods of 1891–1900.[10] The merger wave of 1895 to 1902 changed this situation somewhat. Between 1888 and 1912 at least 29 multiple firm amalgamations took place, involving 616 previously independent companies: all but three of these took place between 1895 and 1902. Many of these amalgamations achieved, so their prospectuses claimed, market shares of between 60 and 90%. They were all in the staple industries and food and drink especially brewing.[11] Many of these firms had previously been associated in price-fixing agreements, the firms for instance in Coats, the English Sewing Cotton Company, the Bleachers' Association, United Alkali and Wallpaper Manufacturers Ltd. In turn, the formation of these larger companies prompted still further association – agreements between Wallpaper Manufacturers Ltd and three other firms gave the firms 98% of the United Kingdom trade. The formation of United Alkali prompted attempts by paper manufacturers to build co-operative factories to make their own bleaching powder, and when these failed the British Paper Makers' Association attempted to raise their prices in response to rises in the cost of raw materials.[12] The Committee on Trusts which reported in 1918 remarked that the greatest proportion of associations listed had come into existence since 1900.[13] Of trade associations affiliated to the FBI in the late 1940s, whose main original purpose was price-fixing, 30.4% were formed between 1900 and 1914 (see table 2.8).

While a trust movement was clearly discernible, it was still relatively limited, and this is demonstrated in the scale of British firms' involvement in international cartels up to 1914; for involvement internationally is dependent on levels of domestic organisation.[14] While one of the most important of these, the International Rail Makers' Association, was first formulated in London in 1886, British participation was mainly limited to shipping conferences and some basic products (see table 2.2).[15] Plummer and Macrosty give details of further international cartels to which British firms were party, including nitrates, bleaching powder, tobacco and incandescent lamps.[16]

The First World War was, however, a major catalyst in the development of Trade Associations. In 1918 the Committee on Trusts referred to over 500 associations 'exerting a substantial influence on the course of industry and price'. John Hilton, its Secretary, reported that 25% of the

Table 2.2. *British participation in international cartels, 1914*

Industry	No. of international cartels	No. with British participation
Coal, iron, other metals	22	9
Chemicals and related industries	19	6
Transportation (mainly shipping conferences)	17	15
Textiles	12	2
Glass and porcelain	8	1
Paper and pulp	7	1
Stones and minerals	6	3
Electrical industry	5	1
Miscellaneous	10	2
Totals	106	40

Source: B. Harms *Volkswirtschaft und Weltwirtschaft* (Jena, 1914) pp. 254–81; OFT *International Cartels* p. 156.

building materials needed in the average house were subject to full control by associations, and 33% to partial control.[17] In 1920 Percy Ashley, Assistant Secretary to the Board of Trade, reported for the Standing Committee on Trusts that he had collected the names of 3,500 federations and associations, of which 700 were local associations in the building trade and 450 were associations in the distributive trade. He had the constitutions of 400 of the remaining 2,266 of which about 100 included avowed objects to regulate the market, through regulation of output and prices.[18]

While cartels proved difficult to sustain in the years after 1918 the 1920s constituted the era of Britain's second merger wave, massively increasing the levels of concentration of ownership in Britain.[19] Many of these mergers were among firms previously linked by agreements, as in industrial alcohol (Distillers) and chemicals (ICI). From the mid-1930s to the late 1940s or early 1950s there was little increase in aggregate levels of concentration and there may have been a slight decrease (see tables 2.1 and 2.2). Prais talks of 'a freezing of the industrial structure during the war period'.[20]

It is this period which marks a high point of British cartelisation.[21] One estimate suggests that about 30% of gross manufacturing output was controlled by trade association cartel arrangements in 1935 (see table 2.3). In 1937 A.F. Lucas was to argue that the trade association 'is without question the most common medium of control in the present time'.[22] This new phase was strengthened by the Second World War and in spite of legislation in 1948 showed no signs of abating right up until the legislation

Table 2.3. *Domestic cartels in British manufacturing industry, 1930s*

Industry	Gross annual production controlled (%)
Food, drink, tobacco	30
Chemicals	21
Iron and steel and products thereof	68
Non-ferrous metals	46
Engineering, shipbuilding and vehicles	26
Textiles	26
Clay and building materials	52
Paper, printing and stationery	17
Miscellaneous	30
Total, all 'factory trades'	30

Source: Calculated from OFT *Survey*, Vols I and II and see H. Mercer 'The Evolution of British government policy towards competition in private industry 1940–56', unpublished Ph.D. thesis (University of London, 1989) Appendix 2. These are provisional calculations, any figures and percentages must be treated with extreme caution.

of 1956. In fact the next date for which reasonably safe quantification is possible is 1956 when in legislation of that year the government established the register of restrictive practices. The major cartel agreements registered (that is excluding the mass of local agreements) covered between 50 and 60% of manufactured output in the mid-1950s[23] (see table 2.4). It is difficult to distinguish between an increase in available evidence or a real increase in the extent of cartelisation. A few firms certainly abandoned restrictive practices, in response to an actual or threatened investigation by the Monopolies and Restrictive Practices Commission (MRPC) between 1949 and 1956.[24] The Commission's reports also reveal that in some industries trade associations had suffered a fall in the extent to which their members dominated the home market, between 1918 and 1948.[25] But on the whole, cartelisation was possibly more pervasive in the 1950s than it had been in the 1930s,[26] a sign that cartels, though sometimes formed in recession will continue to reap the benefits of recovery and growth. This premise is supported by evidence relating to the structure of trade associations discussed later in the chapter.

Indeed, the sheer number of agreements registered after 1956 makes an interesting comparison with Germany in the 1930s – the land of the cartel. There, about 2,100 cartels existed in 1930, controlling possibly 50% of industrial output in 1938. In Britain, 2,240 agreements were entered on the open register between 1956 and 1959 and up to 2,660 by 1969.[27] Although

Table 2.4. *Registered restrictive agreements in British manufacturing industry, 1958*

SIC order	Industry	% sales covered by agreements
I	Agriculture	NA
II	Mining and quarrying	3.1
III	Food, drink, tobacco	67.6
IV	Coal and petroleum products	48.5
V	Chemical and allied industries	26.4
VI	Metal manufacture	76.2
VII	Mechanical engineering	29.6
VIII	Instrument engineering	25.8
IX	Electrical engineering	77.6
X	Shipbuilding and marine engineering	
XI	and Vehicles	49.2
XII	Metal goods n.e.s.	43.6
XIII	Textiles	60.4
XIV	Leather, leather goods, fur	3.2
XV	Clothing and footwear	10.4
XVI	Bricks, pottery, glass, cement, etc.	80.7
XVII	Timber, furniture, etc.	60.1
XVIII	Paper, printing and publishing	70.3
XIX	Other manufacturing	59.6
	Total	54.1

Note: NA: not available.
Source: Derived from D.C. Elliott and J.D. Gribbin, 'The Abolition of Cartels and Structural Change in the United Kingdom', in Jacquemin and de Jong (eds.), *Welfare Aspects of Industrial Markets* (Leiden, 1977) p. 353.

about half of all these applied only to a locality, particularly in the distribution of building materials, their cumulative effect could be national in scope. In addition agreements usually included all the large firms, accounting for up to 80% of sales, and outsiders, including foreign importers, had little capacity to upset the market so controlled.[28] In 1959, when 2,240 agreements were entered on the Register, 127 groups out of the 150 in the Standard Industrial Classification had entries related to them. While some industries were regulated by only a few agreements (cement, carpets, and paint) others (the building trade, iron and steel, textiles and road-making) were each represented by 150 or more agreements, many of these local. At this time manufacturers were party to the overwhelming majority of agreements – 1,800 while wholesalers were party to 350, retailers to 400. The most common types of practice were simple price-fixing – two-thirds of the agreements registered – and just under half concerned standard conditions of sale. In 300 agreements buyers or sellers agreed to restrictions on persons with whom they would deal (known as exclusive dealing arrangements); 300 covered the division of sales territory, 200 imposed limits on the kinds of goods parties could produce or trade, a further 200 imposed quantitative limitations on production, acquisition or supply and 150 determined buying prices. Such a picture gives a quite breathtaking overview of the extent and nature of cartelisation in Britain in the middle of the twentieth century.[29]

In the 1930s Britain also became a major player in the world league of international cartels in industrial products. About 42% of world trade was cartelised between 1929 and 1937 according to a post-war survey.[30] By 1938 between 28 and 34% of the value of British exports were affected by international agreements, according to the investigations of Board of Trade economists in 1944, and 16% of the gross output of British manufacturing was covered by such agreements. This latter figure was based on the fact that international cartels affected production in capital goods and semi-manufactured goods particularly. In turn this meant that 'the greater part of industrial output for export is indirectly influenced by the operations of cartels and other international arrangements'[31] (see table 2.5). Again the sheer number of international cartels to which Britain was party is testimony to the changed situation since before 1914.

However, during the war, with a few exceptions, the international cartel system collapsed as the result of trading with the enemy legislation and controls on foreign exchange needed to pay debts arising under patent or quota agreements.[32] When the war ended, many firms sought to re-establish their arrangements and many important agreements were renewed, for instance in cables, electric lamps and electrical engineering, woodscrews, chemicals, non-ferrous metal manufacture, matches, cement (see appendix 2). Indeed, in 1947 the Board of Trade was concerned lest these arrangements, particularly those in chemicals and electrical engineering were, by forcing British firms towards Empire markets, hindering the drive to increase exports to hard currency markets, such as the United States, Argentina and Sweden. The Board of Trade believed that the pre-war system had actually been re-established, in extent and character, but the evidence is limited. Certainly, after the Second World War Britain's commitments to the United States to prevent cartels were taken seriously and the Board of Trade could no longer give unconditional support or approval to international arrangements.[33] International cartels received unwelcome publicity from MRPC reports, and many British firms, like ICI and British Timken, operating cartels with American firms found themselves indicted for actions in restraint of trade and facing criminal prosecution in the United States. Nevertheless, MRPC reports indicated that little had changed – and major international ramifications were found in the

Table 2.5. *Exports of products wholly or mainly manufactured known to be affected by international arrangements, 1938*

Industry	% affected, 1938
Coke and manufactured fuel	88
Pottery, glass, abrasives	37
Iron and steel and manufactures thereof	85
Non-ferrous metals and manufactures thereof	28
Electrical goods and apparatus	47
Machinery	24
Textiles (cotton)	7
(woollens)	0
(silks)	0
Manufactures of other textile materials	26
Chemicals, drugs, dyes	44
Oils, fats, resins – manufactured	79
Paper, cardboard, etc.	10
Vehicles (incl. locomotives, ships and aircraft)	27
Rubber manufactures	7
Misc. articles	7
Total	28

Note: If all chemicals are included the total is 34%.
Source: OFT, *Survey Vol. I* (1976) p. xxiii.

cases of tyres, electrical engineering and medical gases. International cartels were still considered important enough to British interests in 1956 to warrant special treatment in the Act of that year to exclude them from registration on the grounds of national interest.

Finally, the end of our period sees a further change in direction. From 1949, and more obviously by 1953, the trend towards increased concentration was re-asserted, that is *before* the passing of the 1956 Restrictive Trade Practices Act.[34] In particular from 1952 onwards a sustained rise in merger activity began and from 1959–69 the number of firm disappearances by merger outstripped those of the 1920s. Some consensus exists that the 1956 Act, in effectively undermining the domestic cartel system and contributing to 'business uncertainty' in the 1950s was a factor in the merger movement.[35] Industries with agreements terminated under the 1956 Act showed a significantly higher increase in the level of concentration by 1968, probably the result of greater merger activity, and many mergers were among erstwhile cartel partners.[36]

Other factors contributed to the renewed merger movement, especially increased competitive pressures in conditions of overall growth brought about by the ending of protectionist policies, widening markets and hence increasing benefits from economies of scale.[37] Thus the re-assertion of the trend towards increasing concentration was itself a factor in the passage of the 1956 Act, weakening firms' reliance on and commitment to cartels as a means of market control.

However, cartelisation persisted. 'Information agreements' became common, and eventually these too became registrable under the 1965 Mergers and Monopolies Act, but until then were an important loophole. A few agreements were allowed by the Restrictive Practices Court in, for instance, books, floor tiles and bolts and nuts, while international cartels and a host of restrictive agreements like sole agency and solus sites arrangements were not effectively caught by the 1956 Act, although some were later referred to the Monopolies Commission.[38]

While periods of marked cartelisation and marked increases in concentration alternated, each was dependent on and related to the other. Indeed Robert Brady was to comment in 1943 that 'the trade association becomes in effect a cartel instrument to promote the monopoly policies of a single or a small group of giant concerns'.[39] We now look at how cartels and large-scale industrial organisation were interdependent.

First, British participation in international cartels in the 1930s was generally through the dominant firms in an industry, such as ICI, Unilever, AEI, EMI, Distillers' Company, Courtaulds, Bowater, Metal Box, Pilkington and the British Match Corporation (see appendix 1). They arranged agreements, sometimes on behalf of their domestic cartel partners, a situation which served to reinforce the dominance of the home market by large firms in those sectors affected, such as chemicals and electrical engineering. This helped to create monopolistic conditions in the home market. In 39% of the international agreements described in the Board's survey the British secured the home market for home producers, for instance some iron and steel producers wished to stop cheap imports through which the smaller firms were managing to become more competitive.[40] Indeed, on the whole, participation in international cartels reflected the decline in direct British investment abroad and was a preferred and profitable strategy for British transnational firms.[41] Industries where international agreements were concluded through trade associations, such as iron and steel and coal, had required government intervention to secure the necessary degree of domestic organisation.[42]

Moreover, British participation in international cartels was heavily dependent on the monopoly of imperial ties. The inter-war period saw the intensified exploitation of empire as world trade was increasingly oriented towards economic blocs. British trade with the Empire had increased from

Table 2.6. *The extent of RPM, 1900–64*

Year	Consumer expenditure on price-maintained goods (%)	Consumer expenditure on price-maintained goods and services	Source
1900	3		A
1938	30		B
1938	32		C
1954	55		D
1956	44	34	A
1960	33	25 (23)	E, A
1964	38		F
1964	40	32	G, A
1964	36	28	A

Sources:
A J. Pickering *Resale Price Maintenance in Practice* (1966) pp. 44, 45, 47, 48, 160.
B National Institute of Economic and Social Research, cited in BT64/455 RPM(E)7. Memorandum to the Lloyd Jacob committee by NIESR.
BPP (1948–49), *Board of Trade, Report of the Committee on Resale Price Maintenance,* Cmd.7696 Vol.xx.
C J.B. Jefferys *Distribution of Consumer Goods* (1950) p. 112.
D Dr M. Abrams in *The Times* cited in Pickering *Resale Price Maintenance* p. 45.
E B.S. Yamey *RPM and Shoppers' Choice* (1960) p. 8 and Pickering *Resale Price Maintenance* p. 47.
F Edward Heath *Parl. Deb.* (1963–64) Vol. 691 Col. 258.
G *The Economist* 29/2/1964 and Pickering *Resale Price Maintainance* p. 160.
For 1960 the figure in brackets is the alternative estimate in P.W.S. Andrews and F.A. Friday *Fair Trade. Resale Price Maintenance Re-examined* (1960) p. 8.

34.7% of exports in the 1900s to 42.7% in the 1920s and 46.6% in the 1930s.[43] In part this was of course due to the effect of imperial preference and long-standing marketing strategies of British firms. Indeed ICI saw its future in furthering imperial trade.[44] But international cartels exacerbated the trend. A typical pre-war cartel assigned exclusive sales rights in North America to American firms, in Southern and South Eastern Europe to German firms, and in the Dominions and the Empire to British firms. Areas such as Latin America would be left free for competition, although there might be local agreements governing inter-firm relationships there.

A second indication of the close links between concentration and cartelisation was the rapid development of resale price maintenance (RPM). RPM involves fixing the price at which retailers may sell and was enforced through such devices as loyalty rebates or the withholding of supplies from price-cutters through stop lists. A dramatic rise in its extent occurred in the inter-war years, with smaller, but steady growth from the war to a peak in the mid-1950s (see table 2.6). A Board of Trade report of

1949 concluded that collective resale price maintenance had, 'turned price maintenance from a reasonable means of preventing damage to well-known quality brands ... into a comprehensive system for regulating and policing entire industries'. Such price-fixing, together with branding and packaging, 'must result in the virtual elimination of price competition in the greater part of the distributive trades of the country'.[45]

The growth and strength of RPM was closely connected with the progress of concentration of production. Calculations undertaken by the National Institute of Economic and Social Research (NIESR) in evidence to the Lloyd Jacob Committee (reproduced in appendix 2) indicate, as far as their information was available, the correlation between goods in which RPM was 'significant' (although the authors of the report failed to distinguish collective and individually enforced schemes), mainly branded, nationally advertised consumer goods – food and durables – and levels of concentration of employment. By 1960 further areas affected were radio and television sets, gramophones and records, photographic and sports equipment, watches and clocks, beer, wines and spirits. Frank Friday's estimates give a good general impression (see table 2.7).[46] The practice was becoming increasingly evident in services dependent on supplies of branded products, for instance to high street hairdressers.

RPM was the most well known of retailing restrictions, but other forms existed. In petrol, for instance, the oil companies introduced the 'tied garage' system in the course of the 1950s, offering inducements to would-be garage owners to buy exclusively from one oil company in return for help with refurbishment of the owner's garage.[47] In brewing the 'tied house' system had operated since the eighteenth century and increased concentration proceeded with the extension of the tie. By 1950 95% of pubs in England in Wales and 80% in Scotland were tied.[48]

All these trades mentioned were dominated by oligopolistic firms. Although *collective* RPM (operated through trade associations of retailers and manufacturers) caught public attention, it was RPM operated by individual firms without the help of retailing associations which in fact predominated. An estimated 13% of products were regulated by collective enforcement of RPM in 1955,[49] making individual RPM more significant. The effect of the banning of collective enforcement of RPM and the registration procedure for other cartels was to reduce the incidence of RPM by about 25%, yet still in 1964 RPM had 'extensive sway',[50] for the terms of the 1956 Act encouraged individual manufacturers to prescribe retail prices.

Basil Yamey has asserted that the pressure for RPM came originally at the end of the nineteenth century from small retailers, threatened by the competition from multiple and department stores and the Co-operatives.

Table 2.7. *Proportion of consumer expenditure on goods and services* .
subject to RPM and direct RPM, United Kingdom, 1960

| | | % on | |
Consumer expenditure on	Amount spent 1958 (£ million)	RPM goods and services (%)	direct RPM goods and services (%)
Food	4,672	15	8
Alcoholic drink	941	46	20
Tobacco	1,031	99.5	—
Housing	1,374	1	—
Fuel and light	677	—	53
Footwear and clothing	1,383	8	33
Motor cars and cycles	384	67	—
Furniture and floor coverings	428	15	9
Radio, electrical and other durables	335	89	1
Other household goods	451	1	—
Books, newspapers and magazines	233	97	1
Chemists goods	224	70	11
Miscellaneous recreational goods	161	25	—
Other miscellaneous goods	206	17	2
Running costs of vehicles	342	28	23
Travel	521	—	93
Postal, telephone and telegraph services	132	—	100
Entertainments	193	—	45
Insurance	164	—	100
Other services	868	—	12
Total	14,719	23	17

Note:
Direct RPM is 'when a company owning a chain of retail outlets stipulates the prices at which the manager of each must sell the products . . . [which have] the name or trade mark of that company [e.g. the practice of Marks & Spencer]' (pp. 10–11).
Source: Reproduced from P.W.S. Andrews and F.A. Friday *Fair Trade, Resale Price Maintenance Re-examined* (1960) p. 8.

They lobbied manufacturers to join them in price maintenance schemes.[51] However, large manufacturers were behind many price maintenance schemes, such as the Net Book Agreement, the Motor Traders' Association and the Tobacco Trade Association and large manufacturing firms took a leading role in the Proprietary Articles Trade Association in chemists' goods (Burroughs Wellcome) and the Groceries Federation (W.H. Lever).[52] Large brewers scrambled to establish tied houses to secure outlets for their large-scale production. A similar motive underlay RPM by chocolate and tobacco firms, for whom a large number of outlets was important in their marketing strategy, and RPM, by assuring margins to retailers, secured this policy. Manufacturers of electrical goods used a system of licensed dealers to ensure a certain level of servicing. RPM allowed quasi-vertical integration and shifted pricing decisions – once the key function of the retailer – to the manufacturer. Thus as Kaldor argued in 1964 the real issue in RPM was not price competition among retailers but among manufacturers.[53] In the words of an authority on retailing, J.B. Jefferys, RPM meant that:

the problems of marketing for manufacturers became better defined and therefore more susceptible of solution, the flow of goods became smoother and the market for them more stable, and the quality and standard of the products could be more readily guaranteed.[54]

Indeed, RPM grew alongside the 'branded' product[55] and there was a common force behind both – the tendency to mass-marketing, uniform production, concentration and centralisation of production and distribution, and hence the tendency to the large-scale unit.

Meanwhile RPM provided small retailers with a defence against competition from large retailers, especially from the multiple stores. Union Cold Storage was formed in 1923 with 2,000 branches and a series of amalgamations between 1924 and 1931 formed the Home and Colonial group with 3,000 branches.[56] By 1939 multiple stores accounted for up to 36% of total retail sales. Large retailers had potential economies of scale and could reduce their prices. RPM limited the extent to which they could in fact do so and this, together with secure margins provided by the system of RPM, shielded smaller retailers from competition. RPM therefore represented an alliance of small retailers and large manufacturers of branded goods.

A third indication of the symbiotic relationship between large-scale organisation and cartelisation lies in the way the long-term extension of state economic activity after the war, creating large-scale, monopsonistic organisations, aided the development of British cartels. From the 1940s trade associations sprang up or re-organised themselves in response to the monopsony of such bodies as local authority housing departments, hospitals, schools, and the National Coal Board. Such public bodies encountered strong cartels in the distribution of milk, coal and coke, and the supply of paper, dental instruments, carpets, cement, bricks, dustbins, some motor vehicles and cables. This was in addition to the many restrictions in supplies needed by local authorities' building programmes.[57] However sometimes authorities were able to demand more competitive prices. London County Council stated that some suppliers, for instance of school equipment, had been known to sell at a loss to them to reap the benefits of advertisement which such contracts presented.[58]

The extent of cartelisation in these areas was demonstrated when local authorities began to complain about the practice of uniform or level tendering in the mid-1950s. The items which came to the government's and the media's attention were in constructional steel, cement and building contracts generally: Manchester Corporation reported the practice in school milk.[59] There is also evidence that in such areas as electrical engineering, non-ferrous metals, and the supply of heavy plant for chemicals, trade associations operated a reporting system by which the association handled customer enquires. This clearly provided the means for consultation over tenders to occur.[60] According to *The Economist* the development of this practice in the 1950s showed a return to practices of the 1930s when suppliers did not even have the good manners to show some small diversity of prices.[61]

Much of this analysis leads to the conclusion that in Britain from the 1930s to 1950s the cartel was the economic strategy predominantly of the large firm, and that cartelisation flourished in conditions of large-scale production, distribution and mass demand. Smaller firms found trade associations useful, not only for providing them with market, technical and export information but also for circulating information about 'business enquiries' and 'costs and prices'.[62] In many trade associations prices were so fixed that even less efficient firms could make a reasonable profit. However, the ending of a cartel sometimes prompted massive competition from small firms, though followed by further consolidation and price rises.[63] One small manufacturer of paper boxes complained that large firms were involved in many associations, sometimes as producers of a basic material, sometimes as consumers of that same material, while smaller firms, tending to be either consumers or producers, suffered as the larger firm proposed pricing policies which reconciled the two stages of his interest.[64]

The concomitant flowering of international cartels, both in manufactured goods and commodities, of domestic agreements and retailing associations led therefore to a situation where a large firm, as in the classic German case, may have stood with its head in one cartel, its trunk in another and its feet in still more. Large firms were dominant in some of the largest trade associations of the inter-war period: Lever Bros in the United Kingdom Soap Manufacturers' Association, ICI in the Sulphate of Ammonia Federation, various iron and steel firms in the BISF.[65]

ICI's business in the 1930s was regulated by over 800 cartel agreements, domestic and international, and the company kept out of certain products to avoid competition with other large firms, such as Courtaulds in rayon and Distillers in heavy organic chemicals.[66] Some of the cartels she participated in were in Chilean nitrates, Spanish potash, numerous international agreements for chemical products, while domestically her agreement with Fisons, for instance, regulated selling conditions in fertilisers. Cadbury's was a leading participant in the buying agreement for West African cocoa of September 1937, an agreement which formed the basis of war-time and post-war marketing schemes for cocoa.[67] Meanwhile, domestically Cadbury's operated RPM schemes in retailing.

In the 1950s Unilever was a member of at least 22 trade associations which were concerned with various types of commercial regulation: prices, margins, quotas, conditions of sale or agreements on standards and quality. These associations covered the regulation of trade in raw materials – the Cocoa Association of London, London Average Market Letter Committee (for tallow), Incorporated Oil Seed Association, Federation of Bone Users – in processed goods – Edible Oil Association and National Oil Distributors Federation, Seed Oil, Cake and General Products Association, Association of British Chemical Manufacturers – and the disposal of by-products – United Kingdom Glycerine Producers' Association. Her subsidiary, the United Africa Co., was the other main participant, with Cadbury's, in the 1937 cocoa buying pool.[68]

The development of the system

The extent and stability of the British cartel system cannot be gleaned accurately simply from a quantitative account, for cartel arrangements were continually being re-worked. Equally important is to recognise the longevity, stability, and structure of the trade associations through which many restrictive practices were operated or co-ordinated. In particular the integration of economic and political functions in the trade associations is of great importance in the subsequent story of British competition policy.

By 1944 there were 2,500 trade associations of regional and national scope.[69] FBI research in about 1950 revealed that price-fixing associations affiliated to the FBI had a long life. As table 2.8 shows, 34.7% of trade associations in the sample formed to fix prices had their origins before the First World War, 58.8% between 1915 and 1939, and thus 93.5% had their origins before the Second World War. Thus in the 1930s over half of trade associations formed were formed to fix prices or otherwise manipulate market conditions.[70] The research group, Political and Economic Planning (PEP) conducted a major survey of industrial trade associations in the 1950s and declared that price-fixing was the raison d'être of trade associations.[71] Conversely, when, in 1956 trade associations withdrew their price lists, to conform with the new Act, many organisations lost members and

Table 2.8. *Dates of and reasons for the formation of trade associations affiliated to the FBI, 1875–1950*

	Reasons for formation				
Year	(1)	(2)	(3)	(4)	% of total
Up to 1875	2.1		4.3		3.4
1875–99	4.3	15.4		17.9	
1900–14	6.4	42.4	30.4	28.6	24.5
1915–20	21.3	30.8	10.9	7.1	17
1921–30	6.4		21.8	10.7	11.6
1931–9	8.5	11.4	26.1	17.9	15
1940–5	48.9		4.3	10.7	19.7
1946–50	2.1		2.2	7.1	2.7
	100	100	100	100	100

Notes:
(1) Formed to negotiate with government (of total, 32%).
(2) Formed to deal with wages, etc. (of total, 17.7%).
(3) Formed to negotiate prices/price maintenance (of total, 31.3%).
(4) Other (of total, 19%).
Source: CBI MSS200/F/3/S2/14/70, Trade Associations: their place in the industrial world. Unsigned, undated memorandum, 1947.

quickly collapsed.[72] According to the FBI researcher cited above, the figure for the number of price-fixing associations may be an underestimation, for the FBI having itself the primary function of representing industry to government, tended to attract associations with similar functions.[73] Thus, while it is clear that the 'political' functions of trade associations were increasing, claims by PEP that by the 1950s only a small proportion of them were price- or market-fixing need to be treated with caution.[74] Indeed, PEP's evidence was based on that of trade associations themselves. But price-fixing associations had refused to co-operate with the study, and PEP's access even to non-restrictive associations was 'dependent on convincing them that we are not primarily concerned with restrictive practices'.[75]

This is not to deny that one of the main developments in the 1940s was the trade association as a political organisation. The desire for political representation can be seen in the rise in the number of trade associations affiliated to the FBI, from 178 in 1939 to 270 in 1948.[76] While price-fixing associations dated their formation to pre-war, notably the 1930s, the origins of half of those associations whose main function was to liaise with government lay in the war-time period. It was also during the war and the later 1940s that attempts were made to regularise and systematise the relations between associations, amalgamating or federating already existing organisations. In contrast the trade association as a politico–economic entity was advanced in Germany by the end of the nineteenth century.[77]

The 1940s saw an intensification of trade association activities. Frequently more firms and industries were drawn into the system,[78] but more importantly, existing agreements were intensified, predominantly through vertical arrangements co-ordinating the activities of producers and distributors. We can examine this process using information obtained in the course of PEP's survey.

PEP chose 50 'representative' trade associations, of which 42 had, according to the researchers' notes, practised some form of commercial regulation at some stage in their history (see appendix 3). 27 of these were founded before 1939, and of these seven had their origins before the First World War. Of the 15 founded since 1939 several represented older trade associations which were reconstituted or revived, and others were amalgamations of associations formed pre-war. Altogether 17 of the associations had been either formed, reformed, undergone amalgamation or some form of re-organisation during and after the Second World War.[79] The 1940s was an important period in the formation and re-formation of trade associations, often in response to direct government pressure, or to the needs of government policy like the export drive or raw material allocation. Over 300 export groups were formed many of which later formed themselves into peace-time associations.[80]

Most typical, however, were the amalgamations of two or more trade associations into larger organisations, or the formation of 'umbrella' associations organised federally or operating many sectional groups. In this system it was common for the 'umbrella' to be responsible for broad policy matters, leaving commercial regulation to the affiliates if they desired it.[81]

'Umbrella' organisations were often formed in industries already highly regulated, and tending to bring more rationality and completeness to the system. The British Iron and Steel Federation (BISF) was reorganised in 1945, when the Joint Iron Council (JIC) was also formed for producers *and* customers of pig iron for uses other than steel-making. The latter's two constituent organisations, the Council of Ironfoundry Associations and the Council of Iron Producers, were themselves umbrella organisations. The JIC had a system of co-operation and discussion with the BISF which continued to represent producers of iron for steel-making.[82] The developments in the radio industry also demonstrate the tendency to unite trade customers and suppliers in umbrella organisations. Two major umbrella organisations were formed, the Radio Industry Council (1943) for manufacturers and the Radio and TV Retailers' Association (1942–4), with an exclusive dealing arrangement between the two.[83]

In some major industries trade associations adopted large, federal and more systematic structures. The British Non-Ferrous Metals Federation was formed in 1945 with 10 trade associations, each operating their own arrangements on prices, tenders, RPM and restrictions on capacity. Previously, it seems, each section of the industry was organised separately, negotiating its own international cartels. Alternatively these were negotiated via the large companies in the industry such as ICI, British Aluminium and the National Smelting Co. Post-war it was the Federation which instigated the international cartel known as the 'Lausanne Agreement'.[84]

The British Engineers' Association adopted a federal character in 1944. Its 17 associations, which in 1953 had 600 firms employed 1 million workers. Several of the federated organisations are known to have operated restrictive agreements, particularly through the 'reporting' system of tenders for contracts. (Examples are the Hydraulic Association, Tank and Industrial Plant Manufacturers' Association, and the Federation of Manufacturers of Contractors' Plant.)[85] The Federation of British Rubber and Allied Manufacturers' Association was formally constituted a federal organisation in 1942. One of its 24 associations was the Tyre Manufacturers' Conference, itself a war-time 'umbrella', operating a restrictive distribution scheme well into the 1950s when it was referred to the Monopolies Commission.[86] The BISF adopted a new constitution in 1945 by which 'the sectional associations were co-ordinated and grouped ... and the Federation became a Federation of trade associations (or conferences as the grouped associations were called) instead of a Federation of individual undertakings and trade associations'.[87]

In the case of colliery equipment, war and nationalisation prompted the formation of the Federated Associations of Colliery Equipment Manufacturers (FACEM) to allow its constituent associations to co-operate. The Council of Underground Machinery Manufacturers was also formed during the war and recognised by government as the representative body. FACEM had as one of its members the Mining Electric Lamps Manufacturers' Association (MELMA) also formed towards the end of the war. One company informed PEP that MELMA aimed to make the NCB buy from its members rather than directly from the cable and bulb manufacturers.[88] This, and the example of the coking industry's relationship with the NCB, the Gas Council and the Ministry of Fuel and Power demonstrates how nationalisation, far from breaking down cartel relationships acted to enhance the degree of co-ordination – meshing together state and private interests.

Prior to the war, major organisations had been formed in engineering, such as the British Electrical and Allied Manufacturers' Association, the British Engineers' Association, the Society of Motor Manufacturers and Traders and the Society of British Aircraft Constructors, in engineering. In the chemical industry there were the Association of British Chemical Manufacturers for heavy chemicals, the Association of British Pharmaceutical Industries for general drugs and the Proprietary Articles Trade Association and the Chemists' Friends' Association regulating resale prices and conditions for the sale of branded chemists' products.

These umbrella organisations and amalgamations did not necessarily increase the extent of price-fixing, but they did enhance their potential to make price-fixing more effective. Moreover, the evidence that these organisations were adopting more political functions endowed trade associations with political attributes, and formed the basis for the 'corporatist' suggestions for reconstruction put forward by all major industrial organisations during the Second World War. During the Second World War the controllers of industries were selected from within the industries concerned, a contrast with the First War when controllers had more claim to be 'independent'. This effectively made trade associations, and the large concerns within them an arm of the war-time state. *The Economist* in 1938 had criticised the evolving organisation of industry as a 'new feudal system, with the British market instead of British land, parcelled out among the barons', and in December 1939 argued that the new system of controls, 'under the guise of war-time needs' gave the system of industrial self-government 'official blessing'. Indeed, a range of voices criticised war-time controls as 'merely a glorified form of private monopolies run on a restrictive basis', 'almost indistinguishable from cartels', 'the self-rule of the monopolies masquerading as public control'. This picture supports the accepted one of a changed relationship between government and industry during the war. [89]

Trade associations' influence with government rested on their administrative uses, this in turn rested on the extent to which the associations did indeed represent the industry, which in turn rested historically on their price-fixing activities, and thus their initial attraction to firms. This situation was to give trade associations a powerful veto over government policy in the war and post-war periods. According to two PEP researchers, trade associations, in their relations with government departments 'had the field to themselves' compared with other interest groups such as trade unions, and could 'make the work of government difficult by organising criticism and by becoming less and less co-operative'.[90] The re-organisation and rationalisation of trade associations under the impact of war affected key sectors of the economy. Thus, as the British Engineers' Association remarked, in so far as it represented leading interests and could formulate effective policy, the association could 'bring strong pressure to bear on the Government, both on high-level and legislative matters and on detailed administrative questions'.[91]

Causes and consequences of British cartels

This chapter finally looks at some causes and consequences of cartelisation in British manufacturing, concentrating on the hot-house growth of cartels between the 1930s and the 1950s.

Cartels have been termed 'children of need', their seeds nurtured in conditions of slump and recession. Many cartels came into existence in the inter-war period as a preferred form of market control in conditions of excess capacity prevailing in the 1930s. In such conditions it is harder to drive firms out as weak firms will feel undervalued in the stock market, and thus prefer to hang on, while the acquiring firm would not see the addition of equipment to its stock as a growth point, but as a liability to be scrapped. Both may therefore prefer to collude.[92] However their persistence into the 1940s and 1950s is indicative of the increased ability of industrialists to make effective arrangements. This was the result not only of a given level of oligopoly and concentration, but also of government intervention. Indeed, when we look at government policies, it becomes clear how reliant cartelisation is on government.

First, the government's general policy to raise prices and profits in the 1930s gave a general red light to cartelisation.[93] Nowhere was this more effective than in the sphere of international cartelisation. The devaluation of sterling of 1931 was a powerful inducement to foreign industrialists to seek arrangements with their British counterparts.[94] The introduction of a general tariff created conditions of potential monopoly of the home market and provided the general framework in which British firms could strike international treaties in their products. The Ottawa agreements of 1932, the Import Duties Act of 1932 and the establishment of the Import Duties Advisory Committee (IDAC) to consider special duties on imports were major bargaining counters for British firms.[95] The IDAC was frequently and successfully used to enable British firms or trade associations to secure better terms from the international cartel, or to ensure that an arrangement was indeed concluded by threatening to impose high tariffs in that product.[96] Successful participation at an international level was predicated on effective domestic organisation and thus the IDAC itself encouraged the formation of associations to facilitate negotiations with foreign counterparts, as in iron and steel, rolling mill machinery, and in the case of British competition with Japan in textiles.[97]

Secondly, control over excess capacity – a major aim of many cartelists in the conditions of the 1930s – was generally only successful where government and banks intervened. Competition proved a very slow way of shedding firms and excess capacity, as many observers of the 1930s and 1940s noted. Banks, industry and government drew closer together behind the banner of rationalisation, but the nature of their interaction promoted not amalgamation but cartelisation.

British governments in the inter-war period preferred to hand over direct intervention for ratonalisation to the banks. The Bank of England's rationalisation policies were aimed not at industrial efficiency, but at preserving the stability of the banking of the system against high levels of indebtedness among firms in the staple industries, while simultaneously heading off direct state intervention.[98] Without statutory control of capacity forthcoming from the state or sufficient financial resources forthcoming from the banks amalgamations proved difficult to promote. The Lancashire Cotton Corporation, established through the Bank of England, became a means for banks to offload bankrupt spinning companies, followed by large-scale scrapping of plant. Elsewhere in cotton, amalgamation schemes foundered in the face of Bank of England unwillingness to provide financial backing without good prospects of profitability, which in turn seemed possible only if state powers to regulate production were invoked. Instead mill-owners tried various price-maintenance and capacity-reducing schemes, at first on a voluntary basis and then, as loyalty to these cartels proved elusive, statutorily through the Spindles Act of 1936 and the Cotton Industry (Reorganisation) Act of 1939.[99] The most important result of 10 years of government, banking and industrial attempts to restructure the industry was a far-reaching state-sponsored cartel.

In the iron and steel industry Tolliday stresses the divisions within the industry and, again, the banks' unwillingness to depart from traditional patterns of hands-off involvement in industry. The government tried to use the IDAC, making the granting of a tariff dependent on the establishment of a body to promote rationalisation in the industry – the BISF. Government willingness to leave industry to manage its own affairs led to the 'hijacking' of the BISF by the industry, which came to be a price-maintenance organisation.[100] In coal the immense financial problems of the industry, combined with long-standing pressure from government commissions for amalgamation prompted the 1930 Coal Mines Act which, while supposed to promote rationalisation, in fact became a state-sponsored device to maintain prices and control output, complete with selling agencies regionally and nationally.[101]

Thus, the most sophisticated cartel form adopted in Britain, involving the almost complete abrogation of power over firms by the cartel and strict control of capacity, was achieved in instances of state or Bank of England involvement or endorsement, while most cartels in Britain in the 1930s and 1950s remained simple price-fixing agreements. Otherwise in the 1930s controls over capacity existed in earthenware goods, iron and steel making, sections of the textile trade, and flour-milling. However, by the 1950s private agreements to restrict capacity seemed, if anything, more widespread, possibly because of the enhanced organisation of the trade associations: in the 1950s the MRPC found restrictions on capacity in dental goods, electric cables, calico printing and semi-manufactured copper goods.[102]

Finally, trade associations became transmission belts of government economic policies from the 1930s to the 1950s. In the 1930s they were seen by the government and the Bank of England as a preferable way to articulate the collective interests of an industry, and to effect rationalisation. In the war and post-war period they were used to assist allocation of materials and price controls systems, and the Labour government had plans for heightened industrial organisation, through the Development Councils.[103] The development of RPM was stimulated by the war which allowed the introduction of licensing and limits on entry and ended price-cutting in ways found impossible before the war.[104]

Specifically we find the government giving encouragement to the development of federated trade associations and umbrella groups. One example is particularly interesting. The National Council of Building Material Producers (NCBMP) was set up in 1942 on the request of the government. Representing the producers of between 60 and 95% of building supplies, depending on which items were included, its original purpose was to act as a mechanism for the negotiation of government contracts. It had no price-fixing or restrictive objects, but its constituent associations did. There were eight main sections, and included such groups as the National Federation of Clay Industries, the Cement Makers' Federation, the British Iron-founders' Association, the White Lead Convention, the Sheet and Plate Glass Manufacturers' Association, BEAMA, ELMA, the Cable Makers' Association and the British Plastics Federation. Alongside this organisation of manufacturers were two umbrella organisations of merchants. One, the Building Industry Distributors, had been formed in 1942 and operated a monthly price list for the London area. The other, the Distributors of Building Supplies Joint Council, had existed under various names since before the First World War. In 1946 this was 'almost fully comprehensive' and fixed the resale prices of all its goods, except where these were fixed by the manufacturers' associations (all members of the NCBMP) who made agreements with individual merchants on resale price maintenance, rebates and exclusive dealing.[105] Ironically the building industry, especially the networks of distributors was a major focus of government monopoly investigations after the war.

While the causes of cartelisation in Britain remain a relatively under-researched area, the consequences have received much attention. For contemporaries cartels caused high profits in the 1940s, unemployment in the 1930s and were the handmaidens of German industrial and military aggression leading up to the Second World War.[106] Liberal economists at that time and since, joined more recently by the 'institutional rigidities' school, have made cartels and restrictionism a bête-noire of British economic development.[107] Cartels stand condemned as a worse form of market control than mergers, because they allegedly fail to reap economies of scale and have been the means of support for family firms, acting as an obstacle to rationalisation and integration. This in turn affected productivity performance: evidence exists for instance in blast furnaces, electric lamps and retailing.[108]

It was such concerns which actually occupied the minds of policy-makers during and after the war, and it is therefore worth looking at these accusations in a little more detail.

The notion that the motivation of large firms, mergers and internal growth is for real economies of scale is open to serious doubt, while the loose holding companies which resulted from many mergers allowed the continuance of the family firm.[109] Nor is it proven that cartels yielded no economies of scale and hindered rationalisation. A recent article by Ben Fine argues on general theoretical grounds and on the evidence of the inter-war coal industry that the cartel could in fact form 'a framework by which rationalisation could proceed, whether by amalgamation or mechanisation'.[110]

A comparison with Germany in the late nineteenth century, when it was the land of the cartel and also registered strong economic growth, indicates that no clear-cut association can be made between economic problems of productivity, pursuit of economies of scale and research and development and cartel structure. Here the formalised cartel structure, while restraining horizontal mergers and hence some rationalisation, sometimes played a dynamic role, prompting vertical integration. In the interests of avoiding cartel prices or ensuring outlets for production which cartels might restrict, engineering firms built their own blast furnaces, the Mannesman tube works took over coal mines, the biggest coal-mining company annexed two big iron-working companies, and tar manufacturers incorporated roofing-pulp factories.[111] In some finishing industries cartels successfully introduced specialisation of production to eliminate competing lines. In chemicals the formation of IG Farben secured standardisation, rationalisation and concentration of production, and allowed ambitious research projects. In steel the cartel may, by reducing the risks of investment, have encouraged innovation and the pooling of research and development.[112]

Indeed, it may be that the problem for the British economy, as compared with the German was not cartels but their lack of thoroughness, as no less an economist than Alfred Marshall asserted. In the early twentieth century Germany was frequently identified as the land of the cartel, America as the land of the trust – and Britain the land of 'le gentlemen's agreement'.[113] These categorisations are useful in identifying the ad hoc and informal nature of British arrangements, at least until the 1940s. This was one reason why they were termed 'restrictive practices' to distinguish them from the institutionalised German cartel form.[114] In Germany cartels, whether simply restrictive in respect of prices, markets or production, or whether undertaking more complex tasks, often had a Supervisory Committee or Sales Agency with representatives of consumers, labour and suppliers of raw materials, and its functions were sometimes carried out by banks or commercial houses.[115] It can therefore be understood why in Germany cartels were often characterised as a lower stage along the path to integration and permanent association, a weapon against family firms and individualism.[116]

In comparison most British cartels in the early years of the century were so informal, mainly concerned with simple price-fixing agreements and only rarely, except where state-sponsored, with the control of capacity, that they were more in the nature of Liefmann's characterisation of 'primitive' cartels or associations. It was only under the impact of war and government price controls that the British cartel system became more organised, with many more trade associations setting up recognisable Sales Agencies, such as the Tyre Manufacturers' Conference, often co-ordinating policies for the whole industry rather than for one or a few products.[117]

Nor is the picture much clearer when we turn to specific problems allegedly caused by cartels at specific times between the 1930s and the 1950s. International cartels may have limited Britain to certain export markets when expanding demand called for aggressive overseas marketing: certainly the Board of Trade was concerned about this in the immediate post-war period. The division of territories under post-war arrangements illustrates this: patent agreements concluded with American firms often excluded Britain from the whole of the Americas, and even from Australia and New Zealand, and hence restricted Britain's ability to penetrate hard currency markets.[118] But in the inter-war period international agreements may have preserved some Empire markets. Already in some industries, shipbuilding, rolling stock and some iron and steel products, Empire markets had to be shared with other countries.[119] But a war-time paper on the question concluded that tariffs and imperial preference 'enabled U.K. producers to obtain a major share of Empire markets when negotiating cartel agreements'.[120] Moreover, the defence of the home market, allowed by cartels and tariffs was especially important for the research-intensive, so-called 'new' industries, who could participate in the European and world patent cartels in electrical engineering and chemicals. The situation sustained the iron and steel industry, which was especially important in 'recovery'.[121]

The relationship between cartelisation and unemployment also requires further empirical study. The closure of the Jarrow shipyards and the subsequent role of the International Steel Cartel in scuppering plans for a steelworks there indicates a negative impact of cartels on employment. However, overall, Alan Booth has argued that the government's managed economy encouraging cartels was actually geared to maintaining employment artificially through the maintenance of profits and prices.[122]

The study of cartels also sheds light on two neo-liberal interpretations of Britain's 'recovery' in the 1930s. According to H.W. Richardson recovery was a 'natural' process: government policies, such as coming off Gold, protectionism and cheap money were less significant. It was the structural shift to 'new', technically advanced industries, dominated by large firms which constituted a 'new development block'.[123] The thesis has been extensively criticised, principally on the basis that while these industries (cars, chemicals, consumer durables) grew rapidly, their overall contribution to industrial production remained relatively low. It is worth adding that how 'natural' the shift was is called into question by evidence on international cartelisation. It was precisely in the areas central to Richardson's analysis – electrical engineering and chemicals – that industries were dependent on cartelisation. International agreements gave access to patents and collaboration with American and German firms on technical developments, profits could be assured by a combination of limitations on imports through international cartels, and price maintenance domestically.

Another neo-liberal interpretation urges that 'the role of the tariff in stimulating the manufacturing sector must have been very small'.[124] But the exact direction of the IDAC needs attention. The IDAC, as we have seen, preferred to withhold a tariff until the industry or trade had tried first to negotiate an agreement with their foreign counterparts. Hence the effectiveness of tariffs is to be guaged not only from the effective level of protection, but from the extent to which the tariff facilitated international cartels. In turn these effectively acted as a means to limit and control foreign competition without the open economic warfare tariffs implied. If such spin-offs of protectionism are included in the equation, they would validate that side of the debate which sees tariffs as an important element 'in stimulating economic revival'.[125]

Turning to the post-war period, the main charge levelled by contemporaries was that cartels and trade associations were a cause of 'those dreadfully high profits' of the 1940s. Since then research has shown only a limited connection between profit levels and high entry barriers and price-fixing provided through trade associations, in conditions of high market concentration. This prompts the conjecture that in such industries firms are so isolated from market pressures that there is little overt rivalry, firms fail to minimise costs and set prices to maintain average profits but not to maximise them.[126] This would indeed provide evidence of the general 'lack of enterprise' of which Britain's highly-cartelised industrialists stood accused. For the general public the ending of many restrictive agreements in the wake of the 1956 Act may have had a short-term downward pressure on prices, but in the longer-term mergers and the power of more concentrated industries ended these gains. In some cases cartels were found to have kept prices down.[127]

Finally, the politico–economic nature of cartel/trade associations indicates a range of adverse consequences. It has been demonstrated that they presented a formidable blocking mechanism against modernisation plans pursued by the Labour governments of 1945 to 1951.[128] Indeed, the political problems presented by Britain's cartels system is a major theme of this book, and will be pursued in subsequent chapters.

These issues require more thorough enquiry, and have been touched on here to outline some of the concerns of policy-makers in the key period of development of policy, and the historical evolution of our ideas about cartels and industrial performance.

Conclusions

In the period when policy on competition in private industry was being formulated, Britain had a relatively high level of both industrial and retailing concentration, and economic activity was heavily influenced by a variety of more or less effective restrictive agreements. The history of trade associations in this period demonstrates that while the actual level of price-fixing may be difficult to gauge, the potential for such activities to be very effective indeed may be assumed from the systematisation of organisation which had occurred.

The international dimension of the inter-war cartel system provides important material for understanding the attitudes of British businessmen to plans to restrict cartels in the 1940s. The cartels of the 1920s and 1930s were the response to foreign competition in both home and foreign markets, and the gloomy export prospects of the 1930s, and it was the desire to retain the right to make international cartels which most concerned British businessmen in reconstruction discussions. Indeed many domestic cartels were formed in the 1930s to make participation in international agreements possible.

Cartels in Britain thus became the dominant form of monopolistic organisation and did indeed develop into an identifiable 'system'. The impact of the 'system' until 1945 is difficult to condemn per se: cartels were symptomatic of a general world crisis and of concrete features of Britain's long-standing declining competitiveness. On the contrary, much available evidence indicates that Britain's ability to stem her declining share of world manufacturing exports was due in some part to the developing domestic and international cartel system. By 1945, however, the tenacity of potentially price-fixing and output-restricting trade associations presented a contradictory force in an expansionist world economy, while the trade associations themselves formed a formidable *political* barrier to Labour's plans for post-war modernisation. Legislation was directed against cartels, while the peculiarities of the British cartel system affected the outcome of negotiation over the terms of legislation. This chapter is therefore central to understanding the mechanics of British competition policy.

3 The state and the 'monopoly problem', 1880–1939

The rise of monopoly produced far-reaching departures in economic thought and in political and legal theory. In his classic work on the separation of ownership and control in the running of the large-scale corporation, A.A. Berle wondered 'Must we not ... recognise that we are no longer dealing with property in the old sense?'[1] The implications for the principle of laissez-faire were quickly apparent. Mid-nineteenth century political and economic orthodoxy may be summed up in J.S. Mill's dictum that

in all the more advanced communities the great majority of things are worse done by the intervention of government, than the individuals most interested in the matter would do them, or cause them to be done, if left to themselves.[2]

By 1914 the state was already involved in social legislation: the rise of monopoly was to challenge Mill's precept in the business sphere also.

State and monopoly: theoretical positions

Before 1914 four main theoretical positions on the role of the state in relation to the 'trusts' may be isolated. The dominant strand was the neo-classical school. It derived from a positive assessment of new technical methods requiring developments in business organisation. Indeed, Marshall saw combinations as inherent in 'the deep silent stream of the tendencies of Normal Distribution and Exchange',[3] and 'the supersession of small businesses by large is in many industries inevitable'. Britain needed large-scale production in the face of foreign competition, and Marshall's main dislike of British trade associations was their failure to drive out the small, less efficient firm.[4] His pupil, D.H. MacGregor emphasised that combinations were not necessarily monopolies; even when they became monopolies their existence confirmed the vigour of competition, for they must hold off other competitors by competitive methods. Followers of this school thus had a generally positive attitude to the economies of scale which combination brought (MacGregor's work was cited as a classic exposition of this theory).[5]

This reasoning led to an early variant of Robbins' 'competitive order' in proposals for state action. MacGregor argued for 'the openest competition' through 'foreign supply' and the withholding of tariffs by the state – Marshall and other orthodox economists signed a petition in *The Times* against tariff reform.[6] MacGregor argued that:

The best advice for the period of transition to the new system of industrial organisation is to avoid passion and judgement and the terrorism of mere size; to perceive that the extortion of a few strong producers can be remedied otherwise than by the drastic interference with economic tendencies.

MacGregor pinned his hopes on the view that competition was always and everywhere present and so long as entrepreneurial flair was maintained little was to be feared from combination, but much from state intervention. Thus socialisation was condemned, except for 'natural monopolies' like gas and water which had no ready substitute to provide competition. Regulation through legislation similar to the Sherman Act attached a stigma to combinations which 'may be a normal evolute', and such per se condemnations had in fact been counterproductive. In his support MacGregor cited the Final Report of the American Industrial Commission of 1900–2: '"the strongest forms of combination appear to have been fostered by laws intended to prevent them".' MacGregor foreshadowed many neo-classical objections to antitrust legislation, such as the ingenuity of Trust lawyers, and the ability of Trust power 'to offer a strong passive resistance to legal procedure . . . and wear down an independent by the creation of long delays on technical matters'.[7]

The second identifiable group were the 'historical' economists, a small band in Britain, but representative of the dominant mode of economic analysis in Germany as developed by Friedrich List. This school opposed the 'natural law' economics;[8] for them, monopoly and competition, viewed historically, constantly alternated. If anything monopoly was 'more permanent, more fundamental than competition itself', springing 'from competition itself', from technical advance and from recurrent crises intensifying competition, reducing the number of firms and hence easing the making of collusive agreements. Thus monopoly would not be held back by withholding tariffs, nor was it caused by state intervention. Indeed, Henry Foxwell argued that 'nothing has been more favourable to the growth of practical monopolies than the regime of laissez-faire'.[9] Thus the trust movement was seen as positive, removing the uncertainties of free competition and providing greater regularity of production and employment. The state's involvement to promote trustification was welcomed and the historical economists therefore favoured protectionism and imperial preference.[10] However, while William Ashley was willing to accept socialisation of some trusts, Foxwell deplored state administration and proposed industrial self-regulation.[11]

A third approach to the trust problem was that of the Fabians. To them trusts were the welcome assertion of co-operation rather than competition as the principle behind human relationships. They predicted the degeneration of the capitalist class into 'dividend-mongers', the real function of the entrepreneur passing to salaried employees, the 'black-coated proletariat'.[12] Thus the trusts heralded the new Socialist age. There was an inherent contradiction in 'the desire to put an end to competition while maintaining the private ownership and direction of industry'.[13] The foremost Fabian writer on the trusts, H.W. Macrosty, argued that the unified control over business through combination should be welcomed by Socialists in the same manner as the Roman tyrant who 'wished that all his enemies had but one neck'.[14]

The Fabians had a Panglossian[15] view of the trusts, of the possibility of state regulation and about the separation of ownership and control which would create a class of managers 'heterogeneous within, but different both from the workman and the capitalist'.[16] This would tend also to higher organisation and the specialisation of management functions. Most importantly, the Fabians were supremely confident of the reforming powers of the state. Macrosty, in a classic expression of the Fabian glorification of the state wrote:

The State is not an aggregate of sections. The good it aims at is the good of the whole, its standpoint is that of the consumer, its purpose is the making of citizens. To the organised State alone can we entrust the guardianship of the standard of life.[17]

This faith in the state – even under capitalism – meant that the Fabians came to provide some of the most important contributions to the development of anti-monopoly policy. At an early stage they stressed three key points: 'combination' in various forms was here to stay; the development carried with it efficiencies, which could improve workers' lives and secure Britain against foreign competition, but also great economic, social and political dangers; the state should intervene therefore, but its major dilemma was 'how to secure the benefits of combination without its disadvantages'.[18] This phrase was reiterated constantly in government in the major discussions on monopoly policy during the Second World War and this strand of economic and political thought needs more attention as an influence on the evolution of British antitrust policy up to 1948: neoclassical economists were not the only influence as recent analyses tend to imply.[19] Fabians were less concerned about the maintenance of competition and the rights of private property and hence in spite of early vacillation they emphasised the need for nationalisation and price control while sharing MacGregor's fears of state intervention. Macrosty also argued that any enquiry system to control monopoly would need to be accompanied by special taxation of the rich to protect the state against attempts by strong economic interests to 'capture the national administration'.[20]

Fabians also put their faith in control of monopoly through labour organisations – the power of trade unions and co-operatives to provide some counter-weight to the trusts, directly prompting the popularity among Fabian intellectuals of 'Guild Socialism' which had some success between 1905 and 1915. In addition they tended, like the labour movement in Britain, to be 'internationalist' and opposed to protectionism. Macrosty argued that Britain should be made more competitive by a programme of modernisation including high rates of investment and technical education.[21]

Finally, though weakly represented in Britain before 1914, the Marxist school looked directly to socialist revolution as the ultimate resolution of the contradiction between private property and socialised production. It viewed the development of monopoly as consistent with more intensive competition, prompting national rivalries and imperialist wars. William Morris, in a review of Edward Bellamy's *Looking Backward* in 1889, argued that competition would continue to induce recurrent breakups of trusts and 'war for the division of plunder'.[22] The main representative in Britain of the analysis linking imperialism and the trusts was the liberal, J.A. Hobson, who stands on his own in the schema identified here. He identified the 'economic taproot of imperialism' as the export of capital, itself the result of the intensification of unequal income distribution through the development of the trusts.[23]

In the inter-war period – those 'years of high theory' – the schools outlined above can still be distinguished but the divisions became blurred as political expediency brought about a series of alliances and common viewpoints. The leading economists of the day became closely involved with influencing government policy and many of the most important developments in thought occurred through discussions around the economic programmes of political parties.

Marshall, Arthur Pigou and Joan Robinson worked on identifying some of the main problems of monopoly for neo-classical equilibrium theory: higher prices and reduced output than under 'simple competition', increased product differentiation and advertising increasing prices and wasting resources, the diversion of resources to areas accruing a greater share of income so creating excess capacity in some areas and restriction of output by the monopolist to maintain prices creating under-utilisation of resources.[24] But the policy implications of these analyses were far from clear, especially as neo-classical authors were semi-paralysed by their fears of state intervention.[25]

In the 1920s, Marshall and MacGregor were willing to support a permanent tribunal to enquire into cases of monopoly, 'for the continuance of private enterprise under the conditions that are coming about', and Arthur Pigou to consider price control and public operation, but not ownership, of monopolies.[26] As the problem of unemployment proved enduring 'rationalisation' was increasingly advocated as the alternative to reducing wages and other business costs.[27] The increasing role for state intervention to solve problems of unemployment and investment developed by the Cambridge school, especially by Keynes, had its counterpart in industrial policy. Keynes lobbied for schemes for rationalisation and even compulsory state-aided cartelisation in coal and cotton in the 1920s.[28]

Thus it was that Liberal economists subscribed to political programmes which tagged limited antitrust policies onto plans for enhanced industrial organisation. The Liberal Industrial Enquiry noted that competition 'passed on to the consuming public, in the form of low prices, the results of industrial and economic progress', but also that large-scale production was increasingly inevitable and often more efficient. It therefore favoured monopoly being held in check only by publicity to mobilise consumers, and a tribunal as proposed by the 1919 Committee on trusts. However, it also allowed for the enforcement of trade association rules on minorities in certain cases fearing, as Clay had said that 'the necessary reorganisation of the depressed industries will not be affected unless the intitiative is taken and the impulse given by some agency outside them'.[29]

The inter-war inheritors of the 'historical' tradition were the 'conservative planners' who proposed rationalisation, the extension of trade associations and 'industrial self-government' with minimal government control. The various schemes put forward were variations on the theme of trade associations and industrial councils, culminating in some National Council for Industry, sometimes with trade union co-operation. These ideas were usually accompanied by proposals for the banking system to be more nationally oriented, for full-scale protectionism and for the conscious integration and development of the Empire. In the 1930s two groups spearheaded the corporatist movement: Political and Economic Planning (PEP), a private research society which later became the Policy Studies Institute, founded in 1931 and attracting support from such businessmen as the banker Sir Basil Blackett, Israel Sieff of Marks and Spencer and Sir Thomas Barlow, president of the Manchester Chamber of Commerce; and the Industrial Reorganisation League led by Harold Macmillan. Macmillan was later to propose nationalisation for industries such as transport, electricity, industrial insurance, mining royalties and even armaments.[30]

A determining influence on business and Conservative ideas, of which corporatism was a part was the new power of labour after the First World War.[31] By 1918 many business groups favoured the intensification of imperial ties, together with protectionism and the pursuit of industrial efficiency through rationalisation and the development of large firms.[32] These plans showed an uneasy approach to labour, sometimes emphasising class harmony, sometimes a staunch anti-bolshevism. The planned capitalism of PEP and the Industrial Reorganisation League was a part of this tradition: industrialists needed to put their own house in order to avoid at worst 'a completely socialised state' or to pre-empt schemes for limited nationalisation.[33] Their attitude towards the labour movement varied, yet such plans were promoted, on the whole, by industrialists representing larger firms, able to pay higher wages, as well as eager to cheapen the costs of basic services like power and transport and to enforce small-firm participation in cartels. Corporatism was another strand in their search since the General Strike for 'industrial concordat' and attempts at 'producers' co-operation' via existing bodies like the FBI and the TUC and via less official contacts like the Mond–Turner talks.[34]

The inheritors of the Fabian approach to monopolies and the state in the inter-war period were mainly to be found within the ranks of the Labour Party. Intellectuals, especially in the New Fabian Research Bureau (NFRB), set up by G.D.H. Cole in 1931 and the XYZ Club where Fabians met sympathetic figures from the City, developed 'the reformist analysis to an extent never before attempted. The objective was to understand and correct the faults of capitalism'.[35] Three important developments may be identified. First, Labour shifted from nationalisation and to rationalisation as the cornerstone of its industrial policy and rationalisation became the sole basis of the Labour Government's industrial policy between 1929 and 1931.[36] Even in the Party's major policy document of the 1930s *For Socialism and Peace*, although public ownership with fair compensation was hinted at, few definite commitments were made.[37]

Secondly, leading Fabian intellectuals became prime movers in the attempt to assimilate Keynesian budgetary ideas into Labour policy, spurred on by the work of James Meade.[38] Although not fully articulated in the 1930s the project was of future importance for the belief that unemployment could be tackled through macro-economic policies. Thirdly, Labour's attitude to monopolies and industrial policy was influenced by the fondness among Fabians for theories of the separation of ownership and control. Papers by members of the NFRB expressed the hope that managers would be less likely to feel 'at war against the workers' and could become servants of the state and the public. The Industrial Organisation Group of the

NFRB even entered into negotiations with the Management Research Group – a business organisation presided over by B.S. Rowntree, though with limited success.[39]

Our fourth strand, the Marxist contribution, emerged more clearly in Britain in the inter-war period. The Communist Party's publication *Britain without Capitalists* portrayed monopoly capitalism as the cause of unemployment, for restrictionist monopoly policies posed a 'fetter on production'. It was also the cause of the renewed trend to war, for the 'anarchy of acuter rivalry' between giant contestants meant that economic nationalism coexisted with an intensified 'scramble for colonial preserves'.[40] The Marxist analysis of the state prompted a condemnation of business, Liberal and Labour plans as tinkering, not only because any plans for state control left the state in capitalist hands, but also because monopoly had become more 'fundamental ... woven into the very texture of contemporary capitalism'.[41] *Britain without Capitalists* was reprinted in 1939 with a preface arguing that a transitional programme by a Popular Front government would have to 'go forward boldly to the expropriation of the large capitalist concerns' if it was to achieve more permanent results.

Industrial structure and policy was therefore part of the great debate of the 1930s, not between planning and no planning but 'in whose interests are the plans to be made'.[42] J.A. Hobson's attack on rationalisation illustrates the point very clearly: 'all the economic evidence tends to show that rationalisation (the process normally signifies the organisation of a Combine, Cartel or Trust) carries with it a net diminution of employment ... and a distribution of the product which increases the proportionate share of Capital, reduces that of Labour.'[43]

This schematic review of ideas on the state and industrial organisation cannot end without reviewing a development in the economic thought of the inter-war period which ran against the notions of planning and state intervention outlined above. This was the reassertion of the ideals of competition and the development of a framework for the 'competitive order' by some liberal economists. They saw themselves as voices in the wilderness in the 1930s and 1940s but were to become exceptionally influential.

The reassertion of notions of a self-regulating market mechanism is associated with the Chicago, Austrian and Freiburg schools with some influence at the LSE through Lionel Robbins, Friedrich Hayek and John Jewkes. Although these schools had methodological differences, they agreed that large size brought efficiency gains, most of the economy was competitive, and most monopolies persisted only with active government support. Temporary monopoly profits were actually beneficial, providing funds for research for instance and hence for future dynamic innovation and attracting fresh competition, often in new products or models and hence expanding consumer choice. This view tended to emphasise in an extreme form the importance to the economy of the motive force of entrepreneurs, the drive to profit and hence the sanctity of private property.[44]

The policy pushed by this alliance of economists was that associated principally with the Freiburg 'ordo-liberal' school which proposed, in the words of its chief evangelist 'a positive policy' aimed 'at bringing the market form of complete competition into being'.[45] Their view was inspired by highly conservative opposition to socialism, coupled with a neo-liberal dislike of Hitlerian corporatism, both of which, in their view, denied personal and entrepreneurial freedom, and they clearly felt out on a limb in the atmosphere of the 1930s. Their notion of a 'competitive order' sprang from a commitment to preserve laissez-faire capitalism, and the institution of private property.[46]

The progression of thought outlined here is not intended to imply the influence of ideas on events. Economic opinion increasingly failed to give any very helpful guidelines to government, being divided and without any real consensus, as distinct from periods when, for reasons other than the sheer strength of argument, certain ideas have found more favour with governments than others. Thus it is that to understand major developments in policy between 1880 and 1939 it is to forces other than the weight of economic ideas that we must turn.

Antitrust actions, 1880–1920

In line with the predominance of laissez-faire ideology in the economic sphere which prevailed up to 1914, government policies on the trusts were neither over-supportive nor condemnatory. Initiatives were ad hoc and their outcome dependent on the strengths of competing pressure groups. Thus the Royal Commission on the shipping rings of 1906 was secured through lobbying by traders, but the report was anodyne as their arguments were weighed against those of the shipping interests. The history of the Railway and Canal Traffic Act of 1888 is generally seen as a battle between the 'railway interest' with strong parliamentary representation, and their customers – a broad coalition of manufacturers, especially iron-masters, farmers and other traders. So great was the threat of one interest group against another that according to one historian the issue combined with the question of home rule for Ireland to unite the 'propertied classes' and bring down Gladstone's Third Ministry in 1886.[47] After the establishment of the Railway and Canal Commission in 1888 the railways were still able to 'capture' the machinery of regulation, as *The Economist* had feared. Their lobbying secured favourable maximum rates, which they then used to raise all their rates, although further lobbying by countervailing interests prompted another Act in 1894 which froze all rates.[48]

The incident, although inauspicious for any hopes of antitrust regulation, served to give support to those economists who pinned their hopes on the power of public opinion. The lobbiers for regulation were supported by most of the Press who argued that 'regulation of monopolies is one of the functions of government'.[49] Similar 'public outcry' had apparently forced soap manufacturers representing about two-thirds of British soap production to abandon their plans for a selling agency. In fact the public outcry was essentially orchestrated by the retailers and the Press, which feared loss of advertising revenue.[50] Similarly, the defeat of the tariff reform movement in 1906 was ostensibly due to 'public opinion', specifically labour opposition to the 'dear loaf' which could result from the tariff. But more fundamental in the tariff reform debate was a division between those industrialists hard hit by German and American competition and those who adhered to free trade.[51] The defeat of the former at the 1906 election of the Liberal government merely postponed the debate.

The first antitrust initiative proper was a product of the 1914–18 war. The Committee on Trusts was appointed in February 1918 and its report in 1919 was followed in that year by the first Profiteering Act. That Act watered down the Committee's proposal for a permanent investigating tribunal into a sub-committee for obtaining information about the development of trusts – the Standing Committee on Trusts (SCT). The Act was renewed in 1920 and allowed to lapse the next year.[52]

Looking at the evolution of the Profiteering Acts four important characteristics can be established common to the subsequent history of British antitrust.

First, the appointment of the Committee on Trusts was the response to labour unrest and was intended to defuse it, not respond to it in any positive way.[53] Industrial unrest since March 1915 had been sustained by suspicions of profiteering by big business. Labour awareness of profiteering became, throughout the war, if not the cause then the legitimation of strikes and industrial unrest: 'specific grievances over wages dilution, the skilled man's trade card, and so on, was placed within a sense of overall, systematic unfairness.'[54] Lloyd George saw the 'spirit of revolution' sweeping Europe, and J.A. Hobson commented that, for the first time in modern history 'Property is seriously afraid'.[55] Reports by Industrial Commissioners as part of the Commission of Enquiry on Industrial Unrest in 1917, reported that working class discontent was rooted in the feeling that they were 'being bled white' by profiteers.[56] The reports on industrial unrest recommended government action to dispel public disquiet about profiteering and to reduce or fix maximum prices for food. It was in this atmosphere that the recommendations of the Committee on Trusts were made, that public disquiet be dispelled and the aim of the first Profiteering Act, made quite explicit both in Cabinet and Parliament, was to: 'check growing agitation which has already become menacing' and perhaps to show that profits were not so large and so restore confidence in the system of private enterprise.[57]

Secondly labour unrest proved weak in the face of something still more to be feared – 'capital unrest'. In early 1920 strong feelings prompted suggestions for a special committee on high prices and profits, and Robert Horne, President of the Board of Trade, urged a separate Combines Bill to accompany the renewed Profiteering Act. But apprehension of adverse business reaction scuppered these: Sir Alfred Mond, then First Commissioner of Works argued that, along with new taxation proposals (excess profits tax had just been increased), such a measure would 'still further discourage and unsettle the revival of industry'.[58]

Thirdly, the legislation that was enacted, the Profiteering Acts, aimed to educate the most vocal sectors of 'public opinion' – the working men – out of their suspicion of large-scale business. The value of an enquiry into profits, members of Cabinet argued, was that the worker would learn how enhanced profits arose from the variety of industrial conditions: fixed prices brought 'bare subsistence' to some firms while others were able to reap high profits because of 'exceptionally good management or low capitalisation'. Once the working man understood these things it would 'make it easier to obtain a practical response to appeals made to workmen for further sacrifices and exertions'.[59]

Indeed the lasting impact of the first antitrust experiment was a body of reports which were to be used to support the view that monopolies 'have up till now not really abused their position'.[60] However, it is doubtful if this was a fair summary of the conclusions of the SCT. Few reports were strongly critical of the cases of restraint of trade which they examined, but nearly all urged that the recommendations of the Committee on Trusts be implemented and a permanent committee be established. Just before the SCT was dissolved it prepared a statement arguing that further prevention of abuse rested on continuing publicity, that its work was frustrated without powers to compel firms to supply information, and that the reports had led to the reduction of prices in various consumer articles.[61] The members of the Committee with Co-operative, Labour or Fabian links became openly cynical. Pengelly, who had been with the SCT since its inception opined that: 'They [the government] intended to put a stop to the work of the committee which had discovered too many truths for their liking.'[62] Sidney Webb resigned in October 1920 because he disagreed with the Committee and did not wish to be associated with it, and W.H.

Watkins, a representative of the Co-op and the Consumer Council, believed that business interests were influencing the committees and the tenor of their reports.[63]

Even the more orthodox members regarded the government's attitude towards the committee as discourteous and obstreperous. At one point the Board of Trade held up publication of reports and told the committee belatedly that its Law Officers feared confidentiality would be breached by publication. In another case Webb complained that the Board of Trade had omitted one of the committee's recommendations and so falsified its findings.[64] Many members also felt frustrated at the difficulty of obtaining information from businessmen: the sewing-cotton firm Coats sent the investigating sub-committee 'innocuous documents' followed by a mass of unordered figures.[65] Finally, the committee had an increasing number of brushes in the Press with firms and trade associations which had been the subject of investigation – J.P. Coats and the Electric Light Manufacturers' Association are two examples. The Board of Trade increased members' anger by advising them not to enter controversy in the Press, a position, John Hilton remarked, which left the last word in the public debate to an interested party.[66]

The fourth feature of this early antitrust experiment was that the SCT found itself investigating charges by one group of businessmen against others. Herbert Morrison like *The Times* criticised the Profiteering Acts for being a forum against small firms leaving the 'Big Profiteer – the Milk Trust, the Coal Combine' to go free.[67] Local profiteering tribunals complained that they were only able to investigate profiteering by retailers. Indeed, the minutes of the Complaints Committee, which undertook preliminary investigations of complaints about high prices and which passed several topics on to the SCT, indicate that the vast bulk of complaints were by businessmen against other businessmen. The Federation of Grocers' Associations brought five cases in the two years against rival retailers.[68]

Thus both the intention and effect of the Profiteering Acts were to check social criticism of private enterprise, educate the public and especially the working classes in the inevitability and rightness of trusts, high prices and profits, while giving businessmen a court for their grievances against competitors. As soon as the SCT moved outside this remit it received obloquy from businessmen and obstruction from the Board of Trade. By 1921, with an industrial recession and falling prices some of the public pressure was dissipated, while the campaign in the House of Commons was carried on by no more than five Liberal and Labour MPs who were themselves divided. The government refused to renew the Profiteering Acts in April 1921 and reneged on its promise of permanent legislation on trusts.[69]

Instead in the inter-war years, and with vigour from 1931, the government effectively followed the recommendations of another government enquiry established as a part of Reconstruction discussions – the 1918 report of the Committee on Commercial and Industrial Policy by the Ministry of Reconstruction. In its report, the committee recommended various forms of government support for trusts, industrial organisation and cartels, most notably through a system of imperial preference. A Board would examine each industry's application for special duties. It proposed in overseas trade the supplementation or even 'replacement' of 'the individualistic methods hitherto mainly adopted'. They invoked government support to a quite remarkable extent to secure supplies of materials to aid marketing overseas, and to promote and safeguard key strategic industries.

Naturally the committee felt that any 'positive control of combinations' was inexpedient. The government should have power to obtain information and to investigate in special cases, but at the same time cartels should be legalised so that they could be made enforceable between members. They proposed compulsory registration with the Board of Trade of all international cartels or firms, to which British firms were party, the optional registration of agreements or combinations for the regulation of trade among British firms only, whether for the domestic or foreign markets, and such agreements be made enforceable, and the Board of Trade should have power to ask for confidential information regarding domestic and international combinations and associations.[70] Such a system of registration was to be used, therefore, not, as in the case of the 1956 legislation, as the preliminary to enquiry and prohibition of cartels, but to make various forms of association legally enforceable.

Taken together these commercial and industrial proposals involved the state in holding back foreign competition, and thereby weaving it into an intricate web of monopolist interests, domestic and international. Similar ideas were proposed in the more overtly 'corporatist' plans of the Industrial Reconstruction Council's system of self-governing trade associations and trade Parliaments. Dudley Docker, the founder of the Federation of British Industries (FBI), pressed for rationalisation, with support for scientific research, and a policy of imperial protectionism, and similar ideas were proposed by Sir Auckland Geddes when President of the Board of Trade in 1919.[71]

The extent of support among industrialists for such proposals was, however, limited. The signatories to the report on Commercial Policy were almost entirely industrialists with interests in basic industries who clashed with other sectors of British business. Lancashire remained, on the whole, firmly laissez-faire, while shipbuilding and engineering employers disliked the corporatism of the FBI and their plans for works committees. Shipping and financial circles, organised by Lord Inchcape in the Imperial Association of Commerce, took a determined stand against protection. In addition the successful defeat of Germany followed by the crushing terms imposed by the Allies, together with the re-assertion of financial orthodoxy and reductions in government expenditure in 1919, made determined efforts at modernisation both less pressing and less feasible.[72]

However, notable parts of the Productioneers' programme were implemented in the 1920s – tariffs based on safeguarding of key industries, the establishment of Research Associations, support for the chemical industry, the establishment of the national grid, and legislation promoting amalgamations in electricity, gas, the railways and coal. Government reports on aspects of industrial combination and organisation gave a clear green light to rationalisation and cartelisation. Most significant was the report of the Balfour Committee on Industry and Trade of 1929, which not only saw no case for immediate legislation to restrain possible abuses resulting from combines, but urged further rationalisation by industrialists. Its authors also professed to look with 'envy to the vastly more complete machinery of the Chambers of Commerce of Germany or France, where to all intents and purposes membership and contribution are compulsory'. While rejecting such control as hampering independence, they called on all trade associations and chambers of commerce to consider strengthening their organisation.[73] Meanwhile in the courts the trend of legal judgements was 'to assist rather than put down restrictive arrangements'. Resale price maintenance agreements were sometimes held enforceable in the Courts, while traders damaged by stop lists or boycotts could expect little help from the courts.[74]

Policy towards trusts and cartels in the 1930s

Hence, faced with two approaches to trusts and cartels exemplified in the report of the Committee on Trusts and of the Committee on Commercial Policy, governments in the 1920s effectively opted for the approach of the latter. But this policy was not wholehearted: British capitalism was, as R.W.D. Boyce has put it, 'at the crossroads' from 1919 to 1932. Indeed, insistence on the return to a liberal world order, especially the return to gold at an inflated rate, intensified the competitive pressures on British industry, and strengthened the forces of protectionism. It prompted still greater search by the corporatists and 'productioneers' for industrial peace through producers' alliances – exemplified in the Mond–Turner talks – and propaganda for the 'rationalisation movement'.[75] 1931 to 1932 marked a decisive shift to a system of managed currency, protectionism, imperial preference and the development of other imperial ties. Where do government policies towards cartels and trusts fit into this picture?

On the one hand, some historians have portrayed government policies as 'non-committal' or ad hoc.[76] On the other hand Alan Booth has recently argued that governments endorsed rationalisation and cartelisation as a means to maintain prices and profits, relieve unemployment, and make Britain more competitive against the acknowledged superiority of American and German techniques. For Kirby cartelisation became, in the 1930s the alternative to amalgamation and was a process 'aided and abetted albeit reluctantly, by governments'.[77]

As chapter 2 argued, government policies created hot-house conditions for cartelisation. Not only did imperial preference, tariffs and the IDAC promote domestic cartels as a first step to the promotion of international agreements, but specific policies succoured them, for instance the Budget of 1935 and the Finance Act of 1936 gave tax concessions to voluntary schemes which sought to eliminate excess capacity. Governments tried to rationalise and promote amalgamations in coal, cotton and iron and steel. It was divisions among industrialists and the banks' failure to provide long-term finance when they became involved in rationalisation that meant that such schemes were transformed by the industrialists involved into cartel schemes alone.[78]

The argument for the 'hands off' characterisation of government policy rests heavily on the fact that the government refused to collaborate with more grandiose schemes for compulsory reorganisation or cartelisation, except in specific industries. Thus the government would not support the proposals by PEP and the Industrial Reorganisation League (IRL) for an Enabling Bill whereby, should a majority of an industry desire it, firms could be compelled to join the trade association and abide by its rules. The root of government opposition was that the necessary support from 'business sentiment' could not be assured: 'Conservative leaders were not prepared to go beyond the limits of contemporary industrial opinion.'[79]

For in opposition to the IRL's Enabling Bill and compulsory schemes in general stood the FBI which preferred the voluntary schemes already in existence, was scared of any proposals to introduce labour involvement and did not want to 'upset the apple-cart by bringing the issue of business practices to public attention'. In this it was reflecting the interests of its smaller, independent business members who feared that the Bill 'would enable powerful groups to enforce a scheme to their own interests'.[80] The PEP and the IRL represented the durable consumer goods industries, together with longer-established oligopolistic firms in food and drink. Such industries were more committed to high levels of investment and research, were dependent on basic industries for their inputs and on high levels of demand for sales, and produced policies for the maintenance of wages and profits, together with re-organisation of basic industries, especially of coal and iron and steel to cheapen their costs. Such a strategy could build alliances with the larger firms within for instance the iron and steel industry, but clearly met with opposition from smaller firms not only in iron and steel but throughout manufacturing industry.[81] Thus, as Ritschel comments, the Enabling Bill foundered against the very forces – small competitive firms – it aimed to bring to heel.[82]

Thus the governments ad hoc and apparently unco-ordinated policies embodied an attitude which accorded well with the view promoted by the FBI against state intervention and against any hint of compulsory amalgamation or adherence to trade association rules. The system of protection using the ad hoc methods of the IDAC together with aid to rationalisation and cartelisation without direct government involvement in many of the schemes accorded almost entirely with the demands of the 1918 Committee on Commercial and Industrial Organisation, and with FBI insistence on 'industrial self-government'. Arguing against 'left-wing' attacks on the influence of the FBI, Finer notes that other organisations also proposed some of these measures.[83] However, none of the organisations he mentions had either programmes which closely followed that of the FBI or policies akin to those pursued by governments.

In the sphere of international cartelisation the government, and especially the Board of Trade, most obviously showed its support for business collusion, but again on a basis of 'industrial self-government'. The IDAC, supposedly independent of government but in fact closely allied to Treasury policy through its method of appointment and financing,[84] did not simply acquiesce in British involvement in international cartelisation, it saw involvement as a positive policy to combat foreign competition by less aggressive means than tariffs. As Sir Herbert Hutchison, the Assistant Secretary in the 1930s put it:

the Committee ... considered that the regulation of trade by international agreement was of advantage to industry in the United Kingdom, and was very ready to give its assistance, by advertising an application as under serious consideration or by actually recommending an increase in duty, where it was satisfied that there was a good case for a rise in the absence of agreement. It was prepared to make use of its procedure in such a way as to aid a British industry in securing agreement with other members of a cartel on acceptable terms, or in maintaining or reviving a cartel that was failing.[85]

The British government was itself party to most of the major commodity agreements which flourished in the inter-war years, such as tin, tea, rubber and oil.[86] Not surprisingly in 1944 the Board of Trade believed that in the 1930s government had viewed international cartels 'sympathetically ... on the grounds that they tended to preserve for us markets which we might otherwise have lost'.[87]

The close involvement of the British state with international cartels became particularly apparent in the years of appeasement, especially in 1938 and 1939 when Germany's aggressive trading methods intensified.[88] On 16 March 1939 the FBI and their German counterpart, the Reichsgruppe Industrie, announced the so-called 'Düsseldorf Agreement' which looked forward to British and German industries negotiating further cartel agreements to 'eliminate destructive competition' and as a step 'towards a more ordered system of world trade'. The two sides hoped 'to secure as complete co-operation as possible throughout the industrial structure of their two countries', a sentence interpreted by *The Economist* as a recipe for the complete domestic cartelisaton of Britain.[89] Of great importance for future relations between Britain and the United States on cartel questions was Article 8 which provided for the two sides to collaborate in seeking the help of their governments to bring pressure on an industry in a third country which, by refusing to join a specific cartel, threatened to nullify it. This article prompted a protest from the American State Department, which interpreted the article as referring to American competition in South American markets: the Board of Trade tried to reassure them that Japan and Sweden were the intended targets.[90]

The agreement fulfilled both government hopes for the 'settlement of political problems through the treatment of economic difficulties', and FBI calls since 1937 for an Anglo–German cartel covering every industrial sector which would both accommodate Germany's export drive and protect British markets.[91] The Düsseldorf negotiations therefore indicate the way that business interests and government diplomatic concerns became intertwined. Cartels became associated with appeasement[92] and, in the minds of American businessmen, with potential co-ordination of European trading partners against American goods, an issue of importance during discussions with the Americans on international cartels during the Second World War.

The failure of economic (and political) appeasement marked the outbreak of trade war with Germany. The government's need to increase foreign exchange earnings prompted an 'economic offensive' on exports, for instance in the export drive of February 1940, and the withholding of foreign exchange used in compensatory payments under international agreements.[93] These actions and Trading with the Enemy legislation broke the links between British firms and their pre-war European cartel partners, but until the summer of 1940 and the occupation of much of Western Europe by the Germans, the reformulation of cartel agreements was a possibility. Sometimes, the Board of Trade seemed to turn a blind eye to German involvement, albeit indirectly in these arrangements, at other times it used cartels as a form of trade war – but not so much against Germany. In plate glass Pilkington were told to use their 'full bargaining power' in negotiating with Belgium for third markets. The Board of Trade sanctioned the continued participation of a British producer in a cartel involving German firms which regulated sales of telecommunication equipment to South America on the grounds that British withdrawal from the cartel 'would merely have cleared the way for enemy countries to exert increased influence'. A White Lead Convention without its pre-war German members was also allowed on the basis that it would keep the United States out of Convention markets.[94]

However, by July 1940 the pre-war international cartel system had been largely 'wiped out' and the Foreign Exchange Control Committee decided that no more transfers abroad of payments under cartel arrangements could be allowed.[95] But this decision to adopt a hostile attitude towards cartels had come from the Treasury, not the Board of Trade, and was more the reaction to a force majeure – the course of the war – than any conscious opposition to cartels. Meanwhile officials in the Board of Trade and Trading with the Enemy Department, when considering new arrangements in the autumn of 1939 were happy to maintain international cartels, in order not to waste the effort already expended.[96]

By the late 1930s, therefore, the close links between government and industry in the development of cartels, domestic and international, was developing into something of an art-form, a process further encouraged by the war-time controls. The combination of protectionism, direct government involvement in some industries and unwillingness to interfere otherwise with business produced a situation which appeared to many left-wingers of the day as a form of businessmen's government. Barbara Wootton, for instance criticised the government's unwillingness to interfere with 'the private planning of profitable levels of production',[97] G.C. Allen complained that the government's failure to rationalise the iron and steel industry was an example of 'how a government may be outmanoeuvred by industrialists', and in 1948 was to express a commonly-held view that the extension of bolstering trade associations into the field of foreign trade led to the strengthening of private monopoly.[98]

Still more importantly for the post-war settlement and the battle for Reconstruction, industrialists perceived, or were to say they perceived, government policy to be sympathetic to cartels in the inter-war period. Any action to investigate the activities of trade associations, cartels and monopolies, they argued, would represent a 'complete transformation' in government policy, from 'government encouragement to the pre-war drift away from competition'. And civil servants unrepentantly agreed that government had favoured cartelisation.[99]

Conclusions

In the sphere of economic thought briefly surveyed here, four models of government–industry relations in the era of monopoly were developed between 1900 and 1939.

The neo-classical school clung to as much 'laissez-faire' doctrine as possible, seeing only corruption and bureaucracy in government supervision, and refusing to be panicked into abandoning the concept of competitive capitalism. Many of these economists, although not those of the Freiburg, Chicago and LSE schools, found their distaste for state intervention tempered, during the inter-war years, by the severity of economic conditions. Historical economists and their successors, to be found among the propagandists for corporatism in the inter-war years, proposed state involvement to extend and co-ordinate monopolisation at all levels, domestically through rationalisation and compulsory cartelisation, internationally through the use of protectionism and international cartels. The Fabians and the Labour Party maintained a stance favouring the extension of large-scale operations, but with the regulation of monopoly in the 'public interest', with the issue of nationalisation hovering uncertainly in the background. Finally, for the Marxist school, large-scale industrial organisation demonstrated the fundamental contradiction between socialised production and private ownership, fuelling proposals for sweeping expropriation.

Government policy did not, of course, conform to any of these schools but, it has been argued here, bore close resemblance to policies advocated by the most powerful business pressure group of the inter-war period – the FBI. An 'ad hoc' approach accorded nicely with the FBI's view that cartelisation and rationalisation should be voluntary, only legislated for if a majority of firms in the trade, large and small, wanted it. Meanwhile international cartels were clearly favoured, a policy which increased the dominance of large, transnational firms in the domestic economy.

Where the antitrust initiatives occurred their form was determined principally by the outcome of the conflicting demands of 'labour unrest' and 'capital unrest'. They had no impact on industrial structure, but were constructed to educate working men and as a forum for businessmen's grievances against each other. These themes will recur in the chapters that follow.

4 The war and the White Paper, 1940–44

Introduction

In May 1944 the wartime Coalition government published its White Paper on Employment Policy. This became the key economic policy document to emerge from the discussions on post-war Reconstruction and, like many other decisions of the Coalition government, was to bind the subsequent Labour government.[1] It contained a clause which declared that policy towards cartels and combines was to be reviewed, and which implicitly criticised their restrictive effects:

Employers, too, must seek in larger output rather than higher prices the reward of enterprise and good management. There has in recent years been a growing tendency towards combines and towards agreements, both national and international, by which manufacturers have sought to control prices and output, to divide markets and to fix conditions of sale. Such agreements or combines do not necessarily operate against the public interest; but the power to do so is there. The Government will therefore seek power to inform themselves of the extent and effect of restrictive agreements, and of the activities of combines; and to take appropriate action to check practices which may bring advantages to sectional producing interests but work to the detriment of the country as a whole.[2]

The general approach to cartels and large firms enunciated here was to be embodied in the 1948 Monopolies and Restrictive Practices Act, which similarly adopted an agnostic position on the effects of restrictionism, and established a system of enquiry and control. Although nearly 30 years after the 1918 Committee on Trusts had made its recommendations for a similar procedure, this clause in the White Paper has been hailed as a turning point in the evolution of government policy, ending the encouragement shown to cartels in the 1930s and pointing the way to post-war policy. It is indeed in the war-time discussions that major decisions affecting the evolution of British competition policy are to be found. Many of the considerations then were to set the tone of competition policy until 1956.

The White Paper was 'revolutionary', given the official position of the 1930s, to declare that 'The Government accept as one of their primary aims and responsibilities the maintenance of a high and stable level of employ-

54

ment after the war'. But the whole edifice was one of 'simple Keynesianism' and eschewed radical changes in either industrial organisation or budgetary techniques.[3] Paragraph 54, exhorting workers to greater productivity and employers to less restrictionism was the only indication of measures to promote industrial efficiency which had actually figured very large during Board of Trade Reconstruction discussions. The statement represented a break with pre-war tendencies, but embodied neither the more definite competitive order wanted by the neo-classical economists in Whitehall, nor the wide scope of state ownership advocated by some opponents of monopoly.

The policy of paragraph 54 did not evolve smoothly in the course of the war, by way of a gradual shift away from the pre-war position towards greater suspicion of monopolies, but developed via the erosion and dilution of, on the one hand, businessmen's demands for the full extension and elaboration of the existing trade association system and, on the other, of a radical anti-monopoly policy put forward in 1943 by economists in Whitehall. The bland statement in the White Paper and hence the uncontroversial nature of the 1948 Act was the result not of consensus but of deep conflict. According to the Board of Trade anything more radical would have created 'much opposition, and even strong resentment, in some business circles'.[4] The conflict was multifold and focussed on the future role of private enterprise, and the extent and nature of state control in the era of monopoly. Policy on restrictive practices was also evolved during important and, until well into the post-war period, inconclusive deliberations on future relations between Britain and the rest of the world – the Empire, the United States and Europe.

'Twists and turns'

Hitler's proclamation of his 'New Economic Order' in October 1940 prompted the first round of post-war planning in Britain which culminated in Keynes' December 1940 memorandum 'Proposals to counter the German "New Order"', a paper enunciating a liberal post-war trading order.[5] In November 1941 an official committee on post-war internal economic problems began, in a desultory fashion, to examine certain problems further, but it was not until the publication of the Beveridge report and the establishment of a Cabinet Committee on Reconstruction Priorities (later to become the Reconstruction Committee) that discussions took on a more substantial form. The Steering Committee on Employment, a committee of officials, first met in July 1943. Their report was discussed by the Ministerial Reconstruction Committee, whose deliberations were eventually embodied in the May 1944 White Paper.

Policy on restrictive practices had quickly gone onto the agenda. As early as November 1941 James Meade, Economic Assistant at the Economic Section, in a paper for the Internal Economic Problems Committee, linked the achievement of full employment with measures to tackle restrictive practices by employers and workers.[6] That Committee asked the recently-established Reconstruction Unit of the Board of Trade for a paper on industrial structure. This prompted the Board's representative on the Committee, Sir Charles Innes, a businessman drafted into the civil service for the war, to write a memorandum proposing increased powers for trade associations with some government safeguards. The paper sparked off the first debate on competition. Ruth Cohen, Secretary to the Reconstruction Unit, rejected both the pre-war policy of 'modified encouragement' to trade associations, and Innes' 'more forward policy', to favour the discouragement of trade associations whose primary purpose was restraint of trade. However, the head of the Unit, Henry Clay, predicting post-war conditions not dissimilar to those of the 1930s where 'free competition' could not function, wanted to facilitate the development of trade associations, especially as agencies of rationalisation, with independent tribunals to investigate allegations of excessive prices. In the context of the concurrent establishment and extension of trade associations, export groups and controls to wage war, the post-war future of such organisations was too politically sensitive, and no policy was formulated. The incident, however, probably sparked a flurry of business proposals, not dissimilar to Innes' which will be discussed later.[7]

The issue revived in May 1943 when the Economic Section of the Cabinet submitted a paper to the Cabinet Committee on Reconstruction Priorities, very similar to that of Meade's, stressing the dangers of restrictionism in hindering the growth of internal demand. That Committee agreed that the proposed Steering Committee on Employment should study the problem of restrictive practices by employers.[8] Cartels thus entered an area of separate consideration – the issue of monopoly was firmly to the fore.

The Board of Trade was designated the appropriate department for further development of policy. G.C. Allen and Hugh Gaitskell, both employed as economists by the Board of Trade, were told in July 1943 to write a paper, which became the seminal document 'The Control of Monopoly'.[9] This paper contained dire warnings and radical solutions: 'Monopolistic practices cannot be reconciled with the requirements of an expansionist economy, and our industrial organisation must be brought into accord with such an economy if we really wish to establish it.' In particular it warned that unless the government took a firm stand against businessmen's restrictionist outlook, 'The industrial field is likely to be divided to an increasing extent into a mass of autonomous fiefs, and the area of price competition is likely to shrink'.

Their proposals were uncompromising. The law should be revised to remove any favour to monopoly. Certain agreements, particularly those limiting new entrants to an industry, should be prohibited, except under licence. The government should control by various means large firms responsible for the output of a given product, including the final sanction of public ownership. Trade associations should be registered. In addition there were detailed proposals for the control of monopoly prices and the machinery of such control. Thus, at this stage, discussions about cartels had widened into the general problem of monopoly and by implication the future of private ownership over a vast area of the economy.

The civil servant, G.H. Andrew, who then worked on proposals for the Steering Committee kept more religiously to his brief, concentrating on cartels. Nevertheless, guided by the Allen–Gaitskell paper, his draft memorandum of August 1943 argued that, as cartels had the specific purpose of pursuing a restrictionist policy, they should only be allowed if employers could make out a clear case for them. Thus it proposed the prohibition, except under licence, of all domestic and international cartels which fixed minimum prices, which restricted sales or production or divided territories for sale, which destroyed or sealed capacity or which aimed to enforce any such agreements through excluding new entrants by means of exclusive dealing and boycotts. Trade associations should be registered with the Board of Trade. The paper also suggested extending publicity and enquiry to large firms and even raised the possibility of public ownership to ensure that monopolies acted in the public interest.[10]

This paper represented the high point of the evolution of antitrust proposals in Britain for many years to come, indeed ever since. There followed an inexorable process of dilution. After a confrontation on 17 September between Allen and Gaitskell on one side and Board of Trade permanent officials on the other (Sir Arnold Overton and G.L. Watkinson), the Board's paper to the Steering Committee on Employment in October 1943 proposed that all domestic and international agreements of a restrictive character be registered with the Board of Trade; that if the Board considered these might be against the public interest they could be investigated by a Commission; that such reports should be published and if necessary the Board could take remedial action like the suspension of any import duties or have power by Order to declare an agreement void; a process of investigation of large firms could also be adopted.[11]

Nevertheless this was to prove a radical position, for in January 1944 the Steering Committee's report to the ministerial Reconstruction Committee advised Ministers that disagreement on the committee ruled out a clear recommendation: one group argued against any statement on restrictive practices, another wanted prohibition, while the majority favoured the line of the Board of Trade.[12]

In early 1944 the radical proponents staged a comeback. Lionel Robbins' note of dissent was attached to the Steering Committee's report, and this wanted the prohibition of some types of agreement, such as organised boycotts, exclusive dealing and predatory price discrimination.[13] In addition Stafford Cripps, Minister of Aircraft Production submitted his own paper fully supporting Robbins' dissent as the minimum necessary.[14] At the first discussion on the Reconstruction Committee Hugh Dalton, President of the Board of Trade, argued for the 'drastic' course outlined in the Committee's report, and Harcourt-Johnstone, the Minister for Overseas Trade, for the drastic course for domestic cartels and a more moderate line for international cartels. The Reconstruction Committee was divided but decided that the Board's proposals should be developed for a future paper to be submitted to it.[15]

The paper produced by Dalton and Sir William Jowitt, Minister without Portfolio, in response, essentially developed the proposals of the Board of Trade, although it urged, in contrast to the feeling on the Reconstruction Committee, that the policy of registration be adopted for both domestic and international cartels.[16] However, when this paper came before the Committee a strong alliance of politicians opposed it. As a result Dalton was told to redraft his proposals in favour simply of an investigative tribunal, which could institute enquiries when the Board of Trade had reason to suppose they were against the public interest.[17] This policy had previously been described by the Economic Section as 'doing nothing at all', and failing to deal with 'the ossification of British industry'.[18] This meeting's decisions, however, were the origins of the White Paper's proposals, and of the 1948 Monopolies and Restrictive Practices Act.

Thus there was no gradual recognition of the need for gentle steps towards competition policy; rather there was a clash of long-held opinions and interests. What needs to be explained is not the 'baffling' change of opinion indicated in the 1944 White Paper, as previous writers have argued, but why such a radical policy was proposed in July to October 1943 and why in turn that was diluted.

The role of 'public opinion'

The 'twists and turns' described above can in no way have reflected changes in 'public opinion' and must invalidate much of that thesis. So we shall now look in more detail at what Joe Public was actually saying.

'Public opinion' as a summary of an aggregate of views would bear little relation to reality. It is, however, possible to look at the views of organised groups – political parties, trade unions, business organisations, academic 'think-tanks' and, of course, the Press.

Turning first to the 'labour movement', its focus was on public ownership and public control of monopoly. In contrast to labour feeling during the First World War frustration about inflation and suspicions of profiteering by trade associations and large firms was limited, having been contained from the start by legislation controlling prices and production. Instead, during the Second World War, debate in the labour movement shifted to a more thorough and general critique of private enterprise in the age of large-scale industrial organisation, and in the light of the failures of the inter-war period. Various unions had evolved plans for nationalisation of their industries. The TUC's *Interim Report on Post-War Reconstruction*, published shortly after the White Paper, put public control at the top of the agenda as the means to achieve the goals of full employment and improved wages and conditions. Right at the beginning the pamphlet argued that laissez-faire was over; 'higher forms of business organisation' were both advantageous and inevitable, but endangered individual liberty, while failing to develop scientific techniques. Lack of industrial co-ordination on the one hand and the 'restrictive policies of private monopolies' on the other, limited industrial efficiency, and this was the most powerful argument for public ownership. The report proposed nationalisation of fuel, power, transport (including coastal shipping) and iron and steel and, later, cotton. Other industries should be brought under tripartite, but especially greater workers', control through industrial Boards.[19]

The Labour Party was deeply divided during the war, with much frustration over the policies of the leadership in the Coalition. This emerged clearly among the discontents in the Common Wealth Party. Formed in 1941 and attracting mainly progressive intellectuals, it had a membership of 10,000 at its peak and four MPs. The private ownership of monopoly was a pivotal element in its outlook for the future, and it urged state ownership as the only solution.[20] Meanwhile, figures like Strabolgi and Nathan in the Lords urged immediate nationalisation of monopolies as did Professor Laski.[21] A spirited campaign against cartels was waged from the Labour backbenches. They constantly raised questions in Parliament about the pre-war behaviour of *international* cartels and their role in the appeasement of Hitler or the damage done to Allied war preparations.[22] A few such MPs were vehement that an enquiry like the 1918 Committee on Trusts be established.[23] It was through their participation in debate that it becomes clear how large were the ranks of Labour activists who saw the solution to the problem of cartels and monopoly in general in nationalisation. As Arthur Greenwood said, the choice was between public and private monopoly, for the clock could not be turned back.[24]

However, many influential Labour Party members working as economists in Whitehall during the war such as Hugh Gaitskell, Douglas Jay and Evan Durbin, had been members of the pre-war NFRB and XYZ Club. These organisations had, as chapter 3 discussed, developed a position combining Keynesian intervention to secure full employment with a mixture of 'planning and the price mechanism'. Their impact on the wartime debate in the Labour Party over the scale of nationalisation was to favour that side which sought to limit state ownership and to re-assert the benefits of competition and consumer sovereignty. Hugh Gaitskell's contribution to the paper on 'The Control of Monopoly' analysed how the government could use price control to regulate large firms. He effectively only supported public ownership in the cases of single-firm monopoly where, he argued, such extensive investigation and supervision would be necessary that ultimately the state would have to take over the ordinary shares of the company. Increasingly Labour Ministers, like Hugh Dalton, argued that, 'you should have either really free, profit-seeking competition, or else a centrally-planned public enterprise'.[25]

This 'revisionist' strand in the Labour Party, while dominant on the National Executive Committee (NEC), was strenuously resisted by the 'fundamentalists', the latter seeing it as a threat to public ownership. A resolution at the 1944 party conference reaffirming commitment to sweeping nationalisations carried the day against the NEC.[26] Thus while there were various strands in the labour movement, anti-monopoly feeling was strong, solutions running towards extensive nationalisation, extension of Co-operatives and workers' control. The Labour Ministers in favour of profit-seeking private enterprise being made competitive could not be said to have a wide support within the Labour movement broadly defined.

Indeed, snapping at the Labour Party's heels was the Communist Party, whose influence in the labour movement grew markedly, after June 1941 when Germany invaded the Soviet Union, and with increased unionisation and the Joint Production Committees. Monopoly had always been at centre stage of their analysis of the contradictions of 'imperialism'. Their pamphlet on reconstruction accused monopoly of being the cause of scarcity of goods and work and the cause of suppression of invention, and standing in the way of the future: 'The issue of Monopoly or the People will be a vital issue of domestic politics after the war.' In the short term the solution was nationalisation, regulation and workers' control.[27] Elsewhere the Communist Party proposed the expansion of Co-operatives against the 'Combines'. The People's Convention – a People's Parliament, mainly inspired by the Communist Party – proposed, at its first meeting in January 1941, that a People's Britain should have emergency powers to take over banks, land, transport, armaments and other large industries. They aimed to strengthen the Co-operative movement to secure supplies and combat profiteering, while safeguarding the interests of the small farmer, the small shopkeeper and the consumer. The Convention claimed that the delegates represented 1.2 million workers. This may have been exaggerated, but the Convention had extensive grass-roots support in the trade unions, and its activities provoked discussions in the workplace.[28]

Turning to other political parties we find that the Conservative Party was not the bulwark of liberalism it was to become.[29] In the Reconstruction Committee the Conservative Minister of Production, Oliver Lyttelton, argued most vehemently against policies restraining restrictive practices on the basis that there was 'no evidence to show that monopolies had proved more damaging to employment than free competition'.[30] 36 Tory MPs formed the Tory Reform Group to reform the Party's public image as the tool of big business and to urge commitment to the Welfare state, limited demand management, a pragmatic approach to nationalisation but the full cartelisation of the coal industry. Meanwhile an outstanding pre-war iron and steel cartellist, Sir Spencer Summers, organised his Progress Trusts to counter the reformers.[31] The Conservative sub-committee on industry deprecated compulsory trade associations and recommended government supervision of international cartels.[32] Like the Labour Party, this was a confused picture, but one even less inclined to reviving the spirit of competition.

Perhaps one of the strongest war-time statements for antitrust policy came from the much-weakened Liberal Party. Their proposals on state and industry post-war combined counter-cyclical investment schemes with the removal of controls as soon as possible, the limitation of state intervention, but effective action against restraint of trade. While they wanted a strong 'anti-monopoly code', they also proposed the creation of public utility companies where 'complete monopoly' was found to be necessary or desirable, while they asserted only that trade associations should be subject to rules laid down by Parliament. Many of these ideas, including those for a Council of Industry were echoing themes established since the Liberal Industrial Enquiry 15 years previously.[33]

'Opinion' expressed in the Press was also diffuse. The left-wing Press and journals attacked the plans of business for statutory corporate forms of organisation.[34] But the mainstream press was very divided. *The Economist* maintained a constant barrage against restrictionism and the industrial feudalism of cartels and trade associations.[35] It favoured a policy of planned expansion in the international sphere with domestic laws against price-fixing. *The Times*, however, warned against a return to unfettered competition, although it equally opposed the sectional interests served by 'industrial self-government'.[36]

A well-publicised report of the Nuffield Conference, representing a coalition of leading industrialists and economists, while stating its commitment to the profit motive, saw the solution to the abuse of monopoly and cartels in public ownership, supervision and price control, rather than full-scale commitment to competition.[37]

Thus the monopoly problem was at the centre of popular debates about the future of British industry. Anti-monopoly feeling was strong, but adherence to free market competition was a minority interest. Many solutions represented a challenge to private enterprise and managerial prerogatives across a wide range of industries. The extent of agreement on this is summed up in Churchill's comment during his March 1944 broadcast, seeking to bolster the popularity of the Conservative Party, and public faith in the post-war world: 'There is a broadening field for state ownership and enterprise especially in relation to monopolies of all kinds.'[38]

Perhaps for this reason we find, when we leave the Clapham omnibus and enter the doors of Whitehall, that civil servants and politicians of all colours treated 'public opinion' as something to be contained. Specific ideas for nationalisation, for instance of coal, were vetoed by Churchill as issues that would divide the nation. In the case of policy on cartels and monopoly in general, this containment policy is seen most clearly in the defeat of calls for a general enquiry, even a Royal Commission, into cartels and trusts, along the lines of that after the First World War.

A very broad range of opinion favoured a general enquiry into cartels and trusts, like the Committee on Trusts of 1918. Calls were made in Parliament on at least eight occasions; the Liberal Party called for a general enquiry in 1943, the TUC in October 1944; various newspapers and some government economists favoured such an enquiry to mobilise public opinion in favour of strong action against cartels. A delegation of Conservative MPs, many from the Tory Reform Group, proposed an independent enquiry to cover the whole field.[39]

However, industrialists made their opposition to such a move very clear. In 1942 Henry Clay, responding to a report by the Central Committee of Export Groups[40] favourable to trade associations, proposed an enquiry into the whole question of industrial organisation. The response from Sir Charles Innes was swift and uncompromising. He said he was 'incensed' and thought such a policy would mean that, 'the B.I.S.F., the I.C.I., Unilever, the F.B.I., B.E.A.M.A. and all existing trade associations will at once feel insecure and uncertain as to their future ... controversy will be aroused just at a time when it is essential for Government and Industry to work together in the closest co-operation and harmony'.[41]

The threat went home. Time and time again Ministers, both Labour and Conservative, and civil servants fought shy of an enquiry, and were quite clear about their apprehensions. According to Morrison an enquiry would make the question of cartels a 'first class issue of government policy' and harden the relationship between government and industry.[42] In June 1943 the report by a Cabinet Committee on the recovery of post-war export markets appeared which argued that price rings could damage Britain's export prospects and called for a Commission to investigate the question in general, but only when such an enquiry would not interfere with war production.[43] According to Sir Arnold Overton, Permanent Secretary at the Board of Trade, a Commission of enquiry would 'stir up controversy to no purpose and damage such confidence as industry now has in the Board of Trade'. (Dalton wrote 'Yes' in red ink in the margin of the minute.)[44] In July 1943 revelations that international cartels had sabotaged the war effort prompted Dalton to speed up Allen's and Gaitskell's paper. But his diary reveals that this was done to pre-empt the force of opinion. 'I point out,' he recorded, 'that there is now much pressure from many directions, for an enquiry into Monopolies, and that I am anxious to resist this on the ground that we are working it out ourselves.' Of most influence was the statement by the Steering Committee arguing against a Royal Commission on various grounds but 'above all ... industry will be on the defensive ... and we shall have forfeited the co-operation of industrialists with Government and with each other at the time when we have most need of it'.[45] As a result all the calls for a Commission made in the House of Commons were resisted and no wide-ranging enquiry into restrictive practices or into price rings alone, as the Committee on the export trade proposed, was established.

Thus where 'public opinion' was united, demands were strenuously resisted. Resisted because of the clash that would be provoked with the very organisations that would be the subject of enquiry. In the 20-odd years since the Committee on Trusts of 1918 the political and economic power of cartels and large firms had increased. This served to broaden the 'opinion' favouring widespread public control: an enquiry could have tested the allegations of the Communist Party and others of the abuse of controls by the monopolists. However 'trustification' had given British businessmen increased leverage with government to withstand such demands. With nationalisation a non-starter for policy-makers and an enquiry defeated, the question turned to other policies, policies which involved consideration of the future of private enterprise.

The future of private enterprise

Within Whitehall we can identify three scenarios for the future of private enterprise, each one a response to the cartelisation of the British economy which had arisen in the inter-war period and during the war itself, and each with implications for competition policy. All were evolved at a time when the nature of the international settlement was still in the balance, an issue which will be dealt with later.

Economists within Whitehall, many of whom were newly drafted in during the war, put forward one scenario. Although still inexperienced and lacking self-confidence as a profession in government they were generally united in their proposals for a liberal economy both nationally and internationally.[46] Displaying the bias of their profession in favour of competitive markets that has persisted, they were determined that the restrictionism of the inter-war period be dealt with 'as an essential and conspicuous feature of the main plan for economic expansion'.[47] Commitment to a liberal trading order post-war was central to their outlook, and informed their insistence on action against restrictionism domestically, as detailed in the Allen–Gaitskell paper. There was also a measure of agreement on the use of nationalisation as a sanction against monopoly.[48] The one voice of dissent was that of Henry Clay, who was more tender of restrictive practices: he was removed from the Board of Trade's discussions in 1942.[49] While some, led by Lionel Robbins, pushed for the emphasis of government response to monopoly to lie in the reassertion of the principles of laissez-faire – the 'competitive order' – others embarked on more complex plans for state involvement in industrial rejuvenation, believing, like G.C. Allen that the maintenance of a high level of demand would still not solve problems like excess capacity.[50]

Economists in the Board of Trade consciously campaigned to reverse pre-war policies and to resist the influence of business views within the department. From about the Spring of 1943 when the Steering Committee on Employment was about to be set up and once Reconstruction was being taken seriously, Hugh Gaitskell organised some informal meetings on Saturday mornings in the Board of Trade. Attending these were G.C. Allen, Ruth Cohen, James Meade and the assistant Secretary, William Hughes.[51] The group worked towards a paper on the whole question of monopoly, probably that which materialised in the Allen–Gaitskell paper, although this was never finally agreed by the whole group.

The defeat of economists' liberal industrial strategy did not lie primarily in departmental and civil service intransigence,[52] as some have argued, but in the opposition their ideas encountered from businessmen. Civil servants were continually reminded and reminding Ministers of the intransigent and unimaginative attitude they met among British businessmen. For them the future of trade associations and international cartels was the single most important issue. In 1943 Alix Kilroy noted that: 'our industrial discussions . . . lead rapidly to questions of Government policy on international cartels and the monopoly of the home market.'[53] It was on this that they made their substantial contribution to Reconstruction discussions, and indeed substantially affected the nature of official decisions.

As far as the most articulate and well-organised sections of British business were concerned the future lay with the trade association, planned markets and trade, and industrial self-government. There was almost complete unanimity among industrialists on two relevant aspects of the post-war world. First, the system of domestic trade associations and the right to collude as necessary should in no way be disturbed: indeed the government should encourage 'industrial organisation' and 'industrial self-government'. Second, the right to form international cartels should in no way be disturbed, and the trend of industrial opinion was more unanimous on this point than on the domestic policies.[54] Their various proposals indicate a direct line of descent from the 1918 Committee on Commercial and Industrial Policy, through the Industrial Reorganisation League. Thus Lord McGowan's offer that ICI register its various international agreements with an appropriate government department was aimed at more closely involving the state in business cartel activities, rather than as a stage towards inquiry and control, as civil servants intended when advocating registration. McGowan indeed argued, at the same time as he reiterated this offer that without such 'international industrial co-operation ... the post-war period is likely to lead to chaos in place of order'.[55] Echoing his ideas *The Statist* declared that, 'Unless the big unit exists to handle and direct the spate of production which the machine makes possible ... the whole human race will be swamped by its own productivity'.[56]

The 'World Trade Alliance', an organisation of businessmen, advocated the extension of 'orderly' world marketing, that is government acceptance of a systematised development of international cartels.[57] While the FBI refused to support the World Trade Alliance, it and many other industrial organisations, fully endorsed industry's right to form international cartel arrangements as they saw fit.[58] The Management Research Group, an ad hoc organisation of mainly large firms, gave ardent support to the need to maintain international cartels, and an internal paper asserted, 'too much attention has been given to competition and too little to co-operation'.[59] In keeping with this restrictionist outlook, the FBI and most of industry was extremely sceptical of the benefits of multilateralism, at least on a worldwide basis. Some support for trading blocs like the Sterling area, within which British industry might be dominant existed.[60]

Domestically the tenor of businessmen's demands favoured extended cartelisation. Some important groupings of industrialists wanted statutory and enforceable trade associations and cartels, operating with the stamp of government approval.[61] Others envisioned the incorporation into businessmen's programmes not just of the state but of labour also: a form of voluntary corporatism with Industrial Boards consisting mainly of firms in the industry but with some trade union representation.[62] One example of such proposals was the 'National Policy for Industry', an organisation co-ordinated by Lord McGowan, chairman of ICI. The Council of each sectional association would have charge over production and prices, wages and conditions, the control of competition and collaboration with other trades. A Central Council of Industry would formulate views on issues 'where different sections may take different views'. The Central Council would maintain contact with the TUC, run an intelligence service on world trade and make suggestions to government on social and industrial legislation.[63]

These industrial plans went to the very root of the British industrial problem, and long-held fears for British export competitiveness.[64] The overwhelming tenor of these later plans was fear of foreign competition, particularly from the United States. The post-war world was viewed with alarm by most businessmen. A survey of British business executives in 1944 showed that 77% of those polled anticipated competition from the United States in export markets and 60% favoured post-war arrangements with American firms to safeguard export spheres.[65] The report on the recovery of the export trade showed that only a small sector of British industry anticipated any expansion of the export trade. These were the engineering, chemicals and motor and aircraft industries, and even these believed that expansion could only be assured in the short-term as the response to immediate post-war needs.[66]

A second strand informing these ideas was the calculations of businessmen, particularly those in large firms, in basic industries threatened by the rising popularity of nationalisation, to entice labour to their cause through promises of stable profits, wages and employment. The National Policy for Industry (NPI) was clearly concerned at the prospect of nationalisation. Sir Guy Locock, Director of the FBI, noted how the National Policy for Industry's proposals for a Charter of Labour represented the views of monopolists who would be able to pay higher wages and provide better conditions.[67]

During the war there were a series of attempts to resolve the relationship between employers and trade unions for the post-war years, such as soundings between the World Trade Alliance and the TUC, and an attempt by Beaverbrook and Ernest Bevin to establish a newspaper propagating ideas of co-operation between the two sides of industry. Indeed the glass firm, Pilkington agreed, belatedly, to sign the NPI not primarily for its attitude on cartels but for the need to 'improve post-war relations between capital and labour'. The interest which some trade unions had in domestic and international cartels was brought out in Ministerial discussions, when Ernest Bevin noted that, 'Unregulated competition, especially in the field of international trade, was recognised by Trade Unions as liable to produce most undesirable consequences'.[68]

The group of businessmen favouring state and labour incorporation into industrial plans for self-government was certainly powerful, representing large firms in key sectors of the economy, like engineering, iron and steel and metal manufacture and chemicals. Of the 119 signatories of the NPI listed in the original publication whose industrial interests can be traced, 22, or about 30%, were connected with engineering, including directors of GKN, Baker Perkins, Babcock and Wilcox, Ford's and BSA. 15 signatories were directors of iron and steel firms, 12 of chemical firms, and 7 were from various branches of the textile trade. While these sectors of industry were dominant the NPI also claimed support from large firms in other industries, such as food processing (Chivers, United Yeast) (see appendix 4).

The tenor of another report, by the Central Committee of Export Groups bore close resemblance to NPI plans, and hoped to use the war-time export groups as a starting point for enhanced cartelisation. Behind the Central Committee was the Industrial and Export Council, the successor of the Export Council set up to co-ordinate the export drive of 1940. Its members had similar business backgrounds to signatories of the NPI.[69] Many of these were also members of the Association of British Chambers of Commerce (ABCC) as well as having close connections with one another's businesses. Much of the unanimity of industry's views may be attributed therefore to the close liaison developed between the members of the Industrial and Export Council, the ABCC, and the Cotton Board who were to come together in the NPI.

They also represented firms with strong international cartel connections from before the war and were to attempt to re-establish these after the war. There was therefore a clear correlation between firms espousing domestic cartelisation and those least willing to abandon pre-war defensive mechanisms.

Finally, these large industrialists, many in capital goods industries, influenced government departments because it was precisely such industries which were most vital to the war effort and they were therefore well represented within Whitehall. Some businessmen played important general co-ordinating roles in the Board of Trade, particularly through the Industrial and Export Council. Cecil Weir was on the Export Council, a signatory of the NPI, and later Controller-General of Factory and Storage premises.[70] Sir Charles Innes was on the interdepartmental committee on post-war export trade from November 1941, and on the planning sub-committee which produced the committee's report on the export trade.[71] He was also appointed by that committee to be the co-ordinating link, along with Henry Clay, with the Board's Reconstruction Unit and was responsible for correlating reconstruction in home and export markets. The executive members of the Export Council were businessmen, given full-time positions within Whitehall since 1940. They had daily meetings themselves, weekly meetings with Board of Trade officials, fortnightly meetings of the Export Council, which was also attended by the businessmen controllers of industries.[72]

However, there were major limitations to their strength. Most significant was the opposition which plans for statutory trade associations encountered from organisations representing smaller firms, such as the National Union of Manufacturers (NUM).[73] Implicitly accepting that their plans meant the coercion of smaller firms, the NPI suggested that the needs of smaller producers to appeal against the decisions of the Sectional associations should be met by investigation through an Industrial Tribunal. Otherwise, they said, small firms 'might well appear to run the risk of being swamped by the interests of larger and more powerful undertakings'.[74]

The FBI contained a wide range of size of firms, many of whom felt that their interests were not served by participation in trade associations dominated by large firms. Its survey of its constituent associations showed that compulsory associations were not favoured by the majority of them.[75] In addition the FBI felt that the NPI represented a threat to its hegemony as the main peak industrial organisation with relations with government.[76] Sir Charles Bruce-Gardner, chairman of the FBI's reconstruction committee noted how many important industrialists had *not* signed the NPI, like Sir George Nelson of EEC, Sir James Lithgow, shipbuilding, Samuel Courtauld, L.J. Cadbury, Lord Nuffield and William Rootes.[77] Thus there were important sectors of industry who were not impressed. The FBI, steering a compromise course among a variety of opinions, wanted a more favourable attitude by government to trade associations but otherwise complete freedom from government intervention: trade associations should be trusted to take cognisance of the public interest.[78]

But there was no small-business lobby in favour of laws against either trusts or cartels. Doubtful noises were made only by a few scattered individuals. In the FBI committee which discussed its 1944 report on industrial organisation only one member spoke out against the report's support for price maintenance and redundancy schemes which he saw as 'inimical to enterprise and to capitalistic risk-bearing'.[79] The Vice-President of the ABCC, John McLean, also opposed, at a meeting with the Board of Trade, the 'privileges and monopolies' which trade associations sought to acquire, particularly as they aided international cartelisation which, he said, could restrict Britain's overseas markets.[80] Certain figures in the food-processing industries, such as Paul Cadbury, opposed resale price maintenance and the 'regimentation' of trade associations and their restriction of demand.[81] But these were lone voices.

The general business vision of the post-war world appalled the economists employed in government. A.S.J. Baster remarked of the suggestions by the FBI and ABCC that they seemed to have lost all hope to compete successfully in the post-war world: 'They forecast a Britain brooding like an aged miser in the twilight over a dwindling treasure.'[82] Douglas Jay criticised the 'unenterprise of British industrialists' wanting protection 'by agreements from new products internally and by tariffs or cartels from foreign competition'.[83]

The civil servants were just as critical. William Hughes described the NPI as containing 'the main features of the Fascist corporate state against which we are fighting', and Alix Kilroy described the FBI plans as 'on the fence about the corporate state and united only that the Office of Works should not place its orders outside a recognised trade prices ring. Clearly it is difficult to make this an issue of policy'.[84]

Dalton and many of his officials became heartily tired of the attitude of the average industrialist. Dalton was scathing about many of the industrialists he met.[85] Alix Kilroy commented: 'With few exceptions these discussions [industry by industry] have been disappointing and indeed alarming. There is little tendency to aim beyond a return to the status quo ante the war.'[86]

These corporatist plans were killed off within the Whitehall committee structure without too much difficulty,[87] partly because industry was divided and partly because the middle of a war with Nazi Germany was an inauspicious time for such ideas. However, the government found it difficult to resist industrial opposition to any change in industrial policy from the pre-war days, particularly to any condemnation of or even enquiry into restrictive practices.

Thus the third scenario was that developed principally by the civil servants in the Board of Trade – G.L. Watkinson, Sir Arnold Overton and Alix Kilroy. Their proposals on industrial efficiency combined awareness of business commitment to the current form of industrial organisation together with wider concerns about Britain's post-war balance of payments and the implementation of full employment policy, and the problem of excess capacity in war-expanded industries.

The need to increase British exports after the war was at the heart of Board of Trade thinking about the post-war world. The export trade committee's report which appeared in June 1943, calculated that Britain would need to increase its export trade by between £250 and £375 million, nearly a 50% increase over pre-war trade.[88] The report stressed the need to make British exports more competitive. It stated that price rings were extensive 'with the consequence that the prices of a very large range of United Kingdom manufactures have tended to become non-competitive in unprotected markets'. Price rings were accused of basing prices on the less efficient producers, of preventing the full use of up-to-date factories, and of raising the prices of components used by export industries, for instance in the car industry, requiring iron and steel, electric bulbs, glass and alloy steels. In addition, as both this report and the Board of Trade's own survey of cartels concluded, the commitment to a multilateral trading system was incompatible with international cartels whose development had been dependent on tariffs and autarkical trading patterns.[89]

But many permanent civil servants had been actively involved in inter-war schemes for rationalisation and industrial co-operation. Alix Kilroy, for instance, refused to accept the American tradition for a country like Britain which, to compete, needed large export competitive industries occupying an inevitably monopolistic position in a relatively smaller home market.[90] Furthermore any export drive would require industrial co-operation and the use of the export groups formed, often as extensions of trade associations, during the war.

Commitment to employment policy provided a powerful economic argument for a radical anti-cartel policy: the Board of Trade admitted that proposals to prohibit restrictive practices (as Allen and Gaitskell wanted) rather than proposals to register and investigate them (as the Board was to suggest), 'pointed more fully to full employment'.[91] G.C. Allen has argued that had the tackling of restrictive practices not been a part of Employment policy it is doubtful whether 'resistance to change would have been overcome'.[92]

Again however the problems of the transition meant that the Board of Trade wished to use trade associations for the post-war administration of controls and the process of deconcentration and elimination of excess capacity but was well aware that such a policy 'inevitably encourages the formation of permanent associations with the concomitant dangers of trade monopolies and general restrictive practices'.[93] Overton believed that the whole issue should not be tackled at all until the ending of price and profit controls when monopoly might become a problem.[94]

Finally, and crucially, civil servants had to reckon with the outlook of businessmen and their known opposition to any disturbance of their trade association system. This decisively modified formulation of policy at departmental level. Civil servants, closely in touch with business feeling and lacking the economists' more doctrinaire approach, were most unwilling to risk the loss of business co-operation.

They therefore devised a programme outlined in a major paper to the Steering Committee – 'General Support for Trade'. It proposed methods to achieve amalgamations through government finance schemes and legislation to set up industrial boards in industries that wished for them, to pursue such operations undertaken by the large firm, such as research and development, marketing, the improvement of design and standards. Overall responsibility for pursuing industrial efficiency was to be given to an Industrial Commission, modelled on the IDAC, which would also advise the Board of Trade on restrictive practices and monopolies.[95] The aim of its initiator, Watkinson, was to calm industrial hostility while stimulating industry to overcome post-war difficulties: to overcome the weaknesses of the small firm without actually and overtly challenging its continuance.[96] Here was an 'efficiency' package which would not involve nationalisation, would not challenge the existing system of organisation, indeed could provide it with a fillip and give it state recognition. Competition policy – such as it was – would be subsumed under a programme primarily geared to increasing industrial co-ordination, if not cartelisation.

To conclude, within the Board of Trade three scenarios for the future of British industrial organisation and the role of the state in the era of monopoly and British industrial decline may be isolated: a competitive order, industrial self-government and cartels, or state regulated industrial co-ordination.

The outcome, at the stage of discussions within the Board of Trade, was most clearly decided by the business veto. At the special meeting on 17 September 1943 to resolve the controversy between the economists, proposing prohibition, and the civil servants, proposing registration and investigation, the latter, Overton and Watkinson made the basis of their opposition to the programme of Allen and Gaitskell clear: 'Such a policy was likely to excite great opposition among industrialists, would give rise to administrative difficulties and was based on a view of monopoly which they did not wholly share.' Watkinson added that 'if too ambitious a policy were proposed, there was some danger of achieving nothing at all', although he had elsewhere agreed with Allen's analysis.[97] This is clear evidence of the strength of the business veto. Dalton, presumably feeling that the topic was so delicate that he feared a major rift with his Permanent Secretary, came down on the side of the civil servants but, as a compromise to Allen and Gaitskell, he added a final paragraph outlining alternative measures of prohibition and licensing.[98]

The Board of Trade's own ideas for 'The General Support of Trade' threatened to nullify policy on competition, and in response to fears expressed on this score by Gaitskell and S.R. Dennison, a paragraph was included in the Board's paper on the subject recognising that industrial boards would tighten industrial organisation and increase the possibilities for price-fixing, and stressing the need to take powers to stop restrictive practices: 'if such powers are not taken the formation of Industrial Boards may well make matters worse, and the benefits of the improvement in efficiency at which they aim may be cancelled by a policy of excessive prices and restricted output.'[99] Although the Board submitted its separate paper on restrictive practices to the Steering Committee this referred to the Industrial Commission in the accompanying brief. Thus, the dominant line at the Board of Trade saw the control of restrictive practices as subsidiary to promoting industrial organisation, and a policy favouring the encouragement of the large-scale firm and the representative trade association.

The strength of industrial feeling was powerfully felt in the Board of Trade and although it might be scorned, it could not be ignored. Most industrialists recoiled with nausea at the prospect of a dose of competition policy, and any reversal at all of pre-war policy therefore had to be administered with a large spoonful of sugar in the form of government support for the existing industrial structure. Nevertheless the Board of Trade's proposals on restrictive practices as they stood in mid-1942 were stronger than the White Paper promise. To understand the context in which further dilution took place it is necessary to turn to the impact of American pressure.

Britain and the post-war world

Discussions on the future organisation and ownership of British industry were conducted against the backcloth of the Anglo–American discussions geared to achieving a multilateral monetary and trading system in the post-war world. In addition, the United States wanted to enlist Britain in an international trust-busting campaign aimed specifically at prohibiting international cartels in manufactured goods. The general aim of American commercial policy from 1940 onwards was to secure an 'Open Door' for American goods and investment.[100] In its relationship with Britain the most contentious point at issue was the markets of the British Empire, which the United States sought to open up by the removal or reduction of imperial preferences.[101] However, the United States sought also to prevent other commercial activities which could close markets to her exports, including international cartels.

The United States influenced the direction of British policy in three ways: she had direct leverage over British commercial policy, she aroused public hostility to cartels, and she forced policy-makers to focus on cartels, rather than the broader question of industrial organisation.

The American Congress used Britain's dire financial position to attach strings to Lend-Lease regarding the conduct of post-war financial and commercial policy. Under Article VII of the Mutual Aid Agreement signed in February 1942, Britain was committed to discussions with the Americans on how to eliminate trade barriers.

By April 1943 the majority of British policy-makers favoured the restoration of a multilateral trading system in some form and under certain conditions, to ensure the needed export expansion to overcome the dire balance of payments position that was predicted.[102] In September 1943 the first round of Anglo–American discussions on implementation of Article VII began in Washington. These talks were informal, preparatory, exploratory and secret. They ended with a broad statement of agreement on the desirability of a commercial convention on lowering tariffs, for a higher level of employment to encourage freer trade, and on the abolition of quantitative restrictions on trade.[103] It was not to be until November 1944 that talks resumed, by which time Britain had become a 'reluctant partner' especially on issues of agriculture, state trading, quantitative import restrictions and, of course, imperial preference.[104]

However, it was this pressure for agreement with America about the post-war commercial settlement that prompted some of the earliest specific debates about cartels in general. The official committee on Post-War External Economic Problems and Anglo–American Co-operation commissioned D.H. MacGregor, by then Professor of Economics at the University of London, to write a paper on international cartels. He favoured some form of international supervision, such as an organisation modelled on the Federal Trade Commission of the United States, to receive information and to conduct investigations in response to complaints.[105] A Principal at the Board of Trade, C.K. Hobson, quickly pointed out that such a body presupposed the existence of a national organisation of control in each country.[106] Thus at an early stage it was clear that *international* supervision implied *national* regulation.

Britain nevertheless insisted that domestic policy on restrictive practices must dictate the type of agreement to control international cartels. British negotiators at the commercial talks in Washington in October 1943, having been given no clear guidance about the matter, decided that any policy on international cartels should be dictated by policy on domestic cartels. They took as their guide the Board of Trade's proposals for registration and investigation. Similarly Dalton later told Lord Halifax, British Ambassador in Washington, that any decisions on domestic cartels would come first.[107]

At the discussions in October 1943 the Americans proposed some strong policies: the registration of all private international agreements 'which establish enduring relationships between business enterprises' including acquisitions across countries; the prohibition of certain types of international cartels – for instance those fixing prices, markets, production or limiting production under licences and patents; and international conventions and national legislation covering company, patent and trade-mark law.[108] American arguments tended to centre around the notion that cartels were *generally* incompatible with a liberal world economy. They noted that on commodity policy Britain sought to limit private cartels outside the jurisdiction of an international regulatory commission: could not the same procedure be adopted for semi-manufactured and manufactured products?[109]

The British representatives in turn, and Meade played a key role in this committee, argued that they too took a commitment to free trade as their starting point. However, they preferred regulation to prohibition, they predicted that the British government would use a variety of methods to control domestic monopoly, including fact-finding enquiries, the reform of laws, price control and public corporations. They also raised the point that a framework was needed which encompassed a broad range of systems – from the United States to the Soviet Union – and that therefore it would be best to formulate a list of objectives and leave each country to devise the most appropriate means to execute them.[110]

Thus the furthest the two sides got towards agreement was a statement welcoming the discussions and outlining the American proposals. Both groups agreed that 'the pursuit of widely divergent commercial policies in any field, including that of international cartel policy, would be a matter for regret'. The memorandum to the Cabinet stated that Britain, 'must be prepared for further pressure on this subject' from the Americans and failure to co-operate 'would almost certainly prejudice further discussion in the field of commercial and commodity policy'.[111]

This direct leverage on Britain was supplemented by American influence on the formation of public opinion in Britain hostile to cartels, particularly international cartels. The Americans unleashed a flood of propaganda, a sort of international equivalent of the muck-raking which caused excitement and interest during the antitrust campaign in the United States in the early 1900s.[112] By 1943 the Antitrust Division of the Department of Justice and various Senate and Congressional hearings on patents, munitions and national defence had collected an impressive amount of material on the way pre-war international patent agreements had been instruments of German aggression denying to America, and to a lesser extent Britain, the right to produce materials of strategic value.[113] Particular play was made of the Düsseldorf incident of March 1939 (see chapter 3).

These points fell on fertile ground in war-time Britain. In November 1943 a book based on this information was published in Britain: *Germany's Master Plan*.[114] It caused 'quite a blow up' in the House of Commons and led to increased demands for an enquiry.[115] Various left-wing organisations published their own accounts of this evidence: accusations of pro-Nazi sympathies on the part of big business had been a familiar cry of the British left.[116]

It was not only public opinion which was aroused: British government departments shared some of these public concerns, particularly on security grounds. There was evidence that international cartel agreements had created problems in armaments production, causing shortages of magnesium, dyestuffs and zinc, excessive profits in aluminium, and limited British production of rolling mill machinery, certain activated carbons used in gas masks, and certain scientific instruments.[117] However, the Board of Trade's own survey of international cartels, undertaken as a result of American allegations was inconclusive: 'the strategic results are far from clear as far as the United Kingdom is concerned.'[118]

Dalton responded to a request by the FBI that the government reject the American interpretation of Düsseldorf with strong criticism of this incident and the whole policy of appeasement.[119] The United States had chosen an area of attack calculated to bring out some of the most bitter divisions within the British government and the population at large.

American pressure, conveyed through negotiations and through public response to muck-raking, was instrumental in speeding progress on domestic policies. One incident was particularly important. In July 1943 revelations that ICI had continued an arrangement with IG Farben relating to South American markets after the declaration of war reached England. Several parliamentary questions demanded an enquiry into the activities of cartels.[120] Dalton, although he later asserted that it was clear that ICI had 'put profits before patriotism' resisted such demands.[121] A few days later he summoned his officials and demanded speedy formulation of policy on monopolies, that is on domestic policy. The result was the Allen–Gaitskell paper.

American pressure also drove Britain to formulate policy on cartels, as distinct from solutions to the question of monopolies in general and issues such as rationalisation and nationalisation. This emphasis accorded with the trend of economists' ideas who saw advantages in the large firm, so long as there was competition but regarded cartels as inherently anti-competitive. Thus it was that the Economic Section's early paper to the Committee on Reconstruction Priorities in May 1943 isolated restrictive practices by workers and businessmen as a limit to the achievement of full employment. The focus on cartels also arose from the Board of Trade's consideration of the future of trade associations in various specific industries. Thus the Economic Section's original diagnosis, bracketing restrictive labour and business practices, became Dalton's programme to consider business organisation alone.[122] Similarly the focus of the final White Paper was determined by the simple Keynesian compromise – which preferred to manage only the macro-economy and had little to say on industrial organisation – and by the direct need to respond publicly to American demands.

It should be noted that this American focus was also on *industrial* cartels, a point made dourly by British critics of American pressure. Thus this also explains the way that competition policy became so closely identified with industrial monopoly and restriction: agriculture and service sector arrangements could be ignored for little immediate pressure, at least at the international level, was felt.

However, American emphasis on cartels served to put everyone on the defensive. Conservative MPs reacted to attacks on restrictive business practices by arguing that there should also be legislation on restrictive labour practices. Lyttelton argued that in international competition Britain was at a disadvantage because of her rigid wage structure, 'and cartel agreements were often the only way in which British firms could maintain their export trade'.[123] Although evidence on the extent of restrictive labour practices proved very scanty when the British Employers' Confederation attempted to collect it in 1948,[124] the accusations caused Labour Ministers to falter. When we turn to the final Ministerial decisions of 1944 which were to lead to the White Paper, the negative impact of American pressure on domestic conflicts can be appreciated.

The decisions

On 4 February 1944 the Reconstruction Committee of the War Cabinet discussed that section of the Steering Committee's report on Employment relating to restrictive practices. Opening the discussion, Dalton argued that both Parliament and the Press were 'showing a keen interest in the question of restrictive developments in industry' and discussions on Article VII had raised the need for a definite line. The government must announce legislation, and he therefore ruled out any suggestion of a Royal Commission of enquiry. This was agreed. Dalton went on to argue for the Board of Trade's 'drastic' course – for prohibition. Harcourt-Johnstone, the Liberal Secretary for Overseas Trade, Lord Cherwell, Postmaster General, and Lord Woolton, Minister of Reconstruction argued for the 'drastic' course for domestic cartels and the 'minimum' of investigation and registration for international cartels. Conservative Ministers at the meeting clearly did not like policy on restrictive practices, but they seemed prepared to compromise on the 'minimum' proposals.[125] Dalton and Jowitt were given the task of another memorandum developing the views expressed in more detail.

Meanwhile reflections on the Washington discussions proceeded, as Britain held meetings with Dominion governments. While the two moved closer on imperial preference, the issue of international cartels proved to be one of the most contentious topics at discussions between Britain and the

Dominions between the February and April meetings of the Reconstruction Committee.[126] The Dominion governments were favourable to the prohibition of certain practices, and on registration they insisted that not only should information be registered with national governments but should be communicated to countries affected by the arrangements.[127]

Such a stipulation not only made the idea of registration less attractive it sought to nullify the effect of the cartel itself. Registration, as proposed by large firms like ICI, was intended to be with the national government, allowing supervision by a national government which, like the IDAC, could be expected to be cognisant of national sectional interests. The Dominions were giving the idea an interpretation alien to the spirit of British industrialists' intentions. The Dominions' attitude reduced the possibility of resisting American pressure.

At first these developments, particularly the experience with the Dominions, served to force British policy-makers to seek some compromise with the Americans which would at least avoid prohibition of international cartels. James Meade in early 1944 proposed the registration with a national body of international arrangements, these to be communicated to an International Cartels Office which could pass judgement on them. Unless something like this was proposed, he said, 'there is reason to believe that ... we may endanger the success of our proposals for Commercial Policy and for Commodity Policy'.[128]

But Ruth Cohen's consideration of the problem raised all the other points. She favoured prohibition of certain practices on the basis of the logic of the American argument that international cartels could negate other elements of commercial policy. But while agreeing on the dangers if general commercial policy discussions broke down she made five arguments against prohibition; the first of these ran as follows:

The British manufacturer, through his experiences during the last 20 years, has become well disposed towards cartels and towards monopoly in general, and it will be some time before a new generation of enterprising entrepreneurs has ousted their fearful, security-loving and artery-hardened elders. Until this has happened, a too downright policy on cartels would bewilder and terrify our industrial leaders and we cannot afford to jeopardise our chances of successful industrial reconstruction after the war.[129]

These two papers neatly summarise the variety of pressures which came to bear when Dalton and Jowitt were formulating policy on restrictive practices to present to the April meeting of the Reconstruction committee. Their hardest problem was whether to treat international and domestic cartels differently. They argued for the same treatment on the basis that the fortunes of the two were inextricably linked and that the features of some international cartels were as harmful as domestic cartels, encouraging attempts to monopolise the home market, destroying the safeguard of foreign competition and indulging in activities properly the sphere of the state. Finally, and most significantly, 'It would look very odd to the Americans if, after their public outcry and their private representation to us against international cartels, we now proposed legislation treating these more lightly than domestic arrangements'.[130]

But by the time of the Reconstruction committee meeting on 24 April 1944 this argument had lost its appeal. In early 1944 Britain began to hesitate in her whole approach towards a commercial agreement with the United States. In particular there were disputes over the interpretation of the Atlantic Charter as regards that most sacred of institutions, imperial preference.[131] The Commonwealth Prime Ministers (bar Canada), meeting in London in May 1944, dug in behind imperial preference. Churchill proposed looking at alternative external economic arrangements, and spoke vigorously against any interpretation of Article VII as the signal for the end of imperial preference. A very different overseas settlement was therefore on the cards. Arguably the future of international and domestic cartels hinged on the future of imperial preference and tariffs: as agreement on these points seemed further away, so too receded the need for policy on cartels.

British Ministers and businessmen were increasingly alarmed at the emerging lines of American economic foreign policy. The United States, it seemed, wished to deprive Britain of her traditional forms of protection, like imperial preferences, international cartels, while leaving intact America's tariff system. Thus the point that British negotiators insisted on was the principle of 'duality' that is any agreement on cartels should be part of a general agreement on commercial policy including tariffs. In contrast, at all times, the American side attempted to make cartels a separate issue.[132]

Yet there was no fundamental reason why Britain should seek alliance with America. It was not at all clear how secure such an alliance for the promotion of an expansionist world economy would be. There was no guarantee that a post-war recession would be avoided, Britain's financial position was dire, American competition had already undermined Britain's position in her traditional markets, yet British industrialists were even less confident of their ability to penetrate new, more developed markets. As Lord Halifax and Keynes noted, there were two alternatives. The first was to resort to defensive mechanisms and bilateral trade. The second was to adopt an expansionary policy, but that meant 'hitching the British wagon to the American shooting star without any guarantee that this star will follow a steady course'. [133]

The crisis which had arisen in Anglo–American relations sprang in part from suspicions that America had all along sought to exploit Britain's war-time difficulties. Businessmen had frequently complained that Americans had used Britain's war-time weakness to invade British markets, particularly in Latin America, a view endorsed in a British government note to the State department. They were very cynical of America's selective approach to free trade.[134]

Disputes arose over a number of issues in the early months of 1944, such as Lend-Lease and oil.[135] Between February and April 1944 the American offensive against international cartels intensified. Further indictments were made against British companies, notably ICI, under American Anti-trust.[136] On 17 April the Department of State announced the establishment of a special branch to co-ordinate policy on cartels with that on commodities. Prefacing the announcement was the statement: 'The policies of the United States Government on cartels and related international industrial agreements are inseparable aspects of U.S. commercial policy ... During the coming period ... cartel problems will be a major concern in international affairs.'[137]

It was at precisely the moment when all these considerations were at the fore of British policy-making that Dalton and Jowitt put forward their paper. It was certainly a somewhat extreme interpretation of the February discussions, and included the crucial decision to treat domestic and international cartels equally. Thus they may well have done what Watkinson feared and overplayed their hands. In the course of developing that paper's ideas officials attempted to define agreements which should be registered. The overwhelming predominance of agreements isolated were international, affecting mainly chemicals, iron and steel, metal manufacture, and engineering. Moreover, the implication of the joint paper was that such agreements were prima facie against the public interest as they affected production in and imports into Britain. It is hardly surprising, therefore, that at such a time many Ministers should have reacted very strongly to the Dalton–Jowitt paper.

Thus it was that there was a sharp volte face between February and April 1944. On 23 April 1944 Keynes referred to a wave of anti-American feeling which he considered 'superficial' but 'a momentary factor of the highest importance'.[138] This combined with arguments by the businessmen MPs, Lyttelton and Duncan, that to prohibit arrangements, even after a period of investigations 'would stifle trade and industry to an almost unlimited extent'.[139] (Duncan had been chairman of the BISF before the war and became its executive chairman afterwards. In 1936 he had initiated discussions with American steel interests on behalf of the International Steel Cartel. He was also a director of ICI. Oliver Lyttelton had been a director of the British Tin Investment Corporation Ltd, Imperial Smelting Corporation and the German company, Metallgesellschaft AG. Steel and metal manufacture were also notable for their important international cartel arrangements.)[140] The April meeting was a crowded one, most of the extras being there specifically for the item on restrictive practices. Many of the departments represented sponsored industries with a high degree of restrictionism – the extras were drawn from the Ministries of Fuel and Power, Supply, Works and Agriculture – and their representatives expressed positive experience of trade associations during the war. In addition the disunity among Labour Ministers on the virtues of competition affected the outcome. In September 1944 Morrison suggested that differences in the April meeting centred on whether the aims of policy should be to enforce effective competition or whether 'effective competition would not work in any case and that the tendency to common understandings and centralised arrangements in industry was irreversible'.[141] Morrison and Cripps were certainly keen to stress the government must make clear that it was not endorsing laissez-faire or condemning monopolies, simply trying to control their abuse.[142]

The Reconstruction Committee opted for the very mild policy of intermittent enquiries as it appeared necessary. Policy-makers were forced to make a connection, as the result of external pressures, between policy on domestic and on international cartels. At the same time there were threats from businessmen against any proposals to break up or threaten to break up domestic cartels, but particularly unified and intense hostility to any rules against international cartels. Meanwhile it was precisely on international cartels that Americans were demanding British action, for no less than their prohibition.

The most cogent explanation of the crucial weakening of policy that occurred in April 1944 was the impact of American pressure on British businessmen and politicians who were racked by fears for Britain's economic position in the post-war world. The reaction was to retreat from negotiations with the United States entirely. As the Americans had been the most powerful factor encouraging consideration of the cartel problem, the tendency by April 1944 to withstand their pressure had an inevitable outcome on policy towards domestic competition and restrictive practices.

Conclusion

Policy towards restrictive practices was a highly controversial issue in Reconstruction. The enhanced power of the labour movement and of the left-wing within it promoted a general critique of private enterprise which made policy on competition a sensitive issue. To the extent that 'public opinion' was a factor in the development of policy, the opinion of the labour movement was the most vociferous and mobilised force outside

Whitehall: yet here there was no shift to the notion of competition. On the other hand within Whitehall some Labour economists and Ministers were willing to endorse the validity of competition as an economic mechanism, a split which powerfully affected the outcome of Cabinet discussions.

Meanwhile the politico–economic power of the most articulate business-men was also more entrenched and more strongly united around the right to control markets than in 1918. The balance was held by civil servants and Ministers who, as in 1918, proved most fearful of 'capital unrest' and handed a veto to the business interests, particularly those sections with entrenched positions within the war economy. This last factor disrupted war-time Reconstruction planning for future industrial efficiency in a way castigated by later historians.[143]

Into this scene stepped the United States. In a complex series of moves, American pressure interacted with domestic groups and shifting foreign policy. American actions proved self-defeating in many ways by 1944. The United States propelled the government to formulate policy, when indus-trial resistance might otherwise have proved too great. But by early 1944, plans for Reconstruction were producing definite commitments to the British population which the government would have to honour. The industrial sector was generally fearful of the threat of American compe-tition, and of the loss of Empire markets. The government was beginning to grow obstinate in the face of American pressure. At a critical moment in 1944 fear of business opposition was sustained by rising apprehension of American intentions. It is this that explains the modification of policy between February and April 1944. Policy on cartels was one victim of the combination of a desire not to alienate industrial support in the post-war years, together with a new-found suspicion of American foreign economic policy. These came together at a particular moment in history and account for the weakness of British competition policy in the decade after the Second World War and the shelving of more radical anti-cartel policies.

Two other themes important for future developments have been deve-loped in this chapter. In the various scenarios put forward during the war for the future of British industry, each type of solution to the monopoly problem carried its own implications for the organisation of labour, while being premised on plans and assumptions about the post-war world trading order. Industrialists' corporatist plans were directed as much to incorporat-ing and placating trade unions as to the extension of trade associations. Such plans also envisaged the resumption of the pre-war international cartel system. Calls for nationalisation and other forms of state supervision by the TUC and others in the labour movement were accompanied by hopes for increased workforce involvement in management. On inter-national trade a broad spectrum including Marxists, Labour Party and

Keynesian writers were sceptical lest liberal trading policy jeopardise plans for domestic full employment and social and economic reform.[144] Meanwhile, attacks by economists on restrictionism were attacks on both capital and labour, as early Reconstruction Committee documents make clear. The final version of the White Paper on Employment bracketed both, indeed put restrictions by labour first. At the same time economists were the most dedicated force favouring the re-establishment of a liberal world trading order. Discussions during the war make clear that in the long-term the re-establishment of the philosophy of competition and the market at the domestic and international levels carried serious implications for the organisation of labour, and for the future of domestic economic development.

5 The origins of the Monopolies and Restrictive Practices Act 1948[1]

The 1944 White Paper promise to take powers to enquire into restrictive practices was implemented in the Monopolies and Restrictive Practices Act of 1948 – superficially a clear line of progression. In fact we may trace the same twists and turns the previous chapter outlined for the period that occurred between 1940 and 1944. This chapter considers two questions concerning the transition from Coalition to Labour policy on restrictive practices. Why did it take until March 1948 for a bill to be introduced when Dalton had promised legislation for the 1945–6 session[2] and when draft bills were ready in 1945? Why did Labour adhere to a form of legislation on cartels decided by the Coalition government when its own election manifesto promised to prohibit 'anti-social' restrictive practices?

The answer to these questions lies in the nature of the interaction between British businessmen, especially as represented in the FBI, and the United States. The significant forces shaping British anti-cartel legislation in the 1940s were thus similar to those identified in Germany and Japan at the time. This chapter looks closely at how these, rather than the concerns and outlook of the Labour Party and its allies, should determine government policy.

In pursuing these themes, this chapter shows that the period of 1944 to 1948 was key in the development of British competition policy. The post-war Labour Government consolidated a model of state–industry relations which, though markedly more interventionist than previous peace-time governments' had more in common with Lionel Robbins' strategy for state involvement in the economy than anything deriving from socialist thought. The triumph of a limited demand management, limited nationalisation together with the failure of more dirigiste policies for private industries like the Development Councils, set the seal on the more radical labourite solutions to the monopoly problem outlined in previous chapters. Thus it was a Labour government which instituted the first piece of British competition policy, and one with which the Conservative Party and the FBI could concur and to which the United States could give (qualified) approval.

The timing of the legislation

'Public opinion' across a broad spectrum, but led by Labour MPs and trade unions, was vehemently aroused against cartels in the months before and after the 1945 Election. Profiteering seemed to be confirmed when the Ministries of Aircraft Production and Supply obtained refunds from industries of between £7 and £10 million, as a result of unduly high profits by the contracted firms.[3] Calls for the implementation of paragraph 54 of the 1944 White Paper were legion. Most notable was the resolution passed at the TUC conference in October 1944 calling for a full enquiry into cartels.[4] In February 1945 the Leak and Maizels study of concentration in Britain appeared. It gained Press coverage, and worked further to arouse fears of cartels, which would be easier to organise the greater the development of oligopolistic firms. Using their statistics the Labour Research Department developed a 'case for nationalisation and control'.[5] In March 1945 the House of Lords took up the cudgels with a full-scale debate on a motion put by Lord Nathan for an Act declaring that the abuse of monopoly was against the law and that restrictions on supplies, the fixing of minimum prices and the suppression of invention was per se illegal.[6]

The issue was a major one during the election, which was described by an American commentator as 'a debate on nationalisation and cartels'. While many newspapers were willing to accept the promise of an enquiry, some Labour MPs proposed (unsuccessfully) an amendment to the debate on the Consolidated Fund calling for money to be set aside for an enquiry into the pre-war effects of monopolies, cartels and trade associations.[7] Thus by mid-1945 the issue had become a dominant one, centring on fears of profiteering and the impact of cartels on the domestic economy. This feeling sparked off a flurry of departmental activity but most of it quite abortive.[8] Shortly after the election the Labour government decided to subsume the Bill under powers of price control. This certainly quietened public fears of profiteering but, as one civil servant pointed out, was useless in dealing with the wider problems of industrial organisation which cartels posed.[9]

For stronger factors urged procrastination. From May 1944 until the end of the Coalition, the Conservative Ministers Lyttelton, Duncan and Llewellin, put up 'organised obstruction even of our [the Board's] mild proposals'.[10] As a result of their amendments the Bill was to be drafted so that no disapproval be expressed in it of the practices per se, so that cartels affecting international trade were less open to scrutiny and so that only the main findings of reports could be published. Finally, any announcement of action on restrictive business practices was not to be made until policy on the other part of the White Paper pledge to enquire into restrictive labour practices had been agreed.[11] Thus by June 1945 Parliamentary Counsel to the Board of Trade decided it was not worth spending more time on such a 'compromise measure' which neither Party was likely to implement.[12]

Nor were Labour Ministers inclined to hurry. Dalton sacrificed the Bill to his political ambitions. In late 1944 the Board of Trade was pursuing two main pieces of legislation: restrictive practices and location of industry. Dalton's heart was really in the latter: he had been involved in formulation of policy on this area before the war and his seat was in a 'depressed area'.[13] However, Lyttelton was being obstructive towards both items, and Dalton feared both would fall. He first threatened to resign, and then arranged a compromise with Lyttelton so that Dalton dropped restrictive practices in return for support on the location of industry. In this he aimed also to get the support of Bevin, who, as before, was wary about measures to promote competition.[14]

Similar electoral considerations played their part in the delay under the Labour government. While preparing a review of legislation in December 1945, in the light of limited parliamentary time, Norman Brook, additional Secretary to the Cabinet, drew up a list of major Bills, which included restrictive practices. At this stage Morrison, now Lord President, told Brook that, while he would like to see a Bill on restrictive practices in the second session, 'there was something to be said for leaving it over till the end as a major item in the programme for the last Session before the General Election'.[15] Morrison clearly did not consider the Bill a serious part of Labour's economic programme, the result of the weak terms of the Bill, particularly as it stood in June 1945.

There were domestic reasons for introducing the Bill earlier. Most important was the sheer range of problems which the Board of Trade faced which had a 'monopoly' aspect to them, and which had to be dealt with in an ad hoc fashion.[16] However, fears of profiteering and international cartels continued to be pressed in Parliament and the Press and, as Alix Kilroy, Under Secretary at the Board of Trade, pointed out, to argue that such matters would be judged by a Monopolies Commission was only justified if such a Commission existed.[17] It was, therefore, to allay public suspicions and public complaints that legislation needed to be introduced sooner rather than later.

But the main reason both for the delay and for the eventual introduction of the Bill into Parliament in May 1948 was changing responses to American pressure. This intensified from about April 1944 onwards.[18] In May 1944 Wendell Berge, head of the Antitrust division of the Department of Justice, and Roosevelt himself spoke of the abolition of international cartels and vigorous enforcement of antitrust laws within the United States, as a major feature of American policy. By December 1944 the Foreign Office had decided that the cartel issue 'had the makings of a first-class quarrel which may strain ... our good relations with the Americans'.[19]

The British did not seek compromise with the Americans at any cost. If anything the emerging outlines of Britain's post-war economic difficulties hardened Britain's attitude and led to an increased emphasis on the primacy of domestic economic policy objectives.[20] British negotiations with the United States over general issues of commercial policy had ground to a standstill in 1944, and civil servants were instructed not to discuss the issues with their American counterparts. On international cartels, Dalton advised Lord Halifax, British ambassador to Washington, to avoid discussing the question at all.[21] While cartels remained an item of discussion at Anglo–American negotiations throughout the winter of 1944 to 1945, the issue was less to the fore.[22] It was during this time that policy on cartels notably weakened.

Once pressure was re-applied, British policy-makers had to respond. The Anglo–American loan agreement of December 1945 committed Britain to a Conference on Trade and Employment, to which the Americans speedily put their proposals for prohibition, registration and other commitments on international cartels.[23] It was for this reason that the question was resuscitated in the Board of Trade as a major issue for the first time under the Labour government. In March 1946 the officials said one reason for looking at the question was because 'the problem arises in connection with the talks with the Americans'. They felt it would be prudent to await the outcome of talks.[24] These went through the various stages of discussions around the formulation of an International Trade Organisation and around the Economic Co-operation Agreement accompanying Marshall Aid. Britain proved able to limit American demands, as a later section shows, and the passage of the Monopolies Bill came at a time in negotiations when it could be used by the British negotiators as proof of their good intentions, and as an indication that they could go no further.[25]

Thus the re-emergence of American pressure propelled the Bill along, when other factors could have delayed it further. In 1947 Alix Kilroy thought a major reason for introducing the Bill soon was 'to make a good impression on the Americans'.[26] Indeed, the Bill was in many ways a sop to American pressure, for it was clear that for the Labour and Coalition governments the policy had become so weak as to be irrelevant in the range of pressing issues confronting politicians.

The general approach of the legislation

The same interaction of American and domestic policy concerns determined the general approach of the 1948 Monopolies Bill. As we have said, the Bill was based on the policy which emerged under the Coalition government: indeed the Labour government sought to justify the Bill by citing that very fact.[27] It adopted the case by case approach of the Coalition Bill, and the system of examination by Tribunal, with reports and recommendations for action. Such an approach was indistinguishable from that of the Conservative Party. According to the latter's manifesto: 'the right remedy against harmful restrictive practices is to set up an independent tribunal before which charges of monopoly abuse can be laid.' Indeed, the similarity between Labour and Conservative policies was something noted with surprise by later Conservative documents.[28]

There were differences between the 1948 Bill and the draft Bill of June 1945, making the area of investigation potentially wider, providing for full publicity and including international cartels affecting goods imported to or exported from Britain.[29] However, for the advocates of prohibition and registration which included Labour Ministers like Morrison, Cripps (President of the Board of Trade 1945–7) and Dalton (Chancellor of the Exchequer 1945–7) the Coalition policy, even before it was diluted, caused grave concern.[30] The proposals presented to the Lord President's Committee for approval in September 1946 were, as the Economic Section acidly remarked, 'less than the minimum policy urged on the Coalition'.[31]

The policy was also at variance with the spirit of the Labour Party manifesto of 1945. The manifesto bristled with a deep antipathy to privately-owned monopoly, opening with a diatribe against the activities of 'hard-faced' industrialists in the inter-war years, responsible for profiteering and the slump. While nationalisation was the main solution to industries subject to monopoly and cartel influences, there were other big industries, the manifesto explained, which were 'not yet ripe for public ownership which must nevertheless be required by constructive supervision to further the nation's needs and not to prejudice national interests by restrictive, anti-social, monopoly or cartel agreements – caring for their own capital structures and profits at the cost of a lower standard of living for all'.[32] The regulation of private monopolies and restrictive practices was among the first four industrial policies promised: 'Public supervision of monopolies and cartels with the aim of advancing industrial efficiency in the service of the nation. Anti-social restrictive practices will be prohibited.'[33] Such a statement was open to a variety of interpretations, but it is clear from subsequent actions and statements by Labour Ministers that it did indeed imply more drastic action than the leisurely investigations of the future Monopolies Commission. Labour speeches during the second reading were critical of the Bill's mildness. One MP described the Act as a 'puny infant' when he had hoped for 'a lusty and noisy fellow'.[34]

We now therefore turn to a consideration of how the Bill represented the outcome of, on the one hand, the interaction between British Labour and the United States and, on the other, the interaction between British business and the United States.

Interactions: the Labour government and private enterprise

Labour's policies for the private sector must be set in the context of its general economic policies: commitment to maintaining full employment through demand management and limited nationalisation. Together these promised to take the edge off the pre-war radical critique of the monopolisation and cartelisation of the British economy, the former by removing the threat of unemployment, the latter by putting under public ownership those areas of private monopoly and cartelisation most obviously under attack, especially from trade unions in those sectors. These two policies established, therefore, the permissory framework for Labour's attitude to the private sector.

On coming to power the Labour government moved quickly to quell the fears of private businessmen, some of whom were, according to the then Director General of the FBI, Sir Norman Kipping, preparing to man the barricades against the Labour government.[35] In August 1945 Stafford Cripps, newly appointed President of the Board of Trade, told his staff that: 'The object of the Government will be to create orderly conditions by which private enterprise can make the most effective contribution to the country's economic welfare.'[36] In October 1945 the Board of Trade agreed to retain the Business members if only to avert any adverse 'psychological reaction' by businessmen to curtailment of their government role.[37] Thus the representation of business executives in various Ministries continued until 1946 and beyond. The FBI had 87 representatives on 37 committees and in 10 Ministries in 1946.[38] Indeed, as one author comments, short of a 'revolutionary sweep' the Labour government was bound to inherit and adapt to the 'existing pattern of relations with industry' established during the war.[39] The situation hence developed where the role of private businessmen in government was enhanced relative to their and Labour's war-time position.

Increasingly Labour Party research and published documents developed the notion of a contract between government and private enterprise. A committee set up to propose future policies for privately-owned industry defeated radical proposals for sweeping powers of intervention, members of the committee arguing that the document smacked of too hostile an attitude to capitalism. Instead the committee agreed that 'the aim of Government policy should be to stimulate enterprise on the part of management'.[40] Labour would provide certain forms of support and subsidy, while industry must 'put its own house in order'.[41] Labour was to be the Party which would modernise British industry, enabling it to compete on world markets. Hence arose the industrial policy for the emergent 'reformist economic management' which characterised Labour's time in office.[42]

'Consolidationism', the term used to describe Labour's retreat from nationalisation after the 1947 Party conference, set the seal on radical alternatives to private monopoly, not only for the 1940s but arguably for the post-war period as a whole. Although the Research Department came up with various 'shopping lists' of monopolies for nationalisation, the solution of public ownership was effectively dropped.[43] The moves away from planning and towards fiscal management represented fulfilment of the hopes of those Labour intellectuals who saw Keynesianism as a means to limit intervention and retain the price mechanism. Between 1947 and 1948 Labour's policies veered to compromise with financial and industrial circles.[44]

The desire to placate business generally also jeopardised two key elements in Labour's policies on private industry – price controls and the Development Councils. The former were fundamental in Labour's vision of planning. 'In barest outline,' a research paper proclaimed, 'a policy for the control of private enterprise is a policy of price control, designed to reduce costs and to abolish monopoly profits while at the same time retaining the profit motive as a stimulus to enterprise.'[45] In 1950 Harold Wilson was again to propose the retention of price control to prevent the abuse of monopoly, and a Bill to introduce permanent controls was under discussion in 1950.[46] But Labour's 'bonfire' of controls in November 1948, thereby conceding one of business's prime demands, heralded the end of this type of approach.

Labour's 'one distinctive' policy for private industry – the Development Councils – was also a victim of the very trade associations which anti-cartel policy aimed to control. After a series of working party reports into various industries the Industrial Organisation and Development Act of 1947 allowed for Development Councils to be set up. These combined many of the Board of Trade's war-time recommendations for industrial boards to co-ordinate research, marketing, training and other aids to efficiency for industries with smaller firms. The FBI saw the working parties and the Act as a threat to current industrial organisation. Thus, according to one

Labour Party researcher, the desire to ensure the participation of private enterprise in the Development Councils had 'focussed attention on less drastic methods of dealing with monopolistic practices'.[47]

Any closer co-ordination of industry, like the Development Councils could promote greater cartelisation, as Gaitskell and Dennison had reasoned in 1944 (see chapter 4). But as the already tenuous co-operation of industry with the scheme could be jeopardised the Board of Trade decided that it was difficult to prevent the Councils considering restrictive schemes if they might be useful to the industry.[48] Thus nothing was inserted into the Bill to prevent a Development Council devising such schemes, and there remained a large measure of ministerial discretion. This discretion was used in the case of the cotton industry, where the Board of Trade promised that two price-fixing agreements would not be referred to the Monopolies Commission for three years, in return for assurances from the Cotton Board to reorganise the industry.[49]

By 1947 the alarm, bordering on hysteria felt by businessmen had receded, and the FBI was congratulating itself on its congenial relations with the Labour government, 'apart from purely socialist legislation'. The threat of wide-scale nationalisation had waned, while the fuel and convertibility crisis, the need to increase exports and thus to co-operate with industry had brought the Labour government to heel.[50] By 1947 Labour had gone down a road of acquiescence to private business, which partly explains the unwillingness to challenge it through tough anti-cartel legislation.

Interactions: the Labour government and the United States

The second general influence on Labour's policies for the private sector was that of the United States. 'Consolidation' of a different kind had also proceeded in the international sphere with the gradual hardening of relations between the Soviet Union and the Western world. By 1947 the lines of the Cold War were laid down and Britain and the United States had established a 'special relationship' directed to the resistance to Communism in Europe, the colonies and in their home countries. The economic might of the USA gave it the leverage and the motivation to promote the 'Americanisation' of the economies of Western Europe and Japan. The concept of 'Americanisation' has been poorly defined and generally couched in terms of the promotion of so-called 'American' methods of production and management, a 'consumer economy', together with the attempt to impose American antitrust laws.[51] Another approach would see 'Americanisation' as the attempt to shape the world according to the needs of large-scale American corporations whose productive power was massively expanded in the course of the Second World War. This is a viewpoint espoused by 'revisionist' historians of the Cold War who emphasise that securing the 'Open Door' to American goods and capital put capitalism aggressively on the offensive in the post-war years.[52] President Truman, in a speech on 6 March 1947 at Baylor University, and just six days before he outlined his 'Doctrine' to Congress, announced America's crusade for the freedom of enterprise. This was threatened, he stated, by the trend towards governments conducting foreign trade or planning. Unless this trend were reversed the government of the United States would soon be under pressure to use similar devices 'to fight for markets and raw materials'. The only alternative, then, was that 'the whole world should adopt the American system' of free enterprise, for 'the American system could survive in America only if it became a world system'.[53]

How then did this impinge on the policies of the Labour government? At the most general level, United States policy was increasingly hostile, not only to the planned system of the Soviet Union, but also to the nationalisation and planning programmes of the Labour government in Britain. More direct American leverage took two forms. Firstly, Britain was integrated into a general framework of multilateralism. The general effect of Britain's commitments under the Anglo–American Loan Agreement of December 1945, the European Recovery Programme (ERP) and the Organisation of European Economic Co-operation (OEEC) tended to discourage a planned trade system as well as spending on social services. The pressure by the United States through these agreements was resisted by forces in Britain, but the need for American financial support tended to be the decisive factor in all discussions.[54] The convertibility crisis of July 1947 illustrates these points. On the one hand it set back the cause of multilateralism, but on the other hand Cripps, as Chancellor of the Exchequer, introduced a 'disinflationary' policy to reduce the dollar gap, including cuts in government spending, while the nationalisation of steel was postponed because of the need to increase exports.[55] The United States put further pressure on the nationalisation programme by insisting, for instance in the stillborn Charter of the International Trade Organisation, that publicly-owned companies be subject to investigation under the articles relating to restrictive business practices (see below).

While this leverage affected the general framework of Labour's economic policies, 'Americanisation' was attempted also at industry level. Charles Maier, analysing the domestic sources of the economic concepts which America sought to construct in Europe, concludes that 'by 1945 the two themes of productivity and monopoly formed the conceptual axes along which Americans located economic institutions ... Monopoly explained political and economic setbacks; productivity promised advance'. In fact,

he argues, the crusade against monopoly, especially in the ex-Axis countries, was subordinated to aid productivity as a spur to non-Communist
countries – as part of the Cold War.[56] In Britain also productivity
campaigns had a higher profile than anti-cartel policies. The Labour
government's productivity policies had domestic roots, but it was the
reports of the Anglo-American Council on Productivity which received
wide media attention, drawing public attention constantly to the question
and acting as 'one of the largest experiments in adult education ever
attempted'.[57] The picture painted in the reports was of the United States as
an 'archetypal free enterprise economy' where competition was vigorous
and workers worked. This contrasted with a Britain 'stagnating under
cartel arrangements and weighed down by state controls', and restriction-
minded trade unionists.[58]

We may conclude, therefore, that the general thrust of United States
influence on British economic policy in the post-war years was propaganda
and direct financial pressure for Britain to espouse free enterprise, and limit
state intervention, regulation and controls as well as trade union power. In
particular, the influence propelled Labour Ministers further towards the
policy of 'consolidation', the limiting of the sphere of public ownership and
supervision, and its corollary the extension of alternative anti-monopoly,
specifically anti-cartel policies.

Interactions: debate within the Labour Party

Naturally, these general influences at ministerial level were at war with
others emanating from within the Labour movement. They are best
illustrated in G.D.H. Cole's attack on the early Attlee years, calling it
'Bastard Socialism': 'Keynesian Liberalism ... a limited sphere of public
enterprise ... and therewith a retention of the profit motive as the main
driving force in industry.'[59] Thus when Labour came to study the problem
of restrictive practices, cartels, trusts and trade associations as a general
problem a number of warring considerations were brought to bear.

The report by the joint TUC/Labour Party committee on trusts and
cartels, set up on Dalton's instigation in 1945 and ready in October 1947,
argued against a return to competition and in favour of very comprehensive
public supervision: 'the operation of privately-owned industry in what may
be broadly defined as the public interest, including the achievement of
maximum efficiency ... preserving the advantages while eliminating the
disadvantages of monopoly.'[60] This view ruled out any blanket ban on
forms of monopoly. The committee therefore favoured a monopolies
tribunal, a policy which differed from the line of the Coalition only in
stressing that such a policy be 'an integral part of the Government's
economic planning with specialised functions'.[61]

One strong element in the party continued to argue that it was not monopoly, concentration or even cartels per se which were the problem, but who owned them or controlled them: 'If monopoly is the inevitable development in an industry, it is far preferable that it be public than private.'[62] The Labour Party/TUC Committee likewise said that socialisation was 'ultimately ... the only satisfactory policy for avoiding those dangers to the life and well-being of the community to which the growth of private monopoly gives rise'.[63] In 1950 Wilson proposed strengthening the Monopolies Act to allow nationalisation of firms criticised by the Commission.[64] In 1951 a draft Labour pamphlet on 'Monopoly' favoured price control to protect the consumer against monopoly exploitation and nationalisation 'to transform the anti-social character of monopoly power'.[65]

Another strand was represented by the Co-operative Party which favoured the extension of co-operation, and otherwise pressed for legislation against resale price maintenance. The Labour Government's response was piecemeal, for they did not make the extension of co-operation a priority, but did propose to outlaw resale price maintenance (RPM). On the other hand plans by Labour to increase the sphere of state wholesaling were viewed with dismay by the Co-operative Societies, as limiting the sphere for co-operation.[66]

Other tendencies in the Labour Party were keen to stress the benefits of capitalism. Harold Wilson, introducing the 1948 Bill argued that 'competition is the public's natural safeguard in any industry which continues on the basis of private enterprise'.[67] This was a repetition of the views often stated by Dalton, Cripps and others during the Coalition, and was to gain a stronger hold in the Labour Party in the 1950s, with the steady, if uneven, rise of the 'Gaitskellites'.[68] Crosland summarised this view in 1952: 'Within the framework of overall government planning the proper way to make the private sector responsive to the needs of the community is to make it competitive.'[69] Labour's failing on this score he criticised as its 'single greatest failure'. This approach did not please many unions. USDAW, fearing Labour's plans in 1951 to outlaw RPM would lead to pressure on retailers' margins and thus on wages and conditions, accused the Labour government of rejecting 'the Socialist approach of planning and regulation in favour of private capitalistic unfettered competition'.[70]

Nevertheless, in spite of this plethora of strands and influences an important point remains. The Labour government and its allies, backed by the general pressure from the United States could agree that a tough line on restrictive practices shown to be anti-social be taken. A Labour Party research paper of 1947 argued that large firms covered a relatively small section of the economy, secured certain benefits of large-scale organisation and, being more 'in the public eye', were more sensitive to accusations of monopoly. Cartels, on the other hand, were very widespread, their activities unpublicised and often responsible for retarding efficiency in their industries.[71] Many of the working party reports of 1945 to 1947, commissioned by the Labour government, argued that the level of technical efficiency would be raised by the ending of restrictive practices.[72] Several economists, many of them Labour supporters, had investigated retailing in Britain and argued that, in the distributive sector restrictive practices were wasteful of manpower, and so hindered the introduction of self-service, maintained retail prices and shifted competition into wasteful areas like advertising.[73]

Yet even a policy for banning 'anti-social' restrictive practices, as promised in the manifesto, did not emerge. The Labour government had no intention of challenging the legitimacy of private enterprise, and wished to maintain good relations.[74] This imposed limits on Labour's freedom of action. Hence policy towards private industry bore little relation to the views of the mass organisations allied to the Labour Party, nor with substantial views within the parliamentary party. This lacuna and failure of political will meant that the formulation of policy rested more with the civil service.

Interactions: the Labour government and the civil service

Civil servants gained an enhanced role in economic policy-making,[75] and on cartels and monopoly their strength was also a function, in 1948 as compared with 1943, of the absence of the economists who had played such a formative role in the war.[76] During the war economists had exerted little influence on opinion on competition in ministerial Committees, but did affect the nature of the debate put to Ministers, in the form of papers formulated at departmental level. But now, when Wilson or Morrison raised the idea of stronger measures they had no supporters of any stature within their own departments. Those who remained such as John Jewkes, James Meade and S.R. Dennison were too wedded to the ideal of competition to find much favour with Labour politicians. By 1947 Jewkes had added his name to erstwhile government economists who had deep objections to the industrial strategy of the Labour government, and who reasserted a liberal ideology and the price mechanism.[77]

The influence of civil servants on the general outlines of the Act is in many ways remarkable. At one point in Board of Trade discussions Morrison, now Home Secretary and Lord President, proposed that certain types of practices be listed as anti-social and prohibited, other types be allowed under licence and only the residue be subject to the enquiry procedure.[78] When Harold Wilson took over from Cripps as President of the Board of Trade he also made a mild sally in favour of a system of registration and investigation.[79] Civil servants, in each case, were quick to step in and persuade the Ministers that a system of registration and investigation would be unworkable, although the same people had actually advocated it under the Coalition, rather than blanket bans.[80]

The civil servants were guided by the intransigence of industry on the question. Indeed as late as March 1948, just weeks before the Bill was first introduced, a departmental representative of the Ministry of Supply at a meeting to brief other departments expressed the view that the Bill should be delayed, as the present was no time to 'rock the boat' of government–industry relations.[81] They believed therefore that British industry had to be persuaded and educated out of their restrictionist habits, and into awareness of issues of industrial efficiency and productivity,[82] using publicity for the Commission's findings as a lever on industrialists: unleashing 'public opinion' as a sanction. R.C. Bryant (Assistant Secretary, Board of Trade) summarised the philosophy of the forthcoming Bill in an internal memorandum:

The conventional view of monopoly in this country is that it is fairly sensitive to public opinion and is unlikely to charge very high prices ... or to indulge in restrictive practices which are evidently contrary to the public interest.

It was more likely, he said, that monopoly had effects on efficiency and that costs rather than prices were unduly high, a somewhat tenuous distinction. Thus he hoped that an investigation by the Monopolies Commission was

likely to result in recommendations not for the abandonment of a particular practice but for improved methods of organisation, management, accounting or research ... It is unlikely that a monopoly will be condemned as such because it is an unjustified agglomeration of capacity ... therefore if a trust cannot be set right by the adoption of far-reaching recommendations affecting its internal organisation it is to transfer its control to the state.

This view was substantially repeated by Wilson in his speech moving the second Reading.[83]

In many ways the 1948 Act therefore was a continuation, by other means, of the pre-war 'industrial diplomacy', of cajoling private industry towards efficiency. Mainly this was to be done through working parties, development councils, and a productivity drive. If the Labour government and its civil servants sought co-operation with industry it is necessary to look at what industry was advocating.

Interactions: British businessmen and the United States

The attitude of the majority of industry towards cartels continued to be determined by what agreement was acceptable at international conferences.

The US government had returned to the attack on international cartels in August 1945 as discussions on commercial policy re-opened and as Britain began negotiations for an American loan in the wake of the sudden and unexpected cancellation of Lend-Lease. The draft proposals for an Internationl Trade Organisation (ITO) which the Americans handed to British negotiators provided for the complete abolition of certain restrictive business practices. The position was described by the British delegation as involving virtually 'the adoption of an international Sherman Act and an international authority to administer it', and at first the British side feared lest a 'complete break' could occur with the Americans on the cartel question.[84] Britain proposed instead that a consultative body under the ITO receive complaints if an international cartel was believed to be frustrating the terms of the ITO, but that any enquiry would be undertaken by individual member states who would also find a way to end the practices found objectionable.

Although the Americans were to accept this position in the draft charter of an ITO which formed part of the Anglo–American loan agreement, a year later they were reiterating their demand that certain restrictive business practices be declared against the purposes of the ITO unless the contrary could be proved in specified cases. The terms of the Americans' position was expressed thus: 'Members agree to prevent practices which restrain competition ... [a list of such practices] and thus have the effect of frustrating the purposes of the ITO.' This position was taken to the first preparatory session in London in October 1946 but, with the support of European countries, several of which had legislation highly favourable to cartels, Britain secured American acceptance of the reversion to the Proposals of December 1945. A revision was secured so that the Article read, 'Each member shall ... prevent practices which restrain competition ... *whenever they have* harmful effects on the purposes of the ITO' (my emphasis). This revision, 'crucial to the whole chapter', was endorsed at the second preparatory session in Geneva in the Autumn of 1947, and incorporated into the Final Act of the Charter signed by Britain and 56 other countries in Havana in March 1948.[85]

Not only was the British delegation able to secure their empirical approach, but they were also able to ensure that a system of enquiry conducted nationally had precedence over any international authority. The American draft charter, while committing member governments to take individual action to prevent restrictive business practices which limited free trade made the ITO the body to receive complaints from other members or from commercial enterprises, to require the furnishing of information and to make recommendations to member governments for them to take appropriate action over their nationals. However, the final draft of the Havana charter embodied the thesis that 'Member governments will be allowed a good deal of freedom to deal with problems in their own way', as a Board of Trade memorandum expressed it. The Charter obliged member governments to 'take adequate powers within the framework of their legal and economic systems to control any such arrangements'.[86]

Much of the British negotiators' position was simply a continuation of a line worked out under the Coalition. However, the government and civil servants continued to consult closely with industrialists and were particularly responsive to business feelings on international cartels, taking their lead from business reactions to American proposals. Indeed the FBI had a major consultative role throughout the negotiations with the United States, not only on cartels but on tariffs, Imperial Preference and many other questions.[87]

The FBI set up an Industrial Agreements Committee to consider a submission on the American proposals.[88] Large firms were well represented in this committee, which was chaired by Dr, later Sir William Coates, then Deputy chairman of ICI. The committee, in its document sent to the Board of Trade 'Private International Industrial Agreements', defended cartels on the basis that they were essential to large-scale firms which needed to plan production to secure orderly economic development. Behind this justification lurked the spectre of the inter-war recession and foreign competition: 'in the event of failure to avoid a return to inter-war economic conditions, it would be illogical and unjust not to allow producers to take their own private measures where governments have failed.'[89]

These arguments were repeated by many other trade associations who submitted replies to the Board of Trade, most of which were, overtly or otherwise, hostile to any international control. A few accepted the need for some national and international supervision of agreements, although they quibbled about the American definition of harmful business practices.[90] British industrialists wished to preserve their right to make international agreements and it was therefore crucial that no outright prohibition of any type of agreements be made, nor that any type of practice be considered a priori against the spirit of ITO.

The FBI document 'Private International Industrial Agreements' was especially insistent that any supervision or investigation of international cartels be vested primarily in the national government. It adamantly opposed the American procedure, proposing instead that information on cartels should only be communicated to the contracting parties' respective governments, who should only communicate it to the ITO if there were a complaint.[91] Thus, the British government undertook nothing at an international level which conflicted with the views of those industrialists who expressed an opinion to the Board of Trade.

Nor were the domestic obligations implicit in the ITO Charter too adversely received by British business. The emerging lines of industrial feeling meant that supervision of domestic cartels was no longer viewed with such aversion. The FBI was coming to accept that some tribunal for complaint by industrial interests against monopoly practices might be desirable.[92] One FBI paper accepted that some monopolistic trade associations whose prices entered into and significantly affected the 'general cost structure' should be liable to public scrutiny.[93] It was, therefore, on the basis of the need to protect the industrial consumer that the FBI was willing to countenance government powers of supervision and investigation.

Within the Conservative Party sections concurred with this view, if only to quell public disquiet about the growth of monopoly powers. Already, during the Coalition a group of Conservative MPs had asked the government to introduce legislation allowing for the investigation of monopolies for precisely this reason,[94] and Lord Woolton had been irritated at the limited outlook of businessmen in government and elsewhere which meant that 'there was really no argument left against wholesale socialisation, which could hardly give worse results and might give better'. He proposed an immediate, semi-judicial enquiry.[95] Members of the Tory Reform Group, like Peter Thorneycroft and David Maxwell-Fyfe, wanted a new-look Conservatism geared to a reassertion of competitive capitalism.[96] The Conservative Party's *Industrial Charter* incorporated suggestions for a tribunal as did David Maxwell-Fyfe's pamphlet on Monopoly.[97] Thus the Labour government undertook nothing in this field to which business was opposed.

The results of the negotiations around the Charter of the ITO were very significant for the future lines of domestic economic policy in general. Firstly, the insistence that enquiry on cartels be rested primarily with national governments assured a policy on domestic cartels by obliging the British government, as no other factor in the post-war years did, to establish a national method of supervision and control of restrictive practices. This was a commitment bolstered by the terms of Marshall Aid.

Secondly, the thrust of the ITO, GATT and the Economic Co-operation Agreement under Marshall Aid helped to propel Britain down a path of liberalism in domestic policy as well as in the international field. This was a path in many ways alien to the outlook of Labour. As one civil servant commented in August 1946, the Americans' first draft could be regarded as 'doctrinaire' for a government elected on the basis of a 'planned economy' not a 'laissez-faire' programme.[98] Moreover, the Final Act of the ITO applied the provisions relating to restrictive business practices to 'single public commercial enterprises', a provision resisted unsuccessfully by Britain.[99] Thus not only did the Labour government pursue a line with the Americans determined by Coalition policies and the outlook of businessmen, but they also conceded to policies at odds with planning and public ownership policies at a domestic level. In fact, of course, the ITO was never ratified, but the pressure nevertheless set Britain along the path towards competition policy, and American-style antitrust solutions. The Economic Co-operation Agreement signed as a part of Marshall Aid committed Britain to prevent business arrangements affecting international trade, where they could interfere with 'the programme of European recovery'.[100]

It can therefore be demonstrated that the interaction of American and business pressure were the main determinants of both the timing and nature of the 1948 Act. Businessmen were effectively to shape the broad outlines of policy, a view which contradicts previous studies of business influence on competition legislation.[101] In addition, while the Bill was in preparation, and during its progress through Parliament, businessmen lobbied very effectively, shaping the character of their own regulation.

Shaping the details of regulation

Businessmen were able to play a part in the formulation of their own regulation via the Conservative Party. A comparison of views expressed in the FBI Grand Council, and on its committees, with those expressed by Conservative MPs, especially David Maxwell-Fyfe, during the passage of the Bill indicates that the latter were a mouthpiece for business in Parliament.

The aims of industry, as revealed in their lobbying around the Bill, were twofold. First, to limit its impact and secondly to ensure that the sort of complaints the Commission dealt with were those arising between industrial sectors, rather than between private enterprise as a whole and the 'public interest'.

The amendments put down by industry cannot easily be categorised into one of these two aims, for they often served both purposes. There were clearly some which sought to limit the range of industries which could be referred, the type of judgements delivered and the extent of publicity and sanctions. Thus the FBI attempted to limit the range of references by making the definition of monopoly one half, not one third as the Bill proposed, of all goods supplied, processed or exported.

On publicity the FBI and the Conservative Party made little onslaught on the Bill, having secured, by various means, the limiting of publicity through limiting the types of references. This was largely due to the fact that the Board of Trade anticipated industry's feelings on this matter which had been made very clear during the last year of the Coalition when Lyttelton ensured that publication of a future Commission's reports was highly circumscribed. The section on publicity now ensured that only reasons of security should prevent the publication of a report. G.H. Andrew noted however that, 'Industry is, however, likely to press strongly for the withholding of information which might harm "legitimate business interests" ... and the form of words used is intended to meet this point'.[102]

That industry sought to shape a Bill which would indeed provide some recourse for aggrieved industrialists emerged in some of the arguments made in the House of Commons during the debates. The Conservative Party introduced an amendment to make it possible to refer the nationalised industries because, 'we have lost some rights of complaint which existed with regard to those industries under private enterprise'.[103] But the Conservatives opposed the government when it introduced the amendment, widening the Bill to include referral of types of practices, such as RPM. As Maxwell-Fyfe and others pointed out, this provision widened the Bill, taking it away from specific complaints by aggrieved parties towards more general statements about industry's practices, and their relationship to the 'public interest'. Similarly the amendment introducing a complaints mechanism exposed industry to greater publicity about the accusations, pitting industry against the 'public interest'. The Conservatives argued that the mere fact that a complaint had been made would be a slur on the undertaking concerned, to which they would have no right of reply.[104]

These features support the notion that business sought to remove the process from the public eye as far as possible and keep the regulation a matter primarily for industrialists.

The most important concessions negotiated on behalf of industry related to the basis on which the Board of Trade was to make references. This was to determine the form and extent of industry's regulation and the impact of the Act. Sponsoring departments ensured that either 'their' industries were excluded, as occurred in the case of shipping where lobbying by the Ministry of Transport led to the exclusion of 'carriage' from the Act's coverage,[105] while the Minister of Agriculture ensured that no restriction would be referred to the Commission without the agreement of the Department concerned. A later populariser for Co-operative Societies saw the exclusion of agricultural marketing schemes from the Bill as 'sinister'.[106] As many of the most restrictive arrangements were in industries outside of the responsibility of the Board of Trade by 1948, this was to prove a major limitation on the power of the Board over the interpretation of the Act. Sponsoring departments also ensured that they oversaw the operation of any sanctions against a firm or industry like price control or declaring agreements criticised by the Commission null and void.[107]

Another point on which concessions were made departmentally was on the nature of the Commission, a vital question for the FBI. Again the most important point, that the Commission should not be judicial, was conceded at an early stage, and was therefore never an issue.[108] The point, however, is important at a later stage. Clearly, industry expected that an independent tribunal, without the guide of common law bias against restraint of trade, would be more tender of their interests. That it was not to prove so, prompted calls in the 1950s by industry for the judicial procedure.

However, the FBI still lobbied successfully at departmental level to ensure that the chairman was 'independent', one who was not a 'theoretical economist' with a 'traditional bias against industrial agreements'. The points were conceded privately in the Board of Trade, and were won because the Board of Trade wanted a Commission that would command the confidence of industry.[109]

Finally the FBI and the Conservative Party were successful at ensuring that the Bill included a definition of the 'public interest' against which the Commission should judge any monopoly condition.[110] The Board was willing to concede the point as it needed some definition to guide the Commission, and the only other way was through parliamentary directives which would have required a major economic debate each time a directive was to be issued.[111] However, the FBI's purpose is less obvious. The 'public interest' clause which was introduced was of little use to the Commission, nor did it, according to industry's later testimony, give the industry under investigation any clear idea of how to argue its case. The FBI pressed for a definition at times when it was feeling less happy about the number of assurances written into the Bill.[112] It can therefore be concluded that the 'public interest' definition provided industry with a limitation on any per se opposition to restrictive practices and in favour of competition that might exist on the Commission. It also meant that the Bill accepted implicitly that sectional interests could and should be weighed against any interpretation of the national interest. American writers on regulation have noted similar lobbying by businessmen, aimed at reducing the 'managerial freedom of the commission'.[113]

While this analysis demonstrates that industry was able to shape the thrust of the regulation to some extent, it was not wholly successful at altering the terms of the Bill in its favour in this regard. Such a conclusion is borne out by industry's subsequent criticisms of the Monopolies Commission: of its membership, its terms of reference, its procedure and its judgements. It was these criticisms that prompted the changes to the

Commission in 1956. The concessions that industry did win were, however, vital. The way that references were chosen, the loopholes given to industry to remove passages from the final report, the absence of any sanctions and therefore the reliance on negotiations with industry to secure compliance to the Commission's recommendations all were to prove, as chapter 6 will show, a 'headache' and seriously undermined the whole operation of the Bill.

On the other hand, another lobbying body, the Co-operative Societies and the Co-operative Congress in Parliament was able, under the Labour government to secure certain concessions. Their case was taken up by the Board of Trade, concerned about the inefficiency of retailing in part the result of the practices of RPM.[114] Thus the Board also introduced an amendment to allow a specified class of practice, like RPM, to be referred.[115]

In addition, in the aim of educating industrial opinion and discouraging any extension of cartel activities the government was very serious.[116] Hence they strengthened those elements in the Bill which made it sensitive to public pressure, in particular they proposed an amendment that an annual report on the work of the Monopolies Commission be made to Parliament and it should contain a list of complaints submitted by six groups of possible complainants. These included business groups, consumer bodies, the TUC, local authorities and agricultural interests.[117]

One group of lobbyists who were *not* successful were militant anti-monopoly elements in the Cabinet itself. They were led by A.V. Alexander, Minister of Defence, one-time Liberal who, along with Captain Wedge-wood Benn had proposed an antitrust Bill in 1925 in response to the revelations of some of the profiteering investigations. He feared that, without power to break up large firms the state could not control such concentration of economic and political power.[118]

It was in fact this left-liberal attack which Wilson and his civil servants were most at pains to head off. It ran counter to the educative, persuasive function of the Monopolies Commission, which the Board espoused, in which the interests of industry were not to be seen as running counter to those of the nation as a whole. The Monopolies Commission was to gently point out to industry where its own best interest lay, not to berate it for jeopardising the national cause, and the Bill perforce incorporated this view.

This view accorded entirely with industry's concept of the value of the Bill. In particular the absence of sanctions to deal with the large firm was to prove a major weakness in the Act. As a result large firms were often not referred precisely because the Bill had no power to impose sanctions should a report be adverse. Moreover, the limited powers of the Bill forced the

Board of Trade to rely on negotiations with the firms and trade associations concerned to secure compliance with the recommendation of the Commission. In this way the law was indeed whittled down, as Alexander feared, not by judicial but by departmental decisions.

Conclusions

The tentative nature of the 1948 Monopolies and Restrictive Practices Act was dictated by the restrictionist outlook of British businessmen and their desire to moderate American international trust-busting. They were able to maintain their influence over the general terms of the Act by the continuing need for co-operation between government and trade associations, and by the enhanced role of the civil servants in the formulation of competition policy from 1945, that itself was a result of the Labour Party's lack of direction over policy for private industry. However, the United States, in spite of substantial influence in British domestic policies in the 1940s could not impose their vision of industrial organisation: its foreign economic policy too was limited by the policies of British businessmen, a situation reflected in many studies of 'Americanisation'[119] after the Second World War.

At the same time there was sufficient pressure from internal forces, sections of the Labour movement and some newspapers, to ensure that the Monopolies Commission did not become simply an industrialists' court to try fellow businessmen. Industry was able to exercise most leverage over the general terms of the Act, while other pressure groups could step in to secure modifications of the details, without being able to alter the framework of the legislation. However, the Labour Party's closest allies, the trade unions and the Co-operative movement, did not exercise the same influence over the formulation of policy as the business community. The study of competition policy therefore provides little support for theories of corporate bias even in the key period of the Labour government, but does support theories of regulation, to the extent that in Britain, as chapter 6 demonstrates, amendments and agreements which businessmen secured were to vitally limit the effectiveness of the Monopolies and Restrictive Practices Act.

6 Interpretation of policy – the Monopolies and Restrictive Practices Commission, 1949–56[1]

The Monopolies and Restrictive Practices Commission (MRPC) of 1949–56 ranks as one of the main early regulatory commissions of private economic interests in peace-time Britain. In Britain direct state regulation of an industry, its structure, pricing and practices has generally taken the form either of nationalisation or of specific encouragement to rationalisation, for instance the schemes for industries in the 1930s, such as the Coal Mines Act and the Lancashire Cotton Corporation, the Development Councils of the 1940s and the work of the Industrial Reorganisation Corporation in the 1960s. The Monopolies Commission was very different from these experiments, as it was established to survey permanently and continuously the practices of all industrial sectors. In addition it had more in common with the statutory regulatory practices of the United States than with the self-regulation favoured in Britain.[2]

Studies of the work of the Monopolies Commission have extensively analysed the types of decisions made, but are mainly geared to producing prescriptions for reform, or guidelines for future government action.[3] They place the experience of the Monopolies Commission as one chapter in the story of the march towards improved public perceptions of the need to end restrictive practices and make capitalism competitive.

According to American regulation writing, however, either the legislation establishing the agencies is itself the product of the industry's own desire for regulation, or the regulatory commission accommodates itself to the interests of the firms it regulates.[4] One analyst suggests a life-cycle of regulatory commissions: the commission starts by vigorously attempting to regulate the industry in line with its mandate as custodian of the public interest. However, over time the commissions, 'proved susceptible to private pressure and manipulation', and tended to equate the interests of the regulated groups with the public interest.[5] Studies of agencies like the Federal Trade Commisison (FTC) or the Securities Exchange Commission which, like the MRPC, regulated trade or finance as a whole, have given less clear cut evidence of 'capture'. Nevertheless Gabriel Kolko has argued the FTC 'served as a buffer against public antagonism towards business' and as an agency to give business legal advice through the gradual evolution of a code of business law while also settling inter- and intra-industry disputes 'with private, nonsensational conferences'.[6]

Chapter 5 argued that, to the extent that the FBI was willing to entertain a commission to enquire into business monopolistic practices, it had been in response to American pressure, and as a forum for complaints by business-men against businessmen. This chapter argues that, while business did use the Monopolies Commission for complaints, the Commission itself was not 'captured' by the regulated groups. Instead the hostility of businessmen to the Commission was a constant threat to the working of the Act. This hostility smouldered as the Commission kept the issue of restrictive practices constantly before the public and published some reports highly critical of business methods. This hostility hamstrung and immobilised the work of the Board of Trade in administering the Commission and made the work of the Commission economically irrelevant, leading to the eventual demise of the tribunal procedure itself.

The impact of the Monopolies Commission, 1949–56

One of the aims of the Labour government in passing the 1948 Act was modernisation – improved efficiency of industry and management, improved competitiveness and the removal of rigidities in the industrial system. None of these aims were fulfilled, and the Commission, at least during its life-time, was largely irrelevant as a motor for change in the British industrial system.

The economic impact of the MRPC was minimal. There were relatively few referrals and those that there were took on average two years and three months to complete. One report took four years and one month and it was another eight months before it was published. This performance may be compared with the effect of the 1919 Profiteering Act which in two years had produced 57 reports. Much of this slowness may be attributed to the difficulties of obtaining information from the firms involved.[7] Even fewer reports were acted on by the government, partly because of the time it took to negotiate with the firms over how the Commission's recommendations were to be implemented. In addition, reports published in 1955 and 1956 were overshadowed by forthcoming changes in legislation. The Board of Trade preferred to let practices which the Commission criticised be dealt with under the new system rather than court more controversy with the firms concerned.

The slowness of the Commission meant that the government had taken action over only nine of the reports where action was required, before work was halted with the introduction of the 1956 Act (see table 6.1). In three

Table 6.1. *Summary of the work of the MRPC, 1949–56*

Product investigated (supply of)	Date referred month and year	Date report signed by MRPC	Report published	Action taken on MRPC recommendation
Dental goods and Instruments	March 1949	Nov. 1950	Dec. 1950	Order made that practices illegal, July 1951
Cast-iron rainwater goods	March 1949	Feb. 1951	Apr. 1951	Alternative arrangements from Jan. 1952
Electrical filament lamps	March 1949	Aug. 1951	Nov. 1951	Voluntary undertakings. Many later complaints
Insulated electric wires and cables	March 1949	Apr. 1952	July 1952	Minimum prices allowed Jan. 1955 in line with MC conclusions
Matches and match-making machinery, and exports of	March 1949 March 1949	Oct. 1952 Oct. 1952	May 1953 May 1953	New international arrangements made in March 1954
Copper and copper-based alloys, semi-manufactures and exports. Facts only	Dec. 1950	Apr. 1953		Converted to public interest
Copper semis: Public Interest	July 1953	Jan. 1955	Sept. 1955	NONE
Insulin	Dec. 1950	July 1952	Oct. 1952	Not against public interest later investigation
Printing of woven fabrics (calico)	Apr. 1951	Nov. 1953	Apr. 1954	End some practices; redundancy scheme to run its course
Imported timber	Oct. 1951	July 1953	Oct. 1953	Fed. agreed to recommendations but later found not to comply
Electrical and allied machinery and plant and exports	Apr. 1952	July 1956	Feb. 1957	NONE
Tyres, and exports	Sept. 1952	June 1955	Dec. 1955	NONE
New buildings in greater London (costing more than £1,000 each)	March 1953	June 1954	Sept. 1954	Practices ended 1954 and local authorities elsewhere advised to be aware of the problems

Table 6.1. (*cont.*)

Product investigated (supply of)	Date referred month and year	Date report signed by MRPC	Report published	Action taken on MRPC recommendation
Hard fibre cordage	July 1953	Dec. 1955	Dec. 1955	NONE
Lino	Sept. 1953	Jan. 1956	Jan. 1956	NONE
Sand and gravel in central Scotland	Dec. 1953	Nov. 1955	Mar. 1956	NONE
Industrial and medical gases	Feb. 1954	June 1956	Dec. 1956	March 1956: voluntary undertakings: No action to regulate price and profits
Standard metal windows and doors	Feb. 1954	Sept. 1956	Dec. 1956	NONE
Rubber footwear	Apr. 1954	May 1956	June 1956	NONE
Electronic valves and cathode ray tubes	Dec. 1954 Aug. 1956	Sept. 1956	Dec. 1956	Report limited to facts
Electric street-lighting equipment	June 1955	ENDED MARCH 1956		
Steel frames for buildings	June 1955	ENDED MARCH 1956		
Tea	July 1955	Sept. 1956	Dec. 1956	Practices not found against the public interest
Electric batteries	Sept. 1955	ENDED MARCH 1956		
Chemical fertilisers	Oct. 1955	July 1959	July 1959	Undertakings given
Section 15 references:				
Collective Discrimination	Dec. 1952	May 1955	June 1955	1956 legislation
Common minimum prices and level tendering	Oct. 1955	ENDED MARCH 1956		

Note:
Table 6.1 summarises reports on industries referred to MRPC before the 1956 Restrictive Trade Practices Act came into operation.
Source: Monopolies and Restrictive Practices Acts, 1948 and 1953, Annual Report by the Board of Trade for years ending 1955, 1956, 1957, 1958, 1959.

cases there were still complaints, mentioned in the Board's annual reports, of the same practices continuing, or of the industry continuing to charge allegedly high prices. In one of these cases, the timber trade, the Board of Trade invoked Section 22 of the Act to investigate whether the trade had complied with the Commission's recommendations.[8] In a fourth case, that of calico, the redundancy scheme, although criticised by the Commission, was allowed to run its course until 1959.[9]

Frequently the government did not implement Commission recommendations, for instance in the calico redundancy schemes or the aggregated rebates scheme in electric lamps, or price supervision of the British Oxygen Co.[10] Sometimes economic conditions in the industry nullified the effects of any abrogation. Strong information agreements replaced the formal price lists in calico, while price leadership by the dominant firm, BICC eventually developed in electric wires and cable, although at lower price levels.[11] The Board of Trade used its power to make an Order outlawing practices criticised in the case of dental goods. This action was criticised for its unfair discrimination against firms who happened to be the subject of investigation. The threat of an Order had to be used in two other cases, also – calico printing and cables.[12]

Nor did the reports which were published have any major impact on the rest of industry. Sir Frank Lee, chairman of the inter-departmental working group on the Monopolies Commission, noted how speakers from all parties in the debate on the 1948 Act had expressed a belief that responsible people in industry would use the Commission's findings as a guide to their own conduct, but this had not happened. Practices found objectionable in the supply of rainwater goods were common to the supply of many building materials. Arrangements similar to those in dental goods probably existed in the supply of scientific instruments and laboratory ware. Yet, his paper commented, neither the Ministry of Works nor the Ministry of Health had had talks with other trade associations in the light of the two reports. The reasons for the inertia were, the paper suggested, overwork and lack of experience so that 'most Departments will regard it as premature to court more trouble by broaching restrictive practice problems with their other industries'.[13] The glass firm Pilkington did respond to the threat of action under British and Canadian legislation by reviewing its practices, and was later told by the Board of Trade that it was one of the few industries which had 'adjusted their activities to present trends of thought'.[14] The discussions in the FBI's Trade Practices Committee, set up to monitor the work of the Commission, indicate that businessmen came to appreciate, not the error of their ways, but that increasingly critical reports indicated that still stronger legislation was in the offing. At one stage the pressure of publicity raised the possibility that the FBI establish a code of good practice, but the idea was rejected.[15]

Overall this balance sheet points strongly to 'regulatory failure'. The only benefit most commentators have seen in the experience of the Commission has been the gradual awakening of public perceptions of the problem and the use of reports to prompt stronger action in the 1956 Restrictive Trade Practices Act.[16] However, even this conclusion is open to question. According to Lord Kilmuir, then Attorney General, the sole motive for the 1956 Bill was that he and Peter Thorneycroft (President of the Board of Trade from 1951 to 1956) decided that current legislation and the Commission was unpopular with industry, and the use of the Courts would be preferable.[17] Peter Thorneycroft promised procedural changes in a House of Commons debate in February 1955.[18]

The fundamental cause of the failure was the attitude of businessmen to the Commission. They did not 'capture' the Commission, but they did hamstring the administration of the Commission by the Board of Trade by their hostility, implied and stated. It is next necessary to analyse the basis of this influence.

The nature of business influence on the Board of Trade

Central to business success was the clear division of function between the Commission and the Board of Trade. The Board had the duty to identify cases for referral, which it did after consultation with the 'sponsoring' department. The Commission then conducted the enquiry, wrote the report and made recommendations. The procedure then returned to the Board of Trade and the sponsoring departments to decide whether any section of the report should be omitted on grounds of national security or business confidentiality, and then to conduct negotiations with the firms concerned with a view to carrying out the Commission's recommendations.

In Britain it was not the Commission itself which had to bow to business lobbying. The members of the Monopolies Commission may not have had a coherent idea of the 'public interest' and they can be criticised for lack of thorough investigation particularly in cases of oligopoly, but they certainly were not impressed by businessmen's claims for their practices.[19] Recommendations could be far-reaching: a minority called for nationalisation in the case of British Oxygen. According to some American literature, the praise which an industry heaped on a regulatory commission was an indication that it had been 'captured' by that industry.[20] On this crude criterion the Commission enjoyed some success. Business pressure groups greeted many reports with a chorus of disapproval, charging the Commission with doctrinaire bias.

Industry was generally unsuccessful in getting critical parts of reports excised. Requests for excisions were a major irritant within the Board of Trade, but industries' arguments were usually dismissed.[21] In spite of protracted negotiations the government usually secured voluntary abrogation of the agreements or changes in the constitutions of associations to remove objectionable features, although there were definite limits to the compliance of business, as noted above. For many of the trades, where the industry might be expected to be obdurate, the issue never came to a head, as the government decided not to pursue those industries operating agreements likely to be registrable under the forthcoming Restrictive Trade Practices Act. In the case of copper semi-manufactures for instance, the British Non-Ferrous Metals Federation was shaping up for a fight, and had published a voluminous and detailed refutation of nearly all the Commission's criticisms.[22] In tyres the producers published protests 'among the strongest ever drawn up on a monopolies report before it was published'.[23] In these cases and electrical machinery the government escaped a major battle and the reports were rendered innocuous by the new legislation.[24]

Industries usually preferred to come to an agreement with the government than suffer legal enforcement of the Commission's recommendations. One particularly recalcitrant industry was the Calico Printers' Federation, where Thorneycroft had to threaten to issue an Order before the industry agreed 'voluntarily' to abandon their practices.[25] Nevertheless industry was clearly taken aback at the government's insistence on implementing the Commission's recommendations. In early 1955 Thorneycroft noted that the government's decision to support the Commission over cables, 'aroused considerable disquiet in powerful industrial circles'.[26]

But industrialists directed a most effective lobby at those parts of the procedure handled by the Board of Trade – within government itself, often without having to lift a finger or utter a word of protest. An American regulation theorist has commented:

The hostile environment in which regulation operates is pervasive. It provides the frame of reference for the regulatory process conditional upon the acceptance of regulation by the affected groups. It forces a commission to come to terms with the regulated groups as a condition of its survival.[27]

The whole procedure rested crucially on business co-operation, and this had an impact on the speed of the Commission's work. The 1953 report on the Commission by the Select Committee on Estimates, reviewing the experience of the first seven referrals, found that in four cases the difficulty of obtaining information from the parties concerned seriously delayed completion. In the case of electric lamps which took two years and five months, no less than one year and five months elapsed before all the information requested had been furnished. The report on cables took three years one month, of which one year one month was similarly dead time as far as the costings side of the Commission's report was concerned.[28]

The very composition of the Commission and the absence of many full-time members, laid down in the legislation, was also a factor in the slowness, and this in turn reflected business success at the stage of introducing legislation, when representatives of business had argued that membership be mainly part-time. Until 1953 there were only two full-time members, the chairman Sir Archibald Carter and Sir A.L. Saunders, a seconded civil servant. Although the Select Committee on Estimates' report on the Commission recommended that a further full-time member drawn from industry or commerce be appointed, this was not done.[29] Indeed, in January 1954 Saunders resigned leaving only the Chairman, now Sir David Cairns. It is generally agreed that this was a major limiting factor.[30]

More crucially still, business feeling determined the types of references which the Monopolies Commission was given to pursue and hence determined the character of its work. That this was possible was again inherent in the nature of the legislation, which had laid down no guidelines for priorities, and which gave no power to the Minister responsible to prescribe them. When it did come to ministerial attention, under the Conservatives, it was stressed that industries should not be bothered with a referral unless there were prima facie evidence of abuse or very serious public complaint.[31]

Indeed by 1953 it was clear that the whole procedure was becoming unworkable as possible references from government departments dried up. The problem had first been noted in 1952.[32] In 1953 the problem had actually become more acute with impending legislation to increase the size of the Commission and therefore the volume of its work.[33] With the publication of some extremely critical reports most notably those on cables and calico processing, something of a crisis had arisen which threatened to discredit the whole empirical approach and to prompt demands for sweeping general prohibitions.[34]

There was no doubt in the minds of the civil servants involved that limiting the suggestions from departments was fear of antagonising their industries. As A.C. Hill, Private Secretary to the President of the Board of Trade, put it:

there has been evidence of a growing hostility in some commercial and industrial circles towards the Commission and indeed towards the whole process of enquiry and control provided for by the monopolies legislation. This critical attitude has manifested itself not only in some recent letters to the President but in, for example, the remarks of directors at Annual Meetings and in the 'tough' attitude shown by industries in their discussions with Monopolies branch on points of detail. It seems very likely that this critical atmosphere has influenced departments in their attitude towards the making of new references.[35]

This unwillingness to antagonise industry permeated to Cabinet level.[36] Peter Thorneycroft's plea to the Economic Policy Committee that other departments should co-operate at first produced results from within the Ministries, but soon opposition to the 'big' items proposed within that committee[37] meant that the issue was, for the first time in the history of the Monopolies Commission, taken to the full Cabinet. Even then, with the mandate of the 1955 election, and Churchill's personal support, the really big items were removed, that is cement, the yarn spinners and metal boxes, and Thorneycroft's zeal curbed.[38]

Arguments used in Cabinet were replicas of the feelings of industries towards an investigation, such as the unfairness of singling out certain trades or firms, the burden which an enquiry placed upon a firm or industry, the way just an enquiry encouraged the public to consider the industry guilty.[39] Their use in Cabinet showed how influenced Ministers were also by industrialists' complaints.

It was indeed incessant business complaints that prompted the Board of Trade to reconsider the procedure again in 1954 in response to 'widespread disquiet in industry'.[40] Industrialists complained that they could not see the case against them before the public interest hearings, they were not allowed to cross-examine those making a case against them, and that some members of the Commission were prejudiced against industry.[41] Although members of the Commission and the Board of Trade felt that these complaints were quite unreasonable,[42] in a debate in February 1955 the government, while accepting the controversial calico report, also promised a review of procedure.[43] Thus the changes towards a judicial procedure, in which industries 'accused' would have greater rights to present their case, they believed, and where judges might be expected to have less doctrinal commitment to competition, sprang originally from business complaints.

Still more remarkable than the problems of getting references at all, were the actual products chosen. Why were calico printing, sand and gravel in central Scotland and tea chosen, and not the Yarn Spinners' Association, cement or oils and fats? The choice has certainly baffled later commentators.[44]

There were no agreed criteria for the choice of references and the publicly-stated criteria were different from those outlined in departmental memoranda. The former stated that items were chosen to give the Commission a range of types of practices and industries. The latter, however, advised production departments to select cases on this basis but also on

Table 6.2. *Complaints to the Board of Trade of monopoly or restrictive practices, 1949–56*

There were seven annual reports by the Board of Trade from 1949–56, on the work of the Monopolies Commission.
The following items were mentioned as subjects of complaint four or more times.

Item	No. of complaints	Nature of restriction	If referred
Newspapers and periodicals	7	a	
Motor vehicles	7	a	
Agricultural implements	7	a	
Chemists' goods	6	a	
Electrical accessories and appliances	6	a, c	
Plate glass	6	a, b, c	
Gramophone records	5	a, c	
Petrol	5	a, b, c, d	
Structural steelwork erection	5	b	Yes but ended
Tyres	4	a, b, d	Yes
Electrical components for motor vehicles	4	a, c	Yes
Textile-making machinery	4	c	
Wallpaper	4	a, c	
Carpets	4	a	
Typewriters	4	a	
Electric street-lighting equipment	4	b	Yes but ended

a: in distribution, e.g. discriminatory arrangements.
b: minimum price-fixing, restrictions on new entrants, level tendering in manufacturing.
c: products under monopolistic control through large firms.
d: under monopolistic control through trade associations.

Source: Annual Reports of the Monopolies Commission.

such criteria as the level of public complaint, where there was reason to think efficiency could be improved or production expanded, or where there was evidence that agreements adversely affected the prices and volume of exports (see appendix 5).[45] Thus when questioned by the Select Committee on Estimates, which enquired into the work of the Commission in 1953, A.C. Hill admitted that, 'I would find it awfully difficult in regard to any particular reference to weigh the various factors which led to the choice of reference'.[46]

The selection of references was haphazard, and involved estimation of the dangers and benefits to many areas of government policies and in particular to government–industry relations.

A much-vaunted public complaints procedure was irrelevant in determining which items were chosen (see table 6.2). The Board's annual report on the work of the Commission listed all the public complaints received. The majority of complainants were smaller firms and traders, and few of their items were used as a basis for referral.[47] The Board of Trade also failed to refer items which the public bought and which affected their cost of living, such as newspapers, cars, records, petrol or wallpaper. The *absence* of complaint was often sufficient reason against referral, but its presence was irrelevant to the final decision. Indeed, by 1953 the Board of Trade was sensitive to complaints that the complaints procedure was being ignored and advised departments to suggest industries mentioned in annual reports, 'if only to dispel any idea that we keep off potentially explosive subjects and prefer only those which are likely to yield reports of a fairly anodyne nature'.[48]

The main reason for this was that the most common items of complaint were produced by large, oligopolistic and often transnational firms, in industries which were either good export earners, or occupied some other strategic position in the economy. The rest of this section looks at the way, sometimes by accident, sometimes by design, single-firm monopolies escaped the worst.

The 1948 Act contained no provision for dealing with monopoly abuse exercised by the large, oligopolistic firm. Thus it could be 'embarrassing' for government policy to get an adverse report and to do nothing about it, and for it to be revealed that there were few sanctions against the large firm.[49] Also intrinsic to the Act was the presumption in favour of references involving price rings and cartels rather than large firms, and this was continued in directives to departments from the Monopolies branch.[50] For these reasons the objection that the item concerned was controlled by a single-firm monopoly was used against the referral of metal containers, gas mantles, razor blades, sewing thread, perspex and nylon yarn.

It might be presumed that another policy decision on references, that which stated that 'insignificant' items were not to be preferred[51] would work against the large firm. However, it was sometimes precisely in limited fields of production that a large firm might exercise a monopoly, as in many of the industries where this was part or wholly the reason against referral (cellulose film, chain cables, salt, glues, glycerin, rubber belting, rubber thread and lighter flints).[52] Moreover, the policy was not adhered to rigorously. Cellulose films, glues and gelatine had annual production values of £9m, £5m and £4m respectively, and higher than that of some industries referred, such as matches, insulin and rainwater goods, the value of whose annual production was £4m, £1m, and £4m respectively.[53]

A final aspect of the confusion over general guidelines for references was the tendency to assume that the presence of competition in an industry, even one dominated by a few large firms, was sufficient argument against referral. The result of this train of thought again benefited those products where oligopolistic competition prevailed, for instance in alcohol solvents, pesticides, photographic materials and rubber chemicals.[54]

Also militating against the referral of large firms was the fact that cases of monopoly abuse by them might often be associated with the working of an international cartel. Although international restrictions were included in the scope of the legislation there was much reluctance to delve into them. Even where the domestic restrictions were investigated their international ramifications might be excluded from investigation, as happened in the case of electric cables. The problem was, as the minutes of a departmental meeting put it: 'It was quite possible that if this agreement were examined it would become clear that there was a conflict between our national interests, interpreted strictly, and our international commitments.'[55] Thus this international dimension delayed the referral of heavy electrical machinery and scotched that of metal cans and containers. In diamonds and tea, fears that London would cease to be the centre of trade delayed and scotched references.[56]

The most notable example of how this international connection worked came in the case of petrol whose 'tied garage' system was the subject of frequent complaint.[57] The international oil cartel was outside the terms of reference of the Act, for the Act covered only exports *from* Britain. However an enquiry into the distributive arrangements within Britain encroached on its activities and hence aroused opposition from the companies which was sustained by the Foreign Office and the Ministry of Fuel and Power, supported with letters to Thorneycroft from their Ministers. This opposition made it impossible for the Board to act, in spite of Thorneycroft's support for referral.[58] The power of the companies and of these departments is remarkable when set against the level of public concern, and the Board's own willingness and desire to refer the matter, which was raised several times in this period.[59] The Board even suggested to the Cabinet that if petrol were not referred the government should state its policy towards the industry, in order to counter Opposition criticism.[60]

A further factor which served to shield large firms was the significance of their products in defence, the 'strategic' argument against a referral. To refer alkalis might harm the Board of Trade's relations with ICI, who also manufactured chlorine, which was of key strategic importance.[61] Aluminium was another strategic industry, which officials felt it would be 'prudent' to leave alone because of Britain's reliance on the Canadian Aluminium Company.[62] Officials acknowledged that the price of lighter flints was too high but the industry was important to defence.[63]

A further common argument against referral was that the industry was a good export earner, or was efficient, characteristics again often those of large firms, such as ICI and Unilever. Thus it was that efficiency and hence absence of complaints were the arguments against the referral of cement, metal cans and containers, china clay, flat glass, soap, phosphates, perspex, industrial solvents, and a number of basic chemicals. Some of the most important large firms, Metal Box and Pilkington, Unilever, ICI and Distillers, were involved here, and in cement a thorough cartel, dominated by Associated Portland Cement was concerned. The argument that the industry was a good export earner was used against the referral of copper sulphate, a sales monopoly dominated by ICI and sewing thread, dominated by J. & P. Coats. The argument came out clearly in the case of Unilever, which held a monopolistic position in a wide variety of products, particularly foods. An official at the Ministry of Food argued that while Unilever was dominant, 'This in itself is not a bad thing and I admit that it might be in the general interest to show that a semi-monopoly can be benevolent'.[64]

The position of some firms was so vital to the very structure of an industry, or to British industry in general, that officials sought to defend them against the 'pillorying' by the Monopolies Commission, or to defend themselves against the industrial opposition which such firms could mount. The case of ICI, a firm with strong involvement with government, and government concern in its affairs from its inception,[65] is instructive. Few cases of chemicals were referred: only fertilisers, a market controlled by ICI and Fisons, and medical and industrial gases, a monopoly not of ICI's, but of the British Oxygen Company's (BOC). Yet the possible number of chemical cases considered was legion, prompting one official to remark that the difficulty with ICI cases was knowing where to begin.[66] There were many reasons for not looking at ICI but one forceful argument, made against referring caustic soda, soda ash, glycol and other heavy chemicals was that, 'we do not want the Commission to cut its teeth on ICI'.[67] The damage to the government's relationship with ICI if alkalis were referred has already been mentioned and to refer oil baize, they argued 'would bring us up against ICI and British Plastics'.[68] British Nylon Spinners (BNS), a complete monopoly owned jointly by ICI and Courtaulds, had arrangements with foreign producers and collected royalties from British manufacturers who imported foreign nylon yarn. However, the Board of Trade department concerned, opposed referral in view of the co-operative attitude of the BNS on prices.[69]

A further problem with referring large firms was that they could easily complain of being 'singled out' or 'made a guinea pig'.[70] Thus it was that when the Board decided to refer Unilever's monopoly of non-mineral oils and fats, they decided to refer at the same time the fertiliser aspect of ICI's operations, 'to avoid charges of discrimination against one particular giant'.[71] A list went to the Economic Policy Committee which included both items.

This section has shown the power of business feeling in the work of the Commission. Civil servants were made aware of it, sometimes by osmosis, often by direct lobbying and complaint. The FBI set up a committee to keep the work of the Commission under constant review, providing advice and meeting Thorneycroft and Sir David Cairns, the chairman of the Monopolies Commission. The Committee attempted to co-ordinate the first six industries referred to the Commission, but that side of their work did not take off, and the last meeting was in 1953.[72]

The last case of ICI and Unilever raises a further question for, while Ministers objected to the referral involving Unilever, that involving ICI went through. So how did a referral get through the screening procedure?

The balance of public and business pressure

The most important reason *for* a referral was a sufficiently strong 'countervailing power'. There are clear cases of enquiries being instigated into products which affected the costs of production of other industrialists. In the case of fertilisers, the National Farmers' Union desired an investigation. The Board of Trade also felt happier because the industry was not a complete monopoly of ICI's in the way that oils and fats was for Unilever. The actual extent of Unilever's monopoly acted as a protection – against 'pillorying'! A second example of the buyers' lobby is the failed proposal to investigate the Yarn Spinners' Association, whose margins were criticised by 'other sections of the industry'.[73]

In other cases referred the Commission's reports indicated that sections of businessmen in the industry disliked and were disadvantaged by the monopolistic practices they encountered, although it is not clear that they were the prime movers of the referral. Medical and industrial gases was the only referral entirely geared to investigation of one large firm – the BOC. The chief industrial users of gases were iron and steel producers. They made few complaints to the Commission, but the government was interested in increasing the use of oxygen in iron and steel production and the Ministry of Fuel and Power supported such a reference. Their combined weights were sufficient eventually to overcome the objection of the lack of sanctions against large firms.[74] In the case of tyres, dominated by Dunlop, it was a combination of the motor vehicle industry and local authorities and many other public bodies. However, it was not until the Ministry of Transport approved that the item could go ahead, and the reasons for the withdrawal of their veto are not clear. Later it was clear that some tyre distributors were ecstatic about the report, so again divisions within the industry were a factor.[75] In rainwater goods the building contractors were anxious for action to reduce the web of restrictions, and were prime movers of the earlier report on building materials.[76] In the case of lino and dental supplies public bodies and firms outside the main trade association played a role.[77] The calico-printing referral sprang from a long-standing desire to begin to tackle restrictive practices in textiles, especially in the finishing trades, while avoiding taking on the yarn spinners. Some customers of the Calico Printers Federation were critical of the prices charged and the quality of production.[78] Thus business could and did use the Commission to investigate items of concern to industrial consumers.

Another form of 'countervailing power' were overseas buyers and competitors. The reference of semi-manufactures of copper and other non-ferrous metals was the direct and immediate response to a claim from the European Co-operation Administration in Britain that the Lausanne agreement of the British Non-Ferrous Metals Association contravened the terms of the European Recovery Programme.[79] A facts only report was first made, but the results were not published, and it was decided instead to turn the report into one on the public interest. The report eventually appeared in June 1955, but no further action was taken, for already the industry was preparing to do heavy battle on the terms of implementation and it was again with relief that the Board of Trade could decide to take no further action on many cases as the result of new legislation.[80]

Complaints from Commonwealth governments against heavy electrical equipment and electric wires and cables were an important element also in the referral of two major industries, the latter involving investigation of the activities of a newly-formed conglomerate (BICC). Its referral was a combination of the initial sense of purpose and dynamism in the Board's approach and external complaints about the price of British exports. Meanwhile, the controversial nature of the reference was reduced by specifically omitting the international arrangements from the remit of the Monopolies Commission enquiry.[81] It should also be noted in the case of these big enquiries into such basic industries that the reference was into industries whose costs substantially affected the costs of many other industries, and therefore conform to the pattern of the Commission as a means to rectify the effect of a monopoly in a basic industry on other industries. The continual hankering by Conservative MPs for the national-ised industries to be included in the legislation is indicative of their notion of regulation as a means of reducing *costs*.

In comparison public pressure had minimal impact on the work of the Commission. Sometimes, the procedure of selection was responsive to organised public bodies. One case provided by the Co-operative Societies was pursued – electric lamps – and several were in part a response to complaints by local authorities: tyres, structural steel-work and street-lighting new buildings in London, sand and gravel in central Scotland, standard metal windows and doors and imported timber. The input of local authorities, and also of hospitals, schools and other welfare state bodies was felt strongly in the decision to make a Section 15 reference in uniform tendering and minimum prices. As chapter 2 showed these practices had begun to affect these bodies, and a growing band of outraged authorities assembled their evidence.

However, the case of the Section 15 reference into uniform tendering also indicates the limits to public input. (A Section 15 reference was one ranging across industries designed to catch a widespread practice, for instance RPM.) The Iron and Steel Board, created under the denationalisation legislation of 1953, argued that the sale of further firms might be jeopardised were certain pricing arrangements brought within the scope of an enquiry into the general practice of common prices and uniform tendering.[82] The lobbying by the iron and steel board was one factor in the demise of that reference. Pressure from the oil companies, via the Ministry of Fuel and Power, to be excluded from the enquiry prompted discussions about possible excisions from a possible report even before the decision to make such a reference had been provisionally taken.[83] Eventually the reference was framed to exclude the supply of goods by export from the United Kingdom and of goods in which British parties traded, to meet the concerns of the Ministry of Fuel and Power.[84] The discussions on iron and steel and its position under a possible Section 15 reference were continuing until December 1955 when it was decided, with relief, to drop the whole reference pending the introduction of the new legislation in 1956. The item was dropped in full recognition that public opinion would be disappointed.[85]

In other ways also the procedure was not responsive to public concerns. The limited number of references, the slowness of the Commission and its apparent lack of direction was already causing comment only two years after its inauguration.[86] Joan Robinson, who served on the Commission from 1949 to 1952, was frustrated with the procedure and resigned early.[87] The government was well aware of public disquiet. Alix Kilroy, the first Secretary of the Commission, geared her address to the Manchester Statistical Society to trying to deny the charge that the Commission acted as 'a subterfuge under which the whole question can be put to sleep'.[88] As the Board of Trade found it increasingly difficult to persuade Departments to suggest items for referral a crisis developed with implications for the very principles behind the Act. A.C. Hill, Under-Secretary at the Board of Trade, feared that, without more work, the Commission would come to be seen as 'an obvious futility', and its standing reduced in the eyes both of the public and of its members,[89] threatening to discredit the whole empirical approach and prompting demands for sweeping general prohibitions.[90] When Peter Thorneycroft raised the same problem at the Cabinet's Economic Policy Committee six months later he was clearly aware of hostility to the Act among his colleagues. He argued that: 'If we are to resist the clamour for a new policy we can only do so by a vigorous application of the present one.'[91] To the extent that anyone in government believed in the Commission by 1955, it was as an alternative to public clamour for stronger policies, and hence was indeed a sop to public opinion. Nowhere better is this illustrated than in the Section 15 reference into collective boycott. This was a general enquiry across a range of trades into collective methods of enforcing resale prices, such as boycotts and stop lists.[92] It came to be a showpiece of Conservative action on competition and was important in the introduction of the 1956 Act. However, it was originally conceived under very different circumstances; to wit, to avoid taking action on a previous report on RPM, published in 1949.[93] The Lloyd Jacob committee had undertaken a wide investigation and recommended that collective RPM be banned. The Labour government had prepared in 1951 a White Paper promising the prohibition of all forms of RPM.[94] As soon as Peter Thorneycroft came to the Board of Trade discussions arose on this unfinished business. Awareness of the business opposition which was already afoot prompted civil servants to propose that instead of pursuing Labour's promises a Section 15 reference on collective boycott – the most common and unpopular practice – be undertaken. Naturally the question arose, would this not be an obvious repeat of the Lloyd Jacob investigation? The meeting concluded that by 'confining the reference to trades with important exemption claims and drawing attention to the question of determining the weight of special factors in those trades, we should be able to make it clear that the exercise is meant to fill particular gaps in our knowledge and not simply a duplication of work already done on general issues'.[95] Thus it was that the new reference first evolved. It was not based primarily on other reports, it was not indicative of the government's vigour on monopolies but of its desire to avoid a controversial piece of legislation.

The functions of the MRPC

The absence of any general economic impact of the MRPC has already been discussed. However, there is some evidence that some industries were adversely affected by enquiry. The historian of Dunlop, for instance complains that the opening of the British market to foreign competition may be dated from the time of the MRPC enquiry.[96] Thus the Commission may have had some impact as a businessman's court, although mainly for overseas businessmen! Otherwise the best that has been said for it is that the

MRPC reports created a climate of opinion prompting further development of policy – the 1956 Act. Chapter 7 disputes this point.

Neverthelesss the main role of the MRPC appears to have been an educative one. The work of the Commission served as a constant reminder to the public of the underhand, dark and devious methods of businessmen. From 1952 onwards, the decisions to make a Section 15 reference on collective discrimination, together with the amending Act of 1953 allowing more work to be done, meant that the issue was constantly before the Press and Parliament. Reports grew increasingly critical. Of particular significance were those on collective discrimination, tyres and copper semi-manufactures, which all appeared around the middle of 1955. The report on tyres provided graphic accounts of the use of spies and private courts by the British Motor Trade Association and the Tyre Trade Joint Committee, to enforce resale prices: 'A sooty-faced spy' and 'Snooper with a dirty face' were the headlines.[97] By early 1955 and through to early 1956 there were continual revelations about uniform tendering to local authorities, mainly for building materials, stimulated by a Monopolies Commission report on the London Builders' Conference of July 1954, which had revealed widespread uniform tendering, and the announcement that level tendering would form a further Section 15 reference.[98] Businessmen disliked this critical atmosphere, arguing that even a referral to the Commission immediately aroused public suspicions of their guilt.

However, their hostility to the Commission should not obscure the nature of the reports which generally endorsed *competitive* capitalism. Previous chapters have indicated that those elements of 'public opinion' represented in labour organisations were already aware of and opposed to private monopolies and restrictive practices long before the Monopolies Commission started. Its reports educated opinion in a particular direction, giving publicity, validity and legitimacy to the view that restrictionism and monopoly were deviations from a capitalism which, through 'workable competition' ensured that industries would be efficient, innovatory and adaptable to change, charging reasonable prices. Reports consistently condemned practices which conflicted with these aims, such as exclusive dealing, uniform tenders, quota schemes and loyalty rebates, as well as price arrangements unless they were seen as necessary in a programme of joint research or patent-sharing. The general tenor of the reports' recommendations was the creation of workable competition, especially through ending arrangements designed to stop the new entrant. Sometimes the establishment of competition in oligopolistic industries like electric cables could not be achieved simply by removing agreements, and here the Commission relied on 'countervailing power' such as that of government purchasers.[99]

Thus the MRPC was biased in favour of the presence of competition – either within the industry concerned or as between suppliers and customers – as the main guarantee of the public interest. Indeed civil servants in the Board of Trade used the presence of competition as one criterion to decide on references. The presence of competition in an industry, even one dominated by a few large firms, was sufficient argument against referral.[100] Thus the civil servants set the terms of debate for the Commission before they began their part of the work. In this way the MRPC operated as the Profiteering Acts introduced after the First World War were intended to, to provide arguments for the 'working man' for sustaining capitalism and the legitimacy of private ownership. The MRPC was therefore part of 'Americanisation': it formed a sort of adult education programme in the sphere of monopoly that the reports of the Anglo–American Productivity Council provided in the sphere of productivity. It was operating at a time when the Americans laid great stress on the need for propaganda against cartels, having failed to secure tougher measures (see chapter 8).

The type of education the public could receive was dictated therefore by the views of competition and capitalism of those employed in the Board of Trade and on the Commission. Furthermore, a vital determinant of this education was to lie in the attitude of the press.

The government was relying on investigation and publicity as a way of educating business opinion, and was by extension relying on a sympathetic attitude towards the Monopolies Commission by the mainstream press. Yet the newspaper industry was itself subject to monopoly influences. Five large chains controlled over 40% of all newspapers in Britain, and the Royal Commission on the Press of 1949 believed any further concentration posed a threat to pluralist political opinion.[101] In January 1949 the government lifted quota restrictions on sales, imposed since the war, although newsprint continued to be rationed. The result was a huge increase in the size of circulations, but also increasing competition for advertising and a period of mergers and disappearances, especially of provincial papers. Some mergers had a political intent: Beaverbrook was alarmed at the popularity of the *Daily Mirror* and so began the first approach to the ailing Liberal paper the *News Chronicle*. The 1950s was a time when the future of more serious, and often left-wing, newspapers like the *Daily Herald*, was under pressure.[102] From this point of view it might have been a propitious time for an enquiry. The focus of complaints was the restrictive retailing agreements, the Co-op boycott, and the 'distance limit' rule which became widespread in the early 1950s, and which limited the number of retailers who could operate in a given area. Indeed, the item went on the first shortlist precisely to illustrate the type of practice involving a Co-op boycott.

The idea was killed at an interdepartmental meeting by Alix Kilroy, who said, rather mysteriously, that there were 'great objections to referring newspapers at this particular time'. The Co-op should be asked to find another example such as radios or bicycles which, the officials hoped would not involve any other issues than boycotting the Co-op.[103] The question arose again in 1952, a paper to the policy group noting that there had been more complaints on this score than any other and that the question was now wider than the Co-op boycott and also involved rather an 'interesting' practice. The paper put forward three arguments against referral: the effect of the arrangements on the public interest was insignificant, newsprint was in short supply and it was therefore illogical to demand more retail outlets and, as the arrangements probably also benefited the proprietors 'there might be some advantage in not provoking unfavourable press comment about the Commission's activities until there has been more time to accustom the press to thinking and speaking favourably of the Commission'.[104]

Concentration of ownership in the Press was so great that the government could not afford to investigate it for fear of arousing a concerted Press campaign which might jeopardise the whole legislation. The Press had already been the subject of a monopoly enquiry, whose recommendations had got lost in the opposition of the Publishers' Association. That enquiry had been initiated partly because Labour was disturbed at its hostile reception in the Press.[105] No such considerations affected the Conservative government, and hence the one factor which might have produced an enquiry was absent. Accordingly, the weapon of publicity to mobilise 'public opinion' and to educate businessmen was blunted, then and for all time.

Conclusions

The use of the MRPC to outlaw 'anti-social' restrictive practices and to enquire into private monopoly was minimal and hence bore little relation to the sort of legislation demanded by many liberal economists or sections of the labour movement. The whole framework of the civil service and government–industry relations worked to defend business as a whole from still greater pubic hostility to private monopoly.

The Monopolies Commission's main achievement certainly was the reports it produced which were critical and had some impact on the evolution of legislation. However, it is necessary to be very clear about the type of education the public and business, and government was given. The public learnt that business could behave badly, but this was where they deviated from competitive principles. It learnt much about restrictive practices, but not so much about the large firm, except where it operated restrictive practices. Businessmen learnt that a non-judicial tribunal was a dangerous thing and, though limited in its effects, exposed the businesses concerned to public obloquy. Government learnt that the tribunal form of regulation could be a complete headache, and that departments needed to be insulated from lobbying if they were to pursue industries which they otherwise sought to work with.

The Monopolies Commission was an educational experience, but not in the way that writers have inferred to date. The impact of that education on the future of legislation is the subject of chapter 7.

7   The origins of the Restrictive Trade Practices Act 1956 – a re-interpretation

The Restrictive Trade Practices Act of May 1956 laid the basis for the effective abolition of the British cartel system as it had existed since the 1930s. This was achieved through the operation of the Restrictive Practices Court after the Act was passed, rather than being intrinsic to the terms of the Act. The Act was the first piece of competition policy carrying the assumption that restrictive practices were against the public interest unless industrialists could prove otherwise. However, the result of the Act was not to create a paradise of free atomistic competition, but, in the long run, to contribute to the overall tendency of twentieth-century British business towards concentration and oligopoly.

Peter Thorneycroft, President of the Board of Trade since 1951, introduced the Act with a flourish. The purpose of the Bill was 'to secure that the virtues of free enterprise – initiative, adaptability and risk-taking – are not throttled by restrictions imposed by industry upon itself'.[1] But Labour MPs described the Bill as 'bogus' and the Labour Party moved that a Second Reading not be given to the Bill. They argued that the Bill was 'so framed as to encourage the growth of the movement towards actual combines or full monopolies', and designed 'to destroy the Monopolies Commission as an effective weapon against the citadel of monopoly capitalism in the trusts and combines'.[2]

It will be shown that the Act did indeed, potentially or deliberately, favour the development of large, and specifically transnational, firms. This took place in the context of the general trend to liberalisation of trade, the increasing competitive pressures on the British economy signalled in recurrent balance of payments problems, the re-emergence of significant competition from Germany and Japan, and the growing levels of foreign investment in Britain. As in 1948, the Act was part of the re-orientation of British business to new world conditions.

However, the Act represented a break with past policies, which had allowed restrictive practices to grow into an involved system by the 1950s, and its passage involved a confrontation with those sections of British business which operated with a national, protectionist and restrictionist concept of their interests. This confrontation took place within the Conservative Party itelf giving the Act some curious and contradictory features often noted by commentators.[3] Thus sometimes the Act is portrayed as part of a natural evolution via the 1948 Act, the Section 15 reference and the 'education' of public opinion,[4] and sometimes as a break with the past, requiring a combination of the personal intervention of Peter Thorneycroft against the Conservative diehards, an outburst of public indignation and the Section 15 report putting government 'in a position where it could hardly refrain from legislation'.[5]

The evolution of this piece of legislation had little to do with public feeling, for the debate largely took place within the Conservative Party and business circles, with Labour only having a chance to comment in parliamentary debate. Indeed, the stress on competition was accompanied, then as now, by the undermining of organisations of the labour movement: the Act's focus on restrictive business practices laid the ground-work for a review of restrictive labour practices, while the clauses of the Act on retailing represented a direct attack on the Co-operative dividend. Thus the way was cleared to undermine some of the strongest organisations of popular anti-monopoly sentiment.

A 'charter for big business'?

The 1956 Act made compulsory the registration of all agreements between two or more persons producing, supplying or processing manufactured goods which fixed prices and discounts, allocated quotas and markets, or stipulated methods of manufacture. The Registrar was empowered to refer any of them to the Restrictive Practices Court, a division of the High Court. The Act carried the general presumption that a restriction in the agreement was against the public interest. Industrialists were provided with 'gateways' allowing them to enter pleas of 'special circumstances' before the Court. If they were unsuccessful, and the Court found the restriction against the public interest, it automatically became void. An Order could then be made to desist, but this was usually found to be unnecessary. Agreements to enforce resale prices by collective means were made illegal. On the other hand single firms could enforce resale price agreements through the Courts. The Monopolies Commission was drastically limited to investigating only single-firm monopolies and export agreements. Export agreements themselves had to be notified to the Board of Trade but their details were not made public.

Many of these features only make sense as part of the same piece of legislation from the point of view of the large enterprise. The only element in the Act which could claim to follow the majority recommendations of the report on Collective Discrimination was that banning the collective enforcement of resale prices by discrimination, boycott, stop lists, fines and, of course, the notorious private courts. This, together with the registration of agreements, meant that the Act focussed on restrictive practices operated collectively – on cartels. These attracted the full glare of publicity and sanctions, while the activities of large firms – 'interconnected bodies corporate' in monopolistic positions or using monopolistic practices were shielded from such publicity, and often specifically exempted from legislation.

We now consider how the various sections of the Act together acted in this way.

The main intention of the Act, as fought for by Thorneycroft, was to use a system of registration and enquiry to tackle restrictive practices strongly. When the Commission's report on Collective Discrimination was published, the Cabinet established a Cabinet Committee on action which included Viscount Woolton (Chancellor of the Duchy of Lancaster), Thorneycroft, Reginald Maudling (Minister of Supply), Reginald Manningham-Buller (Attorney-General), Sir Edward Boyle (Economic Secretary to the Treasury) and Lord Kilmuir (Lord Chancellor). Its second meeting agreed a paper by Thorneycroft proposing to require the registration of all restrictive practices, possibly extending beyond those referred to in the report. Collective discrimination arrangements would be illegal if not registered, and once registered industrialists would be required to defend their practices before a tribunal where the onus of proof that the practice was *in* the public interest would lie with the industrialist concerned. Throughout subsequent discussions this element remained the basis of policy. It was endorsed a few days later by the full Cabinet.[6]

Discussions then hinged on the nature of the tribunal to decide the question: this was clearly going to be central to the whole effect of the Act. Peter Thorneycroft's arguments for a judicial tribunal, for the use of the High Courts were threefold. First, that such proceedings would be more acceptable to industry, indeed that the representatives of industry strongly favoured the High Court. Secondly, decisions by the High Court would be less open to attack and the Board of Trade and Ministers would so be insulated from political pressures. Thirdly Thorneycroft was later to make plain in discussions with the Treasury that he expected the Courts to be a strong weapon against restrictive practices. The High Court would have the necessary authority and he expected them to take a strong line on the basis that early nineteenth-century courts had condemned practices in restraint of trade. If the courts passed 'bad judgements' then the law would have to be altered, he said.[7] Thus Thorneycroft intended that the procedure he proposed – the use of the Courts – would indeed prove to be a weapon against restrictive practices.

These arguments came out because of strong opposition, especially from the Treasury whose representatives argued that the decisions to be made were of an economic not a legal nature; that it was 'constitutionally unsound' to try to insulate Ministers from pressure; and that authority over vital issues was being derogated from Parliament and could lead to a clash between Parliament and the Courts. These views were sustained by the tendency in the Treasury to prefer a process of 'edging out' the 'most objectionable practices'. Sir Robert Hall (Economic Adviser to the Government) believed restrictive practices checked increases in the rate of productivity growth and inhibited innovation, but felt they were not promoting outrageous profits. Indeed, he argued that restrictive labour practices were more objectionable, but recognised these could not be tackled without first starting on the employers.[8] The issue went to the Prime Minister and then to Cabinet which was willing to accept a judicial tribunal once a 'justiciable issue' had been defined which did not open the door too wide. Thorneycroft at first opposed defining a justiciable issue on the basis that 'the bill might be so weakened that the result would be to permit the continuance of practices which were contrary to the public interest'.[9]

Thus these discussions indicate how the key element in the Bill, the use of the High Courts, was evolved and show that Thorneycroft intended a system which would be tough on restrictive practices, believing that Court decisions would achieve what the Monopolies Commission had not, and being willing to alter the law if this proved not to be the case.

A tough line was to be taken on restrictive practices – but not on large firms and not on all restrictive practices. And it is here that we begin to understand how tender was the Act to the interests of large firms.

Firstly, certain practices were not registrable and some of these were practices especially associated with the strategies of large firms, namely agreements regulating the use of patent and trade-marks and those relating to exports. Certain types of agreements – especially those used by the large transnational firm in Britain were untouched by the legislation – in particular 'sole agency' agreements. Two American firms, for instance, operated 'sole agency' agreements in agricultural machinery which aimed 'to cut off the smaller British manufacturers from the best dealer outlets, and they can do this because they manufacture a complete range whereas the smaller British firms concentrate on one or two machines and could only offer a complete range if several of them worked together'.[10] Such arrangements were not agreements between two parties, but simply forms of contract imposed unilaterally. These sole agency practices were also widely used by other large firms, for instance the oil companies supplying branded petrol to their tied garages. They could be referred to the Monopolies Commission, solus sites in petrol was in 1960, but were not caught by Part I of the 1956 Act.

Secondly, the MRPC was downgraded. It became the Monopolies Commission to investigate the single firm and agreements relating to exports. Its maximum size was reduced from 25 to 10 members, and it could no longer function in small groups as it had been enabled to do in an amendment to the 1948 Act aimed at speeding up the process of enquiry. This downgrading of the Commission was not an incidental extension of the registration procedure but an intrinsic part of the Act.

The end of the independent tribunal was one of the most heartfelt demands of the FBI and other industrial groups, and a change in the procedure had been, as chapter 6 noted, the 'sole motive' of the originators – Lord Kilmuir and Peter Thorneycroft. Indeed at one stage Thorneycroft intended to abolish the Commission entirely. He told civil servants that the winding up of the Commission was attractive: it would again serve to remove the issue of monopolies from politics, and he feared lest the new system of registration would be hampered if a practice had first to be referred to the Commission.[11] His civil servants were adamant in their opposition. An 'old and tried horse', they said was to be abandoned in favour of a measure 'that is party political in the extreme', and to be administered and judgements made by people with little experience.[12] They seem to have dissuaded Thorneycroft who appreciated that 'if the Monopolies Commission is wound up we may be accused of drawing up a charter for Big Business, a danger to which the ABCC have already drawn attention'. However, he went on, 'it may be inconvenient and embarrassing to probe too far into this field', (of single-firm monopolies). S. Stewart was still concerned that 'we may be open to criticism for concentrating the weight of our attack on restrictive practices of small and medium sized firms, leaving the Monopolies, advertising agents, Insurance companies ..., etc. untouched'.[13] Even so, Thorneycroft continued to try to emasculate the Monopolies Commission, telling his civil servants that the current members were not the 'right sort of people to examine industrial combines'; what was needed was 'a number of top-ranking industrialists'.[14]

Thirdly, while Section 24 of the Act banned collective enforcement of RPM, Section 25 actually strengthened the power of the individual manufacturer to enforce his resale prices by allowing him to take legal action against a price-cutter. This section sustained RPM as a system, though by methods not so obviously iniquitous as the private courts run by trade associations. It was a measure clearly incompatible with an Act supposed to encourage price competition.

The most charitable explanation of the sections on RPM is that the combination of the two measures was a compromise, responding to public outcry against the methods of collective enforcement, while placating small shopkeepers – important in Conservative electoral support. In his major review of RPM, Pickering claims that the government in fact hoped that the abolition of collective enforcement of RPM would end all RPM, and so fulfil government plans to reduce the cost of living and speed innovation and efficiency in distribution.[15] The records indicate something rather different. Peter Thorneycroft indicated in his main policy proposals to the Cabinet committee on Monopolies that:

In our judgement machinery for enabling fixed prices to be maintained ought not to go on, and I propose to say so. I would, however, also say that we are examining whether methods can be found whereby these individually fixed prices can be maintained by methods less open to criticism than some referred to in the report.[16]

Thus the government intended to reinforce individual RPM while breaking up collective arrangements.

That the outcome of these two measures would benefit large firms at the expense of small manufacturers was appreciated at the outset. The trade journal of BEAMA (British Electrical and Allied Manufacturers' Association) wrote that the Bill was 'playing right into the hands of the chain stores, the multiples . . . who by bulk-buying can command better terms', and that as a result industry would 'trustify' itself to take advantage of the individual provision.[17] Manningham-Buller argued in the Cabinet committee that the provision discriminated in favour of the 'big monopolist' and against the 'small manufacturer', while civil servants saw the two measures as 'unfortunate'.[18]

Indeed, had the Conservatives been genuine about using the Bill's provisions to reduce the cost of living and encourage retailing efficiency such as self-service stores, they would have heeded the point of view of the Co-operative and Labour MPs who sought exemption for the Co-ops from the section strengthening individual enforcement. The Co-op was the subject of boycott especially by large manufacturers of branded goods, indeed the Co-op had told the earlier Labour government that it was more harmed by boycotts operated through individual RPM than that operated by associations.[19] The Co-op's dividend policy could definitely help to lower the cost of living: in 1960 the dividend in Northern and Scottish stores was 2/- in the £.[20] The Co-ops were also the pioneers of self-service, as well as vertical integration of production and retailing of many basic food items. Yet if powers of individual enforcement were increased, large firms could more easily refuse to supply if the Co-op gave a dividend on the goods concerned. The Labour movement had been united in arguing that, if individual enforcement were retained, there should be special provision for the Co-operative Societies. The Co-operative Party started a campaign and lobbied hard in Parliament, but it did not issue a leaflet until October 1956.[21]

Yet in a Bill riddled with special pleadings, exemptions and allowance for cases to be made for exemption, no such allowance was made for the Co-op. Indeed, a defence of the Co-ops came from no less a figure than Robert Hall who accepted that the dividend represented a form of aggregated rebate but pointed out that 'it would be much more in the spirit of the proposed legislation to allow the rebate . . . since the amount of it is determined by the total economies of the Co-ops'.[22] However, Thorneycroft, although in agreement, foresaw too many 'political' difficulties in exempting the Co-ops.[23]

The conclusion of this review of the sections of the Act on RPM supports the argument – that the strengthening of individual RPM was done deliberately to aid the large manufacturer of branded goods. Certainly during the enquiry into RPM undertaken by the Lloyd Jacob Committee in 1947 such manufacturers had argued against collective and for individual RPM. Nevertheless, whether that was the intention or not the sections on RPM certainly did nothing to harm the large firm, while certainly threatening smaller businessmen.

Finally, in this assessment of the impact of the Act on small and large firms we return to the main provisions of the Bill – the registration and enquiry procedure – which was to lead to a substantial shake-up of the British cartel system. Previous chapters have argued that large manufacturers were important players in the cartel system which developed since the 1930s and their opposition, with that of the trade associations generally, was crucial to the failure of 'drastic' policy – that is a registration and enquiry procedure – in the 1940s. How was it possible therefore that thirteen years later such legislation was enacted?

There is no evidence that businessmen, or sections of business, campaigned *for* the main provision of the Act – registration – although we know that they did campaign for an end to the MRPC. What occurred therefore was that the business veto *against* such a measure was lifted. The solid phalanx of business opposition to competition policy began to break up in the 1950s, mainly because of the rewards the economic expansion of the 1950s offered to the firm who broke away from cartel agreements: British capitalism had reached another crossroads.

Large firms continued to see uses for certain of their agreements, and the new procedure allowed firms to defend some of their practices – as Pilkington and Dunlop were preparing to do. Other firms rewrote old agreements.[24] Courtaulds and ICI found that their old agreement to produce nylon only through the medium of British Nylon Spinners (a major element in their relationship) had to be registered or abandoned under the terms of the 1956 Act. The latter path was taken.[25]

However, all these firms were reviewing their marketing and production strategies. Pilkington had been attempting to rationalise its distribution structure since the war.[26] ICI in 1950 'stood at a critical point . . . Behind . . . lay . . . the age of the great cartels . . . Ahead lay expansion on a scale still not fully grasped, although it was already apparent that great risks would go hand-in-hand with great opportunities'. By the 1950s ICI, in a search for new areas of development, was considering ways of encouraging other producers to break ICI's monopoly of some bulk products such as alkali, chlorine and nitrogen. In early 1956 ICI agreed with Unilever to change their methods of giving quantitative rebates on soda-ash to avoid charges of price discrimination.[27]

W.H. Smith in 1957 drew up plans for a quickened rate of expansion of modern, large shops, the streamlining of sales to allow for maximum bulk purchasing and the benefits of being a large buyer. A report commissioned by W.H. Smith and Son in 1960 on the effect of the Act, concluded that:

In those retail trades where Restrictive Practices and Resale Price Maintenance have been particularly subjected to attack, a growing number of responsible men have expressed the opinion that in certain fields the dangers of free market competition are outweighed by the retailer's increased scope for using his skill and initiative. Therefore, although Restrictive Practices and Resale Price Maintenance are thought in general to benefit the Company, their relaxation should offer welcome opportunities for increasing success, particularly in the field of merchandising.[28]

Similar relaxation of loyalty to domestic cartels was apparent elsewhere, as the retailing sector boomed, export markets expanded, and new products and techniques were developed. A number of firms adopted major expansion plans in the 1950s involving acquisitions, new manufacturing licences, and increased research.[29] The historian of Unilever argues that in detergents, for instance, agreements with other firms were impracticable for 'the reward for the breakaway was too big, too tempting'.[30] Courtaulds' reaction to the MRPC report on the Federation of Calico Printers was that it might prompt other sectors such as the yarn spinners to modify their practices, and 'any relaxation is more likely to help than to harm us'.[31]

Thus larger firms did not lobby to kill restrictive practices, but neither did they strive officiously to keep them alive.

The removal of the veto must also be understood in terms of the winds sweeping through British industry which were strongly international in character. External pressures tended generally towards multilateral trading, the ending of preferences, lowering of tariffs – the very measures under which British international and domestic cartelisation had flourished in the 1930s. Chief among these was imperial preferences. By 1962 the average preference on all trade with the Commonwealth was 6%.[32] The symbol of the change of circumstances was the convertibility of sterling in 1958.

The emphasis of American pressure had changed from pressure to ensure outlets for American exports[33] to pressure to ensure outlets for American capital. Pressure by the United States against international cartels was relaxed. This was partly due to recognition that the international agreements on cartels which she had been striving for were unlikely to work in the context of widely differing national policies, or might indeed work against the interests of her own overseas investors.[34] It was also due to pressure from the transnationals. The National Foreign Trade Council, the representative of American overseas investors, had already opposed those elements of the ITO referring to international cartels as a form of 'harassment and interference with American enterprises operating in foreign countries'.[35] Tangible pressure was exerted of a more long-term nature, and directed now primarily against domestic cartels. In 1952 Senators Moody and Benton secured amendments to the Mutual Security Act making defence support aid to Europe conditional on agreement being reached with recipient countries that counterpart funds of about £100m be used in local currencies on projects to improve productivity and to discourage monopolies and restrictive practices.[36]

The basis of this pressure was the renewed boom in American direct overseas investment, aided by a variety of US government measures geared to fostering economic growth abroad, encouraging exports while reducing the American dollar surplus. Even tough antitrust action contributed to increased overseas investment in place of the outlawed cartels. The book value of direct American manufacturing investment in Britain doubled between 1950 and 1956, and American transnational companies in Britain desired the end of restrictive practices within Britain as part of general measures to ease restrictions on the flow of American currency. After 1956 American investment expanded still further in the wake of sterling convertibility and the possibility of British entry into the European common market.[37]

Increasing levels of American investment in Britain coincided with, and stimulated, the reassertion of the tendency to merger and concentration of the early 1950s in Britain. The presence of American firms posed a particular threat to British firms and cartel agreements, and in some cases British firms merged in defence, as in cars and agricultural machinery. At the same time the British government encouraged American investment partly to provide competition with British firms, and as a route to breaking down domestic monopolies.[38]

The renewed boom in foreign investment by top British companies in the 1950s and 1960s further promoted a belief in free financial and trade markets.[39] In the 1930s participation in international cartels proceeded with a retreat from overseas investment by British companies:[40] conditions of increasing direct overseas investment put international cartels under pressure. British government policy on foreign transnationals was geared to protecting reciprocal expansion of British transnationals,[41] so the United States focus on domestic restrictions was one which concurred with developments within British business. Thus it was that although members of the Cabinet might consider some of the conditions attached to Mutual Aid 'blackmail' and 'quite incompatible with the policy of HMG', the Cabinet eventually agreed to provisions under which Britain committed nearly £100,000 to a variety of academic studies into monopolies and restrictive practices.[42]

Restrictive practices were also under review in the Economic and Social Council (ECOSOC) of the United Nations and in the OEEC.[43] The FBI response to a proposed convention by ECOSOC showed that international cartels were still, as in the 1940s, the form of restriction most dearly cherished by articulate British industrialists. When asked in 1952 for their opinions the FBI asserted that as restrictive business practices were no longer the main barrier to international trade the government should withdraw from the ad hoc discussions. It feared that if any publicity were given to international cartels this would impair industrial efficiency and prejudice public opinion, and no international organisation was needed. They were still adamantly opposed to ECOSOC's design in 1955.[44] In the world economy of the mid-1950s international cartels were still part of the armoury of many companies, and the industrialists had been touchy about the unwelcome publicity acquired through Monopolies Commission investigations of them.

Yet neither the United States nor the emerging international organisations made international cartels the focus of their attack. In the 1940s the bracketing of policy on domestic and international cartels had been a major cause of the weakness of domestic policy. However, by the 1950s the two issues were not so linked. Thus the external factor was more diffuse in one way – the United States was not the only factor in a process of re-orientation of the British business and, as in the 1940s, domestic policy could proceed more strongly when the threat of similar action being taken on international cartels was removed. With little external pressure for the removal of international cartels the main proponents of any weight for their inclusion in the legislation came from the Colonial Office, protecting underdeveloped countries in its purview from manufacturing cartels. The main defence of their exclusion came from the Foreign Office, defending the position most notably of the oil companies. The Board of Trade decided that as national interests could clash with international it would be highly embarrassing to have their terms either dragged through the courts or publicised.[45]

In summary, large firms had no need to fear for their export agreements, the role of the single monopolist was not to be open to such scrutiny as the cartellist, and their rights of individual RPM were assured. In addition domestic agreements which were becoming increasingly irksome in the expansionist conditions of the 1950s were to be forcibly broken up. It is not surprising therefore that Sir Frank Shires a Managing Director of Heinz Ltd, who became a member of the new Monopolies Commission, defended the 1956 Bill on the Grand Council of the FBI as 'an admirable measure'.[46] When the FBI wished to publish a statement on restrictive practices, in anticipation of the MRPC's Section 15 report, many members of the Grand Council argued that it was too negative and smacked of 'a guilty conscience'.[47]

Thus we may conclude this section by stating that the terms of the Act did indeed represent, as the Labour Party argued at the time, a charter for Big Business. Thorneycroft and his civil servants were well aware that this accusation could be thrown at the Bill, and one civil servant described the Board's position as 'very vulnerable'.[48] What the Bill proved most vulnerable to was not the Labour Party but the reaction within the Conservative Party and business circles. It is this that explains many of the other provisions of the Bill, as previous writers have recognised, and it is to the clash with the old order that the chapter now turns.

The clash with the old order

The government's failure to introduce policy on restrictive practices in the 1940s arose principally from the political problems posed by taking on powerful industrial interests, namely the trade associations. By the 1950s this political constraint was being undermined, as economic pressure in the domestic and world economy weakened cartels as economic organisations, and trade associations as political entities.

Trade associations in the 1950s were still a feature of British economic and political life. The PEP report of 1957 showed the growing role of trade associations in providing services to their members other than price-fixing: arranging exhibitions, joint advertising, sharing technical knowledge. Nevertheless it argued that 'There can be little doubt that at present price-fixing or discriminatory trading is the raison d'être of many associations, and if it is removed there will be little purpose in continuing their existence'.[49]

These organisations had detailed and continuous relationships with government departments and were accepted and welcomed by government as part of its system of intermediaries.[50] Thus cartel activities and trade associations were not dying forces in 1956 and the 1956 legislation involved attacking those practices which had held together a network of political and economic interest groups for over two decades. However, the end of controls ended also their direct economic use to government. During the war trade associations had derived their structural strength from their value in the administration of controls, by the mid-1950s no such considerations prevailed.[51]

But Government discussions of the Bill were permeated with a fear of confrontation with interests represented within the Conservative Party. Sir Lionel Heald, Conservative MP for Chertsey and Attorney-General until 1954, attacked his party during the debate on the Bill for 'undertaking what amounted to a serious interference with private enterprise and private industry'.[52] In the days of lobbying before and after the Bill was introduced into Parliament, Thorneycroft had to placate the Conservative back-benchers on many issues. The small retailer was seen as the backbone of Tory support and the clauses on RPM aroused particular disquiet, and Thorneycroft called on the Conservative research department to circulate two special papers explaining the government's proposals on RPM, in order to discourage government supporters from tabling any further amendments on Part 2 of the Bill.[53] His Parliamentary Secretary, Derek Walker-Smith, took the unusual step of a confidential meeting with the correspondent of the *Daily Telegraph* ahead of the other Lobby correspondents to allow him to do some 'forward thinking on the economic significance of the Bill'.[54]

Indeed, Thorneycroft had to act both cautiously and decisively in the face of this Party opposition. In January 1955 an irascible Churchill wrote to him concerned about unfavourable press reports of the use of private courts to enforce prices, and about the danger posed to the government by rising prices. Thorneycroft urged that the government wait for the report on Collective Boycott; he then forged ahead once it was clear what the recommendations of the Section 15 report would be. He urged the new Prime Minister, Anthony Eden, to let a small Ministerial Committee examine Conservative Party policy in the light of the report's recommendations.[55] Although appointed to consider a question which was 'inherently controversial', and one which, according to Thorneycroft, divided government supporters, the committee was then whipped into 'an early and resolute statement on the report'. This he did by constant reference to public opinion and, more importantly to the danger that delay would give the Labour party the initiative.[56] By forcing the government into an early declaration that such a wide range of practices was to be assumed to be against the public interest, Thorneycroft won a major tactical victory. This declaration in the Commons could only be retracted with immense difficulty.

Nevertheless, Thorneycroft had to compromise. He first proposed to implement the recommendations of the majority report, for prohibition of certain practices, arguing that compulsory registration was neither 'good sense or good politics', was a process of enquiry 'which would extend over decades', and which would leave the Party open to attack for having yielded to FBI pressure.[57] This first meeting of the Cabinet Committee on the Monopolies Commission report on 5 July, showed up divisions in response to Thorneycroft's radical position, but no decisions were taken. A meeting of the Conservative Party's Trade and Industry committee on 6 July was adjourned after 50 minutes 'when the main cleavage was clear and before tempers were raised'. A hurried item in Cabinet on 7 July agreed on steering a 'middle course' between the Majority and Minority reports.[58]

Thorneycroft thus submitted a Bill to register specified practices, but it was of a range of practices, not just those covered by the report on Collective Boycott. It was this combination of the Minority procedure, applied to a wider class of practice which 'combines, I believe, the best of both reports. It avoids on the one hand the apparent inertia of the minority and on the other the taint of criminality which the majority propose to attach to the practices of a large part of our industry and commerce'.[59] This policy went forward to Cabinet and was enunciated in Parliament on 13 July.[60]

Although defeated on his earlier proposals, Thorneycroft had secured the Cabinet's agreement to a divisive measure. In discussions before July 1955, Conservative Ministers, those who were 'more tender to the feelings of large industrial organisations' had been arguing against even the process of referral to a Monopolies Commission.[61] Thus there was a clash with sections of industry.

Yet with certain sections opposing further competition policy, the beneficiaries of the bill not obviously campaigning for it, and the diffusion of international pressures, the question still remains where the real force for policy initiatives arose.

Clearly, the appearance of the Section 15 report on Collective Boycott was important to the story, and is commonly cited as the cause of the 1956 Act, fuelling 'public opinion'.[62] But there was little correspondence between report and legislation. The registration procedure was essentially based on the Minority recommendations.[63] The ban on collective *enforcement* of resale prices, whether collectively or individually fixed, followed the line of the Majority, but they had said nothing about strengthening the powers of individual enforcement. On the type of tribunal or court the report made no recommendation, and the Board of Trade was acting on the advice of interested parties and its own predilections. Nor was the reduction in the membership of the Monopolies Commission, and its emasculated role any part of the Section 15 report.

While the recommendations of the report had little effect on the details of the government's legislation the report itself served to arouse some newspaper feeling. Thus its importance lay in its use to those forces in Britain at the time who wished for further developments in policy. In particular Thorneycroft used it to overcome opposition from within a government divided on the issue.

The role of 'public opinion'

The foregoing discussion points to the actual role of public opinion in the evolution of the Act: Thorneycroft used it in his battle with the 'diehards'. Just as during the 1940s British public opinion was deliberately aroused by American interests to further their campaign against international cartels, in 1955–6 it was skilfully wielded in favour of an Act whose provisions had little to offer 'the public'.

Fundamental, therefore, to understanding the forces behind the Act is the role of Peter Thorneycroft and the growing support for a Conservatism closely identified with nurturing free enterprise and competition. The reformulation of Conservative philosophy had been proceeding since the Second World War and was in part a reaction to nationalisation, controls and planning represented in Labour policies and a search for methods of regulation, like competition policy, which involved less detailed state intervention in the affairs of industry.[64]

Although Peter Thorneycroft represented a strand of economic liberalism that was still a minority view within the Party,[65] he had some solid support. Speaking of the opposition the Bill was encountering from the 'Trade Association Tories', Edward Boyle, Economic Secretary to the Treasury wrote:

the general bias of our economic policy ... aims at stimulating a spirit of greater efficiency and competition in industry and at exerting greater pressure on prices and profit margins. I feel very strongly that we should not go out of our way to protect less efficient firms, or to sanction restrictive practices simply because particular interests would suffer damage from their abolition.[66]

This came from a man who is in fact not to be identified with neo-liberal forces in the Conservative Party, and has been described as impatient of Robbins' and Hayek's unqualified admiration of market forces.[67] Indeed, many Conservatives were willing to go along with the new Bill because 'it is difficult to stand for free enterprise and leave such restrictions unchecked'.[68] The majority of Conservatives present at the Trade and Industry Committee meeting were similarly willing to support changes in policy for political reasons, and to 'show that we are really the party for Free Enterprise and opposed to Monopolies'.[69]

But the promotion of enterprise, efficiency and competition did not conflict with support for large firms. If anything, Conservatives were willing to support the Act to legitimise their activities. For many Conservatives the 'future of industry lay with the large concern'. In this context the Monopolies Commission was necessary 'as a ready means of satisfying the public that large-scale organisations did not necessarily work to their disadvantage'.[70] Little was done by the Conservatives to fulfil its pledge to support the small businessmen and there was considerable support for large firms as the key to efficiency, stability, the export trade and the development of technologically intensive industries.[71] Thus there was no contradiction between a Conservative Party which promoted competition policy and that which introduced the National Economic Development Council and the Cotton Industry Reorganisation Act.

It was this body of opinion within the Conservative Party which was most dynamic in pushing policy along, for 'public opinion' was, as ever, diffuse.

Any summary of 'public opinion' by the 1950s on the question of monopoly is almost impossible. It may be argued in general that anti-monopoly sentiment had lost its radical edge of the 1940s when recent memories of the 1930s, the link between international cartels and appeasement, the strength of the trade unions and the popularity of the Soviet Union contributed to an anti-capitalist spirit. By the 1950s there was disillusionment with the socialist experiment under Labour and specifically with nationalisation, together with a rising standard of living and the Cold War suspicion of Communists externally and internally.

'Public opinion' had also been treated since the war to a barrage of books and articles arguing the virtues of free enterprise and private property, and the beneficence of the large firm. Most evangelical were members of the Mont Pelerin Society, a group which disseminated, at an international level, the concept of a 'competitive order': in Germany Walter Eucken, who provided the ideological underpinnings of the German social-market economy, argued that this was a 'positive policy' unlike the principle of laissez-faire, and aimed 'at bringing the market form of complete competition into being'.[72] The Mont Pelerin Society's founding father was Friedrich Hayek; from Britain Lionel Robbins and John Jewkes attended the first meeting in April 1947.[73] Other vigorous defenders of private property and competition were the Institute of Economic Affairs (IEA) founded in 1955 'which acted explicitly' on Hayek's work, and the Aims of Industry whose self-proclaimed purpose was the defence of free enterprise – free, that was, of state interference.[74]

While these trends of thought were gathering pace their influence on public opinion should not be overstated. Even within the Conservative

Party, though Lionel Robbins consorted much with Conservative MPs, neo-Liberalism, though talked about increasingly had little impact on political programmes.[75]

The literature was sustained, though from very different ideological and theoretical standpoints, by the way the academic establishment was encouraged by American funds to write on restrictive practices. Although the works financed under Counterpart funds did not begin to appear until after the 1956 Act they indicate a trend. They were certainly numerous, including Duncan Burns' study of the structure of British industry, Alan Neale's study of American antitrust, the PEP study of trade associations and works on competition and monopoly in various industries by J.B. Jefferys, Ruth Cohen, Aubrey Silbertson, A.J. Brown, George Rainnie, G.C. Allen and B.S. Yamey.[76] Meanwhile the general thrust of the reports of the Monopolies Commission supported a faith in competition.

The faction fights within the Labour Party continue to make generalisations about opinion there on restrictive practices very difficult. The Labour Party was increasingly impressed by the theory of managerial capitalism which argued that the separation of ownership and control in the large corporation removed the central role of profit. The 'soulful corporation' was therefore actually less a thing to be feared than the traditional atomistically competitive small firm! But the hold of these ideas in the Labour Party was uneven. In a selection of *New Fabian Essays* published in 1952 Crosland was the most committed, Austen Albu was openly cynical, while Roy Jenkins pressed for further nationalisation to extend equality. Forceful resolutions against monopoly were passed at successive Party conferences in the 1950s.[77] A pamphlet by Richard Evely and a speech by Gaitskell proposed that the Commission be strengthened, 'vicious restrictive practices' like stop lists and boycotts be banned, all other agreements be registered, that competing private firms be established and there be action on price controls.[78] But meanwhile the Labour Party suffered certain weaknesses in claiming anti-monopoly policy for themselves. Much political support for Labour was rooted in areas reliant on the staple industries, which were usually cartelised, such as textiles. Thus Harold Wilson was not willing to endorse the report of the Monopolies Commission on the calico printers, a reflection of the views of the workforce in Lancashire.[79]

The rise of the 'Gaitskellites' combined with cynicism about challenging private industry and further nationalisation, prompted more emphasis on the merits of competitive private enterprise.[80] However, overall the position had changed but little since the 1940s. The one point on which Evely's proposals differed from those of the 1947 Labour and TUC Committee was in recommending the prohibition of stop lists and boycotts.[81] In 1957 Douglas Jay, Opposition spokesman on trade and industry remarked, in terms little different from Dalton in 1943, that 'where there is monopoly there ought to be public ownership, and where there is private ownership there ought to be competition'.[82]

Measured by the number of parliamentary questions, general feeling against monopolies and restrictive practices was mounting by 1955. This was the response to four factors. First, there was strong and sensationalist coverage by newspapers of the more scandalous private courts and uniform tendering revealed in MRPC reports. Newspaper reaction to the Section 15 report was also strong, but conditions revealed were somewhat less scandalous, and the differences of opinion within the Commission were played up. *The Times* found the Majority in too much of a hurry, and pushed the government to act on the Minority's recommendations. *The Economist* embraced the Majority proposals with glee as 'moderate and embryonic'. While giving no special mention to the report, the *News Chronicle* attacked the government's plans for legislation, and its failure to accept the Majority recommendations as 'a shameful defeat'.[83] Although newspapers were not homogeneous and cohesive, pressure to accept the majority Report was strong and accusations that Conservative MPs with business interests would try to prevent legislation were made freely.[84]

Secondly, the most important domestic economic problem of 1955 to 1957 was inflation.[85] This had its effect on the pace of policy. In early 1955, Churchill began to pester Thorneycroft on the question of the relationship between restrictive practices and monopoly because, as he said, 'the rise in prices is our Achilles' heel'.[86] The Press and the Labour Party quickly linked inflation and monopoly. The numbers of parliamentary questions rose dramatically in 1955, partly under the influence of Monopolies Commission reports, but also linking the question with inflation. While most economists diagnosed it as 'demand inflation' caused by excessive wage demands, some economists proposed also that Britain's experience of 'creeping inflation' was the long-run result of monopoly pricing, that is 'cost-inflation'.[87] It has therefore been suggested that the 1956 Act was a response to some of these views.[88]

Thirdly, the development of 'growth consciousness', born of comparisons between British and American and European productivity gaps and of Britain's slow rate of expansion of exports at a time of rapid expansion of world trade,[89] focussed some attention on restrictive practices: the reports of the Anglo–American Council on Productivity continued to appear in the 1950s with this line. Finally, the 1950s had seen a revival of the trend to merger and especially the takeover bid, with some spectacular cases in the property market.

All these elements served to create a general climate in 1955 which was used by Thorneycroft to push the Conservative Party into action. However it is clear that public concerns were not taken very seriously, nor that the issues were necessarily on the agenda when Thorneycroft introduced the Bill. Thorneycroft and his advisers were keen to stress that no anti-inflationary results could be expected from the Bill. Some price competition did break out after 1956, in some previously cartelised areas prices of some goods fell by up to 30%, but there is no evidence that the Act had any marked impact on the rate of inflation. Indeed while oligopolistic markets might account for higher prices, theory predicts that short-term anti-inflationary results of competition policy do not exist.[90] Moreover nothing was done to restrict single-firm monopolies.

Indeed on the question of inflation, growth and productivity the Conservative Party laid more blame at the door of trade unions and labour. The Act has been seen as 'coincidental' to these emerging problems,[91] but in fact leading Treasury officials and members of the Cabinet felt that restrictive labour practices were more objectionable, but that the government could not get at these without first starting on the employers.[92] The issue of tackling restrictive labour practices was raised in discussion in Cabinet in December 1955, in a way reminiscent of objections by Conservative Ministers under the Coalition to Dalton's Bill. The matter was referred to the Economic Policy Committee (EPC), and a paper by Walter Monckton, Minister of Labour, argued that the forthcoming Restrictive Trade Practices Bill 'will bring the subject of restrictive labour practices to the forefront of discussion'.[93] The EPC decided against including restrictive labour practices in the Bill on the grounds that the two forms of practice were not strictly analogous: trade union practices were not secret, they were agreements reconciling the opposing interests of employers and employees, not the embodiment of common interests, and a system of judicial enforcement against such practices was 'impossible to envisage'. Nevertheless the EPC, in a decision later endorsed by Cabinet, agreed to ask the Minister of Labour to raise the issue on the National Joint Advisory Council and to appoint a committee of officials on restrictive labour practices. This committee duly reported in 1959.[94] In this scenario the Restrictive Trade Practices Act was not coincidental but the necessary precursor to policies focussing on union behaviour.

In fact the evidence on the importance of restrictive labour practices in the British economy continued to be ambiguous. A survey of management views of labour by the business magazine *Future* in 1950 asked respondents 'Do you find TU practices or trade customs restrict output or keep up costs?'. 81% replied that trade unions practices 'do not trouble us' and 86% that trade customs 'do not trouble us'. Larger firms and firms in engineering recorded rather more trouble, but the figures do not indicate a large problem. The Ministry of Labour's own internal enquiry, published in 1959 concluded that 'some encouragement can be derived from the results of its inquiry'. Industries covering 29% of civilian employees reported 'no problems in regard to the efficient use of manpower', industries covering 39% had, or were setting up, joint machinery to deal with problems, with one industry – engineering – facing particular unspecified 'difficulties'. Industries where the enquiry expressed some concern, mainly because negotiating machinery appeared to have broken down, covered about 7% of civilian employment.[95]

Thus in spite of ambiguous official evidence the attack on restrictive business practices, together with increased attention on inflation and the discernible if, as yet, mild resurgence of free market philosophy, opened the way for an attack on the labour movement. Indeed, as Monckton said when introducing the question on the EPC 'from the purely economic viewpoint most of the negotiated terms and conditions of employment are restrictive practices'.[96] Early reports by the Council on Prices, Productivity and Incomes, established in 1959, were openly hostile to trade union wage claims.[97] At the time the analogy between restrictive labour and business practices was rejected in government as 'false', and the way forward was seen in improved industrial relations and management. Nevertheless, viewed from the standpoint of the 1990s the writing is quite legibly on the wall.

Special pleading

The Act may have represented a victory against the 'trade association Tories' and the 'diehards' in industry who favoured protectionism and restrictionism, but it was very limited, as an account of the special pleading which went on will demonstrate. The Act was uniquely vulnerable to special pleading, containing so many exceptions, and gateways. According to Dame Elizabeth Ackroyd, an Under Secretary in 1956, most of the Act's gateways reflect special pleading by one section of business or another.[98] Indeed, this special pleading was positively encouraged to win sections of industry to the main principles of the Bill. Anthony Barber MP, at a meeting of the Doncaster Chamber of Commerce in March 1956, told the businessmen there that, while there was no possibility of revising certain general principles, if good evidence was submitted, 'certain clauses which may cause hardship will be reconsidered'.[99] Lobbying proceeded carefully, as the FBI was fearful of accusations that the Conservative Party was influenced by it. Thorneycroft colluded with the FBI in the adoption of this ruse.[100]

Many areas of the Bill's provisions serve as examples of industry successfully shaping the legislation; indeed, as argued above, their complaints about the old procedure were a major factor in the introduction of new legislation in the first place, while the process of registration was in conformity with the views, for instance of the FBI, who preferred this to the alarming decisions of the Monopolies Commission.[101]

A second area where industry scored some success was in shaping the 'justiciable issue', that is the legal points on which the courts were to judge practices. The range of agreements which could get through depended crucially on how this was defined, and it therefore became the crux of the Bill, and the focus of much 'peak' association lobbying.[102] For instance one 'gateway' proposed by the FBI was for industry to show that a practice prevented 'the reduction of wasteful fluctuation in trade and employment', potentially a catch-all justification. However, while some Conservatives, like Manningham-Buller, wanted such wide exemptions to protect the small and efficient producer, the line that the definition should be as narrow as possible (espoused by Thorneycroft and Boyle) prevailed as a general rule.[103] Nevertheless, by February 1956 the Grand Council of the FBI was congratulating itself on its 'perceptible influence' on the Bill: its President, W.H. Pilkington, argued that the Bill 'should provide a fair and workable measure which would make it possible for those engaged in those practices to make out a complete case in justification for what they did'.[104] In government production departments the seven proposed 'gateways' caused consternation. A meeting of Under-Secretaries in December 1955 felt that 'industries would be able to put up a colourable defence of their restrictive practices', and that the government and Thorneycroft personally would be roundly attacked by magazines like *The Economist* who were expecting much and might feel that 'the Bill might prove too weak for the job'. The meeting therefore believed that the new Bill could only be vindicated by the way the Courts applied the criteria and interpreted the general lines of the Act.[105]

Finally, one important group which lobbied hard to protect itself from the Bill were the iron and steel manufacturers. In early 1956 the question of whether or not to include iron and steel in the new Bill was often before Cabinet and its committees. The extent of pressure that was then applied is indicated by the fact that, during the progress of the Bill through Parliament, from February to May 1956, the Cabinet discussed the Bill only in relation to the question of the iron and steel industry.[106]

The Iron and Steel Board (ISB) was the supervisory body set up under the Iron and Steel Act of 1953, enjoined to promote efficient supply 'under competitive conditions'. Part of this was to review restrictive arrangements, and make decisions on the public interest in conjunction with the relevant Minister and Parliament. The debate on the privatisation of steel in 1953 had made clear also that the industry would be subject to enquiry by the Monopolies Commission.[107] While the Restrictive Trade Practices Bill was still being drafted the Chairman of the ISB, Sir Archibald Forbes, wrote to Thorneycroft asking that the industry be excluded from the scope of the new tribunal, and that instead the ISB be granted powers of adjudication. If not, Forbes said, 'the position of the Board in relation to the industry which they were set up to supervise would ... be fatally undermined'.[108] Thorneycroft was persuaded at the Cabinet committee that 'it would be an embarrassment if the Bill were put through in the teeth of the ISB' and thus a compromise was reached in Cabinet: the industry would definitely be included but the Board of Trade undertook that agreements in the industry would not be called up for registration until the ISB's own review of restrictive practices had been completed and considered by the Board of Trade.[109]

But in March 1956 the ISB had gained the support of the Iron and Steel Holdings and Realisation Agency, the body managing the re-sale of iron and steel companies to private hands. They argued that unless a special 'Industry Fund Agreement', which regulated the prices of foreign and domestic iron ore and of scrap and pig iron, were made exempt the process of privatisation would be jeopardised. Their position was supported by the Bank of England and the Treasury, the latter especially afraid that, with all the uncertainty over the future of the Agreement, the City might withdraw its co-operation entirely and the re-nationalisation programme would be in ruins.[110]

The battle raged between the Treasury and the Board of Trade. Thorneycroft wrote to Eden that, 'If we are to argue that the existence of the judicial procedure proposed under the Bill renders a steel firm unsaleable, I find it difficult to understand how we can possibly justify the application of such a procedure to the rest of industry'. In equally apocalyptic terms Edward Bridges, Permanent Secretary to the Treasury, told the Chancellor, 'the present policy in regard to the Restrictive Trade Practices Bill is going to shipwreck Government policy on denationalising steel'.[111]

A compromise was reached in March putting the Industry Fund Agreement on a statutory basis, by amending the Iron and Steel Act of 1953, and therefore outside the scope of the Bill. But the ISB was still unhappy, feeling that if agreements were registrable doubt would be cast on the possibility of selling remaining companies. Thorneycroft gave way again and agreed that a specific exemption from registration for the Industry Fund arrangements should be made in the Bill. This was still not enough, and when Thorneycroft's compromise was discussed in Cabinet the Chancellor demanded that the amendment cover not only the Industry Fund Agreement but any other agreement approved by the ISB under statutory authority. Thorneycroft remarked that this meant the complete exclusion of iron and steel from the Bill. But Eden accepted the Chancellor's argument and the Cabinet endorsed his position.[112]

The Board of Trade was thus forced to make an amendment to the Bill, at the Lords Committee stage, excluding the Industry Fund Agreements and a related agreement for the common importation of iron ore. However, this exclusion was made dependent on the approval of both the ISB and the Board of Trade; indeed, arguing for the amendment the Lord Chancellor assured the Lords that this provided a public safeguard for the special treatment of iron and steel. Again the Board was forced to submit to the pressure from the ISB, the City, still doubtful about de-nationalisation and the Treasury: it had to amend its own amendment to remove the need for the Board of Trade to approve exclusion of iron and steel arrangements from the Bill.[113]

Moreover, all these moves were made surreptitiously: the government was especially concerned that it would not have to mention that such exclusions were necessary to secure the success of their de-nationalisation programme. As G.H. Andrew wrote of the final amendment to the amendment:

we do not think that anybody in the House of Lords is aware of the significance of these changes.... If we can take the clause into the House of Commons as an amendment to deal with a particular difficulty (Section 11 of the Iron and Steel Act, and all that), we shall have a better chance of getting it through smoothly than if we expose that there is a point of substance in this question of approvals.[114]

Commitment to privatisation and the rights of private property, proved then, as now, greater than commitment to competition, the process which was supposed to justify private ownership. The story of competition, far from being the heroic process liberal writers would have us believe, can be sordid in the extreme.

Conclusions

Thus while the Act involved confrontation with one form of business organisation it was not only a compromise but an identification with the interests of the large firm. The act had the potential, if not directly to strengthen the hand of the larger firm, then at least to weaken that of the smaller. It also drew public attention away from the activities of the larger firms while protecting them from accusations that their interests were being served by the legislation.

In one important way sections of business were able to shape the terms of their own regulation in the 1956 Restrictive Trade Practices Act – the ending of the old Monopolies Commission, against which they had campaigned long and hard. It was the end of the tribunal and the introduction of the judicial procedure which was the main positive input by organised industry into the Bill. Nor was the move from sporadic enquiry to registration totally at odds with industry's, or the FBI's own ideas for how policy should develop. Indeed, given the hostility to the Commission, registration began to appear as an attractive alternative.

However, this conclusion must be modified by our hindsight of the actual consequences of the Bill, for it is not at all clear that the end of a wide range of restrictions was what the FBI and others had in mind when they lobbied for their concept of regulation. Thus the idea that any section of business in Britain actually moulded regulation according to their heart's desire does not accord with experience. Instead it seems from circumstantial evidence that a wily devotee of competition, Peter Thorneycroft, used the business-men's own programme against them. In this he was to be helped by the interpretation of the law by the Restrictive Practices Court in later years.

The origins of the 1956 Act again show that public opinion was an important general factor in the evolution of policy, but had little specific influence. Many newspapers, even sections of the Labour movement called for outright prohibition and this proposal was ignored, although again the indirect method of registration and enquiry was possibly to prove more effective, given industrial attitudes. Of most importance in this context was the revival within the Conservative Party of economic liberalism, which went together with a tenderness for the cause of the large firm. It may be clearly stated that a large element in this Conservative concern was the desire to justify and legitimise a form of capitalism which increasingly tended towards oligopoly and the dominance in the economy of large firms, with an increasing transnational character.

Finally, the United States proved in this period to be less of a direct influence in the timing and nature of legislation. Indeed it was precisely because international arrangements were excluded from legislation that at least some industrial hostility to the idea of registration was neutralised.

Of most importance in explaining why a measure arousing overwhelming industrial opposition in the 1940s should get through with relatively little controversy is the lifting of the business veto. This in itself was the result of developments in the domestic and international economy. Domestic cartels in Britain had been primarily a response to world trade recession, to limited and sectional economic growth in Britain, and to the peculiar conditions of a period of government controls in the 1940s. The expansion of world trade, the lifting of the many autarkical economic policies of the 1930s and 1940s, exposed Britain to foreign competition and made it both less attractive and less possible to organise effective price cartels. Thus it may be argued that the government was putting its shoulder against a partly-open door.

Finally, we may return to some of the themes developed in chapter 4. Although policy discussions do not reveal the same sense of choosing routes at an economic crossroads, recent interpretations of the 1950s indicate that important changes were afoot. In particular the 1950s is proving important in the development of the large, transnational firm, interested in breaking down trade barriers, loosening domestic restrictionism, a move spearheaded by those based in the United States, and encouraged by the trend of European discussions. As predicted at the end of chapter 4, we find that the triumph of the philosophy of the market and competition was indeed predicated on the re-establishment of a liberal world trading order, while heralding, although only faintly at the time, a new attack on the 'restrictions' on the free market deemed to be operated by trade unions.

8 Resale price maintenance

The evolution of competition policy outlined so far has indicated that the *general* regulation of monopoly became a part of British law in the teeth of general business opposition and the initial Act of 1948 was due in no small part to external pressure. Nor did any identifiable business group actively campaign *for* the 1956 Act, although it has been shown that the Act favoured sections of business against others, and businessmen lobbied against the administrative tribunal and for a judicial review of their practices. It would be false, however, to leave the impression that British antitrust policy evolved without successful pressure by sections of business for regulation. The development of resale price maintenance (RPM) legislation indicates that home-grown demands for regulation existed and that, in the relative absence of overseas influence, the pace and form of competition policy was primarily determined by the changing business strategies of large concerns in manufacturing and retailing.

The most detailed account of the history of policy on RPM, from the report on Fixed Retail Prices by the Standing Committee on Trusts in 1920 to the 1964 Resale Prices Act has been provided by Basil Yamey. His useful account nevertheless falls into the same trap as the histories of competition policy in general, and views the evolution of legislation as the response to public opinion and changes in moods and attitudes. He does, however, accept that the public mood will fluctuate, for instance being more aroused against RPM in times of inflation and when governments are pursuing prices and incomes policies.[1] His account traces the growing critical approach of a series of enquiries into RPM in Britain, and sees government policy as a reasonable response, on the whole, to the tenor of their reports. In fact, it will be argued here that the strongest representative of public opinion on retailing was arguably the Co-operative Societies, supported by the Labour Party – in government and opposition. Their views against RPM were well in advance of government committees. Again it was not public, but the balance of business opinion which provides the clue to the nature and timing of legislation in this specific area.

The progression of policy

Between 1920 and 1964 RPM was the subject of four major enquiries and figured in many others into monopoly and restrictionism in particular trades. Opinions expressed in these committees grew increasingly hostile to collective RPM. The two earliest committees to enquire into RPM were the enquiry into fixed retail prices by the Standing Committee on Trusts in 1920, and the Greene Committee on Restraint of Trade appointed by the Chancellor of the Exchequer in 1930. Both were broadly sympathetic to the general system of price maintenance.[2]

The former argued that both collective and individual RPM checked inflation in times of scarcity, while in times of surplus it ensured the survival of all sections of the trade. These conclusions were questioned by one member, John Hilton, who argued that, given the limited ground surveyed, such a conclusion had little justification. He also condemned boycotts against alleged 'price-cutters' like the Co-ops. Nothing further was done at this time, although this report, like many others by the Committee on Trusts, recommended some tribunal to check the prices at which goods were originally put on the market.

It was the Co-op which secured that the 1930 Committee on Restraint of Trade consider the practice of withholding supplies from alleged price-cutters. As RPM, especially in branded durable consumer goods, spread in the 1930s, so did the practice of 'boycotting', the Co-op on the basis that the dividend was a form of price-cutting. The Greene Committee on Restraint of Trade was set up to consider the practice of withholding supplies from alleged price-cutters in response to the Co-op's attack on the practices of the PATA.[3] The report of the committee was, however, favourable to RPM as a whole. While it saw no justification for the Co-op boycott, the report again argued against any legal prohibition of refusal to supply, as the Co-operative Congress had proposed in its evidence, on the basis that this would interfere with the freedom to contract. Like the report on Fixed Retail Prices, however, the Greene Committee added the rider that the question of RPM impinged on wider issues of trusts and monopolies and public policy on these should be examined. The tone of the report, the financial crisis of September 1931 and the fall of the Labour government rendered this initiative abortive, and the incident merely served to arouse the ire of private trade against the Co-op still more. A Press campaign in 1932 was successful in making the Co-operative surplus liable for taxation as profits in the 1933 Finance Act, taking £1.25 million from the Co-ops in tax.[4]

Two other initiatives were made, both under Labour governments, to control prices through the use of consumer watchdogs. These were the

Food Council set up in 1925 and a Consumers' Council in 1930 which allowed the Board of Trade to regulate the prices of a variety of goods.[5] However, neither initiative flourished in the 1930s.

These hesitant beginnings in the inter-war period were superseded in the 1940s by a flurry of initiatives, enquiries and interest in the problems of retailing, distribution and the Co-ops. Of great importance in supplying data were the Board of Trade's Committees into the Retail Trade during the war, set up to consider the impact of concentration, rationing and licensing schemes on the distributive structure, and the Census of Distribution taken in 1950.[6]

The Labour governments of 1945 to 1951 made the future of distribution its special interest. Three ad hoc committees of enquiry into monopoly had as their main focus RPM, namely those on radio valves, conducted by the Central Price Regulation Committee, on building materials, conducted by the Ministry of Works, and on RPM – the Lloyd Jacob Committee. The latter prompted the Labour government's White Paper to abolish all RPM.[7] In addition the Labour Party established an internal sub-committee of its Home Policy Committee to devise policy on distribution – the source of the recommendations later included in the 1949 programme for the nationalisation of sugar refining and meat wholesaling. A Cabinet committee was established in April 1950 to look at ways of simplifying distribution and marketing, including a consideration of RPM with a view to reducing the general level of retail prices.[8]

Certainly by the 1940s more critical voices were prominent. The Simon Committee on building materials criticised the widespread restrictive practices for raising prices, inflating gross and net distributive margins, and preventing the introduction of more efficient methods of distribution while encouraging an over-elaboration of services and therefore a waste of manpower.[9] It recommended the elimination of all restrictive practices in the industry in the long term and in the short term government control of distributors' margins. Little was done, however, beyond proceeding with the Monopolies and Restrictive Practices Act and referring many items used in the building trade to the Commission. However, in cement and radio valves the reports were careful to absolve the firms concerned of profiteering, although by dubious calculations, which showed wide variations of profits between firms or between types of product.[10]

The most important and influential of reports on RPM was that by the Lloyd Jacob Committee, published in 1949. It generally favoured price competition and recommended that collective RPM be made illegal. It also pursued the line taken by the Greene Committee that the individual manufacturer had the legal right to stipulate the conditions under which his goods were sold and therefore wanted individual RPM permitted. The

Labour government decided to take action on the report. After abortive negotiations with retailers and manufacturers for voluntary acquiescence to the report's recommendations, Harold Wilson introduced the White Paper of 1951 promising to ban all forms of RPM. As chapter 6 has indicated these plans foundered even before the Conservative Party came to power. Thus the 1951 White Paper proposals were only implemented in 1956 when collective RPM was banned and 1964 when the ban was extended to individual price maintenance.

Yamey argues that the development of policy on individually enforced RPM was the response to the tenor of the Monopolies Commission reports which touched on RPM which 'gave a further push in the direction of splitting into two halves the problem of policy towards RPM'.[11] Those which addressed RPM were strongly critical of collective, but tolerant of individual enforcement. The exception was the case of tyres where the Commission believed that the major manufacturers could secure compliance with their prices without collective measures and the abolition of collective RPM would do little to ensure price competition in sales to the public.[12] Thus the 1956 Act can again appear as the logical progression from Lloyd Jacob through the reports of the Commission, backed by the report on Collective Discrimination which argued strongly against methods of collective enforcement, recommending prohibition of the practices with provision for exemptions.

Once collective enforcement was banned, the argument continues, enquiries grew hostile to individual enforcement and to the system of RPM in general. Two out of the three enquiries of the reconstituted Monopolies Commission which looked at RPM between 1957 and 1964 condemned RPM as against the public interest.[13] The judgement by the Restrictive Practices Court upholding the Net Book Agreement was done on the basis that 'Books are different', so further supporting the view that enquiries were moving against RPM. Finally two reports of the Council on Prices and Productivity and Incomes in 1958 and 1959 recommended that RPM be reconsidered, the Committee on Consumer Protection and the Consumer Council, set up in December 1963, said the end of RPM would benefit consumers and the National Economic Development Council welcomed the Bill in 1964 on the grounds that it should increase efficiency in distribution. All this supports the view that government policy responded to 'a growing volume of criticism' and 'public sentiment'.[14]

However, there are two main arguments against this interpretation. First, all that is traced here is the opinion of enquiries and no direct correlation can be made between that and public opinion. Indeed, Co-op pressure for the complete abolition of RPM was strong since the inter-war period. Secondly, the timing of legislation corresponds more closely to changes in business strategies. It is to these two issues that the chapter now turns.

The Co-operative Societies

The main protagonist against RPM throughout the twentieth century was the Co-operative Movement. Indeed, the role of the Co-op in the story of the abolition of RPM is rarely mentioned in existing accounts, which continue to demonstrate the same dismissive approach to the Co-ops as Alfred Marshall, who told Beatrice Potter, when she proposed to undertake her study of the Co-operative Movement (a work which became a classic) not to bother with such 'half-baked nonsense'.[15]

Yet the Co-operative Party and Societies played a major role in each enquiry and initiative – whether abortive or not. It prompted the two inter-war enquiries and the Lloyd Jacob Committee was set up in part to safeguard the Co-op against increasing attempts to undermine the divi-dend. In 1951 Co-operative pressure played some role in persuading the Labour Party to propose the abolition of all forms of RPM. The Co-op did not like the 1956 Act, for reasons described in chapter 7, but the 1964 Act again sprang from their initiative. In 1963 John Stonehouse, a Co-operative Party-sponsored MP, won a place in the ballot for a Private Member's Bill and was persuaded by the Co-operative Party to submit a Bill to outlaw all RPM. His Bill had its first Reading on 12 December 1963, and the Second Reading was due to take place on 17 January 1964. On 15 January 1964 Edward Heath, Minister of Trade and Industry, announced the govern-ment would be introducing its own measure to outlaw individual fixing and enforcement of resale prices, a coincidence which strongly suggests that Stonehouse's motion acted as a catalyst in government decisions.[16] This sequence of events is either overlooked or the role of the Co-op ignored. A recent IEA pamphlet, for instance, suggests that an IEA pamphlet of 1960 by Basil Yamey played the key role in encouraging Heath's move.[17]

The role of the Co-op in the mid twentieth century coincided with a peak in its market shares and membership. Its share of all retail sales was around 11% in the 1950s, reaching a peak in 1957 of 11.9% from when it began to decline quite rapidly, to 9.2% by 1966.[18] In 1950 the Co-operative Societies represented 21.3% of food sales, and were at this point larger than the multiples shops who took a 19.5% share. In addition the Co-operative Wholesale Society owned and operated over 200 factories in 1958, and the 1950s saw a dramatic growth in its banking and insurance services. Its membership also stood at a peak – being 1.7 m in 1900, 4.5 m in 1930, 8.6 m in 1940 and 12.5 m by 1958. Again this growth was to stop in the 1960s. The Co-operative Party, formed in 1917, had 23 MPs in 1945 – its peak – but still maintained between 16 and 19 in elections in the 1950s and 1960s.[19]

The Co-operative Movement could therefore claim to be a strong and representative consumers' group. It was, moreover, an efficient business concern – introducing self-service stores well before the private sector, producing its own brands when it could not get goods which they were refused, and owning large-scale production sites, for instance in flour-milling. If imitation is the sincerest form of flattery, then its business opponents were impressed by the Co-op's methods. Not only did multiple stores gradually introduce self-service and own brand production, often in response to RPM and boycotts, some of them even tried to introduce a form of dividend buying.[20]

While the Co-operative movement may have been at the peak of its powers in the 1940s and 1950s it carried with it two decisive weaknesses. These were the dedicated opposition and hostility from private retailers, some manufacturers, right-wing newspapers and Conservative governments to Co-operation and its unhappy relationship with the Labour Party and the Trade Unions.

Business and Conservative opposition was based partly on hostility to Co-operation and common ownership as a competing *principle* to Competition and private property, and partly on hostility to the Co-operative stores as a competing *interest*. It was the latter which prompted the many campaigns throughout the century to clip the Co-op's wings. Private traders were eventually successful in ensuring that the Co-operative trading surplus was treated as profit and thus liable to profit tax. The last move in this process came in 1946 when the Labour government included the Co-op's undistributed surplus in its new Profits Tax.[21] In addition retailers and some manufacturers argued that the dividend represented a form of price-cutting and so refused to supply Co-operative stores with their price-maintained goods. This particularly affected the ability of the Co-op to expand into the new consumer goods and may have been responsible for the Co-op's lagging growth in the inter-war period when it was refused bikes, electrical goods, books and stationery and chemists' goods. In the post-war period the Co-op identified the servicing of motorists as an area of expansion and planned to set up petrol stations and roadside cafes. The petrol companies refused to supply and got the backing of the Ministry of Fuel and Power, an incident which prompted Cripps to propose special defence regulations.[22] Indeed, sympathetic histories of the Co-op reviewing the attitude of businessmen, the Press and Conservative governments to the Co-op have seen in their attacks on the surplus and the dividend a part of the 'unconcealed endeavours of Capitalism to restrict the growth of Co-operation'.[23]

Given this hostility, the Co-op was even more disturbed by the nonchalant attitude of the Labour Party towards the Co-operative movement. The Co-op's relationship with the Labour governments of 1945 to 1951 was particularly unhappy. Labour Ministers, they felt, displayed studied indifference to Co-operative views, for instance in excluding the Co-op from the Economic Planning Board on the basis that the Co-op was a 'special interest'. Indeed, in spite of electoral agreements, the Co-op found itelf at a distinct disadvantage with the Labour government: for instance the Co-op felt that the views of the National Farmers' Union carried more weight than theirs on the issue of agricultural marketing.[24] More important, and deeper, was the divide between the Co-op Party and the Labour Party over the progress to socialism on the broad level. The Co-operatives, by the 1950s proposed a 'consumer approach to monopolies'. To widen the sphere of co-operation as the form of common ownership was preferable to nationalisation as it offered 'better democratic control and the more equitable distribution of surpluses'. Moreover a government could as easily de-nationalise as nationalise, so a widening sphere of co-operative enterprises, including agriculture and housing was a safer programme as a solution to monopoly.[25]

These divisions within the labour movement came out strongly in policies formulated in the late 1940s on retailing. Labour research papers of the 1940s focused on the effects of RPM on consumer prices and the use of manpower. Although average retail margins had come down during the war, they were still viewed as unnecessarily high. The cotton working party report of 1946 cited a child's cotton dress retailing at 12/5½d, of which wholesale and retailing charges represented 5/3½d.[26] The prevalence of $33\frac{1}{3}$% retail margins given by manufacturers prompted one member of the Lloyd Jacob Committee to ask whether the figure 'came over with the Conqueror'.[27] In fact, the large department stores were able to claim still higher margins from the manufacturer. There was also some unanimity among economists that fixed and irreducible retail margins maintained the small, inefficient shop, encouraged new entrants into retailing, and both tendencies absorbed unwarranted amounts of labour.[28] By 1950, although productivity in retailing in Britain was higher than elsewhere in Europe, smaller retail units used a disproportionate amount of manpower: 54% of retail units were responsible for 14% of turnover but 24% of total manpower.[29] Labour researchers proposed various remedies. On the one hand state intervention was discussed, ranging from price controls and licensing of retail outlets to the nationalisation of wholesaling. On the other hand, plans to increase competition through the prohibition of price-fixing were put forward.[30] As the Labour Party eschewed further nationalisation and showed little sympathy with the extension of Co-operation, the main line pursued by the Labour government was the abolition of price maintenance.[31]

This was a line which coincided with one demand by the Co-op but which clashed with that of USDAW, supported by the TUC. The fear of the unions was that the end of RPM could create unemployment among shopworkers and, by increasing competitive pressures on small shop-keepers, worsen general conditions of work. USDAW and the TUC therefore favoured the abolition of collective enforcement to reduce the costs of distribution, but that the individual manufacturer should have the right, enforceable through the courts if need be, to prescribe resale prices for their products. They added that special provision should be made for the Co-op to ensure that the dividend was not seen as a form of price-cutting. Finally, they supported individual RPM only with the safeguard of a national pricing authority.[32]

The absence of Trade Union support for complete abolition of RPM in 1951 was a weakness for the Labour government when deciding on a response to the Lloyd Jacob Report. In mid-1950, Wilson and the Cabinet Committee on Distribution decided that the full backing of the TUC for complete abolition should first be sought. A meeting with the Co-op and USDAW shortly after the White Paper was published resolved the issue in favour of the Co-op and complete abolition of RPM. But USDAW remained bitter and opposed to the position, and the unions' attitude must have weakened Labour resolve in part.[33] Nevertheless there was consensus from the late 1940s to ban collective enforcement, as well as practices like boycotts and exclusive dealing especially as operated against the Co-ops. While the division on individual enforcement was important, trade union support for it was hedged around with provisions which show a clear acceptance of the dangers of RPM generally.

The point is, therefore, that public opinion, at least as expressed through the Labour Party, the TUC and the Co-op did not need educating on the dangers of RPM, and substantial sections, and certainly those most representative of consumer interests, wanted a change of policy much earlier than government committees of enquiry. On the other hand representatives of consumer opinion, especially of housewives, had a very different view, namely a clear appreciation of the uniform products and prices offered through branding and RPM and the consequent reduction of shopping.[34]

Nevertheless this degree of consensus among sections of the Labour Party was shared by many civil servants. Both at the Board of Trade and elsewhere there was a marked antipathy to restrictions in distribution. Alix Kilroy, for instance, was shocked at the attitude of officials at the Ministry of Fuel and Power over the Co-op dividend. She had also been prepared, as chairman of the Official Committee on Supervisory Boards, to take a stronger line on agricultural marketing boards than she was over restrictions in domestic manufacturing industry.[35]

The more decisive approach of the Board of Trade officials on this issue should not be exaggerated, and Robert Hall bemoaned their over-cautious attitude.[36] Nevertheless civil servants saw a special case in distribution, where the protection of the inefficient directly affected the public consumer, and had absolutely no place in the sellers' market of the post-war period. However, their willingness to act was curtailed by concern about the likely reaction from sections of the trade. Hence the evolution of policy was dependent on changes in business opinion, reflecting the changing balance of forces within the industrial structure.

Private retailers

To understand the evolution of business feeling on RPM it is necessary to return to themes outlined in chapter 2 and examine in greater detail changes in the structure of the retail trades. It was shown that the growth of RPM since the late nineteenth century was closely tied up with the threat to small retailers of the growth of multiples, coupled with the manufacturers' need to maintain prices and secure outlets for their produce against competing firms. The growth of branding and mass production of consumer goods made RPM a possibility.

Thus of particular importance in the business struggle over the future of RPM was the growth of the large retailer – namely the Co-ops, the multiple retailers of single commodities, the 'variety chain stores' like Marks and Spencer, and the department stores. These accounted for 18–23% of total retail sales in 1920, 26–36% in 1939 and between 32 and 38% by 1950. Mergers and amalgamations in the inter-war years brought an increase in the number of branches operated in each multiple shop organisation, and a shift to the very large chain stores with 1,000-plus branches. The most marked growth was in the development of the chain stores, both those selling a wide range of goods and those concentrating on shoes, or clothing. They made particular advances against the Co-ops in boots and shoes, men's wear, clothing generally and in chemists' and photographic goods, accounting in 1950 for 60.3%, 39.3%, 33.8% and 34.5% of all retail sales respectively in those areas. While these shops shifted into some new product areas, their share of electrical consumer goods, as well as radios and sewing machines lagged at a 13.9% share, but nevertheless better than the Co-ops' which stood at 0.5% in 1950.[37] Table 8.1 shows the relative strengths of the sectors of retailing by 1960 and how well advanced mass-retailing was in Britain compared with Western Europe. However, smaller retailers still controlled the major share of retail sales. They were well-organised, in their associations, in the super-associations which became an important part of Britain's cartel system in the 1940s, and in political structures. The Fair Trading Congress was established in 1930 in response to the Greene Committee to unite manufacturers' and dealers' associations against 'the menace which sought to destroy price maintenance by legislation'.[38]

The significance of RPM in the competitive struggle between all these different forms of retailing stores – between large and small, between Co-ops and multiples, as well as between retailers and manufacturers – has been a matter of debate. According to Jefferys the large-scale retailers sought complete freedom over their buying, selling and pricing policies, seeking to use their advantages of size in bulk-buying and storage, in access to finance and hence to careful positioning in high streets, and investment in store layout and display, to appeal to the still-widening working class market. In contrast the large manufacturers sought to control the marketing of their products, to ensure that pricing by retailers did not affect their market share against competing producers, especially through 'loss-leaders'. Thus Jefferys argued that large-scale retailing made headway first in areas where their suppliers were a large number of competing firms – producers of mainly unbranded and unadvertised goods, especially of food, hardware and furniture, or in areas where integration of production and distribution was possible such as bread and men's clothing. They notably failed in products which were nationally-advertised, branded and price-maintained – such as tobacco, confectionery, tinned foods and electrical goods.[39]

The view that RPM militated against economies in retailing was certainly the more popular, but some have argued to the contrary. Grether argued that, in spite of RPM, great strides were made in chain store growth in boots and shoes and points to the growth of Boots Ltd in spite of the strong RPM scheme by the notorious PATA.[40] Andrews and Friday took issue with Yamey in 1960 who had guesstimated savings to consumers of £180m if RPM were completely abolished. They argued that there was no evidence that reductions on margins of price-maintained goods would lead to lower prices generally, indeed there was evidence, also cited by Lloyd Jacob, that margins on price-maintained goods were generally lower than those on free-priced goods. Andrews argued that competition among brands, of which individual RPM was a part, increased the trend to standardisation and was thus no obstacle to progress in manufacturing or distribution. Moreover, abolition would actually reduce competition – from neighbour-

Table 8.1. *Estimated shares of total retail sales, by type of retail establishment and by country, 1960*

	Estimated shares of total retail sales made by:				
Country	Consumer co-ops	Multiple shops	Variety chain stores	Department stores	All other retailers
Britain	11.0	20.8	4.8	5.0	58.4
Germany	2.8	6.0	1.7	5.5	84.0
W. Europe	6.2	8.2	2.6	3.6	79.4
USA	—	18.7	3.0	8.9	66.0

Note:
A multiple shop is a firm operating 10 or more retail branches, like Boots. A variety chain store is a firm operating 10 or more branches selling a wide variety of goods, e.g. Woolworth. In the United States mail order firms accounted for 3.4% of retail sales.
Source: Derived from: J. Jeffreys and D. Knee, *Retailing in Europe* (1962) pp. 64–5.

hood shops, between retailers' own brands and manufacturers', and the size of retailing units would rise needlessly and neighbourhood shops which did survive would have a still more monopolistic position in their locality. There would be a reduction in the services provided, especially in terms of specialised products available, for instance in books; any falls in price on some items would be offset by rises in prices in neighbourhood shops and by the overall reduction of competition. In production manufacturers and retailers would try to compete by differentiation, rather than standardisation of products.[41]

Thus a highly complex competitive struggle emerges, both between retailers and manufacturers, among manufacturers and among retailers. It is changes in the allegiances and strategies of the large manufacturers and retailers which, it will now be argued, most closely explains some of the changes in policy. In particular it explains why it proved so difficult to implement any policy in 1951, and why RPM had to be abolished in two bites in 1956 and 1964.

The retail lobby and policy, 1946–64

The Co-ops were steadfast opponents of RPM, but they were joined by the multiple shops and certain manufacturers. Paul Cadbury, for instance, had spoken against collective RPM as part of the contribution to the debate on cartel policy during the war (see chapter 4). The multiple retailers were organised in the Multiple Shops Federation (MSF). This organisation was chaired by Sir George Schuster between 1939 and 1952, who was chairman of the Allied Suppliers' Group (Home and Colonial Stores) in the 1930s which in turn was financially controlled by Unilever.[42] The MSF established an enquiry into distribution in 1946, and this prompted Cripps to raise the whole issue of distribution again and suggest that the Board of Trade take over the enquiry. This was the origins of the Lloyd Jacob Committee. The Board of Trade drew courage when proposing the enquiry from the support which would be forthcoming from the large stores and multiples: the latter accounted for 22.4% of total retail sales in 1950.[43] Thus the input to the first major move on RPM after the war came about through lobbying by a section of the private retail trade.

Evidence to the Lloyd Jacob Committee demonstrated the division of trade opinion. The MSF wanted the abolition of collective RPM schemes but supported the right of the individual manufacturer to maintain resale prices. Thus Sir George Schuster gave evidence supporting individual RPM, while Home and Colonial Stores, of which he was also chairman, submitted against RPM by associations.[44] Indeed a powerful bloc of trade opinion supported this position, one which, as we have seen, was beginning to emerge in the 1930s. On this point an alliance of interests existed between many manufacturers who gave evidence and multiple retailers. The former favoured and defended the rights of the manufacturer of branded goods to maintain resale prices, but were not necessarily in favour of collective methods of enforcement.[45] Almost all the large, multiple retailers who gave evidence: Home and Colonial, Boots, the Association of Engineering Distributors and Currys, argued that any further extension of collective methods of RPM would stop the large stores competing through passing on economies of large-scale distribution.[46]

However, another set of alliances existed among large manufacturers of branded goods and small retailers, favouring collective RPM to enforce manufacturers' prices. Their reasons for favouring collective RPM usually included the need for RPM to keep quality and established retailers in business, to allow them to carry a wide range of lines, and to support retailers with the requisite technical knowledge to sell the goods. Hence this sort of opinion was expressed by retailers and manufacturers engaged in producing and selling branded goods in tobacco, books and stationery, chemists' goods and dental goods, cars and motor cycles, radios and from retailers of confectionery.[47] Evidence to Lloyd Jacob demonstrated on the ground what economists argued theoretically, that branding fostered a coincidence of interest between larger manufacturers and smaller retailers.[48]

Yet again various associations representing only retailers opposed any legislation which favoured one type of goods against another, as the abolition of collective, but not individual RPM did. The abolition of collective RPM, they argued, posed a threat to the survival of the non-branded article which was useful to both small retailers and manufacturers as 'a stick to hold up to the manufacturer of the branded article'. In addition they feared that the large manufacturer, Hoovers was cited as an example, could force down retail margins and give the retailer little incentive to stock such goods.[49] The evidence of the large manufacturers unintentionally supported these claims. Heinz gave margins of only $16\frac{2}{3}$% to the retailer. The household appliance section of the London chamber of commerce, consisting of manufacturers, said that their retail margins were lower than in other trades.[50] The grocery retailers saw the threat posed to small shops by both the large manufacturers and large retailers. In their evidence they asserted that the end of RPM by associations would mean a trade controlled by large quasi-monopolistic firms, and a reduction in the numbers of small shops.[51]

From this conflicting body of *trade* opinion the Lloyd Jacob Committee came down on the side of the instigators of the enquiry – the MSF. It concluded that collective RPM schemes threatened to eliminate price competition in distribution and, as agreements to fix resale prices were frequently accompanied by agreements among manufacturers to limit competition, the situation had very wide implications for government competition policy.[52] Thus the Committee recommended the prohibition of 'the application of sanctions which extend beyond the remedies open to an individual producer for any breach of resale price maintenance'.[53] Thus, while deprecating any extension of the rights of the individual producer to refuse to supply the Co-op, the Committee recommended that 'no action should be taken which would deprive an individual producer of the power to prescribe and enforce resale prices for goods bearing his brand'. They also proposed that the government enter discussions with trade organisations to ensure that this power was not used to impede the development of more efficient means of distribution, that is, to protect the Co-op and other discount houses.[54] This view was in line with the chairman's legal concerns on property rights, and the force with which manufacturers of branded articles had argued the case for individual RPM, but it had aroused strong opposition from the economists on the committee.[55] It was a position which directly favoured one section of the trade: the large retailers (who could benefit from the removal of collective RPM protecting smaller retailers), and many larger producers (who remained relatively unscathed while individual RPM remained in place and was even strengthened). Hence the fact that any legislation on RPM was, willy-nilly, intervening in trade in a way that was bound to favour certain interests was clear, and governments from 1949 till 1964 had to balance various groups.

When the Labour government tried to force a measure through they found the opposition overwhelming. In June 1949 Wilson announced in Parliament that the government would consult with trade associations about rendering individual RPM harmless to the consumer, and called on industry to take voluntary steps against collective sanctions. He reiterated a determination to protect the Co-ops and the consumer.[56] Sir James Helmore (Second Secretary at the Board of Trade) expressed the hope to Sir Norman Kipping, Director-General of the FBI that informal discussions could establish a 'code of behaviour' on individual RPM which would in turn lead to fresh thought within industry on collective sanctions. He did however add that, although the government hoped industry would take the first steps, it intended to see that 'the great body of collective sanctions is, somehow or other, got rid of'.[57]

But the response of the FBI, the NUM, the PATA and other national bodies was swift and uncompromising. At a meeting in July Kipping told the Board's officials that as long as the talks were based on the President's statement supporting Lloyd Jacob, they had no purpose. The report was an unfair representation of the evidence presented, self-service had no future, its selling costs were no lower than normal methods, individual resale prices could not be enforced if collective sanctions were to be banned. The PATA went so far as to announce that they would not abandon collective sanctions, and they encouraged several hostile parliamentary questions.[58] Later meetings did not resolve the impasse over changes in either forms of RPM and by March 1950 the Board had accepted that legislation was inevitable.

But the Labour government was faced with a number of conflicting pressures. On the one hand Wilson was concerned to meet the points of the Co-op, who argued that some of the worst cases of boycott were practised by individual firms. But on the other hand Wilson accepted the argument that the abolition of collective RPM would deprive manufacturers of branded goods of a remedy against 'loss-leading', and he was also aware of union desires to retain RPM as a system. Although Wilson favoured a ban on all forms of RPM – at one stroke placating the Co-ops and refraining from supporting the claims of any section of retailers and manufacturers – the Distribution Committee was more cautious and referred the matter to a working party of officials from a number of departments. Meanwhile the full backing of the TUC was sought for more radical measures on RPM, and the Board of Trade explored the suggestion made by some manufacturers of branded goods that they would cease their boycott of the Co-op in return for the maintenance of RPM.[59]

The report of the working party endorsed Wilson's views, putting as its main argument that 'a general prohibition of RPM would probably do more than any other single step to reduce the costs of distribution'.[60] In spite of potent trade lobbying, the government published in June 1951 a White Paper promising the abolition of all RPM.[61] But even before its publication, the government again entered into negotiations with industry, this time to consider applications for exemptions to legislation. In addition a special policy group was set up, chaired by Sir Frank Lee, Under-Secretary at the Board of Trade, to work out both legislation on RPM and amendments to the existing Act which were then under consideration. The purpose of this committee was to work out government tactics in the face of the likely opposition. However, once Thorneycroft came to power he clearly did not wish to court business antagonism immediately and proposed instead another enquiry by the Monopolies Commission.[62]

What had happened therefore by 1956 that Thorneycroft felt willing to act against collective RPM?

As chapter 7 outlined the ending of controls between the late 1940s and the mid-1950s,[63] together with rising consumer expenditure, access to foreign supplies, new techniques and materials swept away the protected and restricted markets of the 1930s and 1940s. A company like Marks and Spencer is portrayed as positively straining at the leash by the 1950s. In 1955 the Utility clothing scheme was finally ended and 'The company responded to the opportunities created by this withdrawal of controls by applying even more vigorously the policies which had by that time developed into a consciously held philosophy of retailing'.[64] In the grocery trade the end of food rationing in 1954, the development of self-service stores, up from 600 in 1950 to 2,500 by 1955, and the lifting of building controls at the end of 1954, removed war-time limitations to retail development while giving multiple retailers the opportunities for expansion. Before rationing was ended there was little incentive to cut prices but, Pickering argues, with the end of rationing, 'by about 1955 a "cold war" had been reached between some multiple retailers who wanted to cut prices and manufacturers and other retailers who did not want them to'.[65]

The limitations on outlets imposed by collectives schemes were beginning also to strain the loyalty of manufacturers to collective retailing schemes. Currys was unable to get most of the leading makes of radios, TVs, hoovers and other electrical equipment in the 1950s, and had gone into production itself as a result. However, by the mid-1950s supply was finally threatening to outrun demand. First Ekco, then Hoovers and then Electrolux began to supply Currys. The process was a spiralling one as manufacturers realised they could lose their share of the market to manufacturers who supplied retail multiples. In addition new products broke through old restrictions, such as the replacement of valve radios by transistors and the rocketing sales of TVs in the wake of the 1954 Television Act.[66]

Chapter 7 indicated how the ban on collective RPM together with the strengthening of individual RPM was knowingly calculated not to abolish RPM but to allow it to operate in ways less open to criticism such as private courts. It was a move calculated therefore to strengthen larger manufacturers of branded goods, while yielding to some lobbying from large retailers. Pressures from the latter for complete abolition did not go away, but we turn finally to changes which occurred between 1956 and 1964 and help to explain the further steps that were taken in the Resale Prices Act.

First, the 1956 Act significantly weakened RPM in a few trades. The ban on collective RPM removed the manufacturer's security, for once collective action was prohibited it was more likely that a supplier would find alternative outlets. In the grocery trade the strong growth in self-service stores encouraged such retailers to pass on price advantages to the consumer. In 1950 there were 600 self-service stores, 90% of them Co-operatives: by 1955 there were 2,500, only 60% Co-operative owned, and the process was aided by the ending of building controls and rationing in 1954. Between June 1957 and June 1958 RPM ended on most branded goods, and in 1960 the Grocery Proprietary Association was wound up. Thus the evidence appears to point to the catalytic effect of the 1956 Act in ending RPM in groceries. Manufacturers of grocery goods who wished to enforce their prices found Section 25 difficult to use. That this was so in groceries, while often pursued successfully elsewhere, may have been the result of competition from American brands, like Kellogg who attracted customers with special offers. The boost which the 1956 Act gave to supermarkets also helped to break down RPM between 1956 and 1964 in toiletries and household goods, and tyres. In both cases manufacturers were faced with a new type of retailer for their products – the supermarkets and the small tyre specialist. In the case of tyres, a further reason for the breakdown of RPM was overcapacity among manufacturers.[67] There were also temporary breakdowns in RPM in electrical goods where demand fell in 1960–1 and surpluses built up: the subsequent price-cutting, which manufacturers were unable to stop, was the equivalent of a clearance sale.

Secondly, the cold 'war' between manufacturers and certain classes of retailers of branded articles intensified. The government's internal enquiry into RPM of 1961 intimated that 'more manufacturers would be prepared to abandon the practice were it not for pressure from their distributors.' However, Pickering's evidence describes genuine enthusiasm and philosophical commitment to RPM among manufacturers practising RPM. Indeed many manufacturers only began to enforce their resale prices after the 1956 Act, using the new powers of Section 25. Between 1956 and 1964 there are 210 cases where manufacturers applied to the Courts and obtained injunctions against, or undertakings from, price-cutters. Moreover, Pickering calculates that at least 90% of all known cases of price-cutting were settled before reaching the Courts: an injunction was a last resort. Indeed manufacturers used other methods to force large retailers into line. A Tesco store in Leicester tried to sell Gor-Ray shirts at 75/- instead of 84/-: Gor-Ray told other retailers to charge 69/- and promised to make up the difference. Thus manufacturers remained strongly committed to RPM.[68]

Meanwhile, however, retailers were trying to cut prices. Even in goods where RPM was strong and strong representations were made for its retention by associations of manufacturers and retailers, like electrical goods, motor vehicles and bookselling, price-cutting was an ever-present threat: 39 writs were issued by vehicle manufacturers under Section 25.[69] The period also saw the development of other forms of cut-price retailing in discount houses and the door-to-door sales of John Bloom.[70] Pickering found that 60% of all actions under Section 25 were brought against discount stores and supermarkets (40% were brought against market traders). Although the growth of supermarkets was stemmed through the use of Section 25 they had (like Tesco) declared war on RPM and used foreign imports and their own brands to circumvent it.

Thirdly, it quickly became clear that in other ways the 1956 Act had left RPM in general undisturbed. Indeed, it could hardly be ended without repealing Section 25, for the Act did not affect trade association support for prices individually fixed, and this 'made it possible for a large measure of what is to all intents and purposes collective RPM to continue'.[71] Moreover the continuous spread of branding fostered further individual RPM. Thus RPM showed little sign of abatement. In fact it had to end with a bang rather than a whimper, and it was a bang which prompted a backbench revolt larger than that over Suez.[72]

It is clear that as soon as the 1956 Act was in operation, the Conservative government was eager to develop the ban on RPM further. It seems that much of this eagerness was in response to letters wanting the repeal of individual RPM, and in particular to the unexpected effect of the 1956 Act on the competition from the Co-ops. The same competitive pressures which forced manufacturers to supply Currys led to a situation, many retailers argued where, with stronger powers of individual RPM, manufacturers allowed the Co-op to pay its dividend but stopped other retailers price-cutting.[73] Reginald Maudling's papers to the Economic Policy Committee and to the Cabinet between January 1959 and February 1960 and discussions in both committees illustrate these points. Maudling (President of the

Board of Trade) argued that it was difficult to defend the compromise of Sections 24 and 25 of the 1956 Act and especially difficult to argue that efficient retailers should not be allowed to cut margins and so reduce the cost of living. This argument was put first, and was presumably in response to the letters the Board of Trade had received, for he also argued that he had evidence that a growing proportion of the retail trade were actively opposed to individual RPM. Secondly, Maudling intended to strengthen 'progressive distributors' through the repeal of Section 25, for then they could compete effectively with price-cutters and 'with the Co-operative Societies which at present cause serious embarrassment to the orthodox shopkeeper' with high levels of dividend in some areas. Thirdly, Maudling stated that the chief beneficiaries of the end of RPM would be the consuming public and the more efficient shopkeeper, while abolition 'might indeed accelerate the disappearance of many small retailers and wholesalers. This would probably benefit the economy but it would cause some hardship and resentment'.[74] Indeed, so predictable were these outcomes of the end of RPM that the Paymaster-General, Reginald Bevins, argued that there was no need for a preliminary enquiry before legislation as Maudling was proposing. There was general agreement in Cabinet that the abolition of individual RPM 'would adversely affect small traders'.[75]

Thus it was clear that what motivated Maudling in clearing the way for the abolition of all RPM was not public opinion, although the unanimity of the national Press and a recent paper by Yamey predicting reduction of prices were cited in Cabinet, but the balance of economic forces. Thus there was constant reference to those sections favouring RPM – retail chemists, branded textiles and drapery, car manufacturers and distributors, the majority of small retailers and all shopworkers, but also to the large retailers, who opposed it, and to the fact that RPM seemed to be dying in some areas, notably in groceries. Maudling called for a fact-finding enquiry on individual RPM to elicit the facts without inviting policy recommendations which the government might not wish to follow. The intention therefore seemed to be that the Board of Trade's enquiry could be used by the government, not in the education of public opinion but to gauge more precisely the balance of business forces and to use the results as a weapon against the recalcitrant sections of the trade, and of the Conservative Party, whose opposition was anticipated well before the 1964 Bill was introduced.

The report of the government's internal enquiry certainly supported Maudling, although its findings were less than remarkable. It argued forcefully for abolition of all RPM. This would have certain 'beneficial results', but it was not quite clear what these were. While arguing that the 'average level of retail prices' would be reduced, the report was also concerned to stress that abolition would not be 'an antidote to inflation' since its impact would be 'once and for all'. More generally, abolition would have long-term effects – creating freer competition and encouraging innovatory and efficient techniques in retailing. Finally, abolition might be 'of some benefit to consumers' but would not be disastrous to small shopkeepers: the report denied that the end of RPM had had an adverse effect on shopkeepers in the grocery trade.[76] This was certainly the case and was partly the result of the growth of 'voluntary' groups, like Spar and Londis, which were organised by wholesalers and allowed economies of scale in wholesaling which protected smaller grocers especially in more remote or residential areas.[77]

While its use to Maudling, and later Edward Heath, in pursuing the abolition of RPM is clear, the report is also of interest for its conclusions concerning the range of opinions. Most importantly it demonstrates that 'public opinion' was an incoherent factor. Sectors of the Press 'the more serious part' supported abolition – but not all, claimed the report. Indeed in 1964 the Beaverbrook press unleashed a major attack on Heath, supporting the hard-line Tory opponents of the Bill with their slogan 'hands off the shop-keeper'. Consumer opinion showed great 'confusion and division'. (The opinions of bodies like the Co-ops were not cited at all in the conclusions.) Only economists seemed to present a united front favouring abolition, although the report seemed overly influenced by the views of Basil Yamey and paid no attention to the arguments of Andrews and Friday. Thus their summary indicates that only economists among the general public strongly and clearly favoured abolition. But as economists, like the Pope, can muster but few divisions, we must assume that propelling the Bill along was the 'minority business opinion' cited by the report's authors: namely some multiple retailers and department stores.[78] The report again confirms that the final abolition of RPM was a move known and intended to benefit certain large retailers against smaller, and in the teeth of manufacturing opposition.

The actual passage of the 1964 Act needs also to be set in a wider context. By the late 1950s and early 1960s the Conservative Party showed signs of deep divisions on a number of issues. Consciousness of lagging growth and productivity, and creeping inflation raised question marks over fiscal and monetary policy and industrial relations, the latter becoming 'the centre of the Government's preoccupations'.[79] The liberals in the Party, represented in Thorneycroft's Treasury team in 1958 sought tighter monetary control, deflation and cuts in public expenditure, together with rejection of incomes policy. While struggling for approval this outlook failed to make headway, and the path towards incomes policy and maintenance of expenditure and the extension of state intervention, for instance through the establishment of the National Economic Development Council, was generally taken instead. Nevertheless the development of policy on RPM owed much to these concerns and implied re-thinking on certain labour issues. Thus the very first intimation that RPM generally should be considered was raised in the first report of the Council on Prices, Productivity and Incomes in February 1958 and repeated a year later. In addition, recognition that the abolition of RPM would harm small traders prompted some members of the Cabinet to suggest that some countervailing measure to protect them could be taken, namely the relaxation of regulations on shopping hours.[80]

In addition, while it has been argued here that policy on RPM evolved relatively free of external influences, the fact that RPM probably infringed Article 85(1) of the Treaty of Rome meant that the significance of its abolition in Britain was to strengthen the hand of the Europeans in the Party: it was no coincidence that the measure was pushed through by Edward Heath who had led the negotiations for Britain's entry into the EEC in 1963.[81]

To finish the story: the Bill against RPM put forward on behalf of the Co-operative Societies forced Heath into a decision on RPM. Claims by the Conservatives to be tackling prices and wages and to be the party of modernisation would look hollow if the government opposed the Bill, while they did not want the Labour Party to claim the area of competition as their preserve. So once again popular pressure was used as a spur allowing forces within the Conservative Party to push through measures which were bound to threaten certain interests. And indeed the opposition was enormous. In Cabinet Heath's proposals for the abolition of RPM with pleas for exemptions required the crucial support of Alec Douglas-Home to get through. Like Thorneycroft in 1956, Heath had to use various tricks to get his way, like giving the Press forward briefings. In the vote on the Second Reading 21 Conservative MPs voted against and another 25 deliberately abstained: a revolt whose scale 'far outstripped the Suez revolts'. Heath threatened to resign if the Cabinet weakened as the Second Reading approached.[82] The issue of RPM was not the cause of the Conservative defeat in 1964, but it was one of a series of incidents that tarnished their image.[83]

Conclusions

This example of antitrust history is a useful place at which to end an enquiry into the forces behind competition policy for it brings us back full circle to the example cited at the beginning of this account of antitrust policy – the attempt to regulate the railways in the 1880s. Both were relatively independent of wider considerations of foreign economic policy, and so left to the crude interplay of economic interest groups of which the governments in both cases were well aware. Both involved the rallying of public opinion to the sides of two opposing interest groups. Indeed, both implied, through the opening up of competitive pressures, an attack on the wages and conditions of workers in railways and retailing respectively. Both attacked economic interest groups so strong that they could threaten the continuance of the government itself.

9 Conclusions

The history of British competition policy has little to do with the gradual enlightenment of the British public and its business leaders about the virtues of competition. Large sections of the British 'public', especially as represented in labour organisations, needed neither economists nor government commissions to tell them of the dangers of monopoly, restrictionism, and regulation of the market. Instead it is a story of power politics, special pleading and, at times, downright skulduggery.

Nor did policy progress neatly from timid awakenings in 1944 to Monopolies Commission reports to stronger action thereafter. Rather it evolved by fits and starts, twists and turns. Policy of the sort recommended in 1918 was not introduced until 1948; policy of the sort recommended by economists in 1943 was not adopted until 1956; the policy of the 1964 Resale Price Maintenance Act was foreshadowed in a White Paper of 1951. Thus policy ebbed and flowed in a way which may be explained in terms of changing business strategies in response to the world and the British economic climates and the relationship between government and business.

To understand these changes this book has necessarily focussed on government policy formation. It shows the British government at the centre of three contending forces with views on the nature and need for competition policy: British businessmen, the United States, and a variety of pressure groups within Britain, most importantly the organisations of labour – the Labour Party, trade unions and the Co-ops. These three forces were solid centres of political and economic power and, by extension, ideological influence. We now summarise the nature of their interaction and the consequent impact on government policy formation.

Particular emphasis has been laid on the problems of using 'public opinion' as the dynamic factor in the development of policy. According to received wisdom public opinion had to be gradually convinced of the merits of competition, and it was this slow educative process which explains the timing and nature of legislation. Such accounts do not exaggerate the role of 'public opinion', but mis-state it, in a way which actually downplays the extent of its significance.

There is little match between what 'the public' demanded and the form of legislation, and when the public demanded action and the timing of government action. Governments clearly felt under pressure from domestic opinion during and after the two world wars, but at both times strong antitrust legislation was dropped or diluted. 'Public opinion' may have been united in its mistrust of cartels and monopolies but this was for a wide variety of reasons, while a wide range of solutions was proposed of which 'competition' policy was just one, and not necessarily the most favoured.

Moreover, to the extent that governments did react to 'public opinion' it was to pre-empt it through measures which assuaged some public fears without endangering government–business relations. Governments anticipated that anti-monopoly sentiment was a possible and potential challenge to the legitimacy of private enterprise. They also feared public outcries against specific examples of malpractices, which could put the government in a position where it might have to choose between being discredited in the eyes of the public and pursuing a course of action which could damage their relations with industry. These two fears affected the nature of legislation in that the government saw public opinion as a rock around which it had to steer.

However, it is necessary to depart from the nebulous concept of 'public opinion' and look at some of its most important representatives – the labour movement. The role of the labour movement was in fact fundamental in the development of policy in three key ways.

First, the labour movement provided a pressure for some government intervention on the question of monopoly. During the two world wars this pressure was obvious. Anti-profiteering sentiment threatened industrial unrest during the first: during the second, and with the experiences of the 1920s and 1930s a recent memory, some sections of the labour movement saw the solution to monopoly and restrictionism in sweeping attacks on private ownership and control in general. Conservative politicians and some business leaders could see that unless some measures were taken in response to anti-business feeling which cartels evoked, private property would increasingly be seen as illegitimate.

However, sections of the labour movement were divided on the type of intervention desirable. The Co-ops favoured the extension of Co-operation and/or the abolition of retailing cartels; trade unions were suspicious of measures to increase competitive pressures seeing that as the prelude to attacks on wages and conditions; the extent of nationalisation as a response to monopoly was hotly debated. Thus the second way that labour influenced the evolution of policy was that, once in power these divisions provided a vacuum in policy-making which was speedily filled by other interest groups and articulated through the civil service. Thirdly, after the

Second World War in particular, the Labour leadership in government took upon itself to channel and subdue calls for more vigorous resolution of private monopoly and to seek co-operation and compromise with business. Hence was established a pattern in which policy was actually worked out between the civil service and business.

From the earliest days of British antitrust initiatives policy-makers balanced 'labour unrest' against 'capital unrest'. At the very moments when labour feeling was most aroused – during and immediately after the two world wars – businessmen were most entrenched within government and very committed to keeping the right to control markets. The business veto at these moments was not just one of many factors which determined the evolution of policy, it was the most significant single factor. There is no evidence to suggest that in deciding the sort of policy to be pursued, the views of industry carried equal weight to the views of trade unions. In this study of industrial policy business views reigned supreme, and theories of corporate bias have little validity.

Business feeling laid down the parameters within which governments could operate. In the 1940s these parameters were very narrow as industry felt apprehensive about the post-war world, and firms felt they must retain or strengthen their ability and legal right to restrict capacity or maintain prices should the world go into recession again. By the 1950s these parameters had widened with expanding trade prospects which rendered commitment to any cartel arrangements necessarily more fragile and provoked greater complaints from new entrants to industries encouraged by buoyant demand. At the same time sectors of business were able to shape the system of regulation which emerged.

In particular it has been shown that changing business strategies, linked with changes in British industrial structure provided the main dynamic behind policy. The strategies of large firms were central in both the development of the British cartel and trade association system, and in removing objections to their control in the 1950s. The increasing significance from the 1950s of overseas investment by British TNCs and of foreign investment in Britain supported the pressures for freer trading policies. The gradual tightening of legislation on retailing restrictions was closely linked to the strength of large multi-unit retailers, and the fight around the abolition of RPM was effectively confined to the Conservative Party and competing sectors of the business world.

The third centre of power and influence on government policy was that of the United States. Like businessmen, the United States had direct and formalised contacts with the British government and represented a lobby which the British government could not ignore. American propaganda fuelled and gave a focus to public hostility to big business, acting as an international muck-raker, propelling the formulation of policy along in the 1940s, and providing continued pressure into the 1950s. It should also be noted that much of the propaganda effect of this American pressure was not to be felt until after 1956 when the many studies of the competitive structure of British industry, undertaken with funds provided under conditional aid, fed through into the academic literature. It is an interesting point for speculation whether this American educative effort had any effect on the sustained revival of economic liberalism from the 1970s onwards.

However, while the American lobby was vital, it was to an extent counter-productive in the 1940s, putting British industrialists even further on the defensive. The Americans were heavy-handed in their demands for the post-war world, making unfortunate connections between lend-lease allocations and the end of the British empire. Since the late nineteenth century foreign competition had become increasingly intractable and to the minds of many British businessmen protectionism and cartelism in the 1930s had stemmed the tide. Hence American pressure fuelled the worst fears of British businessmen, fears which had been festering for half a century.

This is not to say that without American pressure British competition policy would have been more determined, on the contrary as far as businessmen were concerned the cartel and trade association system needed refinement and extension: its curtailment was not a part of their vision for the post-war world. However they might have tolerated a system of registration for domestic industry, had it not been seen as committing Britain to similar action on the international level. Thus in the 1940s the Americans were attacking that aspect of the 1930s cartel system which British businessmen were most concerned to preserve. The Americans did so precisely because they felt that it had been used pre-war to limit openings for American goods, something which had to be avoided if the American century was to prevail.

These then were the centres of political and economic power whose interactions determined government policies. In the post-war world the character of British antitrust policies represented a bargain struck between British businessmen and the United States. Where American pressure was less evident, such as on the question of RPM, the bargain was negotiated among British businessmen. In both cases the civil service acted as mediator.

Above and around all this fluttered the economists and the Press. Certainly during the war the far-ranging discussions gave a particular and unique niche to economists who played an important role in the formulation of the economic programme of the Coalition government. Press publicity of restrictive practices was certainly useful to the government as a weapon with which to threaten recalcitrant industries. Business opposition to any enquiry during the war and their squeals of pain during Monopolies Commission investigations, their accusations that an enquiry blackened an industry's name, made overseas customers and competitors suspicious, their pressure for excisions, the massive refutations of Commission reports, all showed that civil servants were correct to argue that monopolists were sensitive to public opinion. But public opinion was a very delicate weapon, and competition policy which relied so heavily on this extra-legal sanction required a Press itself free from oligopolistic control. As we have seen, governments in the 1940s and 1950s were wary of tackling the oligopolistic tendencies in the British Press. That governments proclaimed public opinion as a sanction but failed to ensure its free play must cast doubt on the degree of seriousness with which the government attempted to create a competitive economy.

Economists and the Press were therefore not the dynamic forces in shaping policy, and governments responded to their ideas in accordance with the dictates of business strategy, often, and at the formative periods, acting in response to American pressure.

Turning to general issues facing governments, this book has stressed the wide context in which antitrust policies have been pursued. In no small part the attitude of governments towards restrictionism has been a function of world trading conditions. While the tariff was not directly the midwife of the trusts, it is certainly the case that protectionism of the inter-war years accompanied government complicity in cartelisation and rationalisation, while the 1956 and 1964 Acts accompanied strong and decisive moves to freer trading and monetary policies. In the 1940s indecision and wavering on domestic economic policies very much reflected the uncertain future of world trade at the time. The gradual consolidation of socialism in Eastern Europe and of private enterprise in Western Europe ushered in a new phase of freer trade for those countries in the capitalist orbit this time under clear US hegemony.

Overall domestic policies, especially the adoption of demand management, were also important in determining the nature of antitrust policies. The emphasis on the role of government in macro-economic planning and providing full employment removed the focus for intervention at the level of individual industries: Keynesianism and the growth of demand rather than rationalisation, cartelisation and the curtailment of supply was the new hope to deal with periods of excess capacity.

It is also very important to note how policy adopted on the 'trusts' in turn prescribed also the role of the key domestic actors – government, business and labour – in the economy. The debates of the 1930s demonstrate that business plans for corporatist planning involved a form of state intervention dominated by businessmen presiding over a network of cartel trade associations. Labour had at most a consultative role in these schemes, at worst would have certain rights proscribed. Labour, especially TUC, plans for nationalisation and state supervision aimed to use forms of state intervention to secure greater labour representation and involvement in managerial decisions.

Plans for a 'competitive order' put forward in various guises by liberal economists in the 1940s were less openly partisan, and were presented as measures in the national interest and based on 'scientific' economic theory. They had, however, clear implications for Britain's future. State intervention was to be minimal: Robbins' competitive order would leave businessmen free to operate, but with restrictions on restrictionism.

The implications for labour in the liberal schema were less immediately obvious. On the one hand, moves against cartels in the 1940s seemed to be tackling major concerns of trade unionists (unemployment and profiteering) the major concern of the Co-ops (the boycott) and the general concern of Labour politicians concerning the political powers of trade associations. On the other hand, cartels had brought an element of stability to the market place and, in distribution for instance, RPM was seen to maintain wages and conditions in a sector previously notorious on this score. Indeed economic liberalism has gradually revealed its opposition to organisations of labour as restraints on capital, as bad as, if not worse than, those imposed on business by itself. In this, of course they have been articulating a sort of inverted Marxism. Engels commented in 1844:

But what gives these [Trades] Unions and the strikes arising from them their real importance is this, that they are the first attempt of the workers to abolish competition ... And precisely because the Unions direct themselves against competition, against the vital nerve of the present social order, however one-sidedly, in however narrow a way, are they so dangerous to this social order.[1]

Hence the Sherman Act was used against trade unions at various times and in Britain every move in the 1940s and 1950s to strengthen competition policy met with the demand from some quarter at some stage to tackle restrictive labour practices. This was done more to get the promoters of policy against restrictive business practices to retreat, but the writing was on the wall. The 'freeing' of enterprise in the 1980s was accompanied by the shackling of the unions, both moves endorsed by neo-liberal economists.

Finally we can draw two sets of conclusions from this study concerning the function of antitrust regulation, indeed of regulation in general, and hence the future prospects for regulation in Britain. Gabriel Kolko, in his pioneering work on American regulation argued that railroad leaders viewed railway regulation as 'a safe shield behind which to hide from the consequences of local democracy, as well as a means of solving their own internal problems'.[2] His subsequent study of the Federal Trade Commission developed these ideas further, seeing regulation as serving three purposes: a buffer against public hostility to business, a means to settle business disputes and a forum to establish codes of business behaviour. This study demonstrates that these claims have lost none of their validity over time, nor when applied to the British situation.

Turning to the future prospects of regulation in Britain it is the historical role and current fate of the labour movement which requires attention in predicting its success. Historically labour organisations have necessitated some regulation of monopolistic private industry. Hence the current weakness of labour organisations spells accompanying weakness of regulatory bodies. In opening up an attack on labour, the economic liberals stand in danger of killing the very thing they profess to love – the possibility of regulation and the building of a 'competitive order'.

This ironic situation is not without historical precedent. In his critique of the economic liberals of Europe of the 1920s Karl Polanyi asserted that their desire to restore self-regulation of the markets was accompanied by calls for strong government to ensure deflationary policies worked. He comments:

The stubbornness with which economic liberals, for a critical decade, had, in the service of deflationary policies, supported authoritarian interventionism, merely resulted in a decisive weakening of the democratic forces which might otherwise have averted the fascist catastrophe.[3]

The organisations of labour have historically provided a major dynamic in the evolution of policy precisely because their critique of private monopoly threatened the legitimacy of private property generally. In the absence of a strong labour movement the hopes for regulation to serve a 'public interest' must grow dim. Regulatory bodies will increasingly drop any pretence to be anything other than a forum to settle disputes among businessmen. The direction in which these disputes will be settled can also be predicted. Antitrust legislation has promoted the development of large firms, and has not harmed their interests. Antitrust policies operate as micro-economic fine-tuning, changing the market environment according to the business strategies of large and, increasingly, transnational firms. We can predict that future settlement of business disputes will tend to a similar pattern.

Nor does the present trend to deregulation invalidate these points. This study implies that any move by the state, whether towards or away from regulation must be affected by prevailing economic interests. Antitrust regulation developed under circumstances of labour movement strength:

de-regulation has proceeded on the basis of weak labour opposition. Moreover de-regulation, like competition, is the cry of the strong. The 'competitive order', as Joan Robinson could have predicted, has sustained the economic and political position of those who can control the competition.

Appendix 1: British participation in international cartels in manufactured goods, 1930s and 1950s

Products (1)	British firms or trade associations participating (2)	Type of arrangement (see key on p. 185) (3)	Evidence of existence post-war (4)
Coke and manufactured fuel			
Coke	British Coke Export Sales Corporation	1, 3b,c,d, 7	*
Pottery, Glass, Abrasives			
Plate glass	Pilkington	1, 3b,d, 10, 12	
Sheet glass	Pilkington	3d	
Glass bottles	British Ass. of Glass Bottle Mfrs Ltd	1, 4, 8	
Optical goods	Bausch & Lomb	3e, 12	
	Carl Zeis (London)		
	Adair Dutt & Co.		
Iron and Steel and Manufactures thereof			
Steel	British Iron & Steel Fed.	3b,d, 4, 7	Plans were made
(International Steel Cartel)			(see text)
Subsidiary agreements:			
Semi-finished steel	National Billet Ass.	1, 3b,c,d, 7	
Structural shapes	British Joist Makers' Ass.	1, 3b,c,d, 7	
Merchant bars	Nat. Ass. for Rolled and re-rolled steel	1, 3b,c,d, 7	
Thick plates	Heavy Steel Makers' Ass.	1, 3b,c,d, 7	
Universal plates	HSMA	1, 3b,c,d, 7	
Medium plates	Sheet Makers' Conference	1, 3b,c,d, 7	
Hot rolled strips	NARRS	1, 3b,c,d, 7	
Black sheets	SMC	1, 3b,c,d, 7	
Galvanised sheets	SMC	1, 3b,c,d, 7	
Rails	British Railmakers' Ass.	1, 3b,c,d, 11	
Tinplate	Welsh Plate and Sheet MA	1, 3b,c,d, 7	
Wrought iron and steel tubes	Stewarts & Lloyds Ltd.	1, 3b,c,d	

Product	Association/Company	Codes	
Cast iron pipes	Stanton Ironworks Co.	3c,d	*
Malleable tube fittings	British Malleable Tube Fittings Ass.	1, 2, 3c, 7	*
Nickel-coated strip	Wilmot Taylor & Co.	1	
Steel hinges	Patent Hinge Makers' Ass.	1	
Iron and steel scrap	BISF	6	
Ships for breaking up	BISF	6	
Baths	British Shipbuilders' Ass.	1, 2, 3d, 7, 9	
Milk cans	British Bath MA	1, 3d	
Ice cream freezers	Milk Can MA	1	*
Files, rasps, etc.	Joseph Sankey & Sons	1	*
Metal cans	File Makers' Ass.	1	*
Wood screws	Metal Box		
	GKN	3b,c,d	
Wire and wire products			
Wire rods	British Wire Rod Rollers' Ass.	1, 3b,c,d, 7	
IWECO: a comprehensive comptoir of the International Steel Cartel	Iron and Steel Wire MA	1, 3b,d, 5, 7	*
Subsidiary agreements:			
Felt nails	GKN, Rylands Bros, Whitecross Co.	1, 3d, 5	
Cut tacks	Steel Tack Ass.	1, 3d, 5	
Tingles	British Shoe Rivet MA	1, 3d, 5	
Hobs and studs	British United Shoe Machinery Co.	1, 3d, 5	
Bills and cutlans	British United Shoe Machinery Co. (BUSM)	1, 3d, 5	
Springs for upholstery	Springmakers' Ass.	1, 2, 3b,c,d	
Mattress chains	Jack Chain Ass.	1, 3d, 5	
Bolt and nuts	Black Bolt and Nut Ass.	1, 3d	
Non-ferrous metals and manufactures thereof			
Brass and copper products	Cold Rolled Brass and Copper Ass.		*
	Manufactured Copper Ass.		
	Brass and Copper Tube Ass.		
	Brass Wire Ass.		
	Enfield Rolling Mills Ltd.		
	ICI		
	GKN	3d	

Appendix 1 (*cont.*)

Products (1)	British firms or trade associations participating (2)	Type of arrangement (see key on p. 185) (3)	Evidence of existence post-war (4)
Zinc	Imperial Smelting Corp. (subsid. ICI)	3b,d, 4, 8, 12	
Zinc sheets	Enfield Rolling Mills	1, 2, 3b,d	
Cobalt	Rhokana Corporation Ltd	n/a	
Aluminium	British Aluminium Co.	1, 4, 10, 12	
Semi-manufactured aluminium goods	British Aluminium Co.	1, 3d	
	Wrought Light Aluminium Alloys Ass.		
Aluminium foil	Acme Tea Chest Co. and others	2, 3c,d	
Magnesium	F.A. Hughes & Co.	4b, 7a, 8, 12	
Magnesite bricks	Eglinton Magnesite Brick	1, 2, 3d,e, 7	
	John Le Boutillier Ltd		
Titanium	ICI and 4 other companies	3c, 4, 8, 10, 12	
Titanium oxide pigments	National Titanium Pigments Ltd.	3c, 8, 12	
Tungsten carbide	Tool Metal Mfg Co.	1, 3d, 4, 8, 10, 12	
	British Thomson Houston		
Electrical goods and apparatus			
Heavy electrical machinery and equipment	BEAMA	3c,d, 8, 10, 11, 12	*
	Associated Electrical Industries Ltd		
Electric cables (paper insulated)	Cable Makers' Ass.	1, 3b,d,	*
Electric cables (telephone and telegraph)	Cable Makers' Ass.	1, 3b,d	*
Telephone and telegraph apparatus	5 companies, incl. STC, GEC, Siemens	8,12	
Wireless apparatus	Marconi's Wireless & Teleg. Co.	8, 10, 12	
Electric lamps	Members of ELMA	1, 3b,c,d, 8, 9, 10, 12	*
Gramophone records	EMI, Decca	1, 3c, 7a	*
Photometers	Weston Electrical Instrument Co.	8	
Electrical regulators	EA Controls	8, 10	

Dry batteries			*
Electrical switches			*
Radio valves			*
Machinery			
Iron and Steel Works plant:			
Rolling mill machinery	Members of British Steelworks Plant Ass.	10, 12	*
Continuous strip mills	Richard Thomas Ltd	8	
Steel smelting plant and Foundry machinery	Head, Wrightson & Co.	3c,d, 10	*
Cotton-spinning machinery	Textile Machinery Makers Ltd	1, 2	
Shoe machinery	BUSM Ltd	3c, 8, 10, 12	*
Tanning machinery	Turner Tanning Machinery Co.	3c, 8, 10, 12	*
Match-making machinery	British Match Corporation	1, 3a,c,d, 6, 10, 12	*
Precision chain	Precision Chain Industrial and Export Group	1, 3d	
Paper machine wire	Paper Machine Wire MA	n/a	
Water tube boilers	Babcock & Wilcox	3c,d, 8, 10, 11	*
Firefighting appliances	Permutit Co.	8, 10, 12	
Gaskets	J.P. Payon Ltd	7	
Coke ovens			*
Flour-milling machinery			*
Ball-bearings			*
Multiple-spindle automatics			*
Dredging machinery			*
Chemical plant			*
Textiles			
Nylon	ICI	3c,d, 8, 10	
Hosiery	Nat. Fed. Hosiery Mfrs' Assocns	3d	
Mechanical cloth	the British association	1	*
Rayon	Courtaulds and 4 other companies	12	*
Bleachers' Ass.	n/a		
Fibre Agreement	n/a		*

Appendix 1 (*cont.*)

Products (1)	British firms or trade associations participating (2)	Type of arrangement (see key on p. 185) (3)	Evidence of existence post-war (4)
Chemicals			
Dyestuffs	ICI	1, 3b,c,d, 12	*
Nitrogen	Sulphate of Ammonia Fed.	3b,c,d, 4, 5, 10	
	ICI		
Nitric acid	ICI and others	3c, 5	
Alkalis	ICI	3b,e	
Explosives	ICI	3b,e	
Fuses	ICI	1, 3e	
Manufactured coke	British Coke Export Sales Corporation	1, 3b,c,d, 7	*
Denture materials	ICI	1, 3c,d, 8, 9, 10, 12	*
	Amalgamated Dental Co.		
Oil hydrogenation process	ICI	4, 7, 8, 10	
Phosphates (Disodium and Trisodium)	Albright & Wilson	1, 3b	
Superphosphates	Fertilisers' Mfrs, Ass.	1, 7	
Copper Sulphate	British Sulphate of Copper Ass.	1	*
Potash	ICI	3b,d, 10	*
Carbide	British Oxygen Co.	1, 3c	
Drugs and fine chemicals	Bayer Products Ltd	3e, 12	
	Boots Pure Drug Co.		
	ICI		
Quinine	Howard & Sons Ltd	1, 4, 5	
Hormones	Schering Ltd	1, 10, 12	
	Roussel Labs Ltd		
	Organon Labs Ltd		
	Ciba Ltd		

Product	Company / Association	References	Notes
Industrial solvents	Distillers Co.	1, 3c, 4, 8, 10	
	British Industrial Solvents		
	ICI		
Celluloid	British Xylonite	3b	
White lead	Britannia Lead Co.	1, 3a	
Lead oxide	Goodlass Wall & Lead Co.	1, 3a	
Carbons (activated)	Goodlass Wall & Lead Co.	9, 12	
	British Carbo-Union Ltd	8	
Argon	British Oxygen Co.		
Boracic acid			*
Mercury			*
Bone glue	British Glues & Chemicals	1, 3b, 6	Probably ended
Paper			
Newsprint	Bowater Paper Mills Ltd	1	*
Kraft paper	Paper Makers' Ass., Kraft sections of	1, 2, 7	
Greaseproof paper	Dartford Paper Mill Ltd	1, 3d, 4	
	Wiggins, Teape & Co.		
Vegetable parchment	British Vegetable Parchment Mills Ltd	1, 3c	
Photographic base paper	Wiggins Teape	1	
Sensitised paper	Ozalid Co.	10, 12	
Wall-paper	Wall Paper Mfrs Ltd	1, 3c	
Coated paper	Ass. Makers of Coated Paper of GB	1, 3c	
Vehicles			
Shipbuilding	British Shipbuilding Conf.	5, 11	*
Locomotives	Locomotive MA	1, 3d, 11	*
Railway carriages	Birmingham Railway Carriage & Wagon Co.	3b,d, 10, 11	
	Metropolitan Cammell and 2 other firms		
Railcars	Metropolitan Vickers	3e	
	Metropolitan Cammell		

Appendix 1 (*cont.*)

Products (1)	British firms or trade associations participating (2)	Type of arrangement (see key on p. 185) (3)	Evidence of existence post-war (4)
Miscellaneous			
Cement	Cement Makers' Fed.	1, 3a,c,d	*
Asbestos	Turner & Newall	1, 3c,d, 9, 10, 12	
Hard fibre cordage			*
Hats	Hatmakers' Fed		*
Wallboards	subsid. of Bowaters Ltd	1	
Gas mantles	British Gas Mantle Ass.	1, 3c,d	
Lino and baizecloth	Linoleum MA	1, 3c	
X-Ray films	Ilford Ltd	1	
Rubber thread and latex	Lastex Yarn & Lactron Thread (subsids of Dunlop & US Rubber Co.)	1, 2, 3b, 9, 12	*
Tyres			*

Note: * Details are available from the author on request.
Source: OFT *Survey Volume I*; Papers of the Board of Trade and of the Foreign Exchange Control Committee; Reports of the MRPC 1949–56.

Key to Appendix 1, column 3

The nature of the agreements is indicated in column (3). These are categories devised in OFT *Survey Volume 1.*

1 Among manufacturers re selling prices;
2 Among manufacturers re discounts and credit;
3 Among manufacturers re sales:
   a) by export quotas;
   b) by export quotas;
   c) by the allocation of export markets;
   d) by the reservation of home markets wholly or in part to home producers;
   e) by a central selling agency;
4 Among manufacturers to regulate quantity of output;
5 Among manufacturers to control the extension of capacity;
6 Between manufacturers and suppliers re channels of supply or re joint distribution;
7 Between manufacturers and distributors to restrict channels of sale, fix resale prices;
8 Patent agreements;
9 Regulation of quality or specification of the goods produced;
10 Exchange of technical information;
11 Joint consultation before tendering;
12 Important financial links between companies.

Abbreviations:
Ass. – Association
Fed. – Federation
MA – Manufacturers' Association
n/a – information not available

Appendix 2: Correlation of RPM with levels of concentration of employment, 1938

Commodity or commodity group in which RPM was 'significant' (60–100% of sales) (1)	Co-op Boycott (2)	Employment in the 3 largest units as % of total employment (3)
Cigarettes and tobacco		66
Soft drinks		13
Tea		55*
Spirits (off-licences)		60*
Cocoa		93*
Chocolate and sugar confectionery		40*
Biscuits		37
Condensed milk		60*
Preserves		33
Infant and invalid foods		80*
Soups and sauces		60*
Self-raising flour		60*
Packaged breakfast cereals		75*
Syrup and treacle		70
Dentifrice		60*
Soap		70
Proprietary medicines and packed drugs	CB	19
Beauty preparations, Miscellaneous toilet preparations, Hair preparations, Perfumes and toilet waters, Hair dyes and shampoos		20
Razors and blades		55
Tooth brushes		40*
Radios		41
Radio valves and accessories		70
Vacuum cleaners	CB	85
Gramophones and records	CB	81
Electric light bulbs		61
Electrical appliances (irons, kettles, fridges)	CB	52*
Sewing machines		100
Motor cars	CB	48
Cycles and accessories		55
Tyres and tubes		76
Motor cycles and accessories		62
Petrol	CB	88
Motor oil		35*
Newspapers	CB	27
Stationery		40
Stationery (pens and pencils)	CB	30*
Books		20*
Periodicals		27

Appendix 2 (*cont.*)

Commodity or commodity group in which RPM was 'significant' (60–100% of sales) (1)	Co-op Boycott (2)	Employment in the 3 largest units as % of total employment (3)
Photographic apparatus	CB	70
Matches		47*
Household stores		57*
Musical instruments and sheet music	CB	
Drapery goods	CB	
Toys	CB	
Tools	CB	
Builders' materials	CB	

Note: * Estimates

Sources: BT64/455 RPM(E)57 Memorandum by National Institute of Economic and Social Research. Their table was based on their estimates of RPM and on H. Leak and A. Maizels 'The Structure of British Industry' *Journal of the Royal Statistical Society* 108, 3 (1945). 'Co-ops and Price Rings' *Co-operative Monthly Newsletter* 8, 11 (December 1951). The Co-op also said that it had in its possession the rules of Trade associations and letters from firms which banned sales to the Co-op from: PATA, Meccano Ltd, UK Time Ltd, Electrolux Ltd, Dunelt Cycles, Hairdressers' Sundries, Decca Record Co. Ltd.

Appendix 3: The systematisation of British trade associations, 1875–1953

Name of trade association (1)	Date formed (2)	Comment (3)
National Federation of Clay Industries	1938	controlled 90% of output, excluding building bricks
Glass Manufacturers' Fed.	1926	Nearly all glass melting – not flat glass Discussions with European Glass Containers Manufacturers' Committee
Cement and Concrete Ass.	1935	All manufacturers of Portland Cement
National Council of Building Material Producers	1942	Had 41 trade associations as members Formed on government instigation
Ass. of British Pharmaceutical Industries	1948	First formed as Wholesale Drug Trade Ass. – 1930 1950 – absorbed Pharmaceutical Export Group 90% output of standard drugs Confidential price negotiations with the Ministry of Health
British Coking Industry Ass.	1945	90% of hard coke production
Ass. of British Chemical Manufacturers	1916	95% of production 17 TAs affiliated Organised into 7 bi-product groups Close contact with BCPMA (see below)
British Iron and Steel Fed.	1935	90% + of production of products concerned 1945 – new constitution
Council of Ironfoundry Assocns	1941	75% of total volume of iron castings production 1945 – joined with Council of Iron Producers to form Joint Iron Council, see text p. 000
British Non-Ferrous Metals Fed.	1945	Represented 40% at least of any group of products and 76% in aggregate
Following TAs were members of BNFM:		Was the British participant in the international 'Lausanne Agreement'
Brass and Copper Tube Ass.	1875	
Manufactured Copper Ass.	1901	
High Conductivity Copper Ass.	1903	
Brass Wire Ass.	1911	
Nickel Silver Ass.	1911	
Cold Rolled Brass and Copper Ass.	1912	
Condenser Plate Ass.	1927	
Zinc Roller Ass.	1934	
Non-Electrical Copper Ass.	1938	

Appendix 3 (*cont.*)

Name of trade association (1)	Date formed (2)	Comment (3)
Extruded Brass and CopperAlloy Ass.	1945	
British Chemical Plant Manufacturers' Ass.	pre 1914?	75% of 'units' Membership: 1920 – 19 firms
		1948 – 100 firms
		1955 – 217 firms
		1944 – absorbed chemical plant sub-group of Food and Chemicals Processing Machinery Export Group Part of the ABCM until c. 1938, and still had close co-operation with ABCM so that 'British chemicals shall be made with British plant'
British Electrical and Allied Machinery Ass.	1911	Organised into sections 394 firms employing 690,000 workers
Shipbuilding Conference	1928	60 firms + nearly all builders of ocean-going ships Dominated by the 20 largest firms
British Engineers' Ass. Its 17 affiliated TAs were:	1912	Main TA for mechanical engineering excl. motor vehicles and aircraft. 1944 adopted a federal character, with 17 affiliated TAs, see column (1)
Aerial Ropeways Ass.		
Agricultural Engineering Ass.		
Ass. of Crane Makers		
Ass. of Shell Boilermakers		
BCPMA		
British Compressed Air Society		
British Food Machinery Manufacturers' Ass.		
British Internal Combustion Engine Manufacturers' Ass.		
British Pump Manufacturers' Ass.		
British Valve Manufacturers' Ass.		
Fed. of Manufacturers of Contractors' Plant		
Hydraulic Ass.		
Locomotive Manufacturers' Ass. of Great Britain		
Machine Tool TA		
Mechanical Handling Engineering Ass.		
Tank and Industrial Plant Ass.		
Water Tube Boilermakers' Ass.		

Appendix 3 (*cont.*)

Name of trade association (1)	Date formed (2)	Comment (3)
Engineering Industries Ass.	1941	Organisation for small firms, although 12% of member firms 'large' and also in BEA Represented 24% of all firms in engineering
Radio Industry Council consisting of: British Radio Equipment Manufacturers' Ass. Radio Communication and Electronic Engineering Ass. British Radio Valve Manufacturers' Ass. Radio and Electronic Component Manufacturers' Fed.	1943	Brought together 4 autonomous sections who accounted for 95% of production
British Motor Trade Ass.	1910	18,000+ firms in manufacturing and retailing 100% control of supplies of new cars
Society of Motor Manufacturers, and Traders	1902	17,000 members organised in 17 trade sections
Society of British Aircraft Constructors	pre 1939	30 members covering 100% production of aircraft and guided weapons
National Hardware Alliance	1953	Merger of Hardwear Trade Alliance (formed 1944) and National Steel and Hardware Ass. (formed 1906) Wide range of products, no safe estimate of proportion of production covered
Screw Manufacturers' Ass.	1944	Existed in 1930s, reconstituted 1944 Represented 95% of production by volume
British Aluminium Holloware Manufacturers' Ass.	1918	Represented 80% of output by value
British Pressure Cookers Manufacturers' Ass.	1951	Formed from the Export Group (formed in 1948) Membership of 5 firms representing 90% of production and sales
British Industrial Measuring and Control Apparatus Manufacturers' Ass.	1944	Formed from wartime Export Group. Represented 90% of production
Rayon Weaving Ass.	1936	'Most' firms

Appendix 3 (*cont.*)

Name of trade association (1)	Date formed (2)	Comment (3)
British Jute Trade Federal Council	1947	Successor of Ass. of Jute Spinners and Manufacturers (formed 1916) and other groups
Wool Textile Delegation consisting of: British Wool Fed. Wool Carbonisers' Fed. Woolcombing Employers' Fed. Worsted Spinning Fed. Woollen and Worsted Trades Fed. West of England Wool Textile Employers' Fed. National Ass. of Scottish Woollen Manufacturers Northern Ireland Wool Users' Ass. Shoddy and Mungo Manufacturers' Ass. Associated London Selling Wool Brokers	1921	Had 10 TAs as members, see column (1), and was 'broadly comprehensive'
Wholesale Clothing Manufacturers' Fed. of Great Britain	1910	Main association for heavy clothing Close relation with TAs in Wool Textile Delegation
Apparel and Fashion Industries Ass.	1947	Merger of Apparel Manufacturers' Ass. (formed 1943) and British Fashion TA (formed 1933)
Incorporated Federated Ass. of Boot and Shoe Manufacturers of Great Britain and Ireland	1891	Had 18 local TAs as members Worked closely with Lancashire Boot, Shoe and Slipper Manufacturers' Ass. Together these represented 85% of production of footwear, excl. rubber footwear
Scotch Whisky Ass.	1941	Previously the Whisky Ass. (formed 1912) when it included Irish whiskey
Cocoa, Chocolate and Confectionery Alliance	1901	Previously the Manufacturing Confectioners' Alliance Represented 98% of production: one-third of all firms
Cake and Biscuit Alliance Ltd	1938	Formed on the initiative of the Board of Trade to allocate raw materials
Ass. of British Wood Wool Manufacturers	1942	Formed to allocate timber quota Represented 95% of production

Appendix 3 (*cont.*)

Name of trade association (1)	Date formed (2)	Comment (3)
British Paper and Board Makers' Ass.	1872	Together with Coated Paper and Board Manufacturers' Ass. represented almost 100% of production
Fed. of British Rubber and Allied Manufacturers' Ass.	1942	Successor to India Rubber Manufacturers' Ass. and absorbed Export Group Had 24 sectional TAs Represented 95% of volume and value of production
Fed. of British Manufacturers of Sports and Games	1926	Had forerunner in 1919 1929 adopted new constitution and a group system (13 groups)
British Plastics Fed.	1933	Previously Moulding TA (formed 1929) Represented 'nearly all' manufacturers of plastic material, 'most firms' making plant and a high percentage of suppliers of raw materials
Society of British Gas Industries	1905	Had 18 sections Represented 95% of output Main negotiator with Gas Council while its sections liaised with Area Gas Boards

Notes:
1 Information on the production/sale controlled by a TA relates to the mid-1950s unless otherwise stated.
2 Date when TA as it existed in the mid-1950s at time of PEP survey was formed.
Source: BLPES, PEP File P128. PEP surveyed 50 trade associations in depth for their 1957 account, chosen as a representative sample of British trade associations in 1955. Those listed here practised some form of commercial regulations at some time in their history, other than discussion about wages, etc.
Abbreviations used:
TAs – Trade Associations
Fed. – Federation
Ass. – Association

Appendix 4: Analysis of the signatories of the 'National Policy for Industry', 1942

Name	Main industrial interests/directorships
P.J. Adie	Adie Bros. (silversmiths)
Sir Arthur Aiton	Aiton & Co. (steel pipes)
Sir William Alexander	British Celanese
David A. Anderson	Caird (Dundee)
Robert Barlow	Metal Box Co.
Sir Edward Baron	Carreras
D.W. Barrett	Smith's English clocks
Sir Samuel Beale	GKN
J.E. Bennett	Crane's Ltd
Sir Walter Benton-Jones	United Steel
Harold H. Beresford	Stavel Coal & Iron/Power Cos
J.F. Bostock	Lotus Ltd
Francis Brake	STC; Creed
D. Brown	Insurance
Robert S. Brown	Burgess, Ledward & Co.
Sir Nigel Campbell	Baldwins; Stewart & Lloyds
Archibald D. Carmichael	British Enka; Rayon Council
H.M.S. Chalmers	Maconochie Foods
Kenneth M. Chance	British Industrial Plastics
Percival B.W. Charnaud	Royal Sovereign Pencil Co.
William B. Chivers	Chivers & Sons
Alfred Corning Clark	EMI; Columbia; Marconi
James O.M. Clark	J&P Coats
W.A. Collins	Wm Collins (stationers)
Sir Charles Blampeid Colston	Hoover
Sir Ernest Herbert Cooper	Gillette Inds
Sir Richard Ashmole Cooper	Cooper, McDougall, Robertson (disinfectants)
Harold J. Cotes	British Glues and Chemicals
A. Crawford	N/A
Sir Valentine G. Crittall (later Lord Braintree)	Crittall Mfg Co.
Geoffrey Cunliffe	British Aluminium Co.
Sir Graham Cunningham	Triplex Safety Glass
Gilbert Dennison	Dennison (watches)
Wallace Charles Devereux	Almin (Light Alloys)
Sir Roger Duncalfe	British Glues and Chemicals
Earl of Dudley	BISC and others
H. Durston	N/A
Arthur Dyson	Horsley Bridge (eng.)
David Owen Evans	Mond Nickel Co.
V.Z. de Ferranti	Ferranti
Lord John Dewar Forteviot	John Dewar (distillers)
James Foster-Smith	Wellman-Smith (eng.)
D. Frost	British Ropes

Appendix 4 (*cont.*)

Name	Main industrial interests/directorships
Leslie Carr Gamage	GEC
Mrs E.H. Gasking	Batchelor's
Sir Frank Gill	STC; Creed
Edmund Henry Gilpin	Baker Perkins
E.W. Goodale	Warner & Sons
Sir Allan Gordon-Smith	S. Smith; EMI; Columbia
R. Gordon-Smith	Insurance
Sir John Greenly	Babcock & Wilcox
Sir C. Kenneth Hague	Babcock & Wilcox
G.A. Hancock	Frank Tatham (lace)
B.W. Harvey	United Yeast
Cyril Garnett Heywood	Pinchin Johnson
Philip Ernest Hill	Property developer/financier
Sir Robert Stuart Hilton	United Steel Co; Summers
Lord Hugo Hirst	GEC
F. Thomas Jackson	Telephone Mfg Co.
G. Clement Jenks	Jenks Bros (eng.)
Sir Ernest James Johnson	Johnson Bros (potteries)
Sir Francis L'Estrange Joseph	LMS and coal Cos
William Kilpatrick	Davey & United Eng. Co.
Frank Arthur King	S. Smith & Sons
George Basil King	Amalg. Needles & Fish Hooks
Arthur Colin Kingham	Rolls Razor
Gustavus Henry Latham	BISC; Richard Thomas
Sir W. Clare Lees	Bleachers' Ass.
Sir Ernest Harry Lever	Richard Thomas
Peter Lindsay	United Steel; Morgan Crucible Co.
John Charles Lloyd	Stewart and Lloyds & others
Allan Campbell Macdairmid (Sir 1945)	Stewart and Lloyds & others
J.R. Menzies-Wilson	Stewart and Lloyds & others
Lord Melchett	ICI; Mond Nickel
Lord McGowan	ICI; Mond Nickel
Sir Archibald McKinstry	Babcock & Wilcox; Metal Box
James Osborne Martin	W. & J. Martin (tanners)
J.B. Mavor	Mavor & Coulson (mining machy)
Alexander Stephen Maclellan	Glenfield & Kennedy (eng.)
Sir Percy Herbert Mills	W. & T. Avery; EMI
T.D. Morson	Summerfield Cheml. Works
William J.T. Munro	Callard, Stewart & Watt (confectionery)
Alec Nathan	Glaxo; Joseph Nathan
Cyril Scotts Newton	Carpet Trades Ltd
Sir John Gibb Nicholson	ICI; BNS
George William Odey	Barrow, Hepburn & Gale (tanners)
Geoffrey Parkes	Small & Parkes (belting)
William Patterson	Patterson Eng. Co.
Lord Perry	Ford Motor Co.

Appendix 4 (*cont.*)

Name	Main industrial interests/directorships
A.E. Philipps	N/A
Albert Renfrew Porter	Addressograph-Multigraph
G.B.G. Potter	S. Smith; Marine Instruments
Sir William Prince-Smith	worsted machinery
James Voase Rank	Joseph Rank
Adolph Henry Railing (Sir 1944)	GEC
Charles William Reeve	Assocd Equipment Co.
Edward Robson	Pinchin Johnson
Stanley Robson	Natl Smelting Co.
Sir Alexander Roger	British Insulated Cables; BSA
N.H. Rollason	United Steel; John Summers
A.A. Rose	Clyde Paper Co.
Sir Frank Bernard Sanderson	Wray Sanderson
Lord Sempill	Investment trusts
G.E.H. Sington	Platt Bros; Textile Machinery Makers Ltd
H. Smith	British Ropes
John Southern	Worthington-Simpson
George A. Sowerby	leather
Thomas George Spencer	STT
Sir Richard Felix Summers	United Steel; John Summers
J.A. Tait	furniture
Herbert Tomkinson	Tomkinson (carpets)
Sir Cecil Weir	(shipbuilding family)
Douglas William Turner	N/A
Ernest Theodore Walker	Wolsey
Frederick Wallis	Wednesbury Tube Co.
Gerald Valerian Wellesley	N/A
Reginald Stanley Worth	Nestles
F. Wright	Butterley & Co. (eng.)

Source: National Policy for Industry; Who Was Who; Directory of Directors.

Appendix 5: Criteria for the selection of references to the MRPC outlined in published reports and internal Board of Trade memoranda, 1949–56

In 1948 two Board of Trade memoranda outlined the basis for the selection of cases. One stated the principles on which the first four cases should be selected. These were:
- where an independent body had recently recommended an enquiry;
- a case of an international agreement which raised issues of public concern;
- a 'Co-operative' case;
- a case of monopoly buying.

The second, in a circular letter to Board of Trade production departments, urged the following criteria as bases for thinking about referral:
- where there were reasons to think that efficiency could be improved;
- where agreements adversely affected prices and the direction and volume of exports;
- where complaints had been received;
- where a decision was needed in other areas of policy, e.g. foreign exchange spending;
- where a recent committee had disclosed restrictive practices;
- where it was suspected that output was being restricted.

However, in its public report the Board of Trade explained that in 1949 items were chosen to get a range of types of restrictive practices and types of industries.[1]

In the three next annual reports various criteria for selection were given. In 1950 the Board of Trade tried to refer subjects 'which may be expected to break new ground' and give the Board new information on the types of restrictive practices.[2] In 1951 the choice was based on the desire to enquire into restrictive practices in processing (calico-printing) and importing (timber).[3] In 1952 the Board explained that it wanted to study items playing an important role in the national economy (tyres and electrical machinery) and to diversify the subjects studied (collective discrimination).[4]

In July 1952 a paper to the Policy Group of the MRPC suggested the merits of possible candidates for referral should be decided on the basis of four criteria:
- the nature of the restrictive practices or the market situation involved;
- the identity of the production authority responsible (this was to chivvy departments other than the Board of Trade, notably the Ministry of Supply, to suggest items;
- the relative importance of the trade;
- the volume and sources of complaints.

These reasons were, more or less, echoed in the annual report for 1953, an additional reason being given that an enquiry might prompt conclusions of a wider application or serve as a pilot test.[5]

The annual reports for 1954 and 1955 gave no justification for the items chosen. This masked the crisis which had arisen within the Board of Trade. Two internal memoranda give some flavour of the attempts to secure significant referrals to the MRPC while laying to rest fears that the MRPC was pillorying industries concerned. At a meeting between Board of Trade and MRPC personnel it was agreed that choices of subjects for referral should:

- cover all principal sectors of industry;
- cover all principal examples of monopolies and restrictive practices;
- give priority to cases where there were complaints but 'it should not be assumed that a reference was inappropriate unless there was prima facie evidence of abuse'.

A subsequent letter advised production Ministries other than the Board of Trade that industries selected did not necessarily have to be 'bad', but they should try to look at some of the industries mentioned in annual reports as the subject of complaint 'if only to dispel the idea that we keep off potentially explosive subjects and prefer only those which are likely to yield reports of a fairly anodyne nature'.[6]

---

[1] BT64/467 minute from R.R.D. McIntosh to R.C. Bryant 10.3.1948; BT64/2757 unsigned circular to Board of Trade production departments c. March 1948; BPP (1950) *Monopolies and Restrictive Practices (Inquiry and Control) Act, 1948. Report by the Board of Trade for the period ending 31st December 1949* xiii, p. 6.

[2] BPP (1950–51) *Annual report ... for period ending 31st December 1950* xvii, p. 5.

[3] BPP (1951–52) *Annual report ... for period ending 31st December 1951* xvii, p. 4.

[4] BPP (1952–53) *Annual report ... for period ending 31st December 1952* xv, p. 4.

[5] BT64/4837 MC/RPM(52)12 'Further references to the Monopolies Commission' 17/7/1952; BPP (1953–54) *Annual report ... for period ending 31st December 1953* xvi, p. 5.

[6] BPP (1954–55) *Annual report. ... for period ending 31st December 1954* vi; BPP (1955–56) *Annual report ... for the session 7th June 1955–11th November 1956* xxiv; BT64/4812 'Selection of references for the 5th group' and letter from A.C. Hill to the Ministries of Works, Materials and Supply.

Notes

1 INTRODUCTION

1. Joan Robinson *Economic Philosophy* (Harmondsworth, 1962) based on Josiah Mason lectures for 1959, p. 136.
2. H. Levy *Monopolies, Cartels and Trusts in British Industry* (1927) p. 327.
3. This predilection was pursued through ad hoc policies from the 1930s and through more general policy under the 1964–70 Labour governments and the aim of positive restructuring through the Industrial Reorganisation Corporation. See P. Hall 'The State and Economic Decline' in B. Elbaum and W. Lazonick *The Decline of the British Economy* (Oxford, 1986) pp. 274–8; P. Mottershead 'Industrial Policy' in F.T. Blackaby (ed.) *British Economic Policy 1960–1974* (Cambridge, 1978) pp. 431–50; D. Hague and G. Wilkinson *The IRC – An Experiment in Industrial Intervention* (1983) pp. 3–4, 15.
4. P. Sargent-Florence *Industry and the State* (1957) pp. 100–4. Much of the mania for rationalisation of the inter-war period, and for productivity gains post-war sprang from direct comparisons with American and German performance see L. Hannah *The Rise of the Corporate Economy* (2nd ed., 1983) p. 26. American transnationals operating in Britain formed another model, G.G. Jones 'Foreign Multinationals and British Industry' *EHR* 41, 3 (Aug. 1988) p. 440. For works which cast doubt on the benefits of mergers and large-scale firms see K.D. George and C. Joll *Competition, Growth and Structural Change* (3rd ed., 1981) pp. 73–6, 214–16; G. Meeks *Disappointing Marriage: A Study of the Gains from Merger* (Cambridge, 1977) pp. 32–5; K. Cowling (ed.) *Mergers and Economic Performance* (Cambridge, 1980); J. Jewkes, D. Sawyers and R. Stillerman *The Sources of Invention* (1958) pp. 189–90; M. Sawyer *The Economics of Industries and Firms* (2nd ed., 1985) p. 137; S. Aaronovitch and M. Sawyer *Big Business: Theoretical and Empirical Aspects of Concentration and Mergers in the United Kingdom* (1975) pp. 195–217.
5. Marver H. Bernstein *Regulating Business by Independent Commission* (Princeton, 1955) p. 253.
6. Robinson *Economic Philosophy* p. 136.
7. M.A. Utton *The Political Economy of Big Business* (Oxford, 1982) p. 105. For a discussion of classical and Marxist views of monopoly and competition see M. Sawyer *The Challenge of Radical Political Economy* (New York, 1989) pp. 140–52; S. Aaronovitch *Monopoly: A Study of British Monopoly Capitalism* (1955) p. 25; Aaronovitch and Sawyer *Big Business* (1975) p. 290; P.A. Baran and P.M. Sweezy *Monopoly Capital: an essay in the American economic and social order* (Harmondsworth, 1966) p. 76.
8. D. Swann, D.P. O'Brien, W.P.J. Maunder and W.S. Howe *Competition in British Industry: Restrictive Practices in theory and practice* (1974) p. 172; D.C.

Elliott and J.D. Gribbin 'The Abolition of Cartels and Structural Change in the United Kingdom' in A.P. Jacquemin and H.W. de Jong (eds.) *Welfare Aspects of Competitive Markets* (Leiden, 1977) pp. 357–8; A. Chandler *Scale and Scope. The Dynamics of Industrial Capitalism* (Cambridge, Mass.,1990) pp. 72–9.

9. V. Berghahn *The Americanisation of West German Industry 1945–1973* (Leamington Spa, 1986) p. 32; Wendell Berge *Cartels: Challenge to a Free World* (Washington, 1944) p. 2.

10. J.K. Galbraith *The New Industrial State* (Harmondsworth, 2nd ed., 1985) p. 297.

11. Charles E. Lindblom *Politics and Markets* (New York, 1977) pp. 178–9. The theory is criticised in W. Grant and J. Sargent *Business and Politics in Britain* (1987) pp. 20–1.

12. F. Machlup *The Political Economy of Monopoly* (Baltimore, 1952) p. 75 summarises this and other popular views of the relationship between monopoly and political power. See also, for an expression of these views Galbraith *New Industrial State* p. 306.

13. The study of the history of competition policy in Britain is patchy, and is usually in the form of an introduction to studies of the legal implications of competition law or of the extent and effect of monopoly and restrictionism in the British economy, e.g. R.B. Stevens and B.S. Yamey *The Restrictive Practices Court – a study of the judicial process and economic policy* (1965); P.H. Guenault and J.M. Jackson *The control of monopoly in the United Kingdom* (2nd ed., 1974); A. Hunter *Competition and the Law* (1966); V. Korah *Monopolies and Restrictive Practices* (Harmondsworth, 1968); J.D. Gribbin 'Recent Antitrust developments in the U.K.' *Anti-Trust Bulletin* 20 (1975); Catherine Brock *The Control of Restrictive Practices from 1956: a study of the Restrictive Practices Court* (1966); G.C. Allen *Monopoly and Restrictive Practices* (1968). Some works have attempted a more detailed investigation of the origins of policy itself. Straightforward accounts are to be found in J.D. Gribbin *The Post-War Revival of Competition as Industrial Policy* Government Economic Service Working Paper No. 19 (1978); J. Jewkes 'British Monopoly Policy 1944–56' *Journal of Law and Economics* 1 (Oct. 1958) pp. 1–19; Swann *et al. Competition* (1974). Some writers attempt to use the origins of the 1956 Restrictive Trade Practices Act as a test case of 'the policy-making process' or of government relations with the FBI, the powerful industrial pressure-group. J.J. Richardson 'The Making of the Restrictive Trade Practices Act: a case study of the policy process in Britain' *Parliamentary Affairs* 20, 4 (Autumn 1967) pp. 350–74; J.J. Richardson, *The Policy-making Process* (1969); Stephen Blank *Industry and Government in Britain: the Federation of British Industries in Politics, 1945–65* (Farnborough, 1973) pp. 61–4. Very recently more detailed studies have appeared of moments in the history of British antitrust, using published government records, T. Freyer *Regulating Big Business. Antitrust in Great Britain and America, 1880–1990* (Cambridge, 1992); D. Gribbin 'The contribution of economists to the origins of UK competition policy' in P. de Wolf (ed.) *Competition in Europe. Essays in Honour of Henk W. de Jong* (Dordrecht, 1991) pp. 135–62.

14. J.M. Keynes *The General Theory of Employment, Interest and Money* (2nd ed., 1973) p. 383.

15. Richardson *Policy-making process* pp. 12–13.
16. Jewkes 'British Monopoly Policy' p. 2.
17. Hunter *Competition and the Law* p. 78; Gribbin 'Contribution of economists';
    L. Hannah 'Economic ideas and government policy on industrial organisation
    in Britain since 1945' in M.O. Furner and B. Supple (eds.) *The state and
    economic knowledge. The American and British experiences* (Cambridge, 1991).
18. S.R. Dennison 'The British Restrictive Trade Practices Act of 1956' *The Journal
    of Law and Economics* 2 (Oct. 1959) pp. 64–83; Gribbin 'Recent Anti-Trust
    Developments' pp. 377–410; Brock *Restrictive Practices* p. 30.
19. J. High 'Introduction: A Tale of Two Disciplines' in J. High (ed.) *Regulation,
    Economic Theory and History* (Ann Arbor, 1991) pp. 1–17.
20. H.G. Wells *The Sleeper Awakens* (1906); Edward Bellamy *Looking Backwards
    2000–1887* (1887 reprinted Cambridge, Mass., 1967); J.C. Haig *In the Grip of
    the Trusts* (1909). Frank Norris *The Octopus* (New York, 1969). The Fabian
    economist, H.W. Macrosty, predicted revolution as the outcome if monopoly
    were not controlled, H.W. Macrosty *Trusts and the State* (1901) p. 216.
21. A.D. Neale *The Anti-trust Laws of the USA* (1st ed., Cambridge, 1968) p. 476 n.
    F. Voigt 'German experience with cartels and their control during the pre-war
    and post-war periods' in J.P. Miller (ed.) *Competition, Cartels and their
    Regulation* (Amsterdam, 1962) pp. 174–5.
22. R.H. Bork *The Antitrust Paradox: A Policy at War with Itself* (New York, 1978)
    p. 418.
23. Hannah *Corporate Economy* p. 169; Nigel Harris *Competition and the Corpor-
    ate Society: British Conservatives, the State and Industry 1945–1964* (1972) p.
    226.
24. H.B. Thorelli *The Federal Antitrust Policy: Origination of an American Tra-
    dition* (Stockholm, 1954) p. 1.
25. T.P. Kovaleff *Business and Government during the Eisenhower administration: a
    study of the Antitrust policy of the Justice Department* (Athens, Ohio, 1980)
    p. 156.
26. Lindblom *Politics and Markets*.
27. The range of this literature is discussed in T.K. McCraw 'Regulation in
    America: A Review Article' *BHR* 49, 2 (Summer 1975) pp 159–83. See
    especially G. Kolko *Railroads and Regulation, 1877–1916* (Princeton, 1965); G.
    Kolko *The Triumph of Conservatism: a reinterpretation of American History,
    1900–1916* (New York, 1963); G.J. Stigler *The Citizen and the State* (Chicago,
    1975) p. 114.
28. K. Middlemas *Politics in Industrial Society: the experience of the British system
    since 1911* (1979) pp. 373–4; J. Turner 'The Politics of Business' in J. Turner
    (ed.) *Businessmen and Politics: Studies of Business Activity in British Politics
    1900–1945* (1984) pp. 2–3.
29. Berghahn *Americanisation of West German Industry* pp. 100–6; T.F. Marburg
    'Government and Business in Germany: Public Policy towards Cartels' *BHR*
    38, 1 (Spring 1964) p. 88; J. Halliday *A Political History of Japanese Capitalism*
    (New York and London, 1975) pp. 177–84; T. Uchiyama *The US Occupation
    Policy for Japan: the Deconcentration controversy and the origins of the 'reverse
    course'* (Ph.D. thesis, 1986 lodged in BLPES library).

2 THE BRITISH CARTEL SYSTEM, 1880–1964

1. L. Hannah *The Rise of the Corporate Economy* (2nd ed., 1983); S.J. Prais *The Evolution of Giant Firms in Britain: a study of the growth of concentration in manufacturing in Britain* (Cambridge, 1981); A.D. Chandler *Scale and Scope. The Dynamics of Industrial Capitalism* (Cambridge, Mass., 1990). For the most sweeping re-assessment of price-fixing as government policy see A. Booth 'Britain in the 1930s – a managed economy?' *EHR* 57, 2 (Nov. 1987) pp. 237–57.
2. The survey which follows is limited to developments in manufacturing and retailing as these were the main areas affected by British competition legislation for the period covered by this book.
3. Erwin Hexner referred to the 'jungle of cartel definitions' which obtained by the 1940s. E. Hexner *International Cartels* (1946) p. xi; for a wide-ranging review of the literature defining the cartel see R. Pietrowski *Cartels and Trusts* (Woking, 1933) pp. 11–85.
4. OFT *Board of Trade Survey of International and Internal Cartels 1944 and 1946 Volume I* (1976) p. xxxi. The first use of the term in its modern sense was in 1879 during a debate in the German Reichstag on the way producers of rails and railway stock were charging high prices at home in Germany, while dumping abroad. See Pietrowski *Cartels and Trusts* p. 11. The first book on cartels was F. Kleinwächter *Die Kartelle* (Innsbrück, 1883).
5. On this point see A.F. Lucas *Industrial Reconstruction and the Control of Competition* (1937) p. 215.
6. L. Hannah 'Mergers, Cartels and Concentration: Legal Factors in the U.S. and European Experience' in N. Horn and J. Kocka (eds.) *Law and the Formation of the Big Enterprise in the 19th and early 20th centuries* (Göttingen, 1979) p. 312.
7. R. Brady *Business as a system of power* (New York, 1943) p. 175.
8. H. Levy *Industrial Germany* (Cambridge, 1935) p. 2.
9. W.J. Reader 'The United Kingdom Soapmakers' Association and the English Soap Trade' *Bus.Hist.* 1, 2 (Jun. 1959) p. 77; H.W. Macrosty *The Trust Movement in British Industry* (1907) pp. 210–28; BPP (1886) *Final Report of the Royal Commission appointed to enquire into Depression in Trade and Industry* Vol. xxiii C. 4893 p. xxii. This point is also made in H. Levy *Monopolies, Cartels and Trusts* (2nd ed., 1927).
10. Macrosty *Trust Movement* pp. 155–6 and 79–81.
11. M.A. Utton 'Some Features of the early merger movements in British manufacturing industry' *Bus.Hist.* 14, 1 (Jan. 1972) p. 52. His measurements are based on the firms listed by Macrosty in 1907 of mergers formed from five or more companies; Hannah *Corporate Economy* p. 22 and appendices.
12. Macrosty *Trust Movement* pp. 121, 187–91, 308–9.
13. BPP (1918) *Ministry of Reconstruction. Report of the Committee on Trusts* Vol. xiii Cmd. 9236 p. 2.
14. C.A. Wurm 'International industrial cartels, the state and politics: Great Britain between the wars' in A. Teichova, M. Levy-Boyer and H. Nussbaum (eds.) *Historical Studies in international corporate business* (Cambridge, 1989) p. 113.

15. *Committee on Trusts* pp. 40–1; Macrosty *Trust Movement* pp. 200–1.
16. Macrosty *Trust Movement* pp. 195–7, 192, 229–35; A. Plummer *International Combines in Modern Industry* (2nd ed., 1938) p. 9 and pp. 4–10.
17. *Committee on Trusts* pp. 2, 5–6, 20.
18. BT68/82 Note by P. Ashley to the Board of Trade Council BTC 259 16/2/1920.
19. L. Hannah 'Visible and Invisible Hands in Great Britain' in A. Chandler and H. Daems (eds.) *Managerial Hierarchies* (Cambridge, Mass., 1980) p. 42. Hannah *Corporate Economy* pp. 115–18; L. Johnman 'The Largest Manufacturing Companies in 1935' *Bus.Hist.* 28, 2 (Apr. 1986) pp. 228–31; P. Fitzgerald *Industrial Concentration in Britain* (2nd ed., 1927) pp. 59–62, 81, 134. For the debate on the role of merger in rising levels of concentration see B. Curry and K.D. George 'Industrial Concentration: a Survey' *The Journal of Industrial Economics* 31, 3 (Mar. 1983) pp. 473–86; L. Hannah and J. Kay *Concentration in Modern Industry: Theory, Measurement and the U.K. Experience* (1977) p. 71; Prais *Giant Firms* pp. 25 and 167; G. Walshe *Recent Trends in Monopoly in Great Britain* (Cambridge, 1974) p. 99; on the post-war period see S. Aaronovitch and M. Sawyer *Big Business. Theoretical and Empirical Aspects of Concentration and Mergers in the United Kingdom* (1975) pp. 123–50.
20. Prais *Giant Firms* p. 6; for a similar view see Hannah *Corporate Economy* p. 91; P.E. Hart and R. Clark, *Concentration in British Industry, 1935–1975* (1980) p. 13; R. Evely and I.M.D. Little *Concentration in British Industry: an empirical study of the structure of industrial production, 1935–51* (Cambridge, 1960) p. 63; Aaronovitch and Sawyer *Big Business* p. 92.
21. Already in the 1920s the process of merger, while reducing the number of agreements then (Distillers acquired a previous cartel partner), ushered in some potentially powerful monopolistic cartels: agreements between Brunner Mond (later ICI) and Lever Bros on the supply of soda ash, the Cement Makers' Federation, and early probings at international agreements between ICI and IG Farben.
22. Lucas *Industrial Reconstruction* p. 203.
23. J.D. Gribbin 'Pre-war cartels in the United Kingdom' in OFT *Survey Vol. I* p. 14; D.C. Elliott and J.D. Gribbin, 'The Abolition of Cartels and Structural Changes in the United Kingdom' in A.P. Jacquemin and H.W. de Jong (eds.) *Welfare Aspects of Competitive Markets* (Leiden, 1977) p. 354.
24. Allen *Monopoly and restrictive Practices* (1968) p. 88; Pilkington Archives, Executive Committee minutes, PB260 12/1/1949, 7/6/1949, 10/5/1950; MRPC *Linoleum* p. 15.
25. E.g. transformers, MRPC *Heavy Electrical Machinery* p. 162, and cables, MRPC *Insulated Electric Wires and Cables* p. 17.
26. Gribbin 'Pre-war cartels' p. 14; G.C. Allen *Monopoly* p. 92. Hannah *Corporate Economy* p. 136. The Board of Trade's survey of internal cartels of 1946 was aimed more at establishing the types of domestic practices which the government would have to consider in framing legislation, and the number of domestic cartels included was very limited.
27. BPP (1960–61) *Restrictive Trading Agreements. Report of the Registrar for the period 1956–59* Vol. xix, and BPP (1969–70) *Report for the period 1966–69* Vol. xviii p. 10; J. Kocka 'The Modern Industrial Enterprise in Germany' in

Chandler and Daems *Hierarchies* p. 89. A German government estimate for 1925 gave 2500 manufacturing cartels, R.K. Michels *Cartels, Combines and Trusts in Post-War Germany* (New York, 1928) p. 173.

28. This is based on a survey of 40 registered agreements studied in D. Swann, D. O'Brien, W.P.J. Maunder and W.S. Howe, *Competition in British Industry: Restrictive practices in theory and practice* (1974).

29. BPP (1960–61) *Registrar of Restrictive Trading Agreements. Report for the period 1st Jan. 1960 to 30th Jun. 1961* Vol. xix Cmnd. 1273.

30. United Nations, Department of Economic Affairs *International Cartels* (New York, 1947) p. 2.

31. OFT *Survey Vol. I* p. xxii. However, this figure was an exaggeration, including as it did the operations of transnational firms like Unilever and J.P. Coats under the heading of international cartel.

32. BT64/58 'International cartel problems' memorandum by G.L. Watkinson 12/3/1940, and OFT *Survey Vol. I* passim.

33. BT64/451 'International Trade Organisation – Draft Charter'; BT11/3503 'Cartel agreements and the direction of exports' memorandum by the Board of Trade, Jul. 1947. For a discussion on the issue T231/161 Foreign Exchange Control Committee minutes, 1946.

34. Hannah and Kay *Concentration* p. 81; K.D. George 'Changes in British Industrial Structure, 1951–1958' *Journal of Industrial Economics* 15, 3 (Jul. 1967) pp. 200–11.

35. Hannah *Corporate Economy* Appendix 1, p. 178; Aaronovitch and Sawyer *Big Business* pp. 124–9. M.A. Utton *The Political Economy of Big Business* (Oxford, 1982) p. 136; Hannah *Corporate Economy* p. 149; K.D. George 'The Changing Structure of Competitive Industry' *Economic Journal* 82 (Mar. 1972, supplement) p. 363. W.G. Shepherd 'Changes in British Industrial Concentration, 1951–1958' *Oxford Economic Papers* 18, 1 (Mar. 1966) p. 132 believed that the attack was 'modest' and unlikely to have much impact.

36. Elliott and Gribbin 'Abolition of Cartels' pp. 358–60; Swann *et al.* *Competition.*

37. Aaronovitch and Sawyer *Big Business* pp. 241–51.

38. BPP (1966–67) *Restrictive Trading Agreements. Report of the Registrar 1st July 1963 to 30th June 1966* Vol. xl Cmnd. 3188.

39. R. Brady *Business as a system of power* (New York, 1943) p. 176.

40. Tolliday *British Steel* p. 303.

41. G. Jones 'The Performance of British Multinational Enterprise, 1890–1945' in P. Hertner and G. Jones (eds.) *Multinationals: Theory and History* (Aldershot, 1986) pp. 106–8. The case of Metal Box is indicative of the use of merger and cartels as a defence against, in this case, American pressure on markets, W.J. Reader *Metal Box – A History* (1976) pp. 49–55, and 98–9.

42. OFT *Survey Vol. I* pp. 3, 75.

43. F. Capie *Depression and Protection: Britain between the Wars* (1983) p. 26.

44. W. Reader *ICI – a History. Volume 2: 1926–1952* (1975) p. 198.

45. BPP (1948–49) *Report of the Committee on Resale Price Maintenance* p. 30. The extent of restrictive practices in the retailing sector was of most immediate significance to the general public, and it was partly in response to this public feeling that RPM and other retailing restrictions were investigated so fre-

quently by government committees between 1919 and 1956. See: BPP (1920) *Profiteering Act 1919: Findings and Decisions of a Committee appointed to inquire into the principle of Fixed Retail Prices* Vol. xxiii Cmd. 662; Board of Trade *Restraint of Trade: Report of Committee appointed by the Lord Chancellor and the President of the Board of Trade to consider certain retail practices* (HMSO, 1931); BPP *RPM*; MRPC *Collective Discrimination*.

46. Yamey 'RPM in the UK' p. 275; Andrews and Friday *Fair Trade* pp. 8, 10–13. The latter distinguish RPM where manufacturers enforced their prices on retail outlets either individually or through a trade association, from 'direct RPM' where a multiple retailer stipulated uniform prices in all outlets – Marks and Spencer is the obvious example.

47. BT258/223 internal Board of Trade memorandum explaining the background to the practices 10/1/1956.

48. J. Vaizey *The Brewing Industry 1886–1951* (1960) pp. 6–7.

49. J. Pickering *Resale Price Maintenance in Practice* (1966) p. 48.

50. B.S. Yamey 'Resale Price Maintenance in the United Kingdom' in B.S. Yamey (ed.) *Resale Price Maintenance* (1966) p. 276.

51. B.S. Yamey *The Economics of Resale Price Maintenance* (1954) chapters 7 and 8; B.S. Yamey 'The Origins of Price Maintenance in Three Branches of Retailing' *Economic Journal* 62 (Sept. 1952) pp. 522–43.

52. BT64/454 RPM(E)31 Evidence of Imperial Tobacco Co. to the Lloyd Jacob Committee on RPM 1947; H. Levy *Retail Trade Associations* (1942) p. 18.

53. N. Kaldor in *The Times* 17/3/1964, cited in Yamey *Resale Price Maintenance* p. 10 n.

54. J.B. Jefferys *Retail Trading in Britain 1850–1950* (Cambridge, 1954) p. 55.

55. For a debate on this question see Sir Henry Clay 'Resale Price Maintenance' *Journal of Industrial Economics* 3, 1 (Dec. 1954) pp. 9–21; Yamey 'Resale Price Maintenance in the United Kingdom' p. 251.

56. Levy *Retail Trade Associations* p. 64.

57. BLPES Political and Economic Planning Archive, Part II, Section P: Publications, R.35 (hereafter, PEP) File P126 'Association of Municipal Councils. Report of special sub-committee of the General Purposes Committee on Monopolies' 11/1/1955 and evidence of the Lewisham, Paddington and Northern Hospital groups; File P127 evidence of Miners' Safety Appliances.

58. PEP File 126 evidence of the LCC; MRPC *Heavy Electrical Machinery* p. 162 on the relationship with the Central Electrical Authority.

59. MRPC *Report on the Supply of Buildings in the Greater London Area* p. 67 and passim; PEP File P126 evidence of the Association of Municipal Councils. Newspapers and journals picked up local council allegations, e.g. *The Economist* 14/5/1955, 14/1/1956; *The Times* 15/6/1955, 18/2/1956, 21/2/1956; *News Chronicle* 13/5/1955, 8/6/1955, 28/5/1955.

60. PEP File P128 evidence collected on British Chemical Plant Manufacturers' Association; File P129 evidence on British Plastics Federation, British Non-Ferrous Metals Federation, British Electrical and Allied Manufacturers Association. MRPC *Heavy Electrical Machinery* p. 180 and passim.

61. *The Economist* 14/5/1955. Swann *et al. Competition* p. 266 notes how identical tenders were done so openly in the 1950s that cartels clearly felt immune.

62. PEP *Industrial Trade Associations* (1957) facing p. 234.

63. For instance in starter batteries, Swann *et al. Competition* p. 364; MRPC *Heavy Electrical Machinery* pp. 211, 251–3; MRPC *Semi-Manufactures of Copper* p. 96; PEP File P127 evidence of McAlpine Ltd 18/5/1955.
64. PEP File P127, Letter from Boxfoldia to the Board of Trade, 11/11/1946.
65. Lucas *Industrial Reconstruction* pp. 192, 222; S. Tolliday *Business, Banking and Politics: the Case of British Steel* (Cambridge, Mass., 1987) pp. 302–4. See a classic characterisation of the German trust in D.H. MacGregor's introduction to Liefmann *Cartels, Concerns and Trusts* (1932) p. vii.
66. Reader *ICI* p. 194 and p. 6.
67. D. Meredith 'The Colonial Office, British business interests and the reform of cocoa marketing in West Africa, 1937–1945' *Journal of African History* 29, 3 (1988) pp. 285–300.
68. PEP P120 evidence from Unilever; Meredith 'Cocoa marketing' p. 286.
69. T. Praeger 'Trade Associations in Great Britain' *Agenda* 3 (Nov. 1944) p. 137.
70. 54%. Exact figures of the number of trade associations in the sample are not available.
71. PEP *Industrial Trade Associations* (1957) p. 250. The primacy of price-fixing functions was especially marked in retailing associations, Levy *Retail Trade Associations* Part III.
72. Office of Fair Trading, Registry of Restrictive Trading Agreements, files for building material associations.
73. CBI MSS200/F/3/52/14/70 'Trade associations: their place in the industrial world', undated, unsigned memo.
74. PEP *Industrial Trade Associations* p. 164; see also S. Blank *Industry and Government in Britain: the Federation of British Industries in Politics, 1945–65* (Farnborough, 1973) p. 40.
75. PEP P131, Annual progress report to 30/9/1955; and P121, Letter to Mrs Hemming (Treasury) from R. Bailey (PEP researcher), 5/12/1955. Much of their evidence for price-fixing was derived from complaints and other information.
76. Blank *Industry and Government* p. 47.
77. T. Peirenhemper 'Trade Associations in Germany in the Late Nineteenth and Early Twentieth Centuries' in H. Yamazaki and M. Miyamoto (eds.) *Trade Associations in Business History* (Tokyo, 1987) p. 233.
78. E.g. in carpets, tyres, bread and surgical dressings, Swann *et al. Competition* (1973) p. 116, p. 183, p. 206, p. 313.
79. PEP P128 and P129, case studies of some major and some lesser trade associations.
80. Praeger 'Trade Associations' p. 137.
81. It was probably on this basis that many of the 'umbrella' organisations were able to reply to PEP that they had never practised price maintenance or similar schemes.
82. OFT *Survey Vol. II* pp. 70–1.
83. *Ibid.*, pp. 141–7.
84. PEP P129; MRPC *Semi-Manufactures of Copper* pp. 17, 53–8.
85. PEP P129 and File P127 evidence of the Power Gas Corporation; Registry of Restrictive Trading Agreements, Nos. 227 and 232 on hydraulic machinery.
86. PEP P129.

206   Notes to pages 26–29

87. OFT *Survey Vol. II* p. 13.
88. PEP P127.
89. 'The New Feudalism' *The Economist* 2/4/1938; 'The Economic Front' *The Economist* 9/12/1939; *New Statesman and Nation* 8/3/1941, cited in Brady *Business* pp. 182–3 n.; Thomas Balogh, cited in A.A. Rogow and P. Shore *The Labour Government and British Industry 1945–51* (Oxford, 1955) pp. 22–3; J.S. Allen *World Monopoly and Peace* (New York, 1946) p. 145 citing work by the British Communist R. Palme Dutt; Blank *Industry and Government* p. 32.
90. L. Tivey and E. Wohlgemut 'Trade Associations as Interest Groups' *Political Quarterly* 29, 1 (Jan.–Mar. 1958) pp. 66–7. Trade associations have been little studied in economic and political literature, see B. Jessop 'The Capitalist State and the rule of capital: problems in the analysis of business associations' in David Marsh (ed.) *Capital and Politics in Western Europe* (1979) pp. 139–62. For excellent pioneering work on Britain, and comparisons with Germany see Brady *Business* and R. Brady *The Spirit and Structure of German Fascism* (1937).
91. PEP File P129.
92. Aaronovitch and Sawyer *Big Business* pp. 262–3; K. Cowling *Monopoly Capitalism Revisited* Warwick Economic Research Papers No. 365 (1990) pp. 7–8.
93. Booth 'Managed economy'.
94. OFT *Survey Volume I* p. 3.
95. D.H. Aldcroft *The Inter-war Economy* (1970) p. 292.
96. The threat of tariffs was used in a large number of cases: iron and steel, wire and wire products, other iron goods like baths, various non-ferrous metals like brass, copper and zinc, coal, phosphates, celluloid, greaseproof paper, precision chains, sheet glass and synthetic nitrogen. OFT *Survey* pp. 1, 13, 17–19, 30, 36, 57–9, 65–6, 75, 98–100, 104, 116, 147, 155; Sir Hubert Hutchinson *Tariff-Making and Industrial Reconstruction: an account of the work of the Import Duties Advisory Committee 1932–39* (1965) pp. 79–84, 107–13. Contrariwise, the tariff on lead imposed by Britain disrupted the international lead cartel, Plummer *International Combines* p. 125.
97. OFT *Survey Vol. I* pp. 3 and 30. The case of Japan is mentioned in a civil servant's autobiography, Alix Meynell *Public Servant, Private Woman* (1988) pp. 141–4.
98. M. Collins *Banks and Industrial Finance in Britain 1800–1939* (1991) pp. 77–81; M.H. Best and J. Humphries 'The City and Industrial Decline' in B. Elbaum and W. Lazonick (eds.) *The Decline of the British Economy* (Oxford, 1986) pp. 233–4.
99. J.H. Bamberg 'The Rationalisation of the British Cotton Industry in the Interwar Years' *Textile History* 19, 1 (Spring 1988) pp. 83–102; M.W. Kirby 'The Lancashire Cotton Industry in the inter-war years: a study in organisational change' *Bus.Hist.* 14, 2 (Jul. 1974) pp. 145–59.
100. S. Tolliday 'Tariffs and Steel, 1916–1934: The Politics of Industrial Decline' in J. Turner (ed.) *Businessmen and Politics* pp. 50–75; S. Tolliday 'Steel and Rationalisation Policies, 1918–1950' in Elbaum and Lazonick *Decline* pp. 82–108.
101. M.W. Kirby 'Government Intervention in Industrial Organisation: Coal Mining in the Nineteen Thirties' *Bus.Hist.* 15, 2 (Jul. 1973) pp. 160–73.

102. A summary of the types of practice revealed in Monopolies Commission reports can be found in P.H. Guenault and J.M. Jackson *The Control of Monopoly in the United Kingdom* (2nd ed., 1974) pp. 24–5; BPP (1960–61) *Registrar of Restrictive Trading Agreements* p. 9. Private capacity-controlling agreements listed in the Board of Trade's survey of 1946 were in flour-milling and earthenware goods.

103. J. Turner 'Servants of Two Masters: British Trade Associations in the First Half of the Twentieth Century' in Yamazaki and Miyamoto *Trade Associations*; Best and Humphries 'The City' p. 234.

104. Levy *Retail Trade Associations*, chapter 19.

105. OFT *Survey Vol. I* pp. 84, 118–19.

106. A.A. Rogow and P. Shore *The Labour Government and British Industry 1945–51* (1955) p. 68; J. Leruez *Economic Planning and Politics in Britain* (1975) p. 64; E. Wilkinson *The Town that was Murdered* (1939); G.W. Stocking and M.W. Watkins *Cartels or Competition? The Economics of International Controls by Business and Government* (New York, 1948) p. 53.

107. G.C. Allen *British Industry and Economic Policy* (1979); R.E. Caves 'Market Organisation, Performance and Public Policy' in R.E. Caves *Britain's Economic Prospects* (1968) pp. 306–10; M.W. Kirby 'Institutional rigidities and economic decline: reflections on the British experience' *EHR* 45,4 (1992).

108. S.N. Broadberry and N.F.R. Crafts 'Explaining Anglo–American Productivity Differences in the mid-twentieth century' *Oxford Bulletin of Economics and Statistics* 52, 4 (1990) p. 398; Caves *Economic Prospects* p. 310.

109. Utton 'Early merger movement' pp. 51–60; M.W. Kirby 'Institutional rigidities' p. 645.

110. B. Fine 'Economies of scale and a featherbedding cartel?: a reconsideration of the interwar British coal industry' *EHR* 43, 3 (1990) p. 440 and generally pp. 438–49.

111. R. Liefmann *Cartels* pp. 89–92; D. Warriner *Combines and Rationalisation in Germany 1924–28* (1931) p. 43; H. Levy *Industrial Germany* (Cambridge, 1935), p. 52.

112. F.C. Steckel 'Cartelisation of the German Chemical Industry 1918–25' *Journal of European Economic History* 19, 2 (Fall 1990) pp. 329–51; Warriner *Combines* pp. 45–6; S.B. Webb 'Tariffs, Cartels, Technology and Growth in the German Steel Industry, 1879–1914' *Journal of Economic History* 40, 2 (Jun. 1980) pp. 309–29. It was also found however, that the process of integration could actually work against rationalisation of ownership, while working to increase the gains from economies of scale, Liefmann *Cartels* pp. 65–6; Warriner *Combines* p. 43. For general scepticism on the positive role of German cartels before 1914 see A.D. Chandler *Scale and Scope. The Dynamics of Industrial Capitalism* (Cambridge, Mass., 1990) pp. 493–4.

113. P. Deseille *Le Développement des Trusts en Angleterre* (Paris, 1909) p. 14; D.H. MacGregor *Industrial Combination* (Cambridge, 1906) pp. 138 ff.; R Liefmann *Schutzzoll und Kartelle* (Jena, 1903).

114. It also removed the pejorative tone of the term and its association with Nazism. On the avoidance of the use of the term for these and other reasons see Hexner *International Cartels* pp. 6–10.

115. Liefmann *Cartels* p. 33; Warriner *Combines* p. 83.

116. Levy *Industrial Germany* p. 165; Liefmann *Cartels* p. 64; J. Kocka 'Modern

Industrial Enterprise' p. 106. This categorisation is mainly attributable to Grünzel *Über Kartelle* and was also adopted in the Committee on Industry and Trade *Factors in Industrial and Commercial Efficiency* Part 1 (HMSO, 1927) pp. 71–3.

117. On the difference between British and German trade associations see H. Herrmann 'Verbandskonzentration und Grossunternehmen' in N. Horn and J. Kocka (eds.) *Law and the Formation of the Big Enterprises in the 19th and Early 20th Centuries* (Göttingen, 1979) pp. 647–74.

118. T231/160 Foreign Exchange Control Committee minutes Ref. Nos. E45–233, 267, 273; T231/161 Ref. Nos. E46–387, 389, 413, 414, 415; T231/392 Ref. Nos. E47–462.

119. OFT *Survey Vol. I* pp. 1–7, 21, 23.

120. CAB87/3 R.P.(43)25 'Report on the Recovery of export markets and the promotion of the export trade' 15/6/1943.

121. OFT *Survey Vol. I*, pp. 45, 96 and 85. M. Kitson and S. Solomou *Protectionism and economic revival: the British interwar economy* (Cambridge, 1990) p. 100.

122. Wilkinson *Town that was Murdered*; Booth 'Managed Economy?'.

123. H.W. Richardson *Economic Recovery in Britain 1932–39* (1967).

124. Capie *Depression and Protectionism* p. 140.

125. Kitson and Solomou *Protectionism* p. 100.

126. A. Phillips 'An econometric study of price-fixing, market structure and performance in British industry in the early 1950s' in K. Cowling (ed.) *Market Structure and Corporate Behaviour: Theory and Empirical Analysis of the Firm* (1972) pp. 172–3.

127. J.B. Heath 'Restrictive Practices and After' *Manchester School of Economic and Social Studies* 29, 2 (May, 1961) pp. 173–202; Caves *Economic Prospects* p. 309.

128. H. Mercer 'The Labour Governments of 1945 to 1951 and private industry' in N. Tiratsoo (ed.) *The Attlee Years* (1992) pp. 71–89.

3 THE STATE AND THE 'MONOPOLY PROBLEM', 1880–1939

1. A.A. Berle and G. Means *The Modern Corporation and Private Property* (1932) p. 338.

2. J.S. Mill *Principles of Political Economy* cited in G.C. Allen *Economic Thought and Industrial Policy* University College Inaugural Lecture 4 Mar. 1948 p. 3.

3. J.A.G. Dennison 'The Reaction to the Growth of Trusts and Industrial Combinations in Britain 1888–1921' Ph.D. thesis (University of London, 1980) p. 61, citing A. Marshall *Principles of Economics* p. 711. It is Dennison's assessment that a consensus existed around the neo-classical position, p. 20.

4. A. Marshall *Industry and Trade* (2nd ed., 1923) pp. 580–4, 623, 650. It must rank as one of the ironies of economic history that Marshall's *Principles of Economics* was used to test the newly-devised Net Book Agreement in 1890.

5. H. Clay *The Post-war Unemployment Problem* (1929) p. 172; D.H. MacGregor *Industrial Combination* (Cambridge, 1906) pp. 103, 191, 231; M.E. Hirst *The Story of the Trusts* (1913), see also F.W. Hirst *Monopolies, Trusts and Kartells* (1905).

6. B. Semmel *Imperialism and Social Reform, 1895–1914* (1960) p. 208, the petition appeared on 15/8/1903.
7. MacGregor *Combination* pp. 220–41.
8. Semmel *Imperialism* pp. 188–201. The method of the historical economists was praised by Alfred Marshall, and the influence they had on Marshall is noted in P.L. Williams 'The Attitude of the Economics Profession in Britain and the United States to the Trust Movement, 1890–1914' in J. Hey and D. Winch (eds.) *A Century of Economics* (Oxford, 1990) pp. 92–108 ; Marshall *Principles* pp. 767–8; R. Backhouse *A History of Modern Economic Analysis* (Oxford, 1985) p. 216.
9. H.F. Foxwell 'The Growth of Monopoly and its bearing on the functions of the state' in R.L. Smyth (ed.) *Essays in the Economics of Socialism and Capitalism* (1964) pp. 78–9, 82; W.J. Ashley *The Economic Organisation of England: an outline history* (1914) pp. 186–9; H. Levy *Monopolies, Cartels and Trusts* (2nd ed., 1927) Preface to the First English Edition of 1911 p. vii. The work first appeared in English as *Monopoly and Competition* (1911). Levy believed, however, that the development of cartels and trusts in Britain was limited by the absence of a protective tariff, as well as the lower incidence of local monopolies and the rarity of mineral products likely to foster monopoly. However, these limiting factors in no way insulated her from the general tendency towards concentration and hence to monopoly, Levy *Monopolies* pp. 312–14.
10. For a definition of 'social imperialism' see Semmel *Imperialism* pp. 13–14. He distinguishes social imperialists from 'liberal free trade imperialists' whose platform was a combination of free trade, radical social reform, imperialism and militarism, pp. 25–6. Some tariff reformers were very hostile to trade unions; on Ashley's opposition to his fellow tariff reformers' attitude to unions see A. Sykes *Tariff Reform in British Politics 1903–1913* (Oxford, 1979) p. 107. Many 'historical economists' in Britain, like Ashley and William Cunningham were active in the tariff reform movement.
11. Foxwell 'Monopoly' pp. 86–7; Semmel *Imperialism* pp. 193, 198, 206–7.
12. W. Clark 'The Industrial Basis of Socialism' in G.B. Shaw (ed.) *Fabian Essays in Socialism* (1889); H.W. Macrosty *Trusts and the State* (1901) p. 130 and Ramsay MacDonald *The Socialist Movement* c.1911 p. 55.
13. Macrosty *Trusts and the State* p. 10.
14. H.W. Macrosty *State Control of Trusts* Fabian Tract No. 124 (1905) p. 4.
15. This characterisation was suggested to me by John Quail. Their view was Panglossian compared with both the Marxist and the neo-classical analysis of state intervention.
16. Macrosty *Trusts and the State* pp. 129–46.
17. *Ibid.* p. 309.
18. *Ibid.* p. 283.
19. D. Gribbin 'The Contribution of economists to the origins of UK competition policy' in P. de Wolf (ed.) *Competition in Europe. Essays in Honour of Henk W. de Jong* (Dordrecht, 1991) pp. 135–62; L. Hannah 'Economic ideas and governent policy on industrial organisation in Britain since 1945 ' in M.O. Furner and B. Supple (eds.) *The state and economic knowledge. The American and British experiences* (Cambridge, 1990) pp. 354–75.

20. Macrosty *State Control* p. 14.
21. *Ibid.* p. 15.
22. Dennison 'Reaction to Trusts' p. 90. Bellamy's book conjured up a future where all economic activity was concentrated in the hands of one giant trust.
23. J.A. Hobson *Imperialism* (3rd ed., 1905).
24. Marshall *Industry and Trade* pp. 624–7; A. Matyas *History of Modern Non-Marxian Economics* (2nd ed., Budapest, 1985) pp. 219–45.
25. See for instance A. Pigou *Economics in Practice* (1935) p. 126.
26. D.H. MacGregor *Enterprise, Purpose and Profit* (Oxford, 1934) p. 60; Marshall *Industry and Trade* pp. 660–1; A. Pigou *The Economics of Welfare* (2nd ed., 1924) pp. 305–46;
    A. Pigou *Socialism versus Capitalism* (1937) cited in H.W. Spiegel *The Growth of Economic Thought* (3rd ed., 1991) pp. 572–4.
27. Clay *Unemployment Problem* pp. 172–204; J.A. Hobson *Rationalisation and Unemployment* (1930).
28. D. Moggridge (ed.) *The collected writings of John Maynard Keynes. Volume xix. Activities 1922–29* (Cambridge, 1981) various articles in *The Nation and Athenaeum* 24/4/1926 p. 528, 15/5/1926 pp. 535–6, 19/11/1926 p. 586, 27/11/1926 pp. 591–2, 24/12/1926 p. 600, 19/11/1927 pp. 622–7, 2/2/1929 pp. 632–6.
29. Clay is cited in L. Hannah *The Rise of the Corporate Economy* (2nd ed., 1983) p. 32, see also Clay *Unemployment Problem* p. 175. Liberal Industrial Enquiry *Britain's Industrial Future* (1928) pp. 459–60. The Liberal Industrial Enquiry involved Henry Clay and Keynes and G.C. Allen; A. Booth and M. Pack *Employment, Capital and Economic Policy in Britain, 1918–1939* (1985) p. 42; G.C. Allen 'Advice from economists – forty-five years ago' *The Three Banks Review* 106 (Jun. 1975) pp. 35–50. The point that competition was a poor way to bring about rationalisation was widely held, see especially BPP (1928–29) *Final Report of the Committee on Industry and Trade* Cmd. 3282 p. 179, and G.D.H. Cole *The Next Ten Years in British social and economic policy* (1929) p. 128.
30. H. Macmillan *The Middle Way* (1938); H. Macmillan *Reconstruction: A Plea for a National Policy* (1933); H. Macmillan *The State and Industry in 1932* (1932); A. Salter *Recovery: the Second Effort* (2nd ed., 1933); Lord Melchett *Imperial Economic Unity* (1930); *The Industrial Reorganisation League* (1934). Overviews of some of these ideas are in D. Ritschel 'A Corporatist Economy in Britain? Capitalist Planning for industrial self-government in the 1930s' *EngHR* (Jan. 1991) pp. 41–65; L.P. Carpenter 'Corporatism in Britain, 1930–45' *JCH* 11 (1976) pp. 3–25; A. Marwick 'Middle Opinion in the Thirties: Planning, Progress and Political "Agreement"' *EngHR* 79 (Apr. 1964) pp. 285–98; Booth and Pack *Employment* pp. 55–74.
31. M. Cowling *The impact of Labour 1920–23. The beginnings of modern British politics* (Cambridge, 1971); K. Burgess *The Challenge of Labour: Shaping British Society 1850–1930* (1980).
32. F. Coetzee 'Pressure Groups, Tory Businessmen and the aura of political corruption before the First World War' *Historical Journal* 29,4 (Dec. 1986) pp. 833–52; S. White 'Ideological Hegemony and Political Control: the Sociology of Anti-Bolshevism' *Scottish Labour History Society Journal* 9 (Jun. 1975) pp. 3–20.
33. D. Ritschel 'Corporatist Economy' pp. 43–4.

34. Macmillan *Reconstruction: A Plan for a National Policy* pp. 110–15; Ritschel 'Corporatist Economy' pp. 50–1; M. Dintenfass 'The Politics of Producers' Co-operation: the FBI-TUC-NCEO Talks, 1929–1933' in J. Turner (ed.) *Businessmen and Politics. Studies of Business Activity in British Politics 1900–1945* (1984) pp. 76–92.

35. Booth and Pack *Employment Policy* pp. 148–56 and 141.

36. A. Thorpe 'The Industrial Meaning of Gradualism: the Labour Party and Industry from 1918 to 1931', unpublished paper given at Business History Unit, LSE, conference on 'Labour: the party of industrial modernisation?' (1992) pp. 22, 37. Cole *The Next Ten Years* p. 128.

37. Booth and Pack *Employment Policy* pp. 126, 134; Thorpe 'Gradualism'.

38. Booth and Pack *Employment Policy* p. 143.

39. M. Francis 'Labour's Industrial Policies and Plans from 1931 to 1945', unpublished paper given at Business History Unit LSE, conference on 'Labour: the Party of industrial modernisation?' (1992).

40. *Britain without Capitalists. A study of what industry in a Soviet Britain could achieve* (1936) pp. 4–5, 12–15. The book was written by a group of economists and scientists who remained anonymous but were clearly connected with the Communist Party.

41. *Ibid.* pp. 6–8.

42. Ellen Wilkinson, cited in Ritschel 'Corporatist Economy' p. 43.

43. Hobson *Rationalisation and Unemployment* pp. 94, 85. His solutions were for surplus-profits tax and state provision of good conditions for workers.

44. G.J. Stigler 'Perfect Competition Historically Contemplated' *Journal of Political Economy* 65, 1 (Feb. 1957) pp. 1–17. E.H. Chamberlin 'The Origin and Early Development of Monopolistic Competition Theory' *Quarterly Journal of Economics* 75, 4 (Nov. 1961) pp. 540–3. T. Burke, A. Genn-Bash and B. Haines *Competition in Theory and Practice* (1988) pp. 64–8; M. Sawyer *The Economics of Industries and Firms* (2nd ed., 1985) pp. 256–9.

45. W. Eucken *Gründsätze der Wirtschaftspolitik* (Tübingen, 1952) p. 254 cited in S. Liebermann 'The Ideological Foundations of Western European Planning' *Journal of European Economic History* 10, 2 (Fall 1981) p. 350.

46. H.G. Grossekettler 'On designing an economic order. The contribution of the Freiburg School' in D.A. Walker (ed.) *Perspectives on the History of Economic Thought. Volume 2* (Aldershot, 1989) pp. 38–84; G.J. Stigler *Memoirs of an Unregulated Economist* (New York, 1988) pp. 139–45.

47. W.H.G. Armytage 'The Railway Rates Question and the Fall of the Third Gladstone Ministry' *EngHR* 65 (Jan. 1950) pp. 18–51; H. Parris *Government and the Railways in Nineteenth Century Britain* (1965) pp. 212–25; T. Gourvish *Railways and the British Economy 1830–1914* (1980) pp. 47–56; P.M. Williams 'Public Opinion and the Railway Rates Question in 1886' *EngHR* 67 (Jan. 1952) pp. 37–73.

48. Armytage 'Railway Rates' pp. 48–50.

49. *Daily News* 12/3/1886 cited in Armytage 'Railway Rates' p. 26.

50. Macrosty *The Trust Movement in British Industry* (1907) pp. 203–9; A.E. Musson *Enterprise in Soap and Chemicals* (Manchester, 1965) p. 226; C. Wilson *The History of Unilever: Volume 1* (1954) pp. 80–8.

51. For a breakdown of the leading figures in the Tariff Reform League and on the

Tariff Commission of 1903 see Semmel *Imperialism* pp. 102–5.
52. BPP (1918) *Ministry of Reconstruction. Report of Committee on Trusts* Vol. xiii Cmd. 9236.
53. P.B. Johnson *Land Fit for Heroes: The Planning of British Reconstruction 1916–1919* (Chicago, 1968) pp. 466–8.
54. B. Waites 'The Government of the Home Front and the "Moral Economy" of the Working Class' in P. Liddle (ed.) *Home Fires and Foreign Fields* (1985) p. 179.
55. White 'Ideological Hegemony' p. 3.
56. Waites *Home Front*. p. 181; BPP (1917–18) *Commission of Enquiry into Industrial Unrest. Summary of the reports of the Commission* Vol. xv Cmd. 8696. See also the regional reports in the same volume, and the summary by E. Cannan 'Industrial Unrest' *Economic Journal* 26 (1917) p. 456.
57. CAB24/83 G.T. 7685 'Prevention of Profiteering' memorandum by the President of the Board of Trade 12/7/1919; Dennison 'Reaction to Trusts' p. 277; CAB24/103 C.P. 1074 'Trade Monopolies and Profiteering Act (Amendment) Bill' memorandum by the President of the Board of Trade 14/4/1920.
58. CAB24/103 and BT65/3 C.P. 1074 'Trade Monopolies and Profiteering (Amendment) Act memorandum by the President of the Board of Trade' and C.P. 1208 'Trade Monopolies Bill' memorandum by First Commissioner of Works (Sir Alfred Mond) 3/5/1920; CAB23/21 Cabinet 21(20) 20/4/1920.
59. CAB24/66 G.T. 5920 'Proposed enquiry into Profits in relation to the Cost of Living' memorandum by the President of the Board of Trade (A.H. Stanley) 9/10/1918; CAB24/25 G.T. 6834 'The investigation of profits in industry' memorandum by First Commissioner of Works 18/2/1919; CAB24/68 G.T. 6172 'Proposed enquiry into profits in relation to the cost of living' memorandum by the Food Controller, J.R. Clynes; CAB23/10 minutes of the War Cabinet W.C. 575, 3/6/1919.
60. His was the view expressed by the President of the Board of Trade, replying to a request for further legislation in 1920, and was to be re-iterated by Patrick Fitzgerald in his account of industrial combination based on the reports of the SCT and Standing Committee on Prices. *Parl.Deb.* (1920) Vol. 128 29/4/1920; P. Fitzgerald *Industrial Combination in England* (2nd ed., 1927) p. 208. See bibliography for some of the relevant reports of the Standing Committee on Trusts (SCT).
61. BT55/55 'Deputation regarding trusts legislation' report discussed at joint meeting with the Standing Committee on Prices 5/4/1921.
62. BT55/55 Meetings of the SCT last meeting 18/5/1921.
63. BT55/55 SCT 22nd, 38th, 39th and 47th meetings 22/3/1920, 27/7/1920, 10/8/1920 and 19/10/1920.
64. See John Hilton's comment BT55/55 SCT 11th meeting 6/1/1920 and BT55/55 SCT 12th and 13th meetings 13/1/1920 and 20/1/1920.
65. BT55/55 SCT 5th meeting 11/11/1919.
66. BT55/55 SCT 21st meeting 10/3/1920.
67. Nuffield College, Oxford, Morrison Papers, Box D2/11 election address for North Southwark May 1920.
68. BT68/89 and BT68/90.
69. Dennison 'Reaction to Trusts' pp. 287–8. So unpopular with business and

sections of Whitehall were schemes to control prices and profits that considerations of their control in a future war in the inter-war period bore little fruit
until revived concerns about public disquiet forced the speedy introduction of
the Prices and Goods Act in September 1939. See N. Rollings 'Whitehall and
the control of prices and profits in a major war, 1919–1939' unpublished draft
paper (1992).

70. BPP *Final Report of the Committee on Commercial and Industrial Policy after
    the war* (1918) Vol. xiii Cmd. 9035 pp. 34–9 and 62–5.
71. M. Kirby and M. Rose 'Productivity and competitive failure: British govern-
    ment policy and industry, 1914–1919' in G. Jones and M. Kirby (eds.)
    *Competitiveness and the State: Government and business in twentieth century
    Britain* (Manchester, 1991) p. 27. J. Turner 'The Politics of "Organised
    Business" in the First World War' in Turner *Businessmen and Politics* pp. 33–
    49; CAB24/86 G.T. 7906 'Proposed Trade policy' memorandum by President
    of the Board of Trade.
72. Kirby and Rose 'Productivity' p. 31.
73. *Final Report of the Committee on Industry and Trade* Cmd. 3282 p. 194.
74. D. Cairns 'Monopolies and Restrictive Practices' in M. Ginsberg (ed.) *Law and
    Opinion in England in the Twentieth Century* (1954) pp. 176–8.
75. R.W.D. Boyce *British Capitalism at the Crossroads, 1919–1932* (Cambridge,
    1987) pp. 133, 153 ff.; Dintenfass 'Producers' Co-operation' pp. 76–92; Hannah
    Corporate Economy pp. 27–40.
76. Hannah has argued this case against the views of contemporaries and recent
    Marxists, though he accepts government was more overtly supportive of
    cartels, Hannah *Corporate Economy* p. 51. A variant of Hannah's view is
    Richard Roberts' notion of 'industrial diplomacy': informal contacts between
    civil servants and industrialists helped specific industries 'to the detriment of
    overall balance of policy', R. Roberts 'The Administrative Origins of Industrial
    Diplomacy: an Aspect of Government–Industry Relations, 1929–1935' in
    Turner *Businessmen and Politics* pp. 93, 100.
77. A. Booth 'Britain in the 1930s – a managed economy?' *EHR* 57, 2 (Nov. 1987);
    M.W. Kirby 'Industrial Policy' in S. Glynn and A. Booth *The Road to Full
    Employment* (1987) p. 137.
78. D.H. Aldcroft *The British Economy. Volume 1. The Years of Turmoil 1920–1951*
    (Brighton, 1986) pp. 128–9; P.A. Hall 'The State and Economic Decline' in
    Elbaum and Lazonick *Decline* p. 275; M.W. Kirby 'Government Intervention
    and Industrial Organisation: Coal Mining in the Nineteen Thirties' *Bus.Hist.*
    15, 2 pp. 160–73; G.C. Allen *British Industries and their Organisation* (2nd ed.,
    1935) p. 132F; S. Tolliday 'Steel and Rationalisation Policies, 1918–50' in
    Elbaum and Lazonick *Decline* p. 102; M.H. Best and J. Humphries 'The City
    and Industrial Decline' in Elbaum and Lazonick *Decline* p. 234.
79. Ritschel 'Corporatist Economy' pp. 61–2.
80. *Ibid.* p. 57.
81. This analysis derives from H. Overbeek *Global Capitalism and National
    Decline: The Thatcher Decade in Perspective* (1990) pp. 59–83, without using his
    sometimes confusing distinction between 'corporate liberal bourgeoisie' and
    'state monopoly bourgeoisie' whose members often seemed to overlap.
82. Ritschel 'Corporatist Economy' p. 65.

83. S.E. Finer 'The Federation of British Industries' *Political Studies* 4, 1 (Feb. 1956) p. 78.
84. Sir Herbert Hutchinson *Tariff-Making and Industrial Reconstruction* (1965) p. 26. Hutchinson was Assistant Secretary to the IDAC from 1932 to 1939 and became its Secretary in 1939.
85. *Ibid.* p. 79.
86. G. Jones *The State and the Emergence of the British Oil Industry* (1981) p. 239; E. Hexner *International Cartels* (1946) pp. 112–26.
87. FO371/40584 U720/6/70 Brief prepared by Intelligence section of the Board of Trade for Lord Woolton 25/1/1944. A circular from the Department of Overseas Trade to British ambassadors in 1937 made precisely that point BT11/829 'International Industrial Agreements' letter from Cecil Farrar to Embassies 18/12/1937.
88. CBI MSS200/F/1/1/83 'Anglo–German Industrial Convention' and minutes of meeting at the FBI 5/4/1939. See also 'Telegram from the Soviet Ambassador in Britain to the People's Commissariat for Foreign Affairs of the USSR 3/2/1939' *Soviet Peace Efforts on the Eve of World War Two* (Moscow, 1973) Document No. 113 pp. 197–8. D.E. Kaiser *Economic Diplomacy and the Origins of the Second World War* (New Jersey, 1980) pp. 244, 268; R.G. Holland 'The Federation of British Industries and the International Economy, 1929–1939' *EHR* 43, 2 (1981) pp. 287–301.
89. *Parl.Deb.* (1938–39) Vol. 345 21/3/1939 Cols. 1107–9; *The Economist* 25/3/1939 p. 607.
90. B.J. Wendt *Economic Appeasement* (Hamburg, 1971) p. 575.
91. *U.K. Documents on British Foreign Policy* 3rd series Vol. iv, Appendix Frank Ashton-Gwatkin, head economic section Foreign Office to Emil Wiehl and No. 279 letter Lord Halifax, Secretary of State for Foreign Affairs to Sir Neville Henderson, British Ambassador in Berlin 15/3/1939. On British interests in Eastern and South-Eastern Europe see A. Teichova *An Economic Background to Munich* (Cambridge, 1974) p. 382 and Kaiser *Economic Diplomacy* p. 286; FO371/22951 C2881 'FBI/RGI discussions'; Holland 'The Federation of British Industries' pp. 224, 297–8.
92. For this association in the minds of anti-appeasers in the Foreign Office see FO371/23955 W17272 minute by Laurence Collier 22/11/1939 and W17722 letter J. Somerville, Export Credits Guarantee Department to W. Wills (Board of Trade) 28/11/1939.
93. W.K. Hancock and N.M. Gowing *The British War Economy* (1949) p. 100.
94. BT64/58 'International Cartel Problems' memorandum by G.L. Watkinson (Board of Trade) 12/5/1940; OFT *Survey Vol. II* p. 49.
95. BT64/58 minute by C.K. Hobson (Board of Trade) 3/7/1940; BT64/320 'International Match Agreements' memorandum unsigned, undated from Trading with the Enemy Department.
96. BT64/53 'Enquiry concerning G.E.C. and E.L.M.A.' minute 10/11/1939; FO371/23955 W17765 Ashton-Gwatkin (Ministry of Economic Warfare) to W. Wills 23/11/1939.
97. B. Wootton *Plan or No Plan* (1934) p. 320.
98. Allen *British Industries* p. 132F; Allen *Economic Thought* p. 7.
99. BT64/318 minute Sir Charles Innes to Henry Clay June 1942 and minute by Alix Kilroy (Board of Trade) 8/7/1943.

4 THE WAR AND THE WHITE PAPER

1. On the elements of continuity between the Labour and Coalition governments see K. Middlemas *Power, Competition and the State. Volume 1: Britain in Search of Balance 1940–61* (1986) p. 109; P. Addison *The Road to 1945* (1975) p. 273.

2. BPP (1943–44) *Employment Policy* Vol. viii Cmd. 6527 para. 54.

3. A. Booth 'Simple Keynesianism and Whitehall, 1936–47' *Economy and Society* 15, 1 (Feb. 1986) pp. 1–22; J. Tomlinson *Public Policy and the Economy since 1900* (Oxford, 1990) pp. 168–70; A. Booth 'War and the White Paper' in S. Glynn and A. Booth (eds.) *The Road to Full Employment* (1987) pp. 175–95.

4. CAB87/63 EC(43)3 Steering Committee on Post-war Employment 'Restrictive Practices in Industry' memorandum by the Board of Trade 15/10/1943.

5. W.K. Hancock and H. Gowing *The British War Economy* (HMSO, 1949) p. 534; Addison *Road to 1945* p. 168; L.S. Pressnell *External Economic Policy Since the War. Volume I. The Post-war Financial Settlement* (HMSO, 1986) p. 18.

6. CAB87/54 I.E.P.(41)3 Internal Economic Problems Committee 'Internal Measures for the Prevention of General Unemployment memorandum by the Economic Section of the War Cabinet 3/11/1941'. This is also reprinted in S. Howson (ed.) *The Collected Papers of James Meade. Volume I: Employment and Inflation* (1988) pp. 171–83.

7. BT64/318 Minute from H. Clay to R. Nowell 30/12/1941; memorandum by Innes 'Industrial Organisation' 22/12/1941; note R.L. Cohen to Innes 22/12/1941; note by H. Clay 30/12/1941. This small exchange is given great prominence in two recent accounts of war-time discussions on competition. See D. Gribbin 'The contribution of economists to the origins of UK competition policy' in P. de Wolf (ed.) *Competition in Europe. Essays in honour of Henk W. de Jong* (Dordrecht, 1991) pp. 138–41, and T. Freyer *Regulating big business: Antitrust in Great Britain and America 1880–1990* (Cambridge, 1992) pp. 234–40.

8. CAB87/13 PR(43)26 Committee on Reconstruction Priorities note by the Lord President (Sir John Anderson) prepared by the Economic Section, 'The Maintenance of Employment' 18/5/1943; CAB87/12, PR(43)12th meeting, 13/7/1943.

9. Dalton Diaries, I, Box 29 5/7/1943, 9/7/1943, 12/7/1943; BT64/3180 minutes of the 10th meeting of the Board of Trade Reconstruction Committee 6/7/1943; BT64/318 'The Control of Monopoly' by G.C. Allen and Hugh Gaitskell 17/7/1943.

10. BT64/3345 'The Control of Monopoly' draft memorandum by G.H. Andrew (Principal, Board of Trade) 21/8/1943.

11. CAB87/63 EC(43)3 'Restrictive Practices in Industry' memorandum by the Board of Trade 15/10/1943.

12. CAB87/63 Reconstruction Committee papers R(44)6 'Post-war Employment' Report of the Steering Committee on Employment 11/1/1944.

13. *Ibid.*, note of dissent by Lionel Robbins (Director, Economic Section of the War Cabinet).

14. CAB87/6 R(44)27 'Restrictive Developments in Industry' note by the Minister of Aircraft Production 3/2/1944.

15. CAB87/5 R(44)13th meeting 4/2/1944.
16. CAB87/6 R(44)65 'Restrictive Practices' joint memorandum by the President of the Board of Trade and the Minister without Portfolio 29/3/1944.
17. CAB87/5 R(44)34th meeting 24/4/1944.
18. CAB124/204 note from Norman Brook (Deputy Secretary of the War Cabinet) to Lord Woolton (Minister of Reconstruction) enclosing note by Economic Section 5/2/1944.
19. Trade Union Congress *Post-War Reconstruction* (1944) pp. 7–10 and 15–18.
20. Addison *Road to 1945* pp. 159–60; *Monopoly* Common Wealth Information Bulletin No. 7 (Oct. 1944) p. 24.
21. Their views are cited in E. Burns *Labour's Way Forward* (1942) p. 9.
22. *Parl.Deb.* (1942–43) Vol. 390 6/7/1943 Cols. 1939–40; Vol. 391 20/7/43 Cols. 663–4 and 22/7/1943 Cols. 1097–8; *Parl.Deb.* (1943–44) Vol. 392 12/10/1943 Cols. 729–30 and 19/10/1943 Cols. 1190–1; Vol. 393 2/11/1943 Cols. 499–501 and 3/11/1943 Col. 684 and 9/11/1943 Cols. 1063–4; Vol. 397 23/2/1944 Cols. 817–18 and 29/2/1944 Col. 1253; Vol. 400 16/5/1944 Col. 23; Vol. 401 6/7/1944 Col. 1307.
23. *Parl. Deb.* (1942–43) Vol. 387 23/3/1943 Col. 1460; *Parl. Deb.* (1943–44)) Vol. 397 24/2/1944 Cols. 973–4; Vol. 401 11/7/1944 Col. 1562.
24. *Ibid.* Vol. 401 Debate on Employment policy 21–23/6/1944 Cols. 91–2, 363, 425–6, 450, 557, 561.
25. Dalton Diaries, I, Box 31 4/2/1944. Similar views were expressed by Morrison, see H. Morrison *Herbert Morrison: an Autobiography* (1960) p. 229.
26. S. Brooke 'Revisionists and Fundamentalists: the Labour Party and Economic Policy during the Second World War' *Historical Journal* 32, 1 (1989) pp. 157–5.
27. CPGB *Britain for the People* (May 1944).
28. CPGB *Co-operatives against Combines* (Jun. 1944); J. Attfield and S. Williams (eds.) *1939: the Communist Party of Great Britain and the War* (1984) Appendix VIII; K. Morgan *Against Fascism and War. Ruptures and continuities in British Communist politics 1935–41* (Manchester, 1989) p. 204.
29. N. Harris *Competition and the Corporate Society: British Conservatives, the State and Industry 1945–1964* (1972) p. 59.
30. CAB 87/5 R(44)13th meeting 4/2/1944.
31. Addison *Road to 1945* pp. 232–3; Harris *Competition and Corporate Society* p. 59.
32. Conservative sub-committee on Industry *Work: the Future of British Industry* (Jan. 1944) pp. 25 and 42.
33. Liberal Publication Department *Liberal Policy* (1943) pp. 12–15; *The Relation of the State to Industry* Liberal Publication Department (1943).
34. *Labour Monthly* 'Post-war Reconstruction' xxv, 2 (Feb. 1943); M. Dobb 'Industry and Employment after the War' xxv, 11 (Nov. 1943) p. 346 and 'Conservatives and Industry' xxvi, 3 (Mar. 1944) pp. 93–6.
35. *The Economist* Vol. cxliii 25/7/1942 'Economic Responsibility' p. 9; Vol. cxlv 31/7/1943 'In Defence of Big Business' p. 147 and 6/11/1943 'Over-mighty Subjects' p. 609; Vol. cxlvi 24/6/1943 'Policy for Monopoly' p. 834.
36. *The Times* 18/9/1943.

37. Nuffield College *Employment Policy and the Organisation of Industry after the War* (Oxford, 1943) pp. 44–64.
38. Addison *Road to 1945* p. 228.
39. See n. 22 for calls made in Parliament up to June 1944; Liberal Party *State and Industry*; *The Times* 16/3/1944; CAB117/70 memorandum by A. Baster to Morrison 15/5/1943; CAB124/490 delegation led by Sir Edward Grigg to the Chancellor of the Exchequer 3/8/1944.
40. The Central Committee of Export Groups was composed of businessmen representative of the various export groups set up since the export drive of February 1940.
41. BT64/318 'Trade Associations' by Henry Clay 28/6/1942; Note from Innes to Clay, June 1942.
42. *Ibid.* note from Morrison to Jowitt 13/5/1943.
43. CAB87/3 R.P.(43)25 'Report on the Recovery of the Export Markets and Promotion of the Export Trade' 15/6/1943.
44. BT64/318 minute by Arnold Overton 8/7/1943.
45. CAB87/63 R(44)6 report of the Steering Committee on Employment; CAB87/63 EC(43)3 Restrictive Practices' note by Board of Trade; CAB87/3 R.P.(43)25 report on the recovery of export markets, for similar views.
46. A. Booth and A.W. Coats 'Some Wartime Observations on the role of the economist in Government' *Oxford Economic Papers* 32, 2 (Jul. 1980) pp. 177–99 for a history of the evolution of their role between the 1930s and the 1940s. Leslie Hannah identifies a consistent bias since 1945 in many areas of policy, L. Hannah 'Economic ideas and government policy on industrial organisation in Britain since 1945' in M.O. Furner and B. Supple (eds.) *The state and economic knowledge* (Cambridge, 1990) pp. 354–75. The economists of interest to this chapter were G.C. Allen (Assistant Secretary, Board of Trade), Hugh Gaitskell (Principal Assistant Secretary, Board of Trade), Ruth Cohen (Ministry of Food, 1939–42 and Board of Trade, 1942–5), James Meade (Economic Assistant, 1940–5, and Director 1946–7, of the Economic Section of the Cabinet Offices), Lionel Robbins (Director, Economic Section, 1941–5), S.R. Dennison (Chief Economic Assistant, Economic Section, 1940–6), Henry Clay (economic advisor to the Bank of England 1930–44), A.S.J. Baster (economist to the Minister without Portfolio, 1941–3, and to Paymaster General, 1943–5).
47. CAB87/13 PR(43)26 'The Maintenance of Employment'.
48. BT64/318 Gaitskell's contribution to 'The Control of Monopoly'; BT64/251 note from Allen to Alix Kilroy (Principal Assistant Secretary, Board of Trade) 31/3/1943; CAB123/60 note by Robbins commenting on the National Policy for Industry, and his note of Dissent.
49. BT64/318 'Trade Associations' note by Henry Clay 28/6/1942.
50. G.C. Allen 'An Aspect of Industrial Reorganisation' *Economic Journal* 55, 218–19 (Jun.–Sept. 1945) pp. 179–91; CAB87/63 R(44)6 note of dissent by Robbins shows his liberalism. Allen and Gaitskell were more interventionist BT64/318 'The Problem of Monopoly'. The development of the ideas of Labour Party economists is discussed in Durbin *New Jerusalems* passim and p. 279. James Meade's ideas are developed in *Planning and the Price Mechanism* (1947); see also A.S.J. Baster *The Little Less* (1947).

51. This information was given to me in interview with Mr William Hughes, 10/8/1988.
52. Booth 'War and the White Paper' p. 190.
53. BT64/145 letters from Alix Kilroy to G.C. Allen 29/3/1943 and 5/4/1943. Alix Kilroy (later Dame Alix Meynell) is an important figure in the history of competition policy. She was Principal Assistant Secretary to the Board of Trade, 1943–6, Under Secretary 1946–55 and Secretary to the MRPC 1949–52.
54. On the question of international cartels *The Economist* was quite perturbed at industrial unanimity Vol. 146 8/1/1944, 'The Balance of Payments' p. 33.
55. *The Times* 7/1/1944 statement by Lord McGowan in response to the first antitrust indictment against ICI.
56. *The Statist* 31/7/1943, cited in G.W. Stocking and M.W. Watkins *Cartels or Competition? the Economics of International Controls by Business and Government* (New York, 1948) p. 557.
57. Sir Edgar Jones *World Trade Alliance: main outlines of an organisation for international trade* (Jan. 1944).
58. CBI MSS200/F/3/S1/21/44 correspondence on the World Trade Alliance, 1943–4; FBI *International Trade Policy* (Feb. 1944).
59. BLPES Management Research Group papers, Box 10a Memorandum, 'The Structure of Industry' 19/1/1942.
60. R.N. Gardner *Sterling–Dollar Diplomacy* (2nd ed., 1969) p. 123.
61. BT64/3076 'The Organisation of Industry for the immediate post-war period and for its future development' July 1942 paper by the Central Committee of Export Groups. On this group of businessmen employed by the Board of Trade see Cecil Weir *Civilian Assignment* (1953) p. 39; BT64/3076 S.R. Beale (a member of the Central Committee) to Dalton 23/7/1942 explaining the background of the Committee; BT64/318 'Industrial Organisation' note by Sir Charles Innes 22/12/1941.
62. Association of British Chambers of Commerce *Reconstruction* (1942); BT64/318 'Industry, Export Trade and the State' May 1942 proposals by the Cotton Board. In a more liberal tone Samuel Courtauld favoured also pre-emptory granting of worker representation, lest they seize all, S. Courtauld 'An industrialist's reflection on the future relations of government and industry' *Economic Journal* 51, 205 (Apr. 1942) pp. 1–17. See also L. Johnman 'Labour and Industrial Policy' in N. Tiratsoo (ed.) *The Attlee Years* (1991) pp. 29–53.
63. *A National Policy for Industry* (1942).
64. R.W.D. Boyce *British Capitalism at the Crossroads, 1919–1932* (Cambridge, 1987) p. 182, pp. 101–2, 122–5 on problems of British industry and the pleas for protectionism in the 1920s.
65. K. Hutchison *Rival Partners: Britain and America in the Post-war World* (New York, 1946) p. 156.
66. CAB87/3 R.P.(43)25 'Report on the Recovery of Export Markets and the Promotion of the Export Trade' 15/6/1943.
67. CBI MSS200/F/3/D2/3/1 letter from Guy Locock to Lord Herbert Scott (Vice President of the ABCC) 23/11/1942.
68. CBI MSS200/F/3/S1/21/44, letter from Walter Citrine to Locock 31/12/1943 saying that the TUC thought the WTA was sound in principle; Dalton Diaries,

I, Box 31 23/10/1944; Pilkington Archives PB260, Executive Committee minutes 28/10/1942; CAB87/5 R(44)34th meeting 24/4/1944.
69. Directorships of its members included:
Lord Hyndley – GKN and Bank of England
Clive Baillieu – National Smelting Co. and Dunlops
Sir Cecil Weir – Union Bank of Scotland and connected to the great Weir shipbuilding family
Francis d'Arcy Cooper – chairman of Unilever and Lever Bros
Samuel Beale – chairman of GKN (and a past President of the ABCC)
Edwin Fisher – Barclays Bank
Sir Charles Innes – a director of two telephone companies in the Far East
Captain B.H. Peter – Westinghouse
Geoffrey Cunliffe – British Aluminium Co.
Nigel Campbell – Baldwins and Stewart & Lloyds
Melford Watkins – John Lewis department store.
Background details from *Directory of Directors* for 1936, 1943 and 1946 and *Who Was Who*, names from Weir *Civilian Assignment* p. 45.
70. Weir *Civilian Assignment* p. 48.
71. BT60/67/1 Post-war export trade committee 1st meeting 12/12/1941.
72. Weir *Civilian Assignment* pp. 31–5.
73. BT64/3072 'Post-war Trade' 2nd memorandum by the NUM May 1942; Boyce *British Capitalism* p. 9 on the nature of this group.
74. *A National Policy for Industry* p. 42.
75. CBI MSS200/F/3/D3/5/25 points arising out of replies to questionnaire on compulsory membership and powers of trade associations 31/3/1943.
76. CBI MSS200/F/3/D2/3/1 letter from Locock to Herbert Scott 23/11/1942. The emerging relationship between the FBI and the government is well documented in S. Blank *Industry and Government in Britain: the Federation of British Industries in Politics, 1945–65* (Farnborough, 1973) pp. 37–40.
77. CBI MSS200/F/3/D2/3/1 letter from Bruce-Gardner to Locock 19/11/1942.
78. FBI *Reconstruction: A Report by the Federation of British Industries* (1942).
79. CBI MSS200/F/1/1/188 minutes of Grand Council Meeting 12/7/1944.
80. John McLean was the director of George Wills and Sons, a firm of exporters and importers, and was to be Principal of the ABCC from 1948 to 1950. Dalton was so impressed by McLean that he asked for a special report on him, BT64/3088 Meeting of President with ABCC deputation 29/2/1944; BT64/3577 Correspondence with John McLean March to June 1944.
81. Report in *The Economist* Vol. cxlv 4/9/1943 p. 339 and letters to *The Times* 23/10 24/10/1944; see also Laurence J. Cadbury's note of dissent to FBI *The Organisation of British Industry* (1944) p. 14.
82. CAB117/199 Note from Baster to Sir Alfred Hurst (secretariat of War Cabinet in charge of Reconstruction) 9/6/1942.
83. BT64/3497 note on the 'Long-term prospects of British industry' 15/5/1944. Douglas Jay was Principal Assistant Secretary, Board of Trade, 1943–5.
84. BT64/318 W. Hughes to R.M. Nowell (Assistant Secretary, Board of Trade) 28/7/1942; BT64/3089 note by Alix Kilroy in preparation for a meeting with the FBI 28/1/1943.
85. Dalton Diaries, I, Box 28 28/1/1943 and 1/4/1943, Box 29 7/7/1943 and

14/7/1943.

86. BT64/3548 'Industrial Reconstruction' note by Alix Kilroy for the internal reconstruction department 1/6/1944.

87. Dalton Diaries, I, Box 27 26/8/1942; BT64/3076 minute by G.C. Allen on the Central Committee's proposals.

88. CAB87/3 R.P.(43)25 'Report on the Recovery of the Export Markets and Promotion of the Export Trade', 15/6/1943.

89. *Ibid.*, and Board of Trade *Survey of International Cartels*, p. xlvii.

90. BT64/318 'Monopoly – comments on Professor Allen's paper' by Alix Kilroy 8/7/1943. She was to develop these ideas further when Secretary to the Monopolies Commission. See Dame Alix Kilroy 'The Tasks and Methods of the Monopolies Commission' *Transactions of the Manchester Statistical Society* (1952–3) pp. 4–5. BT64/145 minute from Alix Kilroy to G.C. Allen 5/4/1943.

91. CAB87/63 'Restrictive Practices in Industry' 15/10/1943.

92. G.C. Allen *Monopolies and Restrictive Practices* (1968) p. 62.

93. BT64/3076 Unsigned minute in response to the proposals of the Central Committee of Export Groups 30/4/1942.

94. BT64/318 minutes by Overton 8 and 21/7/1943.

95. CAB87/63 EC(43)4 'General Support of Trade' memorandum by the Board of Trade 15/10/1943; C. Barnett *The Audit of War: The illusion and reality of Britain as a great nation* (1986) pp. 268–74. By March 1944 the Board of Trade had drawn up a list of possible members of the proposed Industrial Commission, consisting of 26 industrialists, 5 financiers, 8 economists and 4 labour representatives, BT64/3466 'Possible names for the I.C.' memorandum March 1944.

96. CAB87/63 EC(43)4 'General Support of Trade' 15/10/1943; BT64/3346 note from Watkinson to Dalton 1/9/43.

97. BT64/3345 note of meeting at the Board of Trade 17/9/1943; BT64/145 note by G.L. Watkinson on the Allen–Gaitskell paper 21/7/1943.

98. Dalton Diaries, I, Box 29 21/9/1943.

99. BT64/3346 draft memorandum on industrial efficiency by Watkinson 1/9/1943 and note by Gaitskell 2/9/1943 and note by Dennison, 4/10/1943; CAB87/63 EC(43)4.

100. This interpretation rests heavily on the 'revisionist' analysis of Anglo–American relations since the Second World War pioneered by W.A. Williams *The Tragedy of American Diplomacy* (New York, 1962) pp. 232–4. The idea is developed in F. Block *The Origins of International Economic Disorder* (Los Angeles, 1977) pp. 56–8. For a summary of the early evolution of the 'Open Door' policy and the background to Anglo–American monetary and commercial negotiations during the war see Gardner *Sterling–Dollar Diplomacy* (1969) p. 17 and passim.

101. W.R. Louis *Imperialism at Bay 1941–1945: the United States and the decolonisation of the British Empire* (Oxford, 1977) p. 24; W.F. Kimball 'Lend Lease and the Open Door: the temptation of British opulence, 1937–42' *Political Science Quarterly* 86, 2 (Jun. 1971) p. 249; R.N. Gardner *Sterling–Dollar Diplomacy in Current Perspective* (New York, 2nd ed., 1980) pp. 18, 36–7.

102. Pressnell *External Economic Policy* pp. 101–9; A.P. Dobson *The Politics of the*

Anglo–American Economic Special Relationship 1940–1987 (Brighton, 1988), p. 62; D. Reynolds 'Roosevelt, Churchill and the Wartime Anglo–American Alliance, 1939–1945. Towards a New Synthesis' in W.R. Louis and Hedley Bull (eds.) *The 'Special Relationship'. Anglo–American Relations since 1945* (Oxford, 1986) p. 33.

103. M.W. Kirby *The Decline of British Economic Power since 1870* (1981) pp. 93–4; C. Thorne *Allies of a Kind: the United States, Britain and the war Against Japan* (Oxford, 1979) pp. 92–102

104. Pressnell *External Economic Policy* p. 193.

105. CAB87/107 U.S.E.(43)2 'International Cartels' memorandum by D.H. Mac-Gregor 8/1/1943.

106. BT11/1953 minute by C.K. Hobson undated c. March 1943.

107. CAB78/14 A.D.(43)5 note of meetings of the group to discuss cartels 23/7/1943 and 8/9/1943; BT64/317, letter from Dalton to Halifax 27/5/1944.

108. CAB78/14 Cartel Paper No. 4 'Joint Statement on International Cartel Policy' 15/10/1943.

109. CAB78/14 GEN19/25 Cartels 1st Meeting 30/9/1943 and GEN19/42 Cartels 3rd Meeting 8/10/1943.

110. CAB78/14 GEN19/36 Cartels 2nd Meeting 6/10/1943.

111. CAB66/44 W.P.(43)559 (Revise) 'Anglo–American Discussions under Article VII' memorandum by the Minister of State (Richard Law) 17/12/1943, Section IV – Cartel Policy.

112. H.B. Thorelli *The Federal Antitrust Policy* (Stockholm, 1954) pp. 333–4 for a detailed account of the muckrakers.

113. CAB78/14 Cartel Paper No. 1 'The Activities of International Cartels' by Corwin D. Edwards 1/10/1943. These were findings handed confidentially to British negotiators in Washington. (Edwards was Chairman of the policy board of the Antitrust division of the Department of Justice.) That British negotiators at Washington were impressed is evident in their report, CAB66/44 War Cabinet memoranda W.P.(43)559 (Revise) 'Anglo–American Discussions under Article VII' memorandum by the Minister of State (Richard Law) 17/12/1943, Section IV – Cartel Policy.

114. J. Borkin and C.A. Welsh *Germany's Master Plan. The Story of Industrial Offensive* (1943). It had a foreword by Thurmann Arnold, the zealous director of the Antitrust division at the time.

115. Dalton Diaries, I, Box 29 2/11/1943; *Parl.Deb.* (1942–43) Vol. 392 2/11/1943 Cols. 499–501; (1943–44) Vol. 395 9/11/1943 Cols. 1063–4.

116. G. Reimann *Patents for Hitler* (1942) and F. Brockway and F. Munally *Death Pays a Dividend* (1944) pp. 132–3; G. Schaffer *The Secret Empire* (1943). S. Haxby *Tory M.P.* (1938) p. 200 showed that Lord McGowan, President of ICI a firm riddled with cartel agreements with Germany was also a member of the Anglo–German Fellowship in 1938.

117. OFT *Survey Vol. I* pp. 61, 68, 87; J. Hurstfield *The Control of Raw Materials* (1953) p. 154; BT64/410 file on the international magnesium cartel; CAB117/70 memorandum to the Prime Minister by the Air Services 17/5/1940.

118. OFT *Survey Vol I* p. xxvi.

119. FO371/39156 C8327/6886/18 letter from Dalton to Eden 17/6/1944.

120. *Parl.Deb.* (1942–43) Vol. 390 6/7/1943 Cols. 1940–1; Vol. 391 20/7/1943 Col.

663 and 21/7/1943 Col. 867 and 22/7/1943 Col. 1097.
121. Dalton Papers, II, Box 7/6 No. 11, note from Dalton to the Attorney General, 15/3/1944, suggesting there might be a basis for prosecution under Trading with the enemy legislation. In January 1944 at lunch with Dalton, Lord Melchett, director of ICI had 'admitted that there might be some letters, written without authority by underlings in the employ of ICI, immediately after the outbreak of war, which might bear a sinister interpretation'. Dalton Diaries, I, Box 30 21/1/1944.
122. CAB87/12 PR(43)13th meeting 13/7/1943; Dalton Diaries, I, Box 29 7, 12 and 13/7/1943.
123. CAB87/5 R(44)13th meeting.
124. CBI BEC archives MSS200/B/3/2/C821 Part 2 Restrictive Practices and Monopolies Act.
125. CAB87/5 R(44)13th meeting 4/2/1944.
126. FO371/40586 U2441 'Discussions with the representatives of the Dominions and India on Article 7'.
127. BT64/317 'Draft brief for possible discussions with American officials' memorandum by the Board of Trade Dec. 1944.
128. FO371/40587 U33622 minutes (written by Overton) of a meeting at the War Cabinet 14/3/1944; BT64/317 Note by Meade to Ruth Cohen, undated, 'International Cartels'.
129. BT64/317 Note by Ruth Cohen and G.H. Andrew 'Draft Brief for discussions with the Americans on International Cartels' 19/4/1944.
130. CAB87/6 R(44)65 'Restrictive Practices' joint memorandum by the President of the Board of Trade and the Minister without Portfolio 29/3/1944.
131. Pressnell *External Economic Policy* pp. 129–37; Gardner *Sterling–Dollar Diplomacy* (1969) p. 65. The change of mood is described graphically in L. Robbins *Autobiography of an Economist* (1971) pp. 203–4, and in papers he wrote at the time: T230/92 'Plan for external economic reconstruction' note by Robbins for Richard Law MP (Minister of State) 17/5/1944.
132. Gardner *Sterling–Dollar Diplomacy* p. 108; BT64/4877 Historical note to TN(56)5 'International Action on Restrictive Business Practices' by Board of Trade 28/5/1956; CAB78/14 AD(43)5th meeting 14/9/1943, British delegation to Washington discussing American ideas for how the talks should proceed.
133. Their conversation is cited in Hutchinson *Rival Partners* p. 250.
134. G. Kolko *The Politics of War: The World and United States Foreign Policy, 1943–1945* (New York, 1968) p. 284. BT64/3072 Meeting of President and Board of Trade officials with a delegation from the National Union of Manufacturers, 4/2/1943 as an example of one such complaint. W.J. Reader *ICI – a History. Volume 2: 1926–1952* (New York, 1975) p. 416, but he also argues that ICI was divided on the value of international cartels by the end of the war, p. 417; ICI *Competition and Combination in International Trade* (1946) p. 88.
135. Kolko *Politics of War* pp. 287–8, 302–3; Dalton Diaries, I, Box 30 23/2/1944 records 'pandemonium' at a Cabinet meeting over the issue of Middle East oil and the Americans.
136. BT64/266 Note by R.J. Shackle 1/11/1944. In January and March 1944 two indictments against ICI and others were filed, although the British govern-

ment pressed successfully for a stay in the proceedings. In May 1944 a complaint was filed against the British Match Corporation.
137. BT64/317 US Dept. of State Order No. 1254 17/4/1944.
138. Letter from Keynes to Redvers Opie (Economic Adviser to the British Embassy in Washington) in D. Moggridge (ed.) *The collected writings of John Maynard Keynes. Vol. xxv. Activities 1940–44* (Cambridge, 1980) p. 446.
139. CAB87/5 R(44)13th meeting; CAB87/6 R(44)60th meeting 11/9/1944; R(44)76th meeting 4/12/1944.
140. *Directory of Directors, 1939*; BT64/341 cutting from *Financial News* 4/7/1938 on his role in the International Steel Cartel; MRPC *Semi-Manufactures of Copper* pp. 53–60; BT64/2834 file on renewal of international steel cartel 1945.
141. CAB87/9 R(44)154 'Restrictive Practices' memo by Home Secretary 9/9/1944.
142. CAB87/5 R(44)34th meeting 24/4/1944.
143. Booth 'The War and the White Paper' p. 194.
144. Gardner *Sterling–Dollar Diplomacy* pp. 34–5.

5 THE ORIGINS OF THE MONOPOLIES AND RESTRICTIVE PRACTICES ACT 1948

1. Much of the substance of this chapter, although not the argument appears in H. Mercer 'Anti-monopoly policy' in H. Mercer, N. Rollings and J. Tomlinson (eds.) *Labour Governments and Private Industry. The Experience of 1945–1951* (Edinburgh, 1992) pp. 55–73.
2. CAB75/22 Legislation Committee H.P.C.(45)44 'Legislative Programme, 1944–5 session' memorandum by the Lord Chancellor 27/4/1945; *Parl. Deb.* (1943–44) Vol. 404 7/11/1944 Cols. 1227–8; *Parl.Deb.* (1947–48) Vol. 448 25/3/ 1948 Col. 3360.
3. W.T. Morgan 'Britain's Election: a debate on nationalisation and cartels' *Political Science Quarterly* 61, 2 (Jun. 1946) p. 233. The incident was picked up from the *Daily Herald*. Ernest Bevin made several allegations of profiteering in steel and bricks and cement, *News Chronicle* 11/6/1945.
4. *Parl.Deb.* (1944–45) Vol. 406 12/12/1944 Cols. 1049–50 and 6/12/1944 Cols. 660–1; Vol. 407 24/1/1945 Cols. 816–17 and 25/1/1945 Col. 977; Vol. 409 27/3/ 1945 Cols. 1312–13 and 10/4/1945 Cols. 1655–6. The TUC's call was taken up in Parliament *Parl.Deb.* (1944–45) Vol. 408 22/2/1945 Col. 954.
5. H. Leak and A. Maizels 'The Structure of British Industry' *Journal of the Royal Statistical Society* (series A) 108 (1945) pp. 142–207. For coverage in the Press see *Daily Telegraph* 28/5/1945. Labour Research Department *The case for nationalisation and control* (Jun. 1945) p. 53.
6. *Parl. Deb.* (Lords) (1944–45) Vol. 136 21/3/1945 Cols. 693–749, Lord Nathan's proposals at Col. 695.
7. Morgan 'Britain's election' p. 222; *Financial News* 21/6/1945. See also *Daily Mirror* 27/6/1945; *Daily Herald* May 1945 various articles; *News Chronicle* 15/ 6/1945; *Daily Telegraph* 26/6/1945; *Financial Times* 27/6/1945; *Parl.Deb.* (1944–45) Vol. 411 13/7/1945 Cols. 1688–1746.
8. BT64/3592 'Summary of policy developments 1943–45 – restrictive practices'.
9. BT64/242 'Price control and restrictive practices' undated, unsigned memorandum.

10. Dalton Diaries, I, Box 31 4/12/1944.
11. CAB87/6 Reconstruction Committee papers R(44)76th meeting 4/12/1944; CAB87/10 R(45)8th meeting 5/2/1945.
12. CAB124/494 Letter from A. Johnstone (Principal Assistant Secretary, Office of the Lord President) to J.P.R. Maud (Secretary, Ministry of Reconstruction, acting) 7/6/1945.
13. Hugh Dalton *The Fateful Years, Memoirs 1931–1945* (1957) shows his emphasis on location of industry policy.
14. Dalton Diaries, I, Box 31 23/11/1944, 4/12/1944 and Box 32 5/2/1945.
15. CAB124/561 note of meeting Morrison, Brook and W.S. Murrie, (Under-Secretary, Cabinet Offices) 19/12/1945.
16. For the variety of issues under this heading see H. Mercer 'The evolution of British government policy towards competition in private industry, 1940–1956' unpublished Ph.D. thesis, University of London (1989) pp. 203–29.
17. BT64/251 note from Alix Kilroy to Miss Johnson (Private Secretary to the Permanent Secretary, Board of Trade) 28/4/1947.
18. FO371/40589 U4861/6/70 'The Cartel Question in the U.S.' Washington Dispatch 31/5/1944 and letter J.E. Coulson (First Secretary, Foreign Office) to R.J. Shackle (Principal Assistant Secretary, Board of Trade) 8/6/1944.
19. FO371/40941 UE2758/53/52 minute by Hall-Patch on a draft brief for discussions with Harry Hawkins on cartels 21/12/1944; FO371/40468 U5161/2302/53 speech by Wendell Berge 31/5/1944; FO371/40941 UE1337/53/53 Fortnightly Economic Summary by the British Embassy, Washington 10/9/1944. Roosevelt endorsed the line of Wendell Berge and Cordell Hull in September 1944 in a widely-reported letter to Hull; BT64/317 F.E. Coulson (First Secretary, Foreign Office) to Alix Kilroy 27/9/1944.
20. R. Gardner *Sterling–Dollar Diplomacy in Current Perspective* (3rd ed., New York, 1980) pp. 122–4.
21. L. Robbins *Autobiography of an Economist* (1971) p. 203; BT64/317 letter from Dalton to Halifax 19/5/1944.
22. FO371/45679 AS(US)(44)1st meeting 7/12/1944 and UE727/113/53 Note from Washington to Foreign Office 16/2/1945; BT64/317 AS(US)(44)13th meeting 30/1/1945; Gardner *Diplomacy* p. 146; FO371/45680 UE2816/112/53 AS(US)(45) 8th meeting 27/6/1945 and UE3830/113/53 AS(US)(45) 11th meeting 14/8/1945.
23. BPP (1945–46) *Financial Agreement between the United States and the United Kingdom* Vol. xxv Cmd. 6708 and *Proposals for Consideration by an International Conference on Trade and Employment (Dec. 1945)* Vol. xxvi Cmd. 6709.
24. BT4/251 Note for the President's morning meeting by G.H. Andrew (Principal, Board of Trade) 7/3/1946.
25. *Ibid.* exchange of telegrams between Washington and the Board of Trade, 25 and 26/6/1948; BT64/494 letter commenting on the Monopolies Bill from Robert P. Terrill (US Department of State, associate chief of the International Resource Division) to R.R.M. McIntosh (Assistant Principal, Board of Trade). The agreement is at BPP (1947–48) *Economic Co-operation Agreement between the Governments of the United Kingdom and the U.S.A., 6th July 1948* Vol. xxxi Cmd. 7469.

26. BT64/251 Letter from Kilroy to Johnson (Private Secretary to the Permanent Secretary, Board of Trade, Sir John Woods) 28/4/1947.

27. *Parl.Deb.* (1945–46) Vol. 414 9/10/1945 Col. 122 speech for the Second Reading of the Supplies and Services Bill by James Chuter-Ede, Secretary of State for Home Affairs.

28. 'Mr Churchill's declaration of policy to the electors' in F.W.S. Craig (ed.) *British General Election Manifestos 1900–1974* (2nd ed., 1975) pp. 113–23; *One Nation* a report by a group of Conservative MPs (1954) and Conservative Party Archives, Bodleian Library, Oxford PCC(55)1 'Note on Monopolies and Restrictive Practices' by James Douglas 31/2/1955.

29. BT64/432 unsigned undated memorandum c. Feb. 1948 summarising decisions.

30. Morrison's apocalyptic memorandum on the matter CAB87/9 R(44)154.

31. CAB132/4 Lord President's Committee papers LP(46)202 'Restrictive Practices' memorandum by President of the Board of Trade 26/7/1946. For the Economic Section's comments CAB124/497 memorandum by P. Chantler 16/9/1946 and by James Meade 17/9/1946.

32. This programme was not specifically socialist: Macmillan had proposed a similar one in the 1930s. See H. Macmillan *The Middle Way* (1938) p. 237.

33. 'Let us Face the Future: A Declaration of Labour Policy for the Consideration of the Nation' (1945) in Craig *Election Manifestos* pp. 126–8.

34. *Parl.Deb.* (1947–48) Vol. 449 22/4/1948 Cols. 2059, 2085, 2086.

35. H. Mercer 'The Labour Governments of 1945–51 and private Industry' in N. Tiratsoo (ed.) *The Attlee Years* (1991) p. 73.

36. BT13/220A M/M/24 Memorandum by Cripps 'Draft directive to the Board of Trade' 28/8/1945.

37. BT13/220A M/M/67 'Business members' note by Sir John Woods 26/10/1945.

38. K. Middlemas *Power, Competition and the State. Volume 1: Britain in search of balance* (1986) p. 143.

39. P. Mathias 'Industry and Government. A History of the Federation of British Industries' (1980) lodged at the Business History Unit, London School of Economics, p. 354. See also A.A. Rogow and P. Shore *The Labour Government and British Industry* (1955) p. 60.

40. LPA RD236/Dec. 1948 'Report to Policy Committee of sub-committee on privately-owned industry'; Mercer 'Labour and private industry' pp. 75–6.

41. Labour Party *Speakers' Handbook 1949–1950* (1949); Labour Party *Labour Believes in Britain* (Apr. 1949).

42. B. Pimlott *Labour and the Left* (Cambridge, 1977) p. 201.

43. Morgan *Labour* p. 121.

44. Middlemas *Power, Competition* p. 136; J. Foster 'Labour, Keynesianism and the Welfare State' in J. Fyrth (ed.) *Labour's High Noon. The Government and the Economy 1945–51* (1993) p. 36.

45. LPA RD1/Sept. 1945 'A Labour Policy for Privately-Owned Industry' by G.D.N. Worswick.

46. CAB124/1200 'The State and Private Industry' memorandum by H. Wilson 4/5/1950; N. Rollings ' "The Reichstag System of Government". The Labour government and controls' in Mercer *et al. Labour Governments* pp. 15–36.

47. LPA RD22/Apr. 1946 'Note on the public control of Trade Associations and

Combines'; Mercer 'Labour and private industry'.

48. BT64/426 G.H. Andrew to Alix Kilroy 24/12/1946; BT64/2258 'Industrial Organisation Bill' note undated (c.Jan. 1947), unsigned.

49. BT64/2250 'Cotton Cloth Price Control and minimum prices' 3/6/1948, unsigned memorandum; M. Dupree 'The cotton industry: a middle way between nationalisation and self-government?' in Mercer *et al. Labour Governments* p. 152.

50. CBI MSS200/F/3/S1/13/23 Memorandum 'Relations between the FBI and the British government' 10/7/1947; MSS200/F/3/D3/5/26 Memorandum by Norman Kipping on the post-war world undated, c.1947; Mercer 'Labour and private industry' pp. 71–89.

51. See the implicit definition in the work by V. Berghahn *The Americanisation of West German Industry* (Leamington Spa, 1986). An earlier definition concentrates on the economic, social and cultural impact of American companies operating in Europe, E.A. McCreary *The Americanisation of Europe* (New York, 1964).

52. G. Kolko and J. Kolko *The Limits of Power: the world and United States foreign policy, 1945–1954* (New York, 1972); W.A. Williams *The Tragedy of American Diplomacy* (New York, 1959); D.F. Fleming *The Cold War and its Origins* (1960).

53. Fleming *Cold War* p. 436.

54. T. Brett, S. Gilliatt and A. Pople 'Planned Trade, Labour Party Policy and US Intervention: The Successes and Failures of Post-War Reconstruction' *History Workshop* 13 (Spring 1982) pp. 130–42.

55. *Ibid.* p. 136; Cairncross *The Years of Recovery. British Economic Policy 1945–51* p. 465; Gardner *Diplomacy* p. 325.

56. C. Maier *In Search of Stability: Explorations in Historical Political Economy* (Cambridge, 1987) pp. 133–4, 146.

57. A. Carew *Labour under the Marshall Plan: The politics of productivity and the marketing of management science* (Manchester, 1987) pp. 134–7. See also J. Tomlinson 'Productivity Policy' in Mercer *et al. Labour Governments* pp. 37–54.

58. Carew *Marshall Plan* pp. 141–2 for an eloquent and amusing summary of the AACP reports.

59. G.D.H. Cole *Labour's Second Term* (Fabian Tract No. 273, May 1949) pp. 7–8.

60. BT64/478 'The public control of monopolies' by the Joint Committee of the TUC and Labour Party on cartels and trusts.

61. LPA RD66/Jul. 1947 'The Public Control of Monopoly' revised memorandum for the Trusts and Cartels Committee.

62. E. Davies *National Enterprise* (1946) p. 16.

63. LPA RD22/Apr. 1946 'Note on the public control of Trade Associations and Combines' for the Joint sub-committee on trusts and cartels; RD33/Nov. 1946 'Criteria for Nationalisation'.

64. CAB124/1200 'The State and Private Industry' memorandum by Wilson 4/5/1950.

65. LPA R.53/Jun. 1951 'Monopoly'. Draft of a pamphlet possibly by Richard Evely.

66. G.L. Perkins' Presidential address to the Co-operative Congress in 1947, cited in G.D.N. Worswick 'Economic Policy and the Co-operative Movement' in N. Barou *The Co-operative Movement in Labour Britain* (1948) p. 16.
67. *Parl.Deb.* (1947–48) Vol. 449 22/4/1948 Col. 2020.
68. CAB124/1200 Gaitskell's contribution to a meeting to discuss Wilson's paper on the state and private industry, 17/5/50; S. Haseler *The Gaitskellites: Revisionism in the British Labour Party* (1969) p. 48.
69. C.A.R. Crosland 'The Transition from Capitalism' in R.H.S. Crossman (ed.) *New Fabian Essays* (2nd ed., 1970) p. 64.
70. LPA R.59/July 1951 'Resale Price Maintenance' paper submitted by USDAW to the NEC.
71. LPA RD22/ Apr. 1946 'Note on the public control of Trade Associations and Combines'.
72. BT64/427 'Comments on restrictive practices made in working party reports' 1/3/1948.
73. LPA RD89/Mar. 1948 'Should there be a Distribution Policy?'; H. Smith *Retail Distribution* (1937) p. 154; W. Arthur Lewis 'Competition in the Retail Trade' *Economica* 12, 4 (Nov. 1945) pp. 230–1; BT64/455 RPM(E)60 Evidence to the Lloyd Jacob Committee on resale price maintenance submitted by R. Cohen, R.F. Khan, W.B. Reddaway and J. Robinson, 1947.
74. See for instance, R. Eatwell *The Labour Governments 1945–51* (1978), p. 161; Middlemas' account of Attlee in Middlemas *Power, competition* pp. 115–19; Morgan *Labour* p. 130; Coates *The Labour Party and the Struggle for Socialism* (Cambridge, 1975) p. 56; J. Tomlinson 'Labour's Management of the national economy 1945–51: survey and speculations' *Economy and Society* 18, 1 (Feb. 1989) p. 16.
75. R.S. Barker 'Civil Service Attitudes and the Economic Planning of the Attlee Government' *Journal of Contemporary History* 21, 3 (Jul. 1986) p. 474 notes that this phenomenon was to be found in other aspects of Labour's economic policy. On the Conservative influence of the civil service see R. Miliband *The State in Capitalist Society* (1973).
76. G.C. Allen *Monopolies and Restrictive Practices* (1968) p. 63; Middlemas *Power, competition* p. 119.
77. J. Jewkes *Ordeal by Planning* (1948); L. Robbins *The Economic Problem in Peace and War: some reflections on objectives and mechanisms* (1947); James Meade *Planning and the Price Mechanism* (1947); A.S.J. Baster *The Little Less* (1947).
78. BT64/251 note of President's morning meeting 26/3/1946. Morrison chaired the meeting in Cripps' absence in India.
79. BT64/467 note by R.C. Bryant (Assistant Secretary, Board of Trade) 25/2/1948.
80. BT64/467 Minute R.C. Bryant to Wilson 19/2/1948, and note by R.C. Bryant for meeting with the TUC 25/2/1948; CAB124/498 Brief for the Debate 23/4/1948.
81. BT64/394 exchange between Allen and Watkinson mid- to late 1945; BT64/467 Note by Kilroy on meeting with departmental officials 6/3/1948.
82. CAB124/497 letter from A. Johnstone, in response to Meade's criticisms of the Board's paper, 26/9/1946.

83. BT64/467 Note by Bryant 10/3/1948; *Parl.Deb.* (1947–48) Vol. 449 22/4/1948 Cols. 2019–39; CAB132/1 LP(46)31st meeting 27/9/46.
84. CAB78/37 GEN89/2 'Commercial Policy and the Lend Lease Negotiations at Washington' memorandum by the Board of Trade 13/9/1945; BT64/414 'Proposals to establish an I.T.O.' memorandum handed to UK officials by Mr Clayton on 4/8/1945, and AS(US)(45)11th meeting held at the Board of Trade on Article VII 14/8/1945, and minute from R.J. Shackle to G.H. Andrew and A. Kilroy 28/8/1945.
85. CAB134/711 TN(46)29 'The US Draft Charter' note by the Board of Trade 5/8/1946; CAB134/712 TN(46)52 Trade Negotiations Committee note by the Joint secretaries circulating 'Note by the Board of Trade on Chapter V of the US Draft Charter (Restrictive Practices)' 29/9/1946; CAB134/713 TN(47)3 'Preparatory committee for the Trade and Employment conference (First Session) Summary Memorandum' by the Board of Trade 9/12/1946 and TN(47)32 'Trade Negotiations. Draft Charter for the ITO Report on the Second Session of the preparatory committee of the conference on Trade and Employment in Geneva' 18/9/1947; BT64/500 'Ch.V – Amendments to various articles' Note for delegation to Havana Conference. This file contains a fairly complete account of the ITO negotiations from 1945 onwards.
86. BTBT64/484 TN(48)11 'The Obligations of the I.T.O. Charter and the G.A.T.T.' draft memorandum 9/7/1948.
87. This is according to their own account; CBI MSS200/F/3/S1/13/23 'Relations between the F.B.I. and British Government' by D.L. Walker 10/7/1947.
88. CBI MSS200/F/3/S1/17/8 Minutes of Committee on Industrial Agreements, 1945–8.
89. BT11/3254 FBI memorandum 'Private International Industrial Agreements' Feb. 1947.
90. BT64/307 Comments received from firms and associations on Ch.IV of Cmd. 6709 'Restrictive Business Practices'. Submissions from associations representing tinplate, cement, mechanical cloth, lino, accumulator and electric lamp manufacturers, and one from a firm of accountants claiming to speak for 18 other trade associations. For modified views see tyres, clothing, engineers and steel tube manufacturers.
91. BT11/3254 FBI memorandum 'International Agreements'.
92. FBI *The Organisation of British Industry* (1944) p. 14.
93. CBI MSS200/S2/14/76 'Trade Associations: their place in the industrial world' c.1950.
94. CAB87/9 R(44)156 'Restrictive Practices' note by Norman Brook 11/12/1944 enclosing memorandum by a delegation of Conservative MPs led by Sir Edward Grigg 'Cartels and Trade Associations' 1/8/1944.
95. Dalton Diaries, I, Box 30 27/6/1944 – a record of Woolton's opinion on 'Long term prospects', which he saw as a businessmen's document; CAB87/9 R(44)145 'Restrictive Practices' memorandum by the Minister of Reconstruction 24/8/1944.
96. N. Harris *Competition and the Corporate Society: British Conservatives, the State and Industry 1945–1964* (1972) pp. 59–60; P. Addison *The Road to 1945* (1975) pp. 232–3; Bartlett *A History of Post-War Britain* (1977) p. 79 on the Tory Reform Group; Dalton Diaries, I, Box 31 27/11/1944; Peter Thorney-

croft's speech in the debate on the Address *Parl.Deb.* (1944–45) Vol. 406 Cols. 660–1 6/12/1944. Thorneycroft became President of the Board of Trade in 1951.

97. Conservative Central Office *The Industrial Charter* (1947) pp. 23–4; D. Maxwell-Fyfe *Monopoly* (1948) pp. 52–3.
98. BT64/414 minute to A. Kilroy, unsigned 29/8/1946.
99. CAB134/713 TN(47)32.
100. BPP (1947–48) *Economic Co-operation Agreement* Art. II para. 3.
101. S. Blank *Industry and Government in Britain: the Federation of British Industries in Politics, 1945–65* (Farnborough, 1973) p. 63; J.J. Richardson 'The Making of the Restrictive Trade Practices Act 1956: a case study of the policy process in Britain' *Parliamentary Affairs* 20, 4 (Autumn 1967) p. 360; S.E. Finer 'The Federation of British Industries' *Political Studies* 4, 1 (Feb. 1956) p. 79.
102. BT64/432 'Notes on the Development of restrictive practices policy' 28/1/1948.
103. *Parl.Deb.* (1947–48) Vol. 452 29/6/1948 Cols. 2092. Throughout the debate the Conservatives constantly identified themselves as the spokesmen of industry, thus 'we' implied 'we industrialists in the Conservative Party'. It is difficult to take the amendment too seriously, for in 1953 the Conservatives retracted their own electoral promise to include the nationalised industries in the 1948 Act.
104. *Ibid.* Cols. 2030–45 and 2054–7.
105. BT64/466 'Points of principle for decision' 12/2/1948 and BT64/467 meeting to discuss second draft, 18/2/1948, and interdepartmental meeting 6/3/1948.
106. BT64/480 letter from Tom Williams, Minister of Agriculture, to Wilson 11/3/1948; BT64/467 note of meeting by Alix Kilroy 6/3/1948; A. Bonner *British Co-operation* (Manchester, 2nd ed., 1970) p. 275.
107. BT64/467 interdepartmental meeting 6/3/1948.
108. CBI MSS200/F/1/1/189 Minutes of the Grand Council 14/4/1948, and 12/5/1948; BT13/220A MM(46)27 'Restrictive Practices' 6/3/1946.
109. CBI MSS200/D3/5/33 Note of meeting with the Board of Trade, 27/2/1948; Industrial Agreements Committee, points to be raised with the Board of Trade 9/4/1948; BT64/482 note Alix Kilroy to Sir James Helmore (Second Secretary, Board of Trade) 30/4/1948 on the chairmanship of the Monopolies Commission.
110. *Parl.Deb.* (1947–48) Vol. 452 Cols. 2045–50.
111. BT64/467 report of Lord Chancellor's dinner 15/4/1948.
112. CBI MSS200/F/3/D3/5/33 meetings 27/2/1948 and 9/4/1948, and letter A.L. Pease (Secretary to the Industrial Agreements sub-committee) 22/4/1948.
113. M. Bernstein *Regulating Industry by Independent Commission* (Princeton, 1955) p. 96.
114. BT64/488 note of meeting with the Co-operative delegation 26/5/1948 where these two amendments were discussed with the Co-operative MP, Beswick.
115. *Parl.Deb.* (1947–48) Vol. 452 Col. 2029.
116. CAB124/499 letter from Wilson to Morrison explaining why the Chairman of the Commission was to receive so large a salary 3/3/1949.
117. *Parl.Deb.* (1947–48) Vol. 452 Cols. 2029–139 proceedings of the Committee of

the whole House 29/6/1948, Col. 2051, for this particular amendment.
118. BT64/482 A.V. Alexander to Wilson, Mar. 1948; CAB128/12 CM(48)21st meeting 11/3/1948 and CM(48)24th meeting 22/3/1948.
119. Berghahn *Americanisation* pp. 100–6; Halliday *Japanese Capitalism* pp. 177–84.

6 INTERPRETATION OF POLICY – THE MONOPOLIES AND RESTRICTIVE PRACTICES COMMISSION, 1949–56

1. Much of the substance of this chapter, although not the argument, appears in H. Mercer 'The Monopolies and Restrictive Practices Commission, 1949–56: a study in regulatory failure' in G. Jones and M. Kirby (eds.) *Competitiveness and the State. Government and business in twentieth century Britain* (Manchester, 1991) pp. 78–99.
2. See for instance the system devised in the 1950s for the regulation of takeovers, R. Roberts 'Regulatory responses to the rise of the market for corporate control in Britain in the 1950s' *BusHist* 34, 1 (Jan. 1992) pp. 183–200.
3. P.H. Guenault and J.M. Jackson *The Control of Monopoly in the United Kingdom* (2nd ed., 1974) pp. 22–95; C.K. Rowley *The British Monopolies Commission* (1966); G.C. Allen *Monopoly and Restrictive Practices* (1968) pp. 70–88; A. Hunter 'The Monopolies Commission and Economic Welfare' *Manchester School of Economic and Social Studies* 22, 1 (Jan. 1955) pp. 22–39.
4. G. Kolko *Railroads and Regulation 1877–1916* (Princeton, 1965) p. 3 and passim; G. Stigler *The Citizen and the State* (Chicago, 1975) p. 114; S.P. Huntington 'The Marasmus of the I.C.C.: The Commission, the Railroads and the Public Interest' *The Yale Law Journal* 61, 4 (Apr. 1952) p. 470. The opposing 'public interest' interpretation is outlined in T.K. McCraw 'Regulation in America: A Review Article' *BHR* 49, 2 (Summer 1975) pp. 159–83 and R. Posner 'Theories of Economic Regulation' *Bell Journal of Economics and Management Science* 5, 2 (Autumn 1974) pp. 335–58.
5. M.H. Bernstein *Regulating Business by Independent Commission* (Princeton, 1955) p. 296.
6. G. Kolko *The Triumph of Conservatism: a reinterpretation of American history 1900–1916* (New York, 1963) pp. 271–3. See also G. Cullom Davis 'The Transformation of the Federal Trade Commission 1914–1929' *Mississippi Valley Historical Review* 49 (Dec. 1962) pp. 437–55; M.E. Parrish *Securities Regulation and the New Deal* (New Haven, Conn. 1975).
7. BPP (1952–53) *Sixth Report from the Select Committee on Estimates, session 1952–53: Monopolies and Restrictive Practices Commission* Vol. iv pp. 46–7.
8. These were in electric lamps, annual report by the Board of Trade on the work of the Commission for 1953, BPP (1953–54) Vol. xvi p. 6 and BPP (1955–56) Vol. xxvi p. 5; in dental goods – report for 1952, BPP (1952–53) Vol. xv p. 5 and for 1953 BPP (1953–54) Vol. xvi p. 6 and for 1955 BPP (1955–56) Vol. xxiv p. 5; and for timber – report for 1955 BPP (1955–56) p. 5 and BPP (1957–58) Monopolies Commission *Imported Timber: Report on whether and to what extent the recommendations of the Commission have been complied with* Vol. xvi. See bibliography for full titles.
9. Annual Report for 1955, BPP (1955–56) Vol. xxiv p. 5.

10. Rowley *Monopolies Commission* pp. 335–9; CAB134/846 EA(53) 18th meeting 17 June 1953.

11. Rowley *Monopolies Commission* pp. 353–9; J.B. Heath 'Restrictive Practices and after' *Manchester School of Economic and Social Studies* 29, 2 (May, 1961) p. 199.

12. CAB134/846 EA(53) 32nd meeting of the Economic Policy Committee 16/12/1953; CAB134/855 'Report on the process of calico printing' memorandum by the President of the Board of Trade 2/2/1955.

13. BT64/4837 MC/RPM(52)11 15/7/1952 'Policy Group on new legislation concerning the Monopolies Commission and Resale Price Maintenance' Annex A. The Policy group on new legislation was a Board of Trade inter-departmental committee set up in August 1951 originally to discuss new legislation on resale price maintenance and possible changes to the procedure of the MRPC. It also took on the task of doing the initial screening of references to the Commission. Its main series of papers are in BT64/4833–7.

14. Pilkington Archives, Working papers for the General Board, PB257 30/11/50. See also Executive Committee minutes, PB260 12/1/1949, 7/6/1949, 10/5/1950; General Board minutes, PB350 26/1/1950, 30/3/1950, 25/5/1950 and Working papers, PB257 31/3/1949.

15. CBI MSS200/F/3/E3/9/1 Papers of the Trade Practices Committee, meeting 24/11/1949 and MSS200/F/3/E3/9/6 letter from Norman Kipping, Director General of the FBI, to E. Copley of the Federation of Calico Printers 16/2/1955.

16. E.g. Allen *Monopoly* p. 88.

17. D. Maxwell-Fyfe *Political Adventure* (1964) p. 261.

18. *Parl.Deb.* (1954–55) Vol. 537 24/2/1955 Col. 1578.

19. Rowley *Monopolies Commission* p. 193; Allen *Monopoly* p. 80; Hunter *Competition and the Law* (1966) pp. 25, 82; J. Jewkes 'British Monopoly Policy 1944–56' *The Journal of Law and Economics* 1 (Oct. 1958) p. 4.

20. Huntington 'The I.C.C.' p. 473.

21. BT64/4824 file on excisions from the tyres report; BT64/4854 file on excisions from the report on lino; BT64/4879 file on excisions from the report on gases; BT64/4882 file on excisions from the report on electrical machinery; BT64/4889 file on excisions from the report on tea; BT64/4890 file on excisions from the report on metal windows; BT64/5003 file on excisions from the report on London buildings; BT64/4852 file on excisions from the report on copper semi-manufactures. BT64/4890 contains a summary to excisions in reports up to 1956.

22. BT64/4852 paper by the British Non-Ferrous Metals Federation; letter to A.C. Hill (Private Secretary to the President of the Board of Trade) 19/1/1956.

23. *Daily Mail* 4/11/1955.

24. BT258/71 meetings between the Board of Trade and representatives of Dunlop 15/8/1955 and 6/9/1955; BT258/72 meeting at the Board (President, Under-Secretaries) 19/1/1956 on action on outstanding reports.

25. CAB134/855 EA(55)23 'Report on the process of calico printing' memorandum by the President of the Board of Trade 2/2/1955; CAB128/29 CM(55)38th meeting 27/10/1955.

26. CAB134/855 EA(55)28 'Policy on Monopolies and Restrictive Practices

memorandum by the President of the Board of Trade' 7/2/1955.

27. Bernstein *Regulating Business* p. 100.

28. BPP (1952–53) *Report from the Select Committee* pp. 46–7.

29. *Ibid.* p. x.

30. Allen *Monopoly* p. 67; Guenault and Jackson *Control of Monopoly* p. 21.

31. See for instance discussions in the Economic Policy Committee CAB134/846 EA(52)23rd meeting 30/7/1952 and CAB134/854 EA(55)6th meeting 17/2/1955.

32. BT64/4837 MC/RPM(52)11 15/7/1952 and MC/RPM(52)12 17/7/1952 papers of the Lee policy group on monopolies.

33. BT64/4812 'Monopolies and Restrictive Practices Commission, selection of references 5th group' letter from Monopolies branch of the Board of Trade to Board of Trade production departments, 26/9/1953.

34. BT64/4813 letters from A.C. Hill to Sir Maurice Dean (2nd Secretary, Board of Trade) 24/7/1954 and 5/8/1954; BT64/4887 'The work of the Monopolies Commission' note by A.C. Hill Sept. 1954.

35. BT64/4887 'The work of the M.C.'; Hill was supported by the Assistant Secretary, BT64/4754, Note by T.K. Rees (Assistant Secretary, Board of Trade) on Ministry of Supply cases, 22/3/55.

36. CAB134/854 EA(55)28 'Policy on Restrictive Practices' memorandum by the President of the Board of Trade 7/2/1955 and EA(55)6th meeting 17/2/1955; CAB128/29 CM(55)12th meeting 7/6/1955 and CM(55)15th meeting 16/6/1955.

37. CAB134/854 EA(55)12th meeting 31/3/1955. The first list of references was chemical fertilisers, structural steel, electrical equipment for motor vehicles, non-mineral oils and fats and electric street-lighting equipment or the yarn spinners. The EPC preferred structural steel, electric street-lighting and kegs and drums.

38. CAB128/29 CM(55)12th meeting 7/6/1955 and CM(55)15th meeting 16/6/1955; CAB129/75 CP(55)28 'Monopolies' memorandum by the President of the Board of Trade 4/6/1955 and CP(55)41 'Monopolies and Restrictive Practices' memorandum by the President of the Board of Trade 15/6/1955; PREM11/1042 Norman Brook to Churchill 15/6/1955 proposing that Churchill support Thorneycroft; *Parl.Deb.* (1955–56) Vol. 542 16/6/1955 Col. 729.

39. CAB134/854 EA(55)6th meeting 17/2/1955 and EA(55)12th meeting 31/3/1955; CAB128/29 CM(55)12th meeting 7/6/1955.

40. BT64/4996 Letter from D. Walker (Chairman of BEAMA) to the President, 11/5/1953, and note of meeting between the Board of Trade and BEAMA, 1/2/1954.

41. BT64/4751 note of meeting with the Secretary, Frank Lee, and David Cairns, chairman of the Commission, 20/10/1954.

42. *Ibid.*, and letter from W. Hughes, Under Secretary, Board of Trade, to Frank Lee 25/10/1954 and note of meeting 23/12/1954.

43. *Parl.Deb.* (1954–55) Vol. 537 24/2/1955 Col. 1578.

44. Jewkes 'Monopoly Policy' p. 7; Hunter *Competition and Law* pp. 80–1. G. Polyani *Which Way Monopoly Policy?* IEA Research Monograph 30 (1973) p. 63 speculates on this question for a later period. Evidence which follows on the Board's screening procedure is all drawn from long and tedious

discussions in a few files: BT64/2757, possible cases for enquiry, discussions on the 1949 referrals; BT64/4833, 4834, 4835, 4836, 4837, papers of Sir Frank Lee's policy group on the Monopolies Commission, 1951–52; BT64/4812 and 4813 – selection of references for the 5th group; BT64/4754 – consideration of items for referral 1954–55; BT64/4838 on the future of the Commission, 1955–56.

45. BT64/2757 unsigned circular to Board of Trade production departments March 1948; BT64/4837 MC/RPM(52)12 'Further references to the Monopolies Commission' paper to the policy group on the MRPC, 17/7/1952.
46. BPP (1952–53) *Report of the Select Committee* p. 18.
47. BT64/573 'Review of Complaints up to 31/12/50' unsigned memorandum.
48. BT64/4812 letter from A.C. Hill to Ministries of Works, Materials and Supply, 27/10/1953.
49. This was an argument used against the referral of razor blades, industrial gases, metal cans and containers, gas mantles, potash and footwear repairs, all under the control of one or a few large firms. Potash was an international cartel run jointly for the British side by ICI and Fisons.
50. BT64/4812 'M.R.P.C. selection of references: fifth group' note from Monopolies branch of the Board of Trade to production departments 16/9/1953.
51. BT64/4837 papers of the Policy group on new legislation concerning the Monopolies Commission and resale price maintenance MC/RPM(52)12 17/7/1952.
52. Large firms involved included BICC, ICI, Dunlop.
53. BT64/4812 letter A.C. Hill to Sir Maurice Dean 25/11/1953; BT64/4813 unsigned minute 10/6/1954.
54. BT64/4812 minutes 21/9/1953 and 13/10/1953, and undated note by R. Colegate.
55. BT64/2757 'M.R.P.C. Possible cases for enquiry' minutes of meeting at the Board of Trade 12/12/1948.
56. *Ibid.* 'Programme for the first year of the M.R.P.C.' 21/10/1948. BT64/4762 meeting with the President 8/6/1955 and meeting between A.K. Rees and Ministry of Supply officials 14/6/1955. BT64/2757 'Goods which were considered in drawing up the short-list' note in Board of Trade 1948; BT64/4823 passim and Elizabeth Ackroyd (Under-Secretary, Board of Trade) to F.W. Glaves-Smith (Private Secretary in the Board of Trade) 4/6/1956.
57. BT64/4813 'Suggestions made in Parliamentary questions for reference of subjects to the Monopolies Commission'. This showed that between 1952 and 1954 there had been twelve Parliamentary Questions on prices and other matters in the oil and petroleum industries.
58. BT64/4754 Letter Geoffrey Lloyd (Minister of Fuel and Power) to Thorneycroft 15/3/1955 and letter Gerald Reading (Minister of State at the Foreign Office) to Thorneycroft 17/3/1955; minutes of meeting at the Board of Trade 15/3/1955.
59. BT64/4837 1952 referrals; BT64/4812 and BT64/4813, 1953–54 referrals.
60. BT64/4754 meeting at the Board of Trade 24/3/1955.
61. BT64/4813 'Possible subjects for reference to the M.R.P.C.' 5th group.
62. BT64/4812 letter from R.F. Bretherton (Under Secretary, Board of Trade, Raw Materials Dept.) to A.C. Hill 26/1/1954.

63. *Ibid.* letter from Clarence Monier-Williams (Under Secretary, Board of Trade) to A.C. Hill 26/10/1953.
64. BT64/4754 note from E. Harwood (Deputy Secretary, Ministry of Food) to A.C. Hill 12/3/1955.
65. W.J. Reader *Imperial Chemical Industries: a History: Volume II* (Oxford, 1975) pp. 475–7.
66. BT64/2757 official in Board of Trade Raw Materials Dept. to R.C. Bryant 14/4/1948.
67. BT64/2757 goods considered for shortlist 1948.
68. BT64/4812 letter from D.R. McGregor (Under Secretary, Board of Trade) to A.C. Hill 30/10/1953.
69. BT64/4813 'Possible subjects for referral' 1953.
70. BT64/4754 letter from E. Harwood to A.C. Hill 12/3/1955.
71. BT64/4754 minutes of meeting at the Board of Trade 3/3/1955.
72. CBI MSS200/F/3/E3/9/1 minutes of meetings especially 21/5/1953 note of meeting with Cairns.
73. CAB134/844 EA(52)108 'Monopolies and restrictive practices: selection of a new reference to the Monopolies Commission' note by the President 25/7/1952.
74. BT64/4837 MC/RPM(52)12 'Further references to the Monopolies Commission' 17/7/1952; BT64/2790 report of a meeting by A.D. Neale (Principal, Board of Trade) 25/11/1949; MRPC *Industrial and Medical Gases* p. 40.
75. BT258/70 R.R.D. McIntosh (Principal, Board of Trade) to A.E. Lee (Assistant Secretary, Board of Trade) 24/9/1948 and Alix Kilroy to McIntosh 22/10/1948 expressing the desire to refer the industry in spite of industrial opposition and note on the attitude of the Ministry of Transport 8/8/1952; BT258/72 letter from the National Association of Tyre Specialists to Thorneycroft 19/12/1955.
76. Ministry of Works *Building Materials* p. 25; *Parl.Deb.* (1945–46) Vol. 419 11/2/1946 written answer, 28; J. Jewkes *Ordeal by Planning* (1948) p. 57. Rainwater goods are plumbers' building items such as drainpipes and guttering.
77. MRPC *Linoleum* p. 17; MRPC *Dental Goods*.
78. BT64/2757 'Programme for the first year of the Monopolies Commission' 21/10/1948; MRPC *Calico-Printing* pp. 57–8.
79. BT64/4852 note on the background to the copper semis reference, 24/10/1955; BT64/502 exchange between the Ministry of Supply and the Board of Trade Dec. 1948–Feb. 1949 on a complaint also from the New Zealand High Commission.
80. BT64/148 minute by T.K. Rees 18/10/1955.
81. BT64/2757 'Programme for the first year of the M.R.P.C. – shortlist' 21/10/1948.
82. BT64/4821 letter from A.C. Hill to the Board of Trade Solicitor 25/6/1955 on the views of the iron and steel division of the Ministry of Supply; BT64/4826 file generally on the Iron and Steel Board's comments on the Section 15 reference.
83. BT64/4821 letter from A.C. Hill to the Board of Trade Solicitor 25/6/1955 on the views of the iron and steel division of the Ministry of Supply; letter J.A.

Beckett (Ministry of Fuel and Power) to Rees 25/7/1955; circular letter to Board of Trade production departments on the common prices reference 5/8/1955.

84. BT64/4822 T.K. Rees to E. Harwood 22/10/1955.
85. BT64/4822 R. Gray (Principal, Board of Trade) to E. Ackroyd Jan. 1956 regretting the President's decision of 9/1/56; BT64/4838 note from Edward Boyle (Economic Secretary to the Treasury) to the President 11/1/1956.
86. BT64/4159 note of meeting between the President and the TUC Economic Committee 10/5/1950; *The Economist* 'The Monopolies Commission' Vol. clviii 18/3/1950 p. 609 and 'Quiet Life for the Monopolies' Vol. clx 3/3/1951 p. 475.
87. M.C. Marcuzzo 'Joan Violet Robinson (1903–1983)' unpublished manuscript (University of Modena, 1985) p. 36.
88. Alix Kilroy 'The Tasks and Methods of the Monopolies Commission' *Transactions of the Manchester Statistical Society* (1952–53) p. 2.
89. BT64/4813 letters from A.C. Hill to Sir Maurice Dean 24/7/1954 and 5/8/1954.
90. BT64/4887 'The work of the Monopolies Commission' note by A.C. Hill Sept. 1954.
91. CAB134/854 EA(55)28 'Policy on Restrictive Practices' memorandum by the President of the Board of Trade 7/2/1955 and EA(55)6th meeting 17/2/1955.
92. For the background to Section 15 references see chapter 5. The enquiry into collective discrimination was the only Section 15 reference made to the MRPC.
93. BPP (1948–49) *Report of the Committee on Resale Price Maintenance* Vol. xx Cmd. 7696.
94. BPP (1950–51) *A Statement on Resale Price Maintenance* Vol. xxvii Cmd. 8274.
95. BT64/4887 MC/RPM(51)22 paper presented to the President by Monopolies Branch 7/12/1951 and 'Resale Price Maintenance' unsigned paper July 1952, reporting meeting with the President 8/12/1951.
96. J. McMillan *The Dunlop Story. The Life, Death and Re-birth of a multinational* (1989) pp. 95–106.
97. *News Chronicle* 12/1/1955; *Evening Standard* 3/2/1955; PREM11/1042 note from Churchill to Thorneycroft 22/1/1955 and 5/2/1955 noting these cases. *Daily Herald* 10/12/1955; *Daily Mirror* 10/12/1955; *Daily Express* 10/12/1955.
98. *The Times* 29/4/1955; *News Chronicle* 13/5/1955 and 8/6/1955; *The Economist* 14/5/1955; MRPC *Buildings in Greater London*.
99. Allen *Monopoly* pp. 78–82.
100. BT64/4812 minutes 21/9/1953 and 13/10/1953 and undated note by R. Colegate (Private Secretary to the President of the Board of Trade).
101. BPP (1948–49) *Royal Commission on the Press 1947–1949. Report* Vol. xx Cmd. 7700 Appendix IV.
102. S. Koss *The Rise and Fall of the Political Press in Britain. Volume Two: the Twentieth Century* (1984) pp. 640–9; D. Jay *Change and Fortune: a Political Record* (1980) pp. 229–30.
103. BT64/2757 Minutes of meeting 12/12/48. Officials from the Ministries of Supply, Works, Health, Fuel and Power, Food and the Board of Trade were

present, Alix Kilroy took the chair.

104. BT64/4837 MC/RPM(52)12 'Further references to the Monopolies Commission' 17/7/1952.

105. CAB128/6 CM(46)68th meeting 15/7/1946; *Parl.Deb.* (1946–47) Vol. 435 18/3/1947 Cols. 1622–34. For the internal debates, and the issues on which the monopoly Press, like that owned by Beaverbrook gave allegedly biased accounts, see CAB124/1072, papers of the Royal Commission, memorandum by the NUJ

7 THE ORIGINS OF THE RESTRICTIVE TRADE PRACTICES ACT 1956 – A RE-INTERPRETATION

1. *Parl.Deb.* (1955–56) Vol. 549 6/3/1956 Col. 1927.
2. *Ibid.* Douglas Jay Col. 1957, W.E. Padley Col. 1957 and M. Turner-Samuels Col. 2017.
3. J. Jewkes 'British Monopoly Policy 1944–56' *The Journal of Law and Economics* 1 (Oct. 1958) p. 5; J. Pickering *Resale Price Maintenance in Practice* (1966) pp. 36–7.
4. A. Hunter *Competition and the Law* (1966) p. 83; J.D. Gribbin *The post-war revival of competition as industrial policy* Government Economic Service Working Paper No. 19 (1978) pp. 22–3; G.C. Allen *Monopoly and Restrictive Practices* (1968) p. 88.
5. Jewkes 'Monopoly Policy' p. 4.
6. CAB130/110 Cabinet Committee on Monopolies Commission Report GEN498/2nd meeting 9/7/1955; CAB128/29 CM(55) 22nd meeting 12/7/1955; CAB129/775 CP(55) 69 'Monopolies Commission report on Collective discrimination' memorandum by the President of the Board of Trade 11/7/1955.
7. BT64/4827 'Draft paper for Cabinet committee on monopolies' by I.M.2 5/10/1955; CAB130/110 GEN498/3rd meeting 13/10/1955; T234/69 note, unsigned on President's proposals 3/11/1955, note Boyle to Chancellor of the Exchequer 9/11/1955 and to St John Trend (Under Secretary, Treasury) 14/11/1955, note, unsigned, reporting a discussion with Sir Frank Lee (Permanent Secretary, Board of Trade) on the President's views 21/11/1955.
8. T234/69 Brief for the Economic Secretary 88/11/1955, Robert Bridges (Permanent Secretary, Treasury 1945–56) to Chancellor of the Exchequer 9/11/1955 and Robert Hall (head of the Economic Section, Treasury and chief economic adviser to HMG 1953–61) to Robert Bridges 18/11/1955.
9. T234/69 note reporting discussion with Lee 21/11/1955; CAB128/29 CM(55)46th meeting 14/12/1955 and CM(55)47th meeting 20/12/1955; PREM11/1660 for the discussion as presented to the Prime Minister.
10. BT64/4774 letter from the Director of Fredk.Burgess Ltd, Agricultural Engineers to the President of the Board of Trade 23/4/1956.
11. BT64/4838 minutes of meeting at Board of Trade 10/10/1955.
12. BT64/4838 minutes from T.K. Rees (Assistant Secretary, Board of Trade) to Elizabeth Ackroyd (Under-Secretary, Board of Trade) 10/10/1955 and 11/10/1955, note by I.M.2 'Future of the Monopolies Commission' 15/10/1955 and note from Robin Gray (Principal, Board of Trade) to T.K. Rees 22/11/1955.
13. BT64/4838 note by President to the Cabinet Committee on Monopolies 18/11/

1955; BT64/4832 memorandum to T.K. Rees 13/1/1956. S. Stewart was an official in I.M.2 of the Board of Trade and closely concerned with the development of the 1956 legislation.

14. BT258/9236 minute by M.R.C. Swindlehurst (Assistant Principal, Board of Trade) recording a meeting with the President 23/7/1956.

15. Pickering *Resale Price Maintenance* pp. 37–8.

16. CAB129/75 CP(55)69 memo by President 11/7/1955.

17. BT64/4841 extract from 'Electrical and Radio Trading' 26/5/1956; letter from Donald Johnson MP to Derek Walker-Smith (Parliamentary Secretary to the Board of Trade) supporting the Net Book Agreement 30/4/1956 and extract from 'The PATA Quarterly Record' Jan. 1956; BT64/4840 'Suggestions on legislation' by BMTA (British Motor Trade Association) 27/9/1955.

18. BT64/4840 note from R. Gray (Principal, Board of Trade) to T.K. Rees 7/10/1955; CAB130/110 GEN498/3rd meeting 13/10/1955.

19. CAB134/133 DM(50)4 'Resale Price Maintenance' memorandum by the President of the Board of Trade (Harold Wilson) 8/5/1950.

20. CAB134/1686 EA(60)2 Cabinet Economic Policy Committee 'Resale Price Maintenance' note by the President of the Board of Trade 26/1/1960.

21. *Co-operative Monthly Letter* 13, 3 (Mar. 1956) p. 13; *Co-operative Monthly Letter* 13, 6 (Jun. 1956), p. 6; *Co-operative Monthly Letter* 13, 8 (Aug. 1956); *Co-operative Monthly Letter* 13, 10 (Oct. 1956) p. 15.

22. T234/70 note from Robert Hall to St John Trend 24/11/1955.

23. CAB130/110 GEN498/6th meeting 8/12/1955.

24. A.E. Musson *Enterprise in Soap and Chemicals* (Manchester, 1965) p. 360; PREM11/1655 letter from Lord Salisbury to the Prime Minister reporting a conversation with Clive Baillieu (President of the FBI) 10/1/1956; Pilkington Archives PB89/97 'Position of agreements affecting the Company as at 28/2/57'.

25. D.C. Coleman *Courtaulds: an economic and social history, Vol. III* (1980) pp. 178–9.

26. T. Barker *The Glassmakers, Pilkington 1826–1976* (1977) p. 412.

27. W.J. Reader *ICI – A History. Volume 2 1926–1952* (1975) pp. 466 and 469; Pilkington Archives PB260 3 and 17/1/1956.

28. W.H. Smith Archives, Abingdon, File 935, on Restrictive Trade Practices Act 'Restrictive Practices and Resale Price Maintenance' 7/11/1960 report for Smith's by Research and Marketing Ltd (a W.H. Smith subsidiary); C. Wilson *First with the News* (1985) pp. 400–3.

29. E.g. see A. Muir *The History of Baker Perkins* (1968) pp. 154–5.

30. C. Wilson *Unilever 1945–1965* (1968) p. 102.

31. CBI MSS200/F/3/E3/9/6 note by M.W. Pitts Turner (Courtaulds) for the Trade Practices Committee 6/5/1954.

32. G.D.N. Worswick 'The British Economy 1950–1959' in G.D.N. Worswick and P. Ady (eds.) *The British Economy in the Nineteen-Fifties* (Oxford, 1962) p. 99.

33. D. Coates *The Labour Party and the Struggle for Socialism* (Cambridge, 1975) p. 69. In interview, Sir Alan Neale, then a Principal at the Board of Trade expressed the view that American influence was more important in 1956 than it had been in 1948.

34. BT64/4877 TN(56)5 'Trade Negotiations Committee, International Action on Restrictive Business Practices' note by the Secretary 18/5/1956.
35. Cited in M. Wilkins *The Maturing of Multinational Enterprise: American Business Abroad from 1914 to 1970* (Cambridge, Mass., 1974) p. 288. She infers that ITO was dropped as a result.
36. CAB134/1181 minutes of the subcommittee on Technical Assistance of the European Economic Co-operation Committee TA(L)(52)34 'Conditional Aid' memorandum by the Board of Trade 22/7/1952.
37. Wilkins *Maturing of Multinational Enterprise* pp. 288–9, 331; BT258/567 American Chamber of Commerce in London *Dollar–Sterling Alliance* 20/11/1952. The aim of supporting direct overseas investment dated from American reconstruction discussions of 1943.
38. J.H. Dunning *American Investment in British Manufacturing Industry* (1958) pp. 158–60; N. Hood and S. Young *The Economics of Multinational Enterprise* (1979) p. 194; CAB130/56 GEN303/5 'Criteria used by HMG in judging applications for U.S. investment in the U.K.' memorandum by the Treasury 7/11/1949.
39. A. Gamble *The Conservative Nation* (1974) p. 172.
40. G. Jones 'The Performance of British Multinational Enterprise, 1890–1945' in P. Hertner and G. Jones (eds.) *Multinationals: Theory and History* (Aldershot, 1986) pp. 97–8 and p. 108.
41. G.G. Jones 'The British government and foreign multinationals 1900s–1960s' in M. Chick (ed.) *Governments, Industries and Markets* (1990).
42. CAB134/1181 TA(L)(52)6th meeting 19/8/1952 and TA(L)(52)40 note by the Secretariat 16/8/1952; BPP (1952–53) *Arrangements for the Expenditure of Counterpart Funds derived from U.S. Economic Aid under S.9(c) Mutual Security Act 1952* Vol. xxx Cmd. 8776.
43. The developments of negotiations with Europeans is summarised in BT64/4877 TN(56) 'Trade Negotiations Committee, International Action on Restrictive Business Practices' note by the Board of Trade 18/5/1956 historical annex.
44. BT64/4877 TN(56)5 'International Action on Restrictive Business Practices' 18/5/1956; CBI MSS200/F/1/1/192 Grand Council minutes 20/4/1955 item no. 2175.
45. BT64/5038 'Restrictive Practices, registration of agreements affecting overseas trading' note for departments from Frank Lee 26/10/1955.
46. BT258/924 minute by Frank Lee 31/10/1956.
47. CBI MSS200/F/1/1/192 Grand Council Minutes 8/6/1955 item no. 2184.
48. BT64/4838 note by T.K. Rees to G.H. Andrew (Second Secretary, Board of Trade) 16/1/1956.
49. PEP *Industrial Trade Associations* (1957) p. 250.
50. BPP (1950) *Report of the Committee on Intermediaries* Vol. xii Cmd. 7904 pp. 43–6, although the report accepted a danger of abuse, pp. 69–70.
51. P.H. Henderson 'Government and Industry' pp. 327–32 and I.M.D. Little 'Fiscal Policy' both in Worswick and Ady *The Nineteen-Fifties*; Coates *Labour Party* p. 66.
52. *Parl.Deb.* (1955–56) Vol. 554 13/6/1956 Col. 870.
53. BT64/4841 POM 305 13/4/1956 and 'Memorandum on government policy on

resale price maintenance' by Conservative Party Research Centre 20/4/1956.

54. BT64/4832 note of meeting with Walker-Smith, T.K. Rees and John Appleby of the *Daily Telegraph* 3/2/1956.

55. PREM11/1042 Churchill to Thorneycroft 22, 25, and 28/1/1955 and Thorneycroft to Churchill 5/2/1955 and Thorneycroft to Eden 27/6/1955; CAB128/29 CM(55)18th meeting 28/6/1955.

56. CAB130/110 GEN498/3 'Monopolies Commission Report on Collective Discrimination' Note by the President 2/7/1955; CAB128/29 CM(55)21st meeting 7/7/1955.

57. CAB130/110 GEN498/3 2/7/1955.

58. CAB130/110 GEN498/1st meeting 5/7/1955; PREM11/1042 notes of the meeting of the Trade and Industry committee 6/7/1955; CAB128/29 CM(55)21st meeting 7/7/1955.

59. CAB130/110 GEN498/4 'Monopolies Commission report on Collective Discrimination. Second Note by the President of the Board of Trade' 8/7/1955 which was agreed at GEN498/2nd meeting 9/7/1955.

60. CAB129/75 CP(55)69 memorandum by the President 11/7/1955; CAB128/29 CM(55)22nd meeting 12/7/1955; *Parl.Deb.* (1955–56) Vol. 543 13/7/1955 Cols. 1943–5.

61. PREM11/1042 letter from Norman Brook to Churchill 15/6/1955.

62. Hunter *Competition and Law* p. 83; P.H. Guenault and J.M. Jackson, *The control of monopoly in the United Kingdom* (2nd ed., 1974) p. 94.

63. This difference is rarely remarked upon by the authors, except Hunter *Competition and Law* p. 84; MRPC *Collective Discrimination* p. 88.

64. L. Hannah 'Government and Business in Britain: the Evolution of the Modern Relationship' in K. Nakagawa (ed.) *Government and Business* (Tokyo, 1980) makes a similar point on the 1956 Act.

65. N. Harris *Competition and the Corporate Society: British Conservatives, the State and Industry 1945–64* (1972) pp. 81–3, 124; J.D. Hoffman *The Conservative Party in Opposition, 1945–51* (1964) pp. 136, 149–51.

66. BT64/4830 note from Edward Boyle to Lord Kilmuir, commenting on the recent meeting of the Cabinet's Monopolies Committee 2/12/1955.

67. R. Nield 'At the Treasury' in A. Gold (ed.) *Edward Boyle. His Life by his friends* (1991) p. 88.

68. D. Maxwell-Fyfe (Lord Kilmuir) *Political Adventure* (1964) p. 74.

69. PREM11/1042 minutes of meeting of the Parliamentary Trade and Industry Committee 6/7/1955.

70. CAB128/29 CM(55)12th meeting 7/6/1955.

71. Harris *Competition and Corporate Society* p. 207.

72. W. Eucken *Grundsätze der Wirtschaftspolitik* (Tübingen, 1952) p. 254, cited in S. Lieberman 'The Ideological Foundations of Western European Planning' *JEEH* 10, 2 (Fall 1981) p. 350.

73. G. Stigler *Memoirs of an Unregulated Economist* (New York, 1988) pp. 142–5.

74. A. Seldon 'Before and After "The Road to Serfdom"' in *Hayek's 'The Road to Serfdom' Revisited* IEA (1984) p. xxiii; Hubert Starley *40 Years Fighting for Free Enterprise* (1982).

75. A. Gamble *The Conservative Nation* (1974) p. 63.

76. CAB134/1183 Sub-committee on Technical Assistance TA(L)(54)77 'Con-

ditional Aid Progress report' Note by the Secretariat 10/6/1954.

77. F.W.S. Craig (ed.) *Conservative and Labour Party Conference Decisions, 1945–1981* (Chichester, 1982) conference resolutions in 1950 p. 360, in 1952 and 1954 (defeated) p. 153 and p. 361, and in 1955 p. 154.

78. Report of Gaitskell's speech 30/1/1955 *The Times* 31/1/1955; *The Economist* 5/2/1955; and R. Evely *Monopoly Good and Bad* Fabian Research Series, No. 163 (1954) p. 40.

79. Reported in *The Economist* Vol. 174 5/3/1955 p. 794.

80. S. Haseler *The Gaitskellites. Revisionism in the British Labour Party* (1969) passim; LPA R.53/June 1951 'Monopoly', and National Executive Committee papers, Vol. 104 Economics Committee 3/1 'T.U.C., Distribution and the Cost of Living' 9/1/1952.

81. LPA R.168/October 1952 'Monopoly Policy' by Richard Evely.

82. Cited in J.W. Grove *Government and Industry in Britain* (1962) p. 187.

83. *The Times* 30/6/1955 leading article; *The Economist* 2/7/1955 Vol. 174 p. 10; *News Chronicle* 15/7/1955.

84. E.g. *The Economist* 2/7/1955 Vol. 174 p. 10; *News Chronicle* 13/7/1955.

85. Worswick 'The British Economy' pp. 33–6; J.C.R. Dow *The Management of the British Economy, 1945–60* (Cambridge, 1964) pp. 78–9 and p. 90.

86. PREM11/1042 note from Churchill to Thorneycroft 22/1/1955 and 5/2/1955.

87. E.g. *Parl.Deb.* (1954–55) Vol. 536 8/2/1955 Cols. 1738–9, Vol. 545 3/11/1955 Col. 1187, Vol. 546 27/11/1955 Col. 1255; K.G.J.C. Knowles 'Wages and Productivity' in Worswick and Ady *The Nineteen-Fifties* p. 511; D. Robertson 'Essays in Money and Interest' *London and Cambridge Economic Bulletin* No. 13 (Mar. 1955); R.C. Tress 'Crisis or Cure?' *Ibid.* No. 14 (Jun. 1955). T.W. Hutchison *Economics and Economic Policy in Britain, 1946–1966* (1968) pp. 131–2.

88. Worswick 'The British Economy' p. 38.

89. Hutchison *Economics and Economic Policy* p. 126; Worswick 'The British Economy' p. 51. This was partly aroused by the reports of the Anglo–American Productivity Councils, see for instance Anglo–American Council on Productivity *Steel-Founding* (1949) p. 33 and 37; *The British Cotton Industry* (1952) p. 27. They sometimes emphasised the need for rationalisation and concentration, e.g. *Metal-working Machine Tools* (1953) p. 53.

90. D. Swann, *et al. Competition in British Industry: Restrictive Practices in theory and practice* (1974) p. 157; J.B. Heath 'Restrictive Practices and After' *Manchester School of Economic and Political Studies* 29, 2 (May 1961) p. 184; E. Heusz 'Oligopoly and Inflation' and Carl Christian von Weizsäcker 'Inflation and Competition' both in A.P. Jacquemin and H.W. de Jong *Welfare Aspects of Industrial Markets* (Leiden, 1977) p. 89 and p. 87 respectively; D. Swann *Competition and Consumer Protection* (Harmondsworth, 1979) p. 126. B.S. Yamey (ed.) *Resale Price Maintenance* (1966), argues that abolition could only have a once and for all impact on prices, p. 3.

91. Worswick 'The British Economy' p. 38.

92. T234/69 Robert Hall to Bridges 18/11/1955 and G. van Loo (Assistant Secretary, Treasury) 26/10/1955; CAB128/29 CM(55)47th meeting 20/12/1955.

93. CAB134/1230 EP(56)18 'Restrictive Labour Practices' memorandum by the Minister of Labour 10/2/1956.

94. CAB134/1229 EP(56) 4th meeting 13/2/1956; CAB134/1230 EP(56)18 'Restrictive Labour Practices' memorandum by the Minister of Labour; PREM 11/1660 memorandum Brooks to Eden 13/2/1956; CAB128/30 CM(56)13th meeting 14/2/1956.
95. 'Management looks at Labour' *Future* vi, 3 (Jun./Jul. 1951) p. 56; Ministry of Labour and National Service *Practices impeding the full and efficient use of manpower* (HMSO, 1959). I am grateful to Nick Tiratsoo for pointing out these references to me.
96. CAB134/1230 EP(56)18 'Restrictive Labour Practices' memorandum by the Minister of Labour 10/2/1956.
97. Knowles 'Wages and Productivity' pp. 511–16.
98. Interview with Dame Elizabeth Ackroyd 28/8/1986.
99. Pilkington Archives, PB89/97 File on Restrictive Practices, Circular letter from Doncaster Chambers of Commerce 27/3/1956.
100. CBI MSS200/F/1/1/192 Grand Council minutes 14/9/1955 item no. 2199 and 14/12/1955 item no. 2214.
101. FBI *Restrictive Business Practices and the Public Interest* (Jun. 1955) pp. 15–16; CBI MSS200/C/1/1/7 minutes of the panel on monopolies 13/11/1953 and 20/1/1956.
102. Conservative Party archives PCC/55/5 'Restrictive Practices' by James Douglas 18/11/1955, summarising the views of the ABCC, and mentioning the NUM's opposition to a definition of the public interest. CBI MSS200/F/1/1/193 Grand Council minutes 14/3/1954 item no. 2237.
103. BT64/4829 'Summary by various trade associations on forthcoming monopolies legislation' Nov. 1955; BT64/4830 note from Boyle to Kilmuir 2/12/1955 and note from Manningham Buller to Kilmuir 5/12/1955; CAB130/110 minutes of special meeting of Cabinet committee on monopolies legislation 6/12/1955.
104. CBI MSS200/F/1/1/192 Grand Council minutes 24/2/1956 item no. 2233.
105. BT64/4821 note from L.H. Robinson (2nd Secretary Board of Trade) to F. Glaves-Smith 30/12/1955. An important line for future research is to understand why the Courts took an anti-cartel stance.
106. CAB130/110 GEN498/9th meeting 9/1/1956; CAB128/30 CM(56)3rd meeting 11/1/1956, CM(56)13th meeting 14/2/1956, CM(56)26th meeting 29/3/1956, CM(56)37th meeting 17/5/1956; CAB134/1278 L(56)5th meeting Legislation committee 14/2/1956.
107. D. Burns *The Steel Industry* (Cambridge, 1961) pp. 316–18; CAB130/110 GEN498/9th meeting 9/1/1956 where Thorneycroft reminded the Cabinet committee on the new legislation of this undertaking.
108. The ISB's position was summarised in CAB129/79 CP(56)11 'The Iron and Steel Board' memorandum by the Lord Chancellor 10/1/1956. The issue at first went before the Cabinet committee CAB130/110 GEN/498 9th meeting 9/1/1956.
109. CAB129/79 CP(56)11;CAB128/30 CM (56)3rd meeting 11/1/1956.
110. T273/46 letter from Bridges to Chancellor of the Exchequer 20/3/1956. By 1955 conditions for re-sale had worsened, see D. Burns 'Steel' in D. Burns (ed.) *The Structure of British Industry. Volume 1* (Cambridge, 1958) p. 299.
111. T228/506 letter from Thorneycroft to Eden 19/3/1956 and letter from Bridges to Macmillan 23/3/1956.

112. CAB128/30 CM(56)26th meeting 19/3/1956; CAB129/81 CP(56)126 'The Iron and Steel Industry' memorandum by the President 16/5/1956; CAB128/30 CM(56)37th meeting 17/5/1956.
113. T228/507 'Steel and Restrictive Practices' note from Herbert Brittain to Robert Bridges 19/7/1956. Otherwise the ISB's maximum price agreements were replaced in 1957 by recommendations and guidance, see Burns *Steel* pp. 614–16.
114. CAB128/30 CM(56)37th meeting 17/5/1956; T228/507 letter G.H. Andrew to Herbert Brittain 24/7/1956. (Brittain was Second Secretary to the Treasury. When he retired, in 1957, he became Chairman of the Iron and Steel Holding and Realisation Agency.) For similar fears expressed at an earlier stage see CAB129/81 CP(56)126 'The Iron and Steel Industry' memorandum by the President 16/5/1956.

8 RESALE PRICE MAINTENANCE

1. B.S. Yamey 'Introduction: the main economic issues' in B.S. Yamey (ed.) *Resale Price Maintenance* (1966) pp. 3, 257.
2. BPP (1920) *Profiteering Act 1919: Findings and Decisions of a committee appointed to inquire into the principle of fixed retail prices* Vol. xxiii Cmd. 662; Board of Trade *Restraint of Trade: Report of Committee appointed by the Lord Chancellor and the President of the Board of Trade to consider certain retail practices* (HMSO, 1931).
3. D. Flanagan *1869–1969: A Centenary Story* (Manchester: Co-operative Union, 1969) p. 86.
4. *Ibid.* p. 79; T.W. Mercer *Towards the Co-operative Commonwealth* (Manchester, 1936) p. 182.
5. *Parl.Deb.* (1929–30) Vol. 238 Col. 199 30/4/1930 and Cols. 1165–323 8/5/1930.
6. Board of Trade Retail Trade Committee *First Interim Report* (HMSO, Oct. 1941), *Second Interim Report* (Jan. 1942), *Third Report* (Jun. 1942); Board of Trade *Census of Distribution and other services, 1950. Retail Trade short report* (1952).
7. BPP (1948–49)*Report of the Committee on Resale Price Maintenance* Vol. xx Cmd. 7696; Ministry of Works *Cement Costs* (1946); BT64/279 'Prices of Radio Valves' report by the Central Price Regulation Committee (1946); Ministry of Works *The Distribution of Building Materials and Components* (1948).
8. LPA RD/89 'Should there be a Distribution Policy?' March 1948; RD235 'Draft report of the Distribution sub-committee' December 1948; CAB134/133 DM(50)1st meeting 1/4/1950 and DM(50) 2nd meeting 21/4/1950.
9. Ministry of Works *Building Materials* p. 26 and pp. 50–2.
10. Ministry of Works *Cement Costs* pp. 11–12, and p. 21; BT64/279 'Prices of Radio Valves' and Note by C.K. Hobson on radio valves for the Survey of Internal Cartels.
11. B.S. Yamey 'Resale Price Maintenance in the United Kingdom' in Yamey (ed.) *Resale Price Maintenance* p. 265.
12. MRPC *Tyres*, pp. 116–17.
13. Monopolies Commission *Report on the Supply of Cigarettes and Tobacco and Cigarette and Tobacco Machinery* (1961); Monopolies Commission *Report on*

the Supply of Electrical Equipment for Mechanically propelled land vehicles (1963); Monopolies Commission *Report on the Supply of Wallpaper* (1964).

14. Yamey 'United Kingdom' pp. 286–90.
15. B. Potter *The Co-operative Movement in Great Britain* (1987 reprint of 1891 ed.) preface by Margaret Cole pp. xix–xxii, citing Beatrice Webb's *My Apprenticeship*. The failure by academics, especially economists, to take the Co-op seriously has been a constant cause for comment see S. Pollard 'The Foundation of the Co-operative Party' in A. Briggs and J. Saville (eds.) *Essays in Labour History 1886–1923* (1971) pp. 208–10; T.F. Carbery *Consumers in Politics* (Manchester, 1969) pp. 192–6. However, the Co-op did have the allegiance of many 'Labour' economists, such as Henry Smith and G.D.N. Worswick.
16. Carbery *Consumers* pp. 192–5; A. Roth *Heath and the Heathmen* (1972) p. 176.
17. W. Allen and P. Curwen *Competition and Choice in the Publishing Industry* Hobart Paper No. 116 (IEA, 1991) p. 9. They refer to B.S. Yamey *Resale Price Maintenance and Shoppers' Choice* Hobart Paper No. 1 (IEA, 1960). Yamey's account mentions Stonehouse, but not the role of the Co-op, Yamey 'United Kingdom' p. 289.
18. J.B. Jefferys *The Structure of Retailing in Britain 1900–1950* (1954) p. 468; N. Stettner *Co-operation Today* (Co-operative Union, 1969) p. 20; A. Bonner *British Co-operation* (Manchester, 2nd ed., Co-operative Union, 1970) p. 245.
19. J. Bailey *The British Co-operative Movement* (2nd ed., 1960) pp. 57, 29; Bonner *Co-operation* p. 250; Carbery *Consumers* p. 36.
20. In 1936 Home and Colonial experimented with a 1/- in the £ dividend scheme, P. Mathias *Retailing Revolution* (1967) p. 288.
21. Bonner *Co-operation* p. 274; Flanagan *Centenary Story* pp. 78–80.
22. BT13/220A MM(46)62 'Effect of Price Maintenance on Co-operative Societies' by the President 11/7/1946 and accompanying correspondence.
23. E.g. Mercer *Co-operative Commonwealth* p. 190.
24. G.W. Rhodes *Co-operative–Labour Relations 1900–1962* (Loughborough, 1962) pp. 84–94; Bonner *Co-operation* pp. 272 ff.
25. Bonner *Co-operation* p. 283; Rhodes *Co-operative–Labour Relations* pp. 95ff.
26. LPA RD89 'Should there be a Distribution Policy?'; P. Bareau *Consumer Goods. The Methods and Costs of Distribution* (1950); Labour Research Department *Over the Counter: a survey of distribution* (1950) passim.
27. BT64/537 Oral evidence to the Committee on RPM 11/6/1948.
28. H. Levy *The Shops of Britain* (1947) pp. 126–35; H. Smith *Retail Distribution* (1937) p. 154; W. Arthur Lewis 'Competition in the Retail Trade' *Economica* 12, 4 (Nov. 1945) pp. 230–31; BT64/455 RPM(E)60 evidence to the Lloyd Jacob Committee submitted by R. Cohen, R.F. Khan, W.B. Reddaway and J. Robinson; RPM(E)55 evidence of University of Oxford Institute of Statistics. One voice was to upset this unanimity, see Sir Henry Clay 'Resale Price Maintenance' *Journal of Industrial Economics* 3, 1 (Dec. 1954) pp. 9–21.
29. J.B. Jefferys, G. Lindblad and S. Hausberger *Productivity in the Distribution Trade in Europe* OEEC, European Productivity Agency (Paris, 1954) p. 57.
30. LPA RD89/March 1948 'Should there be a Distribution Policy?'; RD123/June 1948 'Nation of Shopkeepers' by Richard Evely.
31. LPA RD235/December 1948 'Distribution sub-committee: draft report to the

the Policy committee'.

32. LPA R.59/July 1951 'Resale Price Maintenance' Copy of paper submitted by USDAW; MRC MSS292/321/7 TUC Economic Committee 11/3 'Collective Discrimination' 10/8/1953.

33. LPA R.59/July 1951 'Resale Price Maintenance' paper by USDAW; NEC minutes 27/6/51; Policy and Publicity sub-committee of the NEC joint meeting with the Co-operative Union and USDAW 16/7/51.

34. The evidence was ambiguous. See the summaries in BT258/1187 'Report of committee on resale price maintenance' 2/10/1961, Appendix 3.

35. BT13/220A MM(46)63 minute 12/7/1946 from Alix Kilroy to the Secretary; BT11/3065 S.B.C. 1 'Supervisory Boards Committee' memorandum by the Board of Trade.

36. T228/285 Note on DM(50)4 (memorandum by Wilson on resale price maintenance) by the Treasury 10/5/1950.

37. J.B. Jefferys *Retail Trading in Britain 1850–1950* (Cambridge, 1954) pp. 64–78.

38. Cited in E.T. Grether *Resale Price Maintenance in Great Britain* University of California Publications in Economics, 11, 3 (1935) p. 295 (pp. 257–334).

39. Jefferys *Retail Trading* pp. 96–8. For a useful categorisation of the balance of competitive power see P.W.S. Andrews and F.A. Friday *Fair Trade. Resale Price Maintenance Re-examined* (1960) pp. 46–7.

40. Grether *Resale Price Maintenance* pp. 306–11.

41. Andrews and Friday *Fair Trade* pp. 35–9; 55ff; 70–3.

42. Mathias *Retailing Revolution* p. 263. When Schuster stood as a National Liberal MP in 1938 he first obtained the agreement to this move from the chairman of Unilever – Sir D'Arcy Cooper, Sir George Schuster *Private Work and Public Causes. A Personal Record 1881–1978* (Glamorgan, 1979) p. 129.

43. BT13/220A MM(46)74th meeting 30/7/1947 and MM(46)79 'Distribution Policy' memorandum by G.C. Andrew 6/9/1946; Jefferys *Structure of Retailing* p. 468.

44. BT64/456 RPM(E)13 evidence of Incorporated Sales Managers' Association (Schuster was the President) and RPM(E)16 evidence of Home and Colonial Stores.

45. BT64/454 RPM(E)31 evidence of Imperial Tobacco Co., RPM(E)35 London Chamber of Commerce (household appliance section); BT64/455 RPM(E)51 Horlicks, RPM(E)68 Cadbury's, BT64/456 RPM(E)2 Jantzen Knitting Mills, RPM(E)5 Aluminium Industries, RPM(E)6 Jaeger Co., RPM(E)7 George Spencer (manufacturer of 'Vedonis' underwear), RPM(E)8 Tan Sad (manufacturers of prams, etc.), RPM(E)10 group of shoe manufacturers – Clark, Lotus, Norvic. Somervell, RPM(E)12 Harding Tilton and Hartley (manufacturers of 'Van Heusen' shirts), RPM(E)18 Branded Knitting Wool Association; BT64/457 RPM(E)46 H.J. Heinz.

46. BT64/455 RPM(E)71 evidence of Home and Colonial Stores, RPM(E)62 evidence of Boots' Ltd, RPM(E)52 evidence of the Association of Engineering Distributors, RPM(E)72 evidence of Currys Ltd (retailers of electrical goods); BT64/456 RPM(E)16 evidence of British Home Stores. BT64/455 RPM(E)62 W.H. Smith argued in favour of the extension of RPM and branded goods as a guarantee of quality, although it is unclear wheher this support extended to collective methods.

47. BT64/454 RPM(E)25 evidence of National Union of Retail Confectioners, RPM(E)31 Imperial Tobacco Co., RPM(E)39 National Union of Retail Tobacconists, RPM(E)27 National Pharmaceutical Union, RPM(E)28 Association of Wholesale Druggists, RPM(E)29 Association of Dental Manufacturers and Traders.
BT64/455 RPM(E)59 Associated Booksellers of Great Britain and Ireland, RPM(E)61 Publishers' Association, RPM(E)68 Cadbury's, RPM(E)54 British Cycle and Motor Cycles Manufacturers' Trade Union, RPM(E)54 Motor Agents' Association, RPM(E)63 Scottish Radio Retailers' Association, RPM(E)56 British Refrigeration Association.
BT64/456 RPM(E)20 Stationers' Association, RPM(E)10 evidence of shoe manufacturers, C&J Clark, Lotus, Norvic Shoe Co., Somervell Bros.,
BT64/457 RPM(E)41 British Radio Valves Manufacturers' Association, RPM(E)42 British Motor Trade Association, RPM(E)43 Society of Motor Manufacturers and Traders, RPM(E)50 Electric Lamp Manufacturers' Association.
48. BT64/456 RPM(E)11 evidence of Dr W. Arthur Lewis, and of Hermann Levy, RPM(E)9 in evidence submitted by the Joint Council for Monetary and Economic Research. Smith *Retail Distribution* pp. 77–88 emphasised the retailers' total lack of independence from the manufacturers of branded goods and the frequent coincidence of interests between the two sections in securing and sharing monopoly prices.
49. BT64/519 evidence of the Association of Retail Chambers of Trade; BT64/454 RPM(E)24 evidence of Council of Retail Distributors; BT64/456 RPM(E)19 evidence of Grocery Proprietary Articles Association.
50. BT64/454 RPM(E)35 evidence of London Chambers of Commerce; BT64/457 RPM(E)46 evidence of H.J. Heinz.
51. BT64/456 RPM(E)19 evidence of Grocery Proprietary Articles Association.
52. BPP *Resale Price Maintenance* pp. 30–2.
53. *Ibid.* p. 35
54. *Ibid.* p. 33.
55. BT64/550 RPM(M)7 minutes of meeting of Committee on resale price maintenance 30/9/1948.
56. *Parl.Deb.* (1948–49) Vol. 465 2/9/1949 Cols. 2319–21.
57. BT64/556 letter from Helmore to Kipping 21/6/1949.
58. BT64/556 note by B. Floud (Assistant Secretary, Board of Trade) 26/7/1949 and report of meeting at the Board of Trade with Kipping and Roy Glenday (Economic Director of the FBI) 28/7/1949.
59. CAB130/133 DM(50)4 'Resale Price Maintenance' memorandum by the President of the Board of Trade 8/5/1950, DM(50) 2nd meeting of the Cabinet Committee on Distribution and Marketing 11/5/1950 and DM(50) 4th meeting 14/6/1950.
60. CAB130/133 DM(50) 9th meeting 7/12/1950.
61. BPP (1950–51) *A Statement on Resale Price Maintenance* Vol. xxvii Cmd. 8274 pp. 9–10. The Fair Prices Defence League, an umbrella organisation for a number of leading trade associations, including ELMA even got an interview with the Labour Party Policy Committee, to put its case in favour of all the practices, LPA Policy sub-committee meeting 19/3/51.

62. BT64/4665 1st meeting of policy group 23/3/1951; BT64/4887 Paper by Monopolies branch 7/12/1951 and MC/RPM(51)22 8/12/1951.

63. Much evidence given to the Lloyd Jacob Committee points to the role of price controls and price-fixing via the Central Price Regulation Committee as a key element in the evolution and success of their schemes, BT64/454 RPM(E)25 National Union of Retail Confectioners; BT64/455 British Refrigeration Association; BT64/457 RPM(E)20 Stationers' Association, RPM(E)45 London Wholesale Distributing Confectioner's Association.

64. G. Rees *St. Michael. A History of Marks and Spencer* (2nd ed., 1973) p. 215.

65. J. Pickering *Resale Price Maintenance in Practice* (1966) pp. 116–17.

66. H. Lerner *Currys: the first 100 years* (Cambridge, 1984) pp. 53–61.

67. Pickering *Resale Price Maintenance* pp. 154–8. Pickering also notes the concealed breakdown in other trades, through new ways of offering price advantages, like trade-ins and package deals.

68. *Ibid.* pp. 73–91.

69. BT258/1187 *Resale Price Maintenance*, Appendix 7 para. 25.

70. G.C. Allen *Monopoly and Restrictive Practices* (1968) p. 111.

71. BT258/1187 *Resale Price Maintenance* para. 258.

72. Roth *Heath* p. 177.

73. BT64/1103 cutting from Hansard 17/3/1960 re Parliamentary Question 51370; BT258/990 Brief for President to accompany paper to Economic Policy Committee by I.M.2 1/2/1960.

74. CAB129/100 C(60)26 'Resale Price Maintenance' memorandum by President of the Board of Trade 18/2/1960; CAB134/1684 EA(59)88 'Cabinet Economic Policy Committee. Resale Price Maintenance' note by the President of the Board of Trade 11/12/1959; CAB134/1686 EA(60)2 'Resale Price Maintenance' note by the President of the Board of Trade 26/1/1960; CAB134/1685 EA(60) 4th meeting 10/2/1960.

75. CAB128/34 CC(60)13th meeting 15/2/1960.

76. BT258/1187 'Resale Price Maintenance' para. 257.

77. Pickering *Resale Price Maintenance* pp. 133–7.

78. BT258/1187 'RPM', paras. 235–41. See also Roth *Heath* p. 177.

79. N. Harris *Competition and the Corporate Society: British Conservatives, the State and Industry 1945–1964* (1972) p. 155.

80. CAB134/1684 EA(59)88 'Resale Price Maintenance' memorandum by the President of the Board of Trade 11/12/1959; CAB128/34 CC(60)13th meeting 25/2/1960.

81. Roth *Heath* p. 176.

82. *Ibid.* pp. 176–8.

83. D. Butler *The British General Election of 1964* (1965) pp. 21–3.

9 CONCLUSIONS

1. F. Engels 'The Condition of the working-class in England' (Leipzig, 1845) in *Karl Marx, Frederick Engels Collected Works Volume 4* (1975) p. 507.

2. G. Kolko *Railroads and Regulation 1877–1916* (Princeton, 1965) p. 232.

3. K. Polanyi *The Great Transformation* (2nd ed., 1957) p. 234.

Bibliography

1. BOOKS AND ARTICLES

Aaronovitch, S. *Monopoly: A Study of British Monopoly Capitalism* (1955).

Aaronovitch, S. and Sawyer, M. *Big Business: theoretical and empirical aspects of concentration and mergers in the United Kingdom* (1975).

Addison, P. *The Road to 1945: British Politics and the Second World War* (1975).

Aldcroft, D.H. *The Inter-war Economy* (1970).

Aldcroft, D.H. *The British Economy. Volume 1. The Years of Turmoil 1920–1951* (Brighton, 1986).

Alford, B.W.E. *British Economic Performance 1945–1975* (1988).

Allen, G.C. *British Industries and their Organisation* (1933) (2nd ed., 1935).

Allen, G.C. 'An Aspect of Industrial Reorganisation' *Economic Journal* 55, 218–19 (Jun.–Sept. 1945) pp. 179–91.

Allen, G.C. *Economic Thought and Industrial Policy* University College Inaugural Lecture (4 Mar. 1948).

Allen, G.C. *Monopoly and Restrictive Practices* (1968).

Allen, G.C. *The Structure of Industry in Britain* (3rd ed., 1970).

Allen, G.C. 'Advice from economists – forty five years ago' *The Three Banks Review* 106 (Jun. 1975) pp. 35–50.

Allen, G.C. *The British Disease* Hobart Paper No. 67 (IEA, 1976).

Allen, G.C. *British Industry and Economic Policy* (1979).

Allen, J.S. *World Monopoly and Peace* (New York, 1946).

Allen, W. and Curwen, P. *Competition and Choice in the Publishing Industry* Hobart Paper No. 116 (IEA, 1991).

Andrews, P.W.S. and Friday, F.A. *Fair Trade. Resale Price Maintenance Re-examined* (1960).

Armytage, W.H.G. 'The Railway Rates Question and the Fall of the Third Gladstone Ministry' *EngHR* 65 (Jan. 1950) pp. 18–51.

Arthur Lewis, W. 'Competition in the Retail Trade' *Economica* 12, 4 (Nov. 1945) pp. 202–34.

Ashley. W.J. *The Economic Organisation of England: an outline history* (1914).

Attfield, J. and Williams, S. (eds.) *1939: the Communist Party of Great Britain and the War* (1984).

Backhouse, R. *A History of Modern Economic Analysis* (Oxford, 1985).

Bailey, J. *The British Co-operative Movement* (2nd ed., 1960).

Bamberg, J. 'The rationalisation of the British Cotton Industry in the Interwar Years' *Textile History* 19, 1 (Spring, 1988) pp. 83–102.

Baran, P.A. and Sweezy, P.M. *Monopoly Capital: an essay in American economic and social order* (Harmondsworth, 1966).

Bareau, P. *Consumer Goods. The Methods and Costs of Distribution* (1950).

Barker, R.S. 'Civil Service Attitudes and the Economic Planning of the Attlee Government' *Journal of Contemporary History* 21, 3 (Jul. 1986) pp. 473–86.

Barker, T. *The glassmakers: Pilkington: the rise of an international company, 1826–1976* (1977).

Barnett, C. *The Audit of War: the illusion and reality of Britain as a great nation* (1986).

Barou, N. *The Co-operative Movement in Labour Britain* (1948).

Bartlett, C.J. *A History of Post-war Britain* (1977).

Baster, A.S.J. *The Little Less* (1947).

Bellamy, E. *Looking Backwards 2000–1887* (1887, Cambridge, Mass., 1967).

Berge, Wendell *Cartels: Challenge to a Free World* (Washington, 1944).

Berghahn, V. *The Americanisation of West German Industry 1945–1973* (Leamington Spa, 1986).

Berle, A.A. and Means, G. *The Modern Corporation and Private Property* (New York, 1935).

Bernstein, M.H. *Regulating Business by Independent Commission* (Westport, Conn., 1955).

Best, M.H. and Humphries, J. 'The City and Industrial Decline' in Elbaum and Lazonick *Decline* pp. 223–39.

Blank, S. *Industry and Government in Britain: the Federation of British Industries in Politics, 1945–65* (Farnborough, 1973).

Block, F. *The Origins of International Economic Disorder: a study of United States international monetary policy from World War Two to the present* (Los Angeles, 1977).

Bonner, A. *British Co-operation* (Manchester, 2nd ed., Co-operative Union, 1970).

Booth, A. and Coats, A.W. 'Some Wartime Observations on the role of the economist in Government' *Oxford Economic Papers* 32, 2 (Jul. 1980) pp. 177–99.

Booth, A. and Pack, M. *Employment, Capital and Economic Policy in Great Britain, 1918–1939* (1985).

Booth, A. 'Simple Keynesianism and Whitehall, 1936–47' *Economy and Society* 15,1 (Feb. 1986) pp. 1–22.

Booth, A. 'War and the White Paper' in Glynn and Booth *Full Employment* pp. 175–95.

Booth, A. 'Britain in the 1930's – a managed economy?' *EHR* 57, 2 (Nov. 1987) pp. 237–57.

Bork, R.H. *The Antitrust Paradox: a Policy at War with Itself* (New York, 1978).

Borkin, J. and Welsh, C.A. *Germany's Master Plan. The Story of Industrial Offensive* (1943).

Bowley, M. *The British Building Industry: four studies in response and resistance* (Cambridge, 1966).

Boyce, R.W.D. *British Capitalism at the Crossroads, 1919–1932: a study in politics, economics and international relations* (Cambridge, 1987).

Brady, R. *The Spirit and Structure of German Fascism* (1937).

Brady, R. *Business as a system of power* (New York, 1943).

Brett, T., Gilliatt, S. and Pople, A. 'Planned Trade, Labour Party Policy and US

Intervention: The Successes and Failures of Post-War Reconstruction' *History Workshop* 13 (Spring, 1982) pp. 130–42.

Bridges, E. *The Treasury* (1964).

Britain without Capitalists. A study of what industry in a Soviet Britain could achieve by a group of economists, scientists and technicians (1936).

Broadberry, S.N. and Crafts, N.F.R. 'Explaining Anglo–American Productivity Differences in the mid-twentieth century' *Oxford Bulletin of Economics and Statistics* 52, 4 (1990) pp. 375–402.

Brock, C. *The Control of Restrictive Practices from 1956: a study of the Restrictive Practices Court* (1966).

Brockway, F. and Munally, F. *Death Pays a Dividend* (1944).

Brooke, S. 'Revisionists and Fundamentalists: the Labour Party and Economic Policy during the Second World War' *Historical Journal* 32,1 (1989) pp. 157–75.

Burgess, K. *The Challenge of Labour: Shaping British Society 1850–1930* (1980).

Burke, T., Genn-Bash, A. and Haines, B. *Competition in Theory and Practice* (1988).

Burn, D. *The Structure of British Industry. Volume 1* (Cambridge, 1958).

Burn, D. *The Steel Industry, 1939–1959* (Cambridge, 1961).

Burns, E. *Labour's Way Forward* (1942).

Butler, D. *The British General Election of 1964* (1965).

Butler, R.A. *The Art of the Possible: the Memoirs of Lord Butler* (1971).

Butterfield, H. *The Whig Interpretation of History* (1931).

Cairncross, A. *The Years of Recovery. British Economic Policy 1945–51* (1985).

Cairns, D. 'Monopolies and Restrictive Practices' in M. Ginsberg (ed.) *Law and Opinion in England in the Twentieth Century* (1954) pp. 173–92.

Cannan, E. 'Industrial Unrest' *Economic Journal* 26 (1917) pp. 451–70.

Capie, F. *Depression and Protection: Britain between the Wars* (1983).

Carbery, T.F. *Consumers in Politics* (Manchester, 1969).

Carew, A. *Labour under the Marshall Plan: The politics of productivity and the marketing of management science* (Manchester, 1987).

Carpenter, L.P. 'Corporatism in Britain, 1930–45' *Journal of Contemporary History* 11 (1976) pp. 3–25.

Carter, G.R. *The Tendency to Industrial Combination* (1913).

Caves, R.E. 'Market Organisation, Performance and Public Policy' in R.E. Caves (ed.) *Britain's Economic Prospects* (1968) pp. 279–323.

Chamberlin, E.H. 'The Origin and Early Development of Monopolistic Competition Theory' *Quarterly Journal of Economics* 75, 4 (Nov. 1961) pp. 515–43.

Chandler, A. *The Visible Hand: the managerial revolution in American business* (Cambridge, Mass., 1977).

Chandler, A. *Scale and Scope. The Dynamics of Industrial Capitalism* (Cambridge, Mass., 1990).

Chandler, A. and Daems, H. (eds.) *Managerial Hierarchies: comparative perspectives on the rise of the the modern industrial enterprise* (Cambridge, Mass., 1980).

Chester, N. *The Nationalisation of British Industry 1945–51* (HMSO, 1975).

Clark, W. 'The Industrial Basis of Socialism' in G.B. Shaw (ed.) *Fabian Essays in Socialism* (1889) (Jubilee ed., 1948) pp. 58–95.

Clarke, Sir Richard *Anglo–American Economic Collaboration in War and Peace, 1942–1949* edited by Sir Alec Cairncross (Oxford, 1982).

Clay, H. *The Post-war Unemployment Problem* (1929).

Clay, H. 'Resale Price Maintenance' *Journal of Industrial Economics* 3, 1 (Dec. 1954) pp. 9–21.

Coates, D. *The Labour Party and the Struggle for Socialism* (Cambridge, 1975).

Coetzee, F. 'Pressure Groups, Tory Businessmen and the aura of political corruption before the First World War' *Historical Journal* 29, 4 (Dec. 1986) pp. 833–52.

Cole, G.D.H. *The Next Ten Years in British social and economic policy* (1929).

Coleman, D.C. *Courtaulds: an economic and social history. Volume 3: Crisis and change, 1940–1965* (Oxford, 1980).

Collins, M. *Banks and Industrial Finance in Britain 1800–1939* (1991).

Cook, P.L. and Cohen, R. *Effects of Mergers: six studies* (1958).

Courtauld, S. 'An industrialist's reflection on the future relations of government and industry' *EJ* 51, 205 (Apr. 1942) pp. 1–17.

Cowling, K. *Mergers and Economic Performance* (Cambridge, 1980).

Cowling, K. *Monopoly Capitalism Revisited* Warwick Economic Research Papers No. 365 (1990).

Cowling, M. *The Impact of Labour 1920–24. The beginning of modern British politics* (Cambridge, 1971).

Craig, F.W.S. (ed.) *British General Election Manifestos 1900–1974* (2nd ed., 1974).

Craig, F.W.S. (ed.) *Conservative and Labour Party Conference Decisions, 1945–1981* (Chichester, 1982).

Crosland, C.A.R. 'The Transition from Capitalism' in R.H.S. Crossman (ed.) *New Fabian Essays* (2nd ed., 1970) pp. 33–68.

Cullom Davis, G. 'The Transformation of the Federal Trade Commission 1914–1929' *Mississippi Valley Historical Review* 49, 3 (Dec. 1962) pp. 437–55.

Curry, B. and George, K.D. 'Industrial Concentration: a Survey' *The Journal of Industrial Economics* 31, 3 (Mar. 1983) pp. 473–86.

Dalton, H. *The Fateful Years. Memoirs 1931–1945* (1957).

Davies, E. *National Enterprise* (1946).

Dennison, J.A.G. 'The Reaction to the Growth of Trusts and Industrial Combinations in Britain 1888–1921' (unpublished Ph.D. thesis, University of London, 1980) pp. 64–83.

Dennison, S.R. 'The British Restrictive Trade Practices Act of 1956' *The Journal of Law and Economics* 2 (Oct. 1959).

Deseille, P. *Le Développement des Trusts en Angleterre* (Paris, 1909).

Dintenfass, M. 'The Politics of Producers' Co-operation: the FBI–TUC–NCEO Talks, 1929–1933' in Turner *Businessmen and Politics* pp. 76–92.

Dobb, M. 'Industry and Employment after the War' *Labour Monthly* xxv, 11 (Nov. 1943).

Dobb, M. 'Conservatives and Industry' *Labour Monthly* xxvi, 3 (Mar. 1944).

Dobson, A.P. *The Politics of the Anglo–American Economic Special Relationship 1940–1957* (Sussex, 1988).

Dow, J.C.R. *The Management of the British Economy 1945–60* (Cambridge, 1964).

Dunning, J.H. *American Investment in British Manufacturing Industry* (1958).

Dupree, M. (ed.) *Lancashire and Whitehall. The Diary of Sir Raymond Streat, Volume 2: 1939–1959* (Manchester, 1987).

Dupree, M. 'The cotton industry: a middle way between nationalisation and self-government?' in Mercer *et al. Labour* pp. 137–61.

Durbin, E. *New Jerusalems: the Labour Party and the Economics of Democratic Socialism* (1985).

Eatwell, R. *The 1945–1951 Labour Governments* (1979).

Edwards, C.D. (ed.) *A Cartel Policy for the United Nations* (New York, 1945).

Elbaum, B. and Lazonick, W. (eds.) *The Decline of the British Economy* (Oxford, 1986).

Elliott, D.C. and Gribbin, J.D. 'The Abolition of Cartels and Structural Change in the United Kingdom' in Jacquemin and de Jong *Welfare Aspects* pp. 345–66.

Engels, F. 'The Condition of the working-class in England' (Leipzig, 1845) in *Karl Marx, Frederick Engels Collected Works Volume 4* (1975).

Evely, R. and Little, I.M.D. *Concentration in British industry: an empirical study of the structure of industrial production 1935–51* (Cambridge, 1960).

Fine, B. 'Economies of scale and a featherbedding cartel?: a reconsideration of the interwar British coal industry' *EHR* 43, 3 (Aug. 1990) pp. 438–49.

Finer, S.E. 'The Federation of British Industries' *Political Studies* 4, 1 (Feb. 1956) pp. 61–84.

Fitzgerald, P. *Industrial Combination in Britain* (2nd ed., 1927).

Flanagan, D. *1869–1969: A Centenary Story* (Manchester: Co-operative Union, 1969).

Fleming, D.F. *The Cold War and its Origins* (1960).

Foreman, S. (ed.) *Striking a Balance: the role of the Board of Trade 1786–1986* (HMSO, 1986).

Foster, J. 'Labour, Keynesianism and the Welfare State' in J. Fyrth (ed.) *Labour's High Noon. The Government and the Economy 1945–51* (1993) pp. 20–36.

Foxwell, H.F. 'The Growth of Monopoly and its bearing on the functions of the state' reprinted in R.L. Smyth (ed.) *Essays in the Economics of Socialism and Capitalism* (1964) pp. 77–89.

Francis, M. 'Labour's Industrial Policies and Plans from 1931 to 1945', unpublished paper given at Business History Unit, LSE, conference on 'Labour the party of industrial modernisation?' (1992).

Freyer, T. *Regulating Big Business. Antitrust in Great Britain and America, 1880–1990* (Cambridge, 1992).

Galbraith, J.K. *The New Industrial State* (Harmondsworth, 2nd ed., 1985).

Galbraith, J.K. *American Capitalism: the concept of countervailing power* (1952).

Gamble, A. *The Conservative Nation* (1974).

Gamble, A. *Britain in Decline: economic policy, political strategy and the British state* (2nd ed., 1985).

Gamble, A. and Walkland, S.A. *The British Party System and Economic Policy 1945–83* (Oxford, 1984).

Gardner, R.N. *Sterling–Dollar Diplomacy: The origins and the prospects of our International Economic Order* (New York, 2nd ed., 1969).

Gardner, R.N. *Sterling–Dollar Diplomacy in Current Perspective: The origins and the prospects of our International Economic Order* (New York, 2nd ed., 1980).

George, K.D. 'Changes in British Industrial Structure, 1951–1958' *Journal of Industrial Economics* 15, 3 (Jul. 1967) pp. 200–11.

George, K.D. 'The Changing Structure of Competitive Industry' *Economic Journal* 82 (Mar. 1972, supplement) pp. 353–68.

George, K.D. and Joll, C. *Industrial Organisation: Competition, Growth and Structural Change* (3rd ed., 1981).

Glynn, S. and Booth, A. (eds) *The Road to Full Employment* (1987).

Gourvish, T. *Railways and the British Economy 1830–1914* (1980).

Grant, W. and Sargent, J. *Business and Politics in Britain* (Basingstoke, 1987).

Grether, E.T. *Resale Price Maintenance in Great Britain* University of California Publications in Economics No. 11, 3 (1935) pp. 257–334.

Gribbin, J.D. 'Recent Antitrust developments in the U.K.' *Anti-Trust Bulletin* 20 (1975).

Gribbin, J.D. *The Post-war Revival of Competition as Industrial Policy* Government Economic Service Working Paper No. 19, (1978).

Gribbin, J.D. 'The contribution of economists to the origins of UK competition policy' in P. de Wolf (ed.) *Competition in Europe. Essays in honour of Henk W. de Jong* (Dordrecht, 1991) pp. 135–62.

Griffiths, B. *Competition in Banking* Hobart Paper No. 51 (IEA, 1970).

Grossekettler, H.G. 'On designing an economic order. The contribution of the Freiburg School' in D.A. Walker (ed.) *Perspectives on the History of Economic Thought. Volume 2* (Aldershot, 1989) pp. 38–84.

Grove, J.W. *Government and Industry in Great Britain* (1962).

Guenault, P.H. and Jackson, J.M. *The control of monopoly in the United Kingdom* (2nd ed., 1974).

Hague, D. and Wilkinson, G. *The IRC – an Experiment in Industrial Intervention* (1983).

Haig, J.C. *In the Grip of the Trusts* (1909).

Hall, P. (1986) 'The State and Economic Decline' in Elbaum and Lazonick *Decline* pp. 266–302.

Halliday, J. *A Political History of Japanese Capitalism* (New York and London, 1975).

Hancock, W.K. and Gowing, H. *The British War Economy* (HMSO, 1949).

Hannah, L. 'Mergers, Cartels and Concentration: Legal Factors in the U.S. and European Experience' in Horn and Kocka (eds.) *Law and the Formation of the Big Enterprise* pp. 306–16.

Hannah, L. 'Visible and Invisible Hands in Great Britain' in Chandler and Daems *Managerial Hierarchies* pp. 41–76.

Hannah, L. 'Government and Business in Britain: the Evolution of the Modern Relationship' in K. Nakagawa (ed.) *Government and Business* International Conference on Business History 5 (Tokyo, 1980) pp. 107–24.

Hannah, L. *The Rise of the Corporate Economy* (2nd ed., 1983).

Hannah, L. 'Economic ideas and government policy on industrial organisation in Britain since 1945' in M.O. Furner and B. Supple (eds.) *The state and economic knowledge. The American and British experiences* (Cambridge, 1991) pp. 354–75.

Hannah, L. and Kay, J. *Concentration in Modern Industry: Theory, Measurement and the U.K. Experience* (1977).

Hargreaves, E.L. and Gowing, M. *Civil Industries and Trade* (HMSO,1952).

Harms, B. *Volkswirtschaft und Weltwirtschaft* (Jena, 1914).

Harris, N. *Competition and the Corporate Society: British Conservatives, the State and Industry 1945–1964* (1972).

Hart, P.E. and Clark, R. *Concentration in British Industry, 1935–1975: a study of the growth, causes and effects of concentration in British manufacturing industries* (Cambridge, 1980).

Haseler, S. *The Gaitskellites. Revisionism in the British Labour Party* (1969).

Haxby, S. *Tory M.P.* (1938).

Hayek, F. *The Road to Serfdom* (Chicago, 1944).

Heath, J.B. 'Restrictive Practices and After' *Manchester School of Economic and Social Studies* 29, 2 (May 1961) pp. 173–202.

Henderson, P.H. 'Government and Industry' in Worswick and Ady *Nineteen-Fifties* pp. 326–77.

Herrmann, H. 'Verbandskonzentration und Grossunternehmen' in Horn and Kocka (eds.) *Law and the Formation of the Big Enterprise* pp. 647–76.

Heusz, E. 'Oligopoly and Inflation' in Jacquemin and de Jong (eds.) *Welfare Aspects* pp. 89–100.

Hexner, E. *International Cartels* (1946).

High, J. 'Introduction: A Tale of Two Disciplines' in J. High (ed.) *Regulation, Economic Theory and History* (Ann Arbor, 1991) pp. 1–17.

Hirst, F.W. *Monopolies, Trusts and Kartells* (1905).

Hirst, M.E. *The Story of the Trusts* (1913).

Hobsbawm, E. *Industry and Empire* (1968).

Hobson, J.A. *Imperialism* (3rd ed., 1905).

Hobson, J.A. *Rationalisation and Unemployment* (1930).

Hoffman, J.D. *The Conservative Party in Opposition 1945–51* (1964).

Hogg, Q. *The Case for Conservatism* (West Drayton, 1947).

Holland, R.G. 'The Federation of British Industries and the International Economy, 1929–1939' *EHR* 34, 2 (May 1981) pp. 287–301.

Hood, N. and Young, S. *The Economics of Multinational Enterprise* (1979).

Horn, N. and Kocka, J. (eds.) *Law and the Formation of the Big Enterprises in the 19th and Early 20th Centuries* (Göttingen, 1979).

Howell, D. *British Social Democracy: a study in development and decay* (1976).

Howson, S. (ed.) *The Collected Papers of James Meade. Volume 1: Employment and Inflation* (1988).

Hugill, A. *Sugar and All That. A History of Tate and Lyle* (1978).

Hunter, A. 'The Monopolies Commission and Economic Welfare' *Manchester School of Economic and Social Studies* 22, 1 (Jan. 1955) pp. 22–39.

Hunter, A. *Competition and the Law* (1966).

Huntington, S.P. 'The Marasmus of the I.C.C.: The Commission, the Railroads and the Public Interest' *The Yale Law Journal* 61, 4 (Apr. 1952) pp. 467–509.

Hurstfield, J. *The Control of Raw Materials* (1953).

Hutchinson, Sir H. *Tariff-Making and Industrial Reconstruction: an account of the work of the Import Duties Advisory Committee 1932–39* (1965).

Hutchinson, K. *Rival Partners: Britain and America in the Post-war World* (New York, 1946).

Hutchison, T.W. *Economics and Economic Policy in Britain, 1946–1966: some aspects of their interrelations* (1968).

Jacquemin, A.P. and de Jong, H.W. (eds.) *Welfare Aspects of Industrial Markets* (Leiden, 1977).

Jay, D. *Change and Fortune: a Political Record* (1980).

Jefferys, J.B. *Retail Trading in Britain 1850–1950* (Cambridge, 1954).

Jefferys, J.B. *The Structure of Retailing in Britain 1900–1950* (1954).

Jefferys, J.B., Lindblad, G. and Hausberger, S. *Productivity in the Distribution Trade in Europe* OEEC, European Productivity Agency (Paris, 1954).

Jefferys, K. (ed.) *Labour and the Wartime Coalition: from the diaries of James Chuter-Ede, 1941–1945* (1987).

Jenks, J.W. *The Trust Problem* (New York, 1903).

Jessop, B. 'The Capitalist State and the rule of capital: problems in the analysis of business associations' in D. Marsh (ed.) *Capital and Politics in Western Europe* (1979) pp. 139–62.

Jewkes, J. *Ordeal by Planning* (1948).

Jewkes, J., Sawers, D. and Stillerman, R. *The Sources of Invention* (1958).

Jewkes, J. 'British Monopoly Policy 1944–56' *Journal of Law and Economics* 1 (Oct. 1958) pp. 1–19.

Johnman, L. 'Labour and Industrial Policy' in Tiratsoo, *Attlee Years* pp. 29– 53.

Johnman, L. 'The Largest Manufacturing Companies in 1935' *Bus. Hist.* 28, 2 (Apr. 1986) pp. 226–45.

Johnson, P.B. *Land Fit for Heroes: the Planning of British Reconstruction 1916–1919* (Chicago, 1968).

Jones, G. *The State and the Emergence of the British Oil Industry* (1981).

Jones, G. 'The Performance of British Multinational Enterprise, 1890–1945' in P. Hertner and G. Jones (eds.) *Multinationals: Theory and History* (Aldershot, 1986) pp. 96–112.

Jones, G. 'Foreign Multinationals and British Industry' *EHR* 41, 3 (Aug. 1988) pp. 429–53.

Jones, G. 'The British government and foreign multinationals 1900's–1960's' in M. Chick (ed.) *Government, Industries and Markets: Aspects of government–industry relations in the UK, Japan, West Germany and the USA since 1945* (Aldershot, 1990) pp. 294–214.

Jones, G. and Kirby, M. (eds.) *Competitiveness and the State: Government and business in twentieth century Britain* (Manchester, 1991).

Kaiser, D.E. *Economic Diplomacy and the Origins of the Second World War* (New Jersey, 1980).

Keynes, J.M. *The General Theory of Employment, Interest and Money* (2nd ed., 1973).

Kilroy, Dame Alix 'The Tasks and Methods of the Monopolies Commission' *Transactions of the Manchester Statistical Society* (1952–53).

Kimball, W.F. 'Lend Lease and the Open Door: the temptation of British opulence, 1937–42' *Political Science Quarterly* 86, 2 (Jun. 1971) pp. 232–59.

Kirby, M. 'The Lancashire Cotton Industry in the inter-war years: a study in organisational change' *Bus.Hist.* 14, 2 (Jul. 1974) pp. 145–59.

Kirby, M. *The Decline of British Economic Power since 1870* (1981).

Kirby, M. 'Government Intervention in Industrial Organisation: Coal Mining in the Nineteen Thirties' *Bus.Hist* 15, 2 (Jul. 1973) pp. 160–73.

Kirby, M. 'Industrial Policy' in S. Glynn and A. Booth (eds.) *Full Employment* pp. 125–39.

Kirby, M.W. 'Institutional rigidities and economic decline: reflections on the British experience' *EHR* 45, 4 (Nov. 1992) pp. 637–60.

Kirby, M. and Rose, M. 'Productivity and competitive failure: British government policy and industry, 1914–1919' in Jones and Kirby *Competitiveness* pp. 20–39.

Kitson, M. and Solomou, S. *Protection and economic revival: the British interwar economy* (Cambridge, 1990)

Kleinwächter, F. *Die Kartelle* (Innsbrück, 1883).

Knight, A. *Private Enterprise and Public Intervention: the Courtaulds Experience* (1974).

Knowles, K.G.J.C. 'Wages and Productivity' in Worswick and Ady *Nineteen-Fifties* pp. 502–36.

Knox, F. and Hennessy, J. *Restrictive Practices in the Building Industry* IEA Research Monograph 1 (1966).

Kocka, J. 'The Modern Industrial Enterprise in Germany' in Chandler and Daems *Managerial Hierarchies* pp. 77–116.

Kolko, G. *The Triumph of Conservatism: a Reinterpretation of American History, 1900–1916* (New York, 1963).

Kolko, G. *Railroads and Regulation 1877–1916* (Princeton, 1965).

Kolko, G. *The Politics of War. The World and United States Foreign Policy, 1943–1945* (New York, 1968).

Kolko, G. and Kolko, J. *The Limits of Power: the world and United States foreign policy, 1945–1954* (New York, 1972).

Korah, V. *Monopolies and Restrictive Practices* (Harmondsworth, 1968).

Koss, S. *The Rise and Fall of the Political Press in Britain. Volume Two: the Twentieth Century* (1984).

Kovaleff, T.P. *Business and Government during the Eisenhower Administration: a study of the Antitrust policy of the Justice Department* (Athens, Ohio, 1980).

Leak, H. and Maizels, A. 'The Structure of British Industry' *Journal of the Royal Statistical Society* (series A) 108 (1945) pp. 142–207.

Lerner, H. *Currys: the first 100 Years* (Cambridge, 1984).

Leruez, J. *Economic Planning and Politics in Britain* (1975).

Levy, H. *Monopolies, Cartels and Trusts in British Industry* (2nd ed., 1927).

Levy, H. *Industrial Germany* (Cambridge, 1935).

Levy, H. *Retail Trade Associations* (1942).

Levy, H. *The Shops of Britain* (1947).

Liebermann, S. 'The Ideological Foundations of Western European Planning' *Journal of European Economic History* 10, 2 (Fall 1981) pp. 343–72.

Liefmann, R. *Schutzzoll und Kartelle* (Jena, 1903).

Liefmann, R. *Cartels, Concerns and Trusts* (1932).

Lindblom, C. *Politics and Markets: the world's political and economic systems* (New York, 1977).

Little, I.M.D. 'Fiscal Policy' in Worswick and Ady *Nineteen-Fifties* pp. 231–300.

Louis, W.R. *Imperialism at Bay 1941–1945: the United States and the decolonisation of the British Empire* (Oxford, 1977).

Lucas, A.F. *Industrial Reconstruction and the Control of Competition* (1937).

McCraw, T.K. 'Regulation in America: A Review Article' *BHR* 49, 2 (Summer, 1975) pp. 159–83.

McCreary, E.A. *The Americanisation of Europe* (New York, 1964).

MacDonald, Ramsay *The Socialist Movement* (c.1911).

McEachern, D. *A Class Against Itself: power and the nationalisation of the British steel industry* (Cambridge, 1980).

MacGregor, D.H. *Industrial Combination* (Cambridge, 1906).

MacGregor, D.H. *Enterprise, Purpose and Profit* (Oxford, 1934).

MacKenzie, N. and MacKenzie, J. *The First Fabians* (1977).

Macmillan, H. *The state and Industry in 1932* (1933).
Macmillan, H. *Reconstruction: A Plea for a National Policy* (1933).
Macmillan. H. *The Middle Way* (1938).
McMillan, J. *The Dunlop Story. The Life, Death and Re-birth of a multinational* (1989).
Machlup, F. *The Political Economy of Monopoly* (Baltimore, 1952).
Macrosty, H.W. *Trusts and the State* (1901).
Macrosty, H.W. *The Trust Movement in British Industry* (1907).
Maier, C. *In Search of Stability: Explorations in Historical Political Economy* (Cambridge, 1987).
Marburg, T.F. 'Government and Business in Germany: Public Policy towards Cartels' *BHR* 38,1 (Spring, 1964) pp. 78–101.
Marshall, A. *Industry and Trade* (2nd ed., 1923).
Marshall, A. *Principles of Economics* (6th ed., 1910).
Marwick, A. 'Middle Opinion in the Thirties: Planning, Progress and Political "Agreement"' *EngHR* 79 (Apr. 1964) pp. 285–98.
Mathias, P. *Retailing Revolution: a history of multiple retailing in the food trades based upon the Allied Suppliers group of Companies* (1967).
Mathias, P. 'Industry and Government. A History of the Federation of British Industries' (1980) lodged at the Business History Unit, London School of Economics.
Matyas, A. *History of Modern Non-Marxian Economics* (2nd ed., Budapest, 1985).
Maxwell-Fyfe, D. *Monopoly* (1948).
Maxwell-Fyfe, D. *Political Adventure* (1964).
Meade, J. *Planning and the Price Mechanism* (1947).
Meeks, G. *Disappointing Marriage: A Study of the Gains from Merger* (Cambridge, 1977).
Melchett, Lord *Imperial Economic Unity* (1930).
Mercer, H. 'The evolution of British government policy towards competition in private industry, 1940–1956' unpublished Ph.D. thesis (University of London, 1989).
Mercer, H. 'The Monopolies and Restrictive Practices Commission 1949–56: a study in regulatory failure' in Jones and Kirby *Competitiveness* pp. 78–99.
Mercer, H. 'The Labour Governments of 1945–51 and private industry' in Tiratsoo *Attlee Years* (1991) pp. 71–89.
Mercer, H., Rollings, N. and Tomlinson, J. (eds.) *Labour Governments and Private Industry. The Experience of 1945–1951* (Edinburgh, 1992).
Mercer, H. 'Anti-Monopoly Policy' in Mercer *et al. Labour Governments* pp. 55–73.
Mercer, T.W. *Towards the Co-operative Commonwealth* (Manchester, 1936).
Meredith, D. 'The Colonial Office, British business interests and the reform of cocoa marketing in West Africa, 1937–1945' *Journal of African History* 29, 3 (1988) pp. 285–300.
Meynell, A. *Public Servant, Private Woman* (1988).
Michels, R.K. *Cartels, Combines and Trusts in Post-War Germany* (New York, 1928).
Middlemas, K. *Politics in Industrial Society: the experience of the British system since 1911* (1979).
Middlemas, K. *Power, Competition and the State. Volume 1: Britain in Search of Balance 1940–61* (1986).

Miliband, R. *The State in Capitalist Society* (1969).

Moggridge, D. (ed.) *The collected writings of John Maynard Keynes. Vol. xix. Activities 1922–29* (Cambridge, 1981).

Moggridge, D. (ed.) *The collected writings of John Maynard Keynes. Vol. xxv. Activities 1940–44* (Cambridge, 1980).

Morgan, K.O. *Labour in Power, 1945–1951* (Oxford, 1984).

Morgan, K.O. *Against Fascism and War. Ruptures and continuities in British Communist politics 1935–41* (Manchester, 1989).

Morgan, W.T. 'Britain's Election: a debate on nationalisation and cartels' *Political Science Quarterly* 61, 2 (Jun. 1946) pp. 222–27.

Morrison, H. *Herbert Morrison: an Autobiography* (1960).

Mottershead, P. (1978) 'Industrial Policy' in F.T. Blackaby (ed.) *British Economic Policy 1960–1974* (Cambridge, 1978) pp. 431–50

Muir, A. *The History of Baker Perkins* (1968).

Musson, A.E. *Enterprise in Soap and Chemicals: Joseph Crosfield Sons Limited, 1815–1965* (Manchester, 1965).

Neale, A.D. *The Anti-trust Laws of the USA* (1st ed., Cambridge, 1968).

Nield, R. 'At the Treasury' in A. Gold (ed.) *Edward Boyle. His Life by his friends* (1991) pp. 85–90.

Norris, F. *The Octopus* (New York, 1969).

Overbeek, H. *Global Capitalism and National Decline: The Thatcher Decade in Perspective* (1990).

Parris, H. *Government and the Railways in Nineteenth Century Britain* (1965).

Parrish, M.E. *Securities Regulation and the New Deal* (New Haven, Conn., 1975).

Peacock, A. (ed.) *The Regulation Game* (Oxford, 1984).

Phillips, A. 'An econometric study of price-fixing, market structure and performance in British industry in the early 1950's' in K. Cowling ed. *Market Structure and Corporate Behaviour: Theory and Empirical Analysis of the Firm* (1972) pp. 177–200

Pickering, J. *Resale Price Maintenance in Practice* (1966).

Pierenhemper, T. 'Trade Associations in Germany in the Late Nineteenth and Early Twentieth Centuries' in Yamazaki and Miyamoto *Trade Associations* pp. 233–61.

Pietrowski, R. *Cartels and Trusts* (Woking, 1933).

Pigou, A. *The Economics of Welfare* (2nd ed., 1924).

Pigou, A. *Economics in Practice* (1935).

Pimlott, B. *Labour and the Left in the 1930's* (Cambridge, 1977).

Plummer, A. *International Combines in Modern Industry* (2nd ed., 1938).

Polanyi, G. *Which Way Monopoly Policy?* IEA Research Monograph 30 (1973).

Polanyi, K. *The Great Transformation* (2nd ed., 1957).

Political and Economic Planning *Industrial Trade Associations* (1957).

Pollard, S. 'The Foundation of the Co-operative Party' in A. Briggs and J. Saville (eds.) *Essays in Labour History 1886–1923* (1971) pp. 185–210.

Posner, R. 'Theories of Economic Regulation' *Bell Journal of Economics and Management Science* 5, 2 (Autumn, 1974) pp. 335–58.

Potter, B. *The Co-operative Movement in Great Britain* (1987 reprint of 1891 ed.).

Praeger, T. 'Trade Associations in Great Britain' *Agenda. A Quarterly Journal of Reconstruction* 3 (Nov. 1944) pp. 137–53.

Prais, S.J. *The Evolution of Giant Firms in Britain: a study of the growth of concentration in manufacturing in Britain* (Cambridge, 1981).

Pressnell, L. *External Economic Policy Since the War. Volume 1. The Post-War Financial Settlement* (HMSO, 1986).

Reader, W. 'The United Kingdom Soapmakers' Association and the English Soap Trade' *Bus.Hist.* 1, 2 (Jun. 1959).

Reader, W. *ICI – a History. Volume 2: 1926–1952* (1975).

Reader, W. *Metal Box – A History* (1976).

Rees, G. *St. Michael. A History of Marks and Spencer* (2nd ed., 1973).

Reimann, G. *Patents for Hitler* (1942).

Reynolds, D. 'Roosevelt, Churchill and the War-time Anglo–American Alliance, 1939–1945. Towards a New Synthesis' in W.R. Louis and Hedley Bull (eds.) *The 'Special Relationship'. Anglo–American Relations since 1945* (Oxford, 1986) pp. 17–41.

Rhodes, G.W. *Co-operative-Labour Relations 1900–1962* (Loughborough, 1962).

Richardson, H.W. *Economic Recovery in Britain 1932–39* (1967).

Richardson, J.J. 'The Making of the Restrictive Trade Practices Act: a case study of the policy process in Britain' *Parliamentary Affairs* 20, 4 (Autumn, 1967) pp. 350–74.

Richardson, J.J. *The Policy-making Process* (1969).

Ritschel, D. 'A Corporatist Economy in Britain? Capitalist Planning for industrial self-government in the 1930's' *EngHR* 106 (Jan. 1991) pp. 41–65.

Robbins, L. *The Economic Problem in Peace and War: some reflections on objectives and mechanisms* (1947).

Robbins, L. *Autobiography of an Economist* (1971).

Roberts, R. 'The Administrative Origins of Industrial Diplomacy: an Aspect of Government–Industry Relations, 1929–1935' in Turner *Businessmen and Politics* pp. 93–104.

Roberts, R. 'Regulatory responses to the rise of the market for corporate control in Britain in the 1950's' *BusHist* 34, 1 (Jan. 1992) pp. 183–200.

Robertson, D. 'Essays in Money and Interest' *London and Cambridge Economic Bulletin* 13 (Mar. 1955).

Robinson, J. *Economic Philosophy* (Harmondsworth, 1962).

Rogow, A.A. and Shore, P. *The Labour Government and British Industry 1945–51* (Oxford, 1955)

Rollings, N. '"The Reichstag System of Government". The Labour governments and controls' in Mercer *et al. Labour Governments* pp. 15–36.

Rollings, N. 'Whitehall and the control of prices and profits in a major war, 1919–1939' unpublished draft paper (1992).

Roth, A. *Heath and the Heathmen* (1972).

Rowley, C.K. *The British Monopolies Commission* (1966).

Salter, A. *Recovery: the Second Effort* (2nd ed., 1933).

Sargent-Florence, P. *Industry and the State* (1957).

Sawyer, M. *The Economics of Industries and Firms* (2nd ed., 1985).

Sawyer, M. *The Challenge of Radical Political Economy* (New York, 1989).

Scheider, E. 'Real economies of integration and large-scale production versus advantages of domination' in E.H. Chamberlin (ed.) *Monopoly and Competition and their Regulation* (Macmillan, 1954) pp. 203–14.

Schuster, Sir G. *Private Work and Public Causes. A Personal Record 1881–1978* (Glamorgan, 1979).

Seldon, A. 'Before and After "The Road to Serfdom"' in Hayek's *'Serfdom'
Revisited* Hobart Paperback 18 (IEA, 1984) pp. xv–xxxii.
Semmel, B. *Imperialism and Social Reform, 1895–1914* (1960).
Shepherd, W.G. 'Changes in British Industrial Concentration, 1951–1958' *Oxford
Economic Papers* 18, 1 (Mar. 1966) pp. 126–32.
Smith, H. *Retail Distribution* (1937).
Spiegel, H.W. *The Growth of Economic Thought* (3rd ed., 1991).
Steckel, F.C. 'Cartelisation of the German Chemical Industry 1918–25' *JEEH* 19, 2
(Fall 1990) PR 329–51.
Stettner, N. *Co-operation Today* (Co-operative Union, 1969).
Stevens, R.B. and Yamey, B.S. *The Restrictive Practices Court -a study of the judicial
process and economic policy* (1965).
Stigler, G.J. 'Perfect Competition Historically Contemplated' *Journal of Political
Economy* 65, 1 (Feb. 1957) pp. 1–17.
Stigler, G.J. *The Citizen and the State* (Chicago, 1975).
Stigler, G.J. *Memoirs of an Unregulated Economist* (New York, 1988).
Stocking, G.W. and Watkins, M.W. *Cartels or Competition? The Economics of
International Controls by Business and Government* (New York, 1948).
Swann, D., O'Brien, D.P., Maunder, W.P.J. and Howe, W.S. *Competition in British
Industry: case studies of the effects of restrictive practices legislation* (Loughbor-
ough, 1973).
Swann, D., O'Brien, D.P., Maunder, W.P.J. and Howe, W.S. *Competition in British
Industry: restrictive practices legislation in theory and practice* (1974).
Swann, D. *Competition and Consumer Protection* (Harmondsworth, 1979).
Sykes, A. *Tariff Reform in British Politics 1903–1913* (Oxford, 1979).
Teichova, A. *An Economic Background to Munich: international business and
Czechoslovakia, 1918–1938* (Cambridge, 1974).
Thorelli, H. *The Federal Antitrust Policy: Origination of an American Tradition*
(Stockholm, 1954).
Thorne, C. *Allies of a Kind: the United States, Britain and the war against Japan*
(Oxford, 1979).
Thorpe, A. 'The Industrial Meaning of Gradualism: the Labour Party and Industry
from 1918 to 1931', unpublished paper given at Business History Unit, LSE,
conference on 'Labour: the party of industrial modernisation?' (1992).
Tiratsoo, N. (ed.) *The Attlee Years* (1991).
Tivey, L. and Wohlgemut, E. 'Trade Associations as Interest Groups' *Political
Quarterly* 29, 1 (Jan.–Mar. 1958) pp. 59–71.
Tolliday, S. 'Tariffs and Steel, 1916–1934: the politics of industrial decline' in
Turner *Businessmen and Politics* pp. 50–75.
Tolliday, S. 'Steel and Rationalisation Policies, 1918–1950' in Elbaum and Lazo-
nick *Decline* pp. 82–108.
Tolliday, S. *Business, Banking and Politics. The Case of British Steel 1918–1939*
(Cambridge, Mass., 1987).
Tomlinson, J. 'Labour's Management of the national economy 1945–51: survey and
speculations' *Economy and Society* 18, 1 (Feb. 1989) pp. 1–23.
Tomlinson, J. *Public Policy and the Economy since 1900* (Oxford, 1990).
Tomlinson, J. 'Productivity Policy' in Mercer *et al. Labour Governments* pp. 37–54.
Tress, R.C. 'Crisis or Cure?' *London and Cambridge Economic Bulletin* 14 (Jun.
1955) pp. 2–4.

Turner, J. (ed.) *Businessmen and Politics: Studies of Business Activity in British Politics 1900–1945* (1984).

Turner, J. 'The Politics of Business' in Turner *Businessmen and Politics* pp. 1–19.

Turner, J. 'The Politics of "Organised Business" in the First World War' in Turner *Businessmen and Politics* pp. 33–49.

Turner, J. 'Servants of Two Masters: British Trade Associations in the First Half of the Twentith Century' in Yamazaki and Miyamoto *Trade Associations* pp. 173–98.

Uchiyama, T. *The US Occupation Policy for Japan: the Deconcentration controversy and the origins of the 'reverse course'* (Ph.D. thesis, 1986, lodged in BLPES library).

Utton, M.A. 'Some Features of the early merger movements in British manufacturing industry' *Bus.Hist.* 14, 1 (Jan. 1972) pp. 51–60.

Utton, M.A. *The Political Economy of Big Business* (Oxford, 1982).

Vaizey, J. *The Brewing Industry 1886–1951* (1960).

Vogel, D. *National Styles of Regulation* (Ithaca, New York, 1986).

Voigt, F. 'German experience with cartels and their control during the pre-war and post-war periods' in J.P. Miller (ed.) *Competition, Cartels and their Regulation* (Amsterdam, 1962) pp. 169–213.

Waites, B. 'The Government of the Home Front and the "Moral Economy" of the Working Class' in P. Liddle (ed.) *Home Fires and Foreign Fields* (1985) pp. 175–94.

Walshe, G. *Recent Trends in Monopoly in Great Britain* (Cambridge,1974).

Warriner, D. *Combines and Rationalisation in Germany 1924–28* (1931).

Webb, S.B. 'Tariffs, Cartels, Technology and Growth in the German Steel Industry, 1879–1914' *Journal of Economic History* 40, 2 (Jun. 1980) pp. 309–29.

Weir, Sir Cecil *Civilian Assignment* (1953).

von Weizsacker, C.C. 'Inflation and Competition' in Jacquemin and de Jong *Welfare Aspects* pp. 75–88.

Wells, H.G. *The Sleeper Awakens* (1906).

Wendt, B. *Economic Appeasement: Handel und Finanz in des britischen Deutschland–Politik, 1933–1939* (Hamburg, 1971).

White, S. 'Ideological Hegemony and Political Control: the Sociology of Anti-Bolshevism' *Scottish Labour History Society Journal* 9 (Jun. 1975) pp. 3–20.

Wilkins, M. *The Maturing of Multinational Enterprise: American Business Abroad from 1914 to 1970* (Cambridge, Mass., 1974).

Wilkinson, E. *The Town that was Murdered* (1939).

Williams, P.L. 'The Attitude of the Economics Profession in Britain and the United States to the Trust Movement, 1890–1914' in J.Hey and D. Winch (eds.) *A Century of Economics* (Oxford, 1990) pp. 92–108.

Williams, P.M. 'Public Opinion and the Railway Rates Question in 1886' *EngHR* 67 (Jan. 1952) pp. 37–73.

Williams, W.A. *The Tragedy of American Diplomacy* (New York, 1962).

Wilson, C. *The History of Unilever: Volume 1* (1954).

Wilson, C. *Unilever 1945–1965* (1968).

Wilson, C. *First With the News: the history of W.H. Smith 1792–1972* (1985).

Wootton, B. *Plan or No Plan* (1934).

Worswick, G.D.N. 'Economic Policy and the Co-operative Movement' in N. Barou (ed.) *The Co-operative Movement in Labour Britain* (1948) pp. 14–29.

Worswick, G.D.N. 'The British Economy 1950–1959' in Worswick and Ady *The Nineteen-Fifties* pp. 1–75.

Worswick, G.D.N. and Ady, P. (eds.) *The British Economy in the Nineteen-Fifties* (Oxford, 1962).

Wurm, C.A. 'International industrial cartels, the state and politics: Great Britain between the wars' in A. Teichova, M. Levy-Boyer and H. Nussbaum (eds.) *Historical Studies in international corporate business* (Cambridge, 1989) pp. 111–22.

Yamazaki, H. and Miyamoto, M. (eds.) *Trade Associations in Business History* (Tokyo, 1987).

Yamey, B.S. *The Economics of Resale Price Maintenance* (1954).

Yamey, B.S. 'The Origins of Price Maintenance in Three Branches of Retailing' *Economic Journal* 62 (Sept. 1952) pp. 522–43.

Yamey, B.S. *Resale Price Maintenance and Shoppers' Choice* Hobart Paper No. 1 (IEA, 1960).

Yamey, B.S. (ed.) *Resale Price Maintenance* (1966).

Yamey, B.S. 'Introduction: the main economic issues' in Yamey *Resale Price Maintenance* pp. 3–22.

Yamey, B.S. 'Resale Price Maintenance in the United Kingdom' in Yamey *Resale Price Maintenance* pp. 249–98.

2. PAMPHLETS

A National Policy for Industry (1942).

Association of British Chambers of Commerce *Reconstruction* (1942).

Cole, G.D.H. *Labour's Second Term* Fabian Tract No. 273 (May 1949).

Common Wealth Information Bulletin *Monopoly* No. 7 (Oct. 1944).

Communist Party of Great Britain (CPGB) *Steel* (Jun. 1942).

Conservative Central Office *The Industrial Charter* (1947).

Conservative sub-committee on Industry *Work: the Future of British Industry* (Jan. 1944).

CPGB *Britain for the People* (May 1944).

CPGB *Co-operatives against Combines* (Jun. 1944).

Evely, R. *Monopoly Good and Bad* Fabian Research Series No. 163 (1954).

FBI *Reconstruction: A Report by the Federation of British Industries* (1942).

FBI *International Trade Policy* (Feb. 1944).

FBI *The Organisation of British Industry* (1944).

FBI *Restrictive Business Practices and the Public Interest* (Jun. 1955).

ICI *Competition and Combination in International Trade* (1946).

Industrial Reorganisation League (1934).

Jones, Sir Edgar *World Trade Alliance: main outlines of an organisation for international trade* (Jan. 1944).

Labour Party *Trusts and the Public* (1920).

Labour Party *Speakers' Handbook 1949–1950* (1949).

Labour Party *Labour Believes in Britain* (Apr. 1949).

Labour Research Department *The case for nationalisation and control* (Jun. 1945).

Labour Research Department *Over the Counter: a survey of distribution* (1950).

Liberal Industrial Enquiry *Britain's Industrial Future* (1928).
Liberal Publication Department *Liberal Policy* (1943).
Liberal Publication Department *The Relation of the State to Industry* (1943).
Macmillan, H. *The State and Industry in 1932* (1932).
Macrosty, H.W. *State Control of Trusts* Fabian Tract No. 124 (1905).
Nuffield College *Employment Policy and the Organisation of Industry after the War* (Oxford, 1943).
One Nation a report by a group of Conservative MPs (1954).
Schaffer, G. *The Secret Empire* (1943).
Starley, Hubert *40 Years Fighting for Free Enterprise* (Aims of Industry, 1982).
Trade Union Congress *Post-War Reconstruction* (1944).
United Nations, Department of Economic Affairs *International Cartels* (New York, 1947).

3. GOVERNMENT PUBLICATIONS

Board of Trade *Restraint of Trade: Report of Committee appointed by the Lord Chancellor and the President of the Board of Trade to consider certain retail practices* (1931).
Board of Trade Retail Trade Committee *First Interim Report* (Oct. 1941).
Board of Trade Retail Trade Committee *Second Interim Report* (Jan. 1942).
Board of Trade Retail Trade Committee *Third Report* (Jun. 1942).
Board of Trade *Working Party Reports: Cotton* (1946).
Board of Trade *Census of Distribution and other services, 1950. Retail Trade short report* (1952).
Ministry of Labour and National Service *Practices Impeding the full and efficient use of manpower* (1959).
Ministry of Supply *Interim Report of the Committee of Investigation into the Cotton Textile Machinery Industry* (1947).
Ministry of Works *Cement Costs* (1946).
Ministry of Works *The Distribution of Building Materials and Components* (1948).
OFT, *Board of Trade Survey of International Cartels and Domestic Cartels 1944 and 1946 Volume I* (1976).
OFT, *Board of Trade Survey of International Cartels and Domestic Cartels 1946 Volume II* (1976)

4. PARLIAMENTARY PAPERS

BPP (1886) *Final Report of the Royal Commission appointed to enquire into Depression in Trade and Industry* Vol. xxiii C. 4893.
BPP (1917–18) *Commission of Enquiry in Industrial Unrest. Summary of the reports of the Commission* Vol. xv Cmd. 8696.
BPP (1918) *Final Report of the Committee on Commercial and Industrial Policy after the War* Vol. xiii Cmd. 9035.
BPP (1918) *Ministry of Reconstruction. Report of the Committee on Trusts* Vol. xiii Cmnd. 9236,
BPP (1920) *Profiteering Act 1919. Findings by a Committee appointed to enquire into the effects on road transport rates caused by the alleged existence of a combine* Vol. xxiii Cmd. 549.

BPP (1920) *Profiteering Act 1919. Findings by a committee appointed to enquire into the existence of a trade combination in the tobacco industry and into the effect which its operation has on prices and on the trade generally* Vol. xxiii Cmd. 558.

BPP (1920) *Profiteering Act 1919. Report on Motor Fuel prepared by a sub-committee appointed by the Standing Committee on Prices* Vol. xxiii Cmd. 597.

BPP (1920) *Profiteering Act 1919. Findings and decisions of a sub-committee appointed by the Standing Committee on Trusts to enquire into the existence of any trusts or trade combinations in the electric lamp industry* Vol. xxiii Cmd. 622.

BPP (1920) *Profiteering Act 1919: Findings and Decisions of a Committee appointed to inquire into the principle of Fixed Retail Prices* Vol. xxiii Cmd. 662.

BPP (1928–29) *Final Report of the Committee on Industry and Trade* Vol. vii Cmd. 3282.

BPP (1930–31) *Report of the Committee on Finance and Industry* Vol. xiii Cmd. 3897.

BPP (1943–44) *Employment Policy* Vol. viii Cmd. 6527.

BPP (1945–46) *Financial Agreement between the United States and the United Kingdom* Vol. xxv Cmd. 6708.

BPP (1945–46) *Proposals for Consideration by an International Conference on Trade and Employment (Dec. 1945)* Vol. xxvi Cmd. 6709.

BPP (1947–48) *Economic Co-operation Agreement between the Governments of the United Kingdom and the U.S.A., 6th July 1948* Vol. xxxi Cmd. 7469.

BPP (1948–49) *Report of the Committee on Resale Price Maintenance* Vol. xx Cmd. 7696.

BPP (1948–49) *Royal Commission on the Press 1947–49. Report* Vol. xx Cmd. 7700.

BPP (1948–49) *Report of the Committee on Resale Price Maintenance* Vol. xx Cmd. 7696.

BPP (1950) *Report of the Committee on Intermediaries* Vol. xii Cmd. 7904.

BPP (1950–51) *A Statement on Resale Price Maintenance* Vol. xxvii Cmd. 8274.

BPP (1952–53) *Sixth Report from the Select Committee on Estimates, session 1952–53: Monopolies and Restrictive Practices Commission* Vol. iv.

BPP (1952–53) *Arrangements for the Expenditure of Counterpart Funds derived from U.S. Economic Aid under S.9(c) Mutual Security Act 1952* Vol. xxxxx Cmd. 8776.

BPP (1960–61) *Registrar of Restrictive Trading Agreements. Report for the period 7th August 1956 to 31st December 1959* Vol. xix Cmd. 1273.

BPP (1960–61) *Restrictive Trading Agreements. Report of the Registrar for the period 1st Jan. 1960 to 30th Jun. 1961* Vol. xix Cmnd. 1273.

BPP (1966–67) *Restrictive Trading Agreements. Report of the Registrar, 1st July 1963 to 30th June 1966* Vol. xl Cmnd. 3188.

BPP (1969–70) *Restrictive Trading Agreements. Report of the Registrar 1st July 1966 to 30th June 1969* Vol. xviii Cmd. 4303.

Department of Trade and Industry (1988) *DTI – the Department for Enterprise* Cm. 278.

BPP (1957–58) Monopolies Commission. *Imported Timber: Report on whether and to what extent the recommendations of the Commission have been complied with* Vol. xvi.

BPP (1960–61) Monopolies Commission. *Report on the Supply of Cigarette and Tobacco and Tobacco Machinery* Vol. xix.

BPP (1963–64) Monopolies Commission. *Report on the Supply of Electrical Equipment for Mechanically Propelled Land Vehicles* Vol. xvi.

BPP (1963–64) Monopolies Commission. *Report on the Supply of Wallpaper* Vol. xvi.

Reports of the MRPC 1949–56:

BPP (1950–51) *MRPC. Report on the Supply of Dental Goods* Vol. xvii.

BPP (1950–51) *MRPC. Report on the Supply of Cast Iron Rainwater Goods* Vol. xvii.

BPP (1950–51) *MRPC. Report on the Supply of Electric Lamps* Vol. xvii.

BPP (1951–52) *MRPC. Report on the Supply of Insulated Electric Wires and Cables* Vol. xvii.

BPP (1951–52) *Report on the Supply of Insulin* Vol. xvii.

BPP (1952–53) *MRPC. Report on the Supply of Imported Timber* Vol. xv.

BPP (1952–53) *Report on the Supply and Export of matches and the Supply of Match-Making Machinery* Vol. xv.

BPP (1953–54) *Report on the Process of Calico-Printing* Vol. xvi.

BPP (1953–54) *Report on the Supply of Buildings in the Greater London Area* Vol. xvi.

BPP (1955–56) *Collective Discrimination: A Report on Exclusive Dealing, Collective Boycotts, Aggregated Rebates and other Discriminatory Trade Practices* Vol. xxiv Cmd. 9504.

BPP (1955–56) *Report on the Supply and Export of certain Semi-Manufactures of Copper and Copper-Based Alloys* Vol. xxiv.

BPP (1955–56) *Report on the Supply and Export of Pneumatic Tyres* Vol. xxiv.

BPP (1955–56) *Report on the Supply of Sand and Gravel in Central Scotland* Vol. xxiv.

BPP (1955–56) *Report on the Supply of Hard Fibre Cordage* Vol. xxiv.

BPP (1955–56) *Report on the Supply of Certain Rubber Footwear* Vol. xxiv.

BPP (1955–56) *Report on the Supply of Linoleum* Vol. xxiv.

BPP (1956–57) *Report on the Supply of Electronic Valves and Cathode Ray Tubes* Vol. xvi.

BPP (1956–57) *Report on the Supply and Exports of Electrical and Allied Machinery and Plant* Vol. xvi.

BPP (1956–57) *Report on the Supply of Certain Industrial and Medical Gases* Vol. xvii.

BPP (1956–57) *Report on the Supply of Tea* Vol. xvii.

BPP (1956–57) *Report on the Supply of Standard Metal Windows and Doors* Vol. xvii.

BPP (1958–59) *Report on the Supply of Chemical Fertilisers* Vol. xvii.

Reports by the Board of Trade on the working of the Monopolies and Restrictive Practices Act:

BPP (1950) *Monopolies and Restrictive Practices (Inquiry and Control) Act, 1948. Annual Report by the Board of Trade for the period ending 31st December 1949* Vol. xiii.

BPP (1951–52) *Monopolies and Restrictive Practices (Inquiry and Control) Act, 1948. Annual Report by the Board of Trade for the period ending 31/12/1951* Vol. xvii.

BPP (1952–53) *Monopolies and Restrictive Practices (Inquiry and Control) Act, 1948. Annual Report by the Board of Trade for the period ending 31/12/1952* Vol. xv.

BPP (1953–54) *Monopolies and Restrictive Practices (Inquiry and Control) Act, 1948. Annual Report by the Board of Trade for the period ending 31/12/1953* Vol. xvi.

BPP (1954–55) *Monopolies and Restrictive Practices (Inquiry and Control) Act, 1948. Annual Report by the Board of Trade for the period ending 31/12/1954* Vol. vi.

BPP (1955–56) *Monopolies and Restrictive Practices (Inquiry and Control) Act, 1948. Annual Report by the Board of Trade for the period ending 31/12/1955* Vol. xxiv.

BPP (1956–57) *Monopolies and Restrictive Practices (Inquiry and Control) Act, 1948. Annual Report by the Board of Trade for the period ending 31/12/1956* Vol. xvi.

ARCHIVES

Collections of Documents:

Soviet Peace Efforts on the Eve of World War Two (Moscow, 1973)
UK Documents on British Foreign Policy 3rd Series Vol. iv.

Public Record Office, Kew:

Files of the:
    Board of Trade (BT).
    Cabinet and Cabinet committees (CAB).
    Foreign Office (FO).
    Ministry of Power and its predecessors (POWE).
    Prime Minister's Office (PREM).
    Ministry of Supply and its predecessors (SUPP).
    Treasury (T).
    Works Department and Property Services Agency (WORK).

British Library of Political and Economic Science:

Dalton Papers:
    Part 1 – Diaries, Boxes 26–42, 1942–51
    Part II – A – Section 7 – papers and speeches
    Part III – B – Section 9 – Correspondence
Meade Papers: Section 1 – Diaries (Mission to the USA, 1943).
Management Research Group papers
Political and Economic Planning archives: R35 – papers relating to the Trade Association volume

Modern Records Centre, University of Warwick
    CBI Predecessors archives – MSS200
    TUC archive – MSS 292

Conservative Research Department Archive (war and post-war papers to 1964), Bodleian Library, Oxford

CRD2 – Advisory Committee on Policy (ACP) series
Minutes of Central Council meetings
Minutes of the National Unionist Executive Committee

Labour Party Archives, Walworth Road, London
Files of the Research Department, R.D. series, R. series and RE series, 1942–1956.
Minutes of the National Executive Committee, the Home Policy sub-committee and the Policy and Publicity sub-committee.

Nuffield College, Oxford
Stafford Cripps' private papers
Herbert Morrison's private papers

Churchill Archives Centre, Churchill College, Cambridge
Kilmuir papers (private papers of Sir David Maxwell-Fyfe).
Chandos papers (private papers of Sir Oliver Lyttelton).

Pilkington Group Records Service, St Helens.
General Board working papers and minutes (PB257, PB349 and PB350).
Executive Committee working papers and minutes (PB258 and PB260).
File on restrictive practices (PB89/97).

W.H. Smith Company Archives, Abingdon, Oxfordshire
File on Restrictive Trade Practices Act

NEWSPAPERS AND PERIODICALS

Co-operative Monthly Letter
Daily Express
Daily Herald
Daily Mail
Daily Mirror
Daily Telegraph
The Economist
Evening Standard
Financial News
Financial Times
Future
Labour Monthly
News Chronicle
The Times
Directory of Directors
Who's Who
Who Was Who

Index

Ackroyd, Dame Elizabeth, 143
AEI Ltd, 17
agricultural machinery, 128
Aims of Industry, 139
Alexander, A.V., 102–3
Allen, G.C., 52, 56–7, 64, 70–1, 140,
    217n.46
'Americanisation', 90–1, 103, 122, 226n.51
Andrew, G.H., 57, 100, 146
Andrews, P.H.S., 158–9, 167
Anglo–American Council on Productivity,
    92, 122, 141
Anglo–American loan, 86, 91
Antitrust Division, US Dept. of Justice, 74
antitrust policies, function of, 3, 4–5, 6,
    175–6
Ashley, Percy, 12
Ashley, William, 37
Association of British Chambers of
    Commerce (ABCC), 67, 68, 129
Association of Engineering Distributors,
    160

Bank of England, 29, 30, 145
Barber, Anthony, 143
Barlow, Sir Thomas, 40
Baster, A.S.J., 69, 217n.46
Beaverbrook, Lord, 66, 122
Berge, Wendell, 85
Berle, A.A., 36
Beveridge report, 55
Bevin, Ernest, 66
Bevins, Reginald, 166
Blackett, Sir Basil, 40
Bloom, John, 165
Board of Trade, 15, 18–19, 46, 50, 51, 52,
    88
    and 1944 White Paper, 55, 56–7, 62–3,
        64, 67, 69–72, 75, 77–8
    and 1948 Act, 94–5, 100–1, 102
    and 1956 Act, 145–6
    and MRPC, 109, 110–2, 113–120

and RPM, 156–7, 160
businessmen in, 88
Booth, Alan, 33, 49
Boots Ltd, 158, 160
Bowater Ltd, 17
Boyce, R.W.D., 48
Boyle, Sir Edward, 127, 138, 144
Brady, Robert, 17
branded goods, 21, 156–7, 160–1
brewing industry, 19, 20
Bridges, Sir Edward, 145
Britain without Capitalists, 42
British Electrical and Allied Manufacturers'
    Association (BEAMA), 26, 30, 62, 130
British Employers' Confederation, 76
British Engineers' Association, 26, 27
British Insulated Callender Cables (BICC),
    108, 118
British Iron and Steel Federation (BISF),
    22, 25–6, 62
British Match Corporation, 12, 15
British Non-Ferrous Metals Federation
    (BNFMF), 26, 110, 118
British Nylon Spinners, 116, 131
British Oxygen Co (BOC), 108, 109, 116, 117
Bruce-Gardner, Sir Charles, 68
Bryant, R.C., 95
building materials, 12, 13, 14, 22, 30, 106–7,
    108
    Simon committee report on, 151
    see also rainwater goods
buildings in London, MRPC report on,
    106, 119, 121
Burns, Duncan, 140
businessmen, role in policy, 64–9, 71–2, 96–
    103, 172
    influence on MRPC, 109–119
    on 1956 Act, 143–6, 131–2, 146–7
    on Resale Prices Act, 149, 160–2, 167

Cadbury, L.J., 69
Cadbury Ltd, 21, 23

267